# PREFACE TO THE THIRD EDITION

fully revised, completely updated edition was a long time com- Countless changes have occurred on Humboldt and Del Norte ls and beaches since our 1993 major revision. I'm extremely happy have this new guide to my favorite coast.

I've added over 60 miles of new trails in nine new trail reports and 17 new OTHER SUGGESTIONS. New trails include Crescent City's Point St. George bluffs and beaches, Jedediah Smith State Park's gorgeous Boy Scout Tree Trail, Redwood National Park's lovely Trillium Falls Loop, marvelous Berry Glen Trail, and Lyons Ranch Trails on Bald Hills Road. In McKinleyville, the delightful, multi-use Hammond Trail is complete, though plans are afoot to extend it at both ends. In Arcata, new Arcata Ridge Trail is opening in stages through 2015, and new trails expand options at Arcata Marsh and the Community Forest. Exciting news: Eureka Waterfront Trail moves toward completion, with Hikshari' Trail along the western bayshore a vast upgrade over the old Hilfiker trail. Southeast of Eureka, I detail the pleasant Elk River to Headwaters Trail, with ghost town Falk and a corner of infamous Headwaters Forest. We've expanded coverage of now designated King Range Wilderness Area. A spur trail to a camp and water source have enhanced Chemise Mountain Trail. In Southern Humboldt, I've added the pleasantly pastoral trails of Southern Humboldt Community Park.

These new trails join fully updated reports of our original hikes, with many major reroutes like changes on popular James Irvine Trail at Prairie Creek as well as changes on Ossagon, Clintonia and Elk Prairie Trails. In Redwood National Park, big changes include a major reroute on Little Bald Hills Trail, a vastly improved north half of DeMartin Trail, closure to motor vehicles of much of Coastal Drive, with a trail on the closed portion, a big change on Redwood Creek Trail and changes on many other RNP trails. I report trail reroutes at Patrick's Point State Park and other Trinidad trails. I've updated Arcata's Community Forest with new and rerouted trails there, expanded coverage of Ferndale's charming Russ Park, and changes on Avenue and the Giants trails. Other big changes at Humboldt Redwoods State Park include our expanded report of rerouted Bull Creek Flats/Big Tree Loop, and major reroutes on Johnson Camp and Baxter Trails. I also updated Sinkyone Wilderness State Park's New Lost Coast Trail, where a road closure expands hiking options. I summarize changes and improvements on the California Coastal Trail.

Not all changes have been good. In RNP, Footsteps Rock Trail was closed, and in affiliated state park's many trail camps have been closed or abandoned in state park's misguided attempts to cut costs. In many parks federal, state and county, cutbacks have made it harder to find park personnel either on the ground or over the phone. In Southern Humboldt, major cutbacks at Benbow Lake SRA caused us to downgrade it to an OTHER SUGGESTION.

Still, most of the changes we report are positive and exciting developments, providing you even more choices to get out and explore the natural beauty of the North Coast. This guide now covers well over 600 miles of trails and beaches to explore, with expanded options for mobility-challenged nature lovers, cyclists, dog owners, equestrians, backpackers, and beachcombers. Get your copy now, so you'll have at your fingertips all the info you need to explore Humboldt and Del Norte Counties, whether you're here for a weekend or a lifetime.

*On every stump and fallen log, and on every ,*
*and bulge of living tree, little elves' gardens of sm*
*plants and fungi were growing—dainty sprays*
*vaccinium, red and orange toadstools, barberry*
*gaultheria; and the roadside banks were set with*
*myriads of ferns, while mosses grew to such size that*
*I sometimes mistook them for a young growth of some*
*stiff, heathery plant.*

**— J. Smeaton Chase at Prairie Creek, 1913**
*California Coastal Trails*

# The HIKER'S hip pocket GUIDE to the Humboldt Del Norte Coast

Bob Lorentzen

BORED FEET PRESS
MENDOCINO, CALIFORNIA
Third Edition
2014

© 1988, 1993, 2009, 2014 by Robert S. Lorentzen

Third edition, July 2014

Printed in the United States of America on 30% post-consumer recycled paper

Illustrations © by Joshua Edelman

Symbols by Jann Patterson-Watters and Taylor Cranney

Maps by Bob Lorentzen, Marsha Mello, Garth Hagerman, Brian Kang of City of Arcata, California State Parks, and USGS

Design by Judy Detrick

Layout and production by Garth Hagerman and Bob Lorentzen

Edited by Anne Fox

Cover Photograph © by Clinton Smith

Published by Bored Feet Press
Post Office Box 1832
Mendocino, CA 95460
(707) 964-6629, (888) 336-6199
Visit our website: www.boredfeet.com

ALL RIGHTS RESERVED. No part of this book may be reproduced or transmitted in any form or by any means, electronic or mechanical, including photocopying, scanning, recording or by any information and retrieval system without written permission from the publisher, except for the inclusion of brief quotations in a review. Information contained in this book is correct to the best of the author's knowledge at date of publication. Author and publisher assume no liability for damages arising from errors or omissions. You must take the responsibility for your safety and health while on these trails. Safety conditions of trails, beaches and tide pools vary with seasons and tides. Be cautious, assume that changes have occurred, heed the warnings in this book, and always check on local conditions. If these conditions are not satisfactory, you may return this book unread for a full refund.

Cataloging-in-Publication Data

Lorentzen, Bob

The hiker's hip pocket guide to the Humboldt Del Norte coast, third edition

/by Bob Lorentzen

264 pp.

Includes bibliographic references and index.

1. Hiking—California—Humboldt County (Calif.)—Guide-books.

2. Hiking—California—Del Norte County (Calif.)—Guide-books.

3. Humboldt County (Calif.)—Description and travel—Guide-books.

4. Del Norte County (Calif.)—Description and travel—Guide-books. I. Title.

ISBN 978-0-939431-39-7

Dedicated to Spencer, our beloved airedale terrier/Irish wolfhound mix, who shared hundreds of miles of California trails with our family for more than eleven years. He was always ready to go!

*Spencer at Twenty Lakes Basin in Hoover Wilderness*

This book is also dedicated to California Ocean Sanctuary, the movement to prevent the degradation and destruction that would result if oil exploration and development were allowed on the northern California coast. Save the coast for future generations, whether of people, whales, birds, fish or other life.

**NO OFFSHORE OIL!**
**OCEAN SANCTUARY NOW!**

For more information, write:

OCEAN PROTECTION COALITION

an affiliate of the
Redwood Coast Watershed Alliance
P.O. Box 87
Elk, CA 95432

*In memoriam:*

Karl Lorentzen

Carolyn Lorentzen

Marcia Howe

Gary Matson

Sam Watnick

Edward Abbey

# ACKNOWLEDGMENTS

I express my hearty thanks to all who helped create this new edition. In particular, I offer my deep gratitude to Garth Hagerman for bringing his pinpoint focus, design savvy, and persistent humor to producing this book. I also thank David Baselt of Redwood Hikes Press for his wonderful, detailed maps and website, www.redwoodhikes.com, which provided a vast amount of supporting information and reality checking. Jeff Russell of Crescent City's Jefferson State Books helped with Point St. George and other Del Norte trails. Denise Wood and Mark Craven at Prairie Creek Redwoods State Park, and Jim Wheeler and Mike Poole of Redwood National Park and other RNSP staff members helped tame that vast trail resource for the pages of this book. My thanks also to Mark Andre, Darius Damonte, Michael McDowell and Brian Kang of the City of Arcata's Environmental Services Department, Bob Rasmussen, Jane Wilson and all the staff and volunteers at Arcata Marsh, Miles Slattery at the Eureka Planning Department for help with the Hikshari'/Eureka Waterfront Trail, Deborah Gardner, Dave Pritchard and Dave Stockton (now retired) for Humboldt Redwoods State Park, Kathryn Lobato for Southern Humboldt Community Park, Bob Wick, Bruce Cann, and Gary Pritchard Peterson for help with the King Range and other Bureau of Land Management lands on the North Coast.

For their help in creating the original book twenty-six years ago, I forever owe a debt of gratitude to Anne Fox for her sensitive editing, Joshua Edelman for his evocative illustrations, Jann Patterson-Watters and Taylor Cranney for their marvelous renditions of the symbols, and Judy Detrick for the hours spent at her kitchen table and her superb design. Special thanks to Loren Bommelyn for information about Tolowa culture, and to Liz Petersen for meticulous plant identification, perseverance under pressure, and design innovations.

# CONTENTS

PREFACE TO THE THIRD EDITION 1

WHAT KIND OF TRAIL ARE YOU LOOKING FOR? 9

MAPS OF THE HUMBOLDT/DEL NORTE COAST 11

INTRODUCTION 13

*How to Use This Book* 13
*The Dangers* 14
*The Symbols* 15
*The History* 18
*The Climate* 19
*Get Ready, Get Set, Hike!* 20

THE TRAILS

**Tolowa Dunes State Park & Lake Earl Wildlife Area** 21
1. North to Yontocket & the Mouth of Smith River 21
2. Dead Lake Loop 27
3. Point St. George Loop 30

**Redwood National Park & Del Norte Coast** 35
4. Little Bald Hills 36
5. Boy Scout Tree 41
6. Enderts Beach/Last Chance Section, Coastal Trail 45
7. Damnation Creek 49
8. DeMartin Section, Coastal Trail 52
9. Old Hostel/Trees of Mystery Section, Coastal Trail 56
10. Yurok Loop/Hidden Beach Section, Coastal Trail 60
11. Flint Ridge Section, Coastal Trail 64
12. Coastal Drive and Short Trails 66

**Prairie Creek Redwoods State Park** 73
13. Carruthers Cove 73
14. Ossagon 76
15. Brown Creek/Rhododendron/South Fork Loop 79
16. West Ridge to Butler Creek 82
17. Elk Prairie Loop 85
18. James Irvine/Miners Ridge Loop 89
19. Fern Canyon Loop 95
20. Friendship Ridge/Coastal Loop 98

**Redwood National Park, South Portion**
21. Trillium Falls Loop 101
22. Lost Man Creek 104
23. Skunk Cabbage Creek Section, Coastal Trail 106
24. Lady Bird Johnson Grove Loop 110
25. Berry Glen 112
26. Redwood Creek 115
27. Tall Trees/Emerald Ridge Loop 121
28. Dolason Prairie 124

**Humboldt Lagoons to Patrick's Point**
29. Dry Lagoon to Big Lagoon Beach 128
30. Agate Beach 132
31. Rim Loop 134

**Trinidad Area**
32. Elk Head/College Cove 138
33. Mill Creek to Beach 140
34. Tsurai Loop on Trinidad Head 142
35. Indian Beach 144
36. Other Trinidad Trails 146

**Humboldt Bay Area**
37. Hammond Section, Coastal Trail 147
38. Mad River Beach and Dunes 152
39. Arcata's Community Forest 155
40. Arcata Ridge Trail 160
41. Arcata Marsh and Wildlife Sanctuary 163
42. Hikshari'/Eureka Waterfront 168
43. Elk River to Headwaters Forest 173
44. Table Bluff County Park 177

**Ferndale Area**
45. Centerville Beach North 180
46. Centerville Beach South 184
47. Russ Park 185
48. Cape Mendocino 189

**Humboldt Redwoods State Park**
49. Hiker's Guide to Avenue of the Giants 193
50. Bull Creek Flats/Big Tree Loop 197
51. Grasshopper Peak via Johnson Camp 203
52. Squaw Creek Ridge 207

**King Range Wilderness Area/Lost Coast** 211
53. Mattole River South 211
54. Smith-Etter Road to Beach 218
55. Kings Crest North 220
56. Lightning to Kings Peak 223
57. Kings Crest South 225
58. Shelter Cove North 230
59. Hidden Valley to Chemise Mountain to Whale Gulch 232
60. Sinkyone Wilderness State Park's New Lost Coast 238

**Other Southern Humboldt Trails**
61. Southern Humboldt Community Park 243
62. Tanoak Springs/Durphy Creek Loop 247

APPENDICES
*California Coastal Trail: Becoming a Reality …* 250
*What Kind of Trail Are you Looking For?, Continued* 253
*Common & Scientific Names of Plants along the Trails* 254
*Bibliography* 258
*Index* 260
*About Bored Feet* 264

# WHAT KIND OF TRAIL ARE YOU LOOKING FOR?

## TWELVE TRAILS NOT TO MISS—If Your Time Is Limited

5. Boy Scout Tree
6. Enderts Beach/Last Chance Section, Coastal Trail
10. Yurok Loop/Hidden Beach Section, Coastal Trail
18. James Irvine/Miners Ridge Loop
19. Fern Canyon
27. Tall Trees/Emerald Ridge Loop
30. Agate Beach
34. Tsurai Loop on Trinidad Head
47. Russ Park
50. Bull Creek Flats/Big Tree Loop
53. Mattole River South (at least 4 miles to Punta Gorda)
60. Sinkyone Wilderness State Park New Lost Coast

## TRAILS FOR HANDICAPPED ACCESS

12. Coastal Drive and Short Trails
17. Elk Prairie—see OTHER SUGGESTION
22. Lost Man Creek
24. Lady Bird Johnson Grove Loop
26. Redwood Creek—first mile or so of trail
31. Rim Loop—see OTHER SUGGESTIONS
32. Elk Head—see OTHER SUGGESTIONS
39. Arcata's Community Forest
41. Arcata Marsh— Trail to Interpretive Center, Log Pond Loop, & Klopp Lake Loop
42. Hikshari'/Eureka Waterfront Trail
43. Elk River to Headwaters Forest—first part
49. Avenue of the Giants—see M.20.5: Founders Grove
61. Southern Humboldt Community Park

## TRAILS WHERE DOGS ARE ALLOWED

3. Point St. George Loop
4. Little Bald Hills — dogs allowed on National Forest land from south end of trail
37. Hammond Section, Coastal Trail
38. Mad River Beach and Dunes
39. Arcata's Community Forest
40. Arcata Ridge
41. Arcata Marsh & Wildlife Sanctuary— quiet, leashed dogs only
42. Hikshari'/Eureka Waterfront
43. Elk River to Headwaters Forest—only to South Fork bridge
44. Table Bluff County Park
45. Centerville Beach North
46. Centerville Beach South
47. Russ Park
48. Cape Mendocino
53. Mattole River South
54. Smith-Etter Road to Beach
55. Kings Crest North

56. Lightning Trail to Kings Peak
57. Kings Crest South
58. Shelter Cove North
59. Hidden Valley to Chemise Mountain to Whale Gulch—only to 6-mile point
61. Southern Humboldt Community Park

## TRAILS FOR BACKPACKING

4. Little Bald Hills
6. Last Chance Section, Coastal Trail
8. DeMartin Section, Coastal Trail
11. Flint Ridge Section, Coastal Trail
12. Coastal Drive to Gold Bluffs Beach Hike/Bike Camp
13. Carruthers Cove to Gold Bluffs Beach Hike/Bike Camp
14. Ossagon to Gold Bluffs Beach Hike/Bike Camp
18. James Irvine to Gold Bluffs Beach Hike/Bike Camp
26. Redwood Creek
27. Tall Trees/Emerald Ridge Loop
51. Grasshopper Peak
52. Squaw Creek Ridge
53. Mattole River South
54. Smith-Etter Road to Beach
55. Kings Crest North
56. Lightning Trail to Kings Peak
57. Kings Crest South
58. Shelter Cove North
59. Hidden Valley to Chemise Mountain to Whale Gulch
60. New Lost Coast

## TRAILS FOR MOUNTAIN BIKES

1. North to Yontocket & the Mouth of Smith River
2. Dead Lake Loop
4. Little Bald Hills
6. Last Chance Section, Coastal Trail
12. Coastal Drive
14. Ossagon—see OTHER SUGGESTION: 19-mile loop
15. Brown Creek—see OTHER SUGGESTIONS
22. Lost Man Creek
37. Hammond Section, Coastal Trail
39. Arcata's Community Forest—see map
40. Arcata Ridge
42. Hikshari'/Eureka Waterfront Trail
43. Elk River to Headwaters Forest—only to South Fork bridge
51. Grasshopper Peak—see map
52. Squaw Creek Ridge—see map: 11-mile loop
54. Smith-Etter Road to Beach
61. Southern Humboldt Community Park

## TRAILS FOR EQUESTRIANS

1. North to Yontocket & the Mouth of Smith River
2. Dead Lake Loop
3. Point St. George
4. Little Bald Hills
26. Redwood Creek—see OTHER SUGGESTIONS: 34 miles

**continued on p. 253**

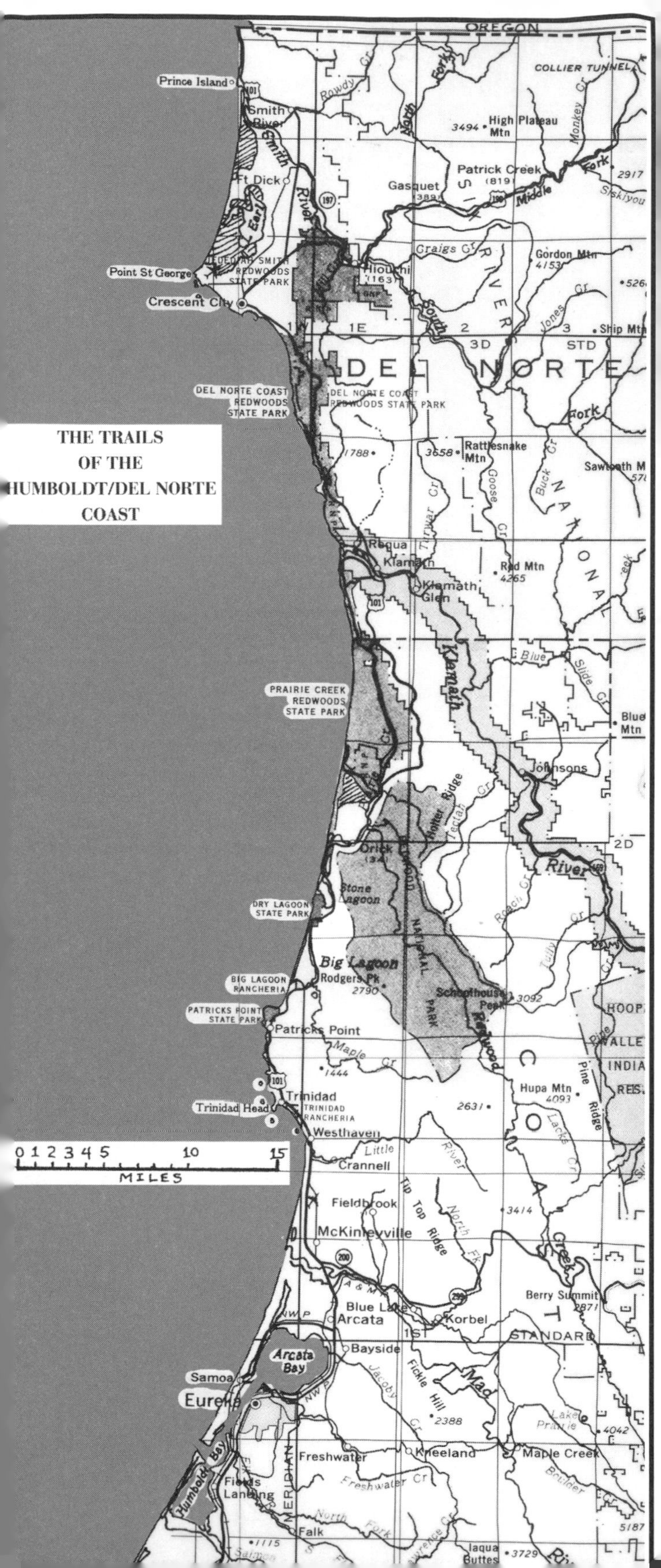
THE TRAILS
OF THE
HUMBOLDT/DEL NORTE
COAST
OREGON
Prince Island
Smith River
Ft Dick
Point St George
Crescent City
JEDEDIAH SMITH REDWOODS STATE PARK
DEL NORTE COAST REDWOODS STATE PARK
DEL NORTE
Gasquet
Patrick Creek
High Plateau Mtn
COLLIER TUNNEL
Hiouchi
Gordon Mtn
Ship Mtn
Rattlesnake Mtn
Sawtooth Mtn
Requa
Klamath
Klamath Glen
Red Mtn
PRAIRIE CREEK REDWOODS STATE PARK
Blue Mtn
Johnsons
Orick
Stone Lagoon
DRY LAGOON STATE PARK
Big Lagoon
Rodgers Pk
BIG LAGOON RANCHERIA
PATRICKS POINT STATE PARK
Patricks Point
Schoolhouse Peak
REDWOOD NATIONAL PARK
Trinidad
Trinidad Head
TRINIDAD RANCHERIA
Westhaven
Crannell
Hupa Mtn
0 1 2 3 4 5 10 15
MILES
Fieldbrook
McKinleyville
Tip Top Ridge
Berry Summit
Blue Lake
Arcata
Korbel
Bayside
Arcata Bay
Samoa
Eureka
Fickle Hill
Humboldt Bay
Fields Landing
Freshwater
Kneeland
Maple Creek
Falk
Iaqua Buttes
MERIDIAN
STANDARD

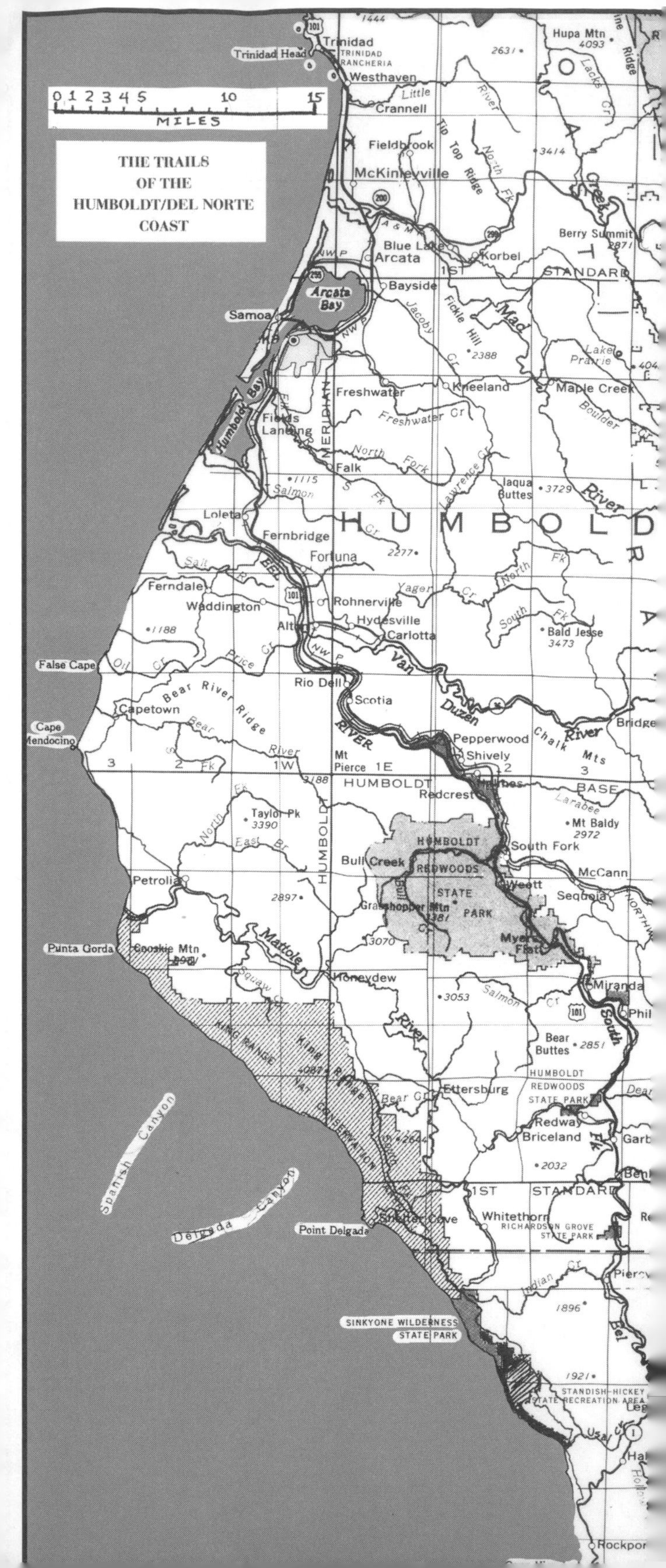
THE TRAILS
OF THE
HUMBOLDT/DEL NORTE
COAST
0 1 2 3 4 5 10 15
MILES
Trinidad Head
Trinidad
TRINIDAD RANCHERIA
Westhaven
Crannell
Fieldbrook
McKinleyville
Tip Top Ridge
Hupa Mtn
4093
Berry Summit
Blue Lake
Arcata
Korbel
Arcata Bay
Samoa
Bayside
Jacoby Cr
Fickle Hill
Mad River
Humboldt Bay
Freshwater
Kneeland
Maple Creek
Freshwater Cr
Fields Landing
Falk
Iaqua Buttes
3729
Salmon Cr
Loleta
Fernbridge
Fortuna
HUMBOLDT
Ferndale
Waddington
Rohnerville
Hydesville
Carlotta
Alton
Yager Cr
Bald Jesse
3473
False Cape
Oil Cr
Price Cr
Rio Dell
Scotia
Van Duzen River
Bear River Ridge
Capetown
Cape Mendocino
Bear River
Pepperwood
Shively
Chalk Mts
Bridgeville
Mt Pierce
HUMBOLDT BASE
Redcrest
Larabee
Mt Baldy
2972
Taylor Pk
3390
HUMBOLDT REDWOODS STATE PARK
South Fork
Bull Creek
McCann
Weott
Sequoia
Petrolia
Grasshopper Mtn
Myers Flat
Punta Gorda
Cooskie Mtn
Mattole River
Honeydew
Salmon Cr
Miranda
Phillipsville
Bear Buttes
2851
KING RANGE NAT CONSERVATION AREA
King Range
Ettersburg
Bear Cr
HUMBOLDT REDWOODS STATE PARK
Redway
Briceland
Garberville
Spanish Canyon
Delgada Canyon
Point Delgada
Shelter Cove
Whitethorn
RICHARDSON GROVE STATE PARK
1ST STANDARD
Indian Cr
Piercy
SINKYONE WILDERNESS STATE PARK
STANDISH-HICKEY STATE RECREATION AREA
Rockport

# INTRODUCTION

Humboldt and Del Norte counties comprise a vast wild land of forests, mountains, rivers and shores in the northwestern corner of California. The area's 165-mile coastline varies greatly from north to south. From Crescent City north, the shore consists of sandy beaches backed by marine terraces. South of Crescent City, the rugged rocky shore lies below high, eroded cliffs that stretch to the Humboldt County line. Humboldt County's coast north of Trinidad is characterized by dark sand beaches with high bluffs, rocky coves and tidepools, three large lagoons and vast forests. Then the coast turns more gentle, with long, dune-backed beaches adjacent to fertile river flood plains and the lowlands of Humboldt Bay. South of Ferndale, high coastal mountains drop steeply to the narrow, secluded beaches of California's Lost Coast.

Highway 101 crosses the heart of this rugged land from north to south, providing access to hundreds of miles of trails. Although the highway stays within 25 miles of the shore, roads to the coast are few, except in the vicinity of Humboldt Bay.

This book tells you how to find and walk, hike or ride more than 600 miles of trails through this wild, scenic land. The trails range from easy walks to difficult backpacks, with choices to fit the taste of every nature lover. The hikes will lead you to the highest peak on the Northern California coast, the world's tallest trees, the broad mouths of wild rivers, marshes and estuaries rich in bird and plant life, pristine ponds and streams, city parks, vast wild beaches, meadows and prairies sprinkled with wildflowers, and jagged rock outcrops.

So get out of your car and use feet, bicycle, horse or wheelchair to explore the Humboldt/Del Norte Coast.

# HOW TO USE THIS BOOK

The trails in this book are organized from the north to the south. Highway 101 is the starting point for the directions to every trailhead. No trail is more than two hours from Eureka or Arcata.

You will find a milepost number on Highway 101 in the directions to each trail. These numbers refer to the white highway mileposts placed frequently (but at irregular intervals) along Highway 101 by CalTrans, the State Department of Transportation. You can quickly determine the location of a trail (and where it is in relation to you) by referring to its milepost number. The detailed directions to each trailhead may include other mileposts on secondary roads.

You do not have to start at the beginning of the book. Simply turn to the trail nearest your location and you will be on your way. Neighboring trails will be on adjacent pages.

For each trail in the book you will find a map (top is north unless noted otherwise), specific directions to the trailhead, the best time to go, appropriate warnings, and a detailed trail description with some history and/or natural history.

You will find a group of symbols below the access information for each trail. They tell you at a glance the level of difficulty, type of trail, whether there is a fee, and whether dogs are allowed. The list of symbols follows.

After the Contents pages are lists of trails most suitable for a particular type of recreation: dog walking, mountain bikes, equestrians, backpacking, beach walks (or runs) and handicapped access. We've added a list of the twelve trails not to miss if your time is short. An appendix details the California Coastal Trail as it currently runs through Del Norte and Humboldt Counties.

## THE DANGERS

### TEN COASTAL COMMANDMENTS

When on the trail, *always* keep your senses wide open so that you can best appreciate nature's pleasures as well as her dangers. Don't let nature lull you into complacency. Here are ten rules to keep you out of danger and enhance your journey so that you may safely enjoy the beauty of the coast and forests.

1. **DON'T LITTER**. Most of these places are unspoiled. Do your part to keep them that way. Show your appreciation for Mother Nature by hiking with a trash bag which you can fill with any trash you find in otherwise pristine places, even cigarette butts, matches and bottle caps.

2. **NO TRESPASSING**. Property owners have a right to privacy. Stay off private property. There are enough public places without walking through someone's yard.

3. **NEVER TURN YOUR BACK ON THE OCEAN.** Oversized rogue waves can strike the coast at anytime. They are especially common in winter. They have killed people; watch for them. More subtle are the changes of the tides: don't let rising tides strand you against steep cliffs or on a submerged tidal island. The ocean is icy and unforgiving, generally unsafe for swimming without a wetsuit.

4. **STAY BACK FROM CLIFFS**. Coastal soils are often unstable. You wouldn't want to fall 40 feet into the icy sea, would you? Don't get too close to the cliff's edge, and never climb on cliffs unless there is a safe trail.

# THE SYMBOLS

WALK:
Less than 2 miles
Easy terrain

EASY HIKE:
2 to 10 miles
Easy terrain

MODERATE HIKE:
2 to 10 miles
Rougher terrain

DIFFICULT HIKE:
Strenuous terrain
Backpacking possible

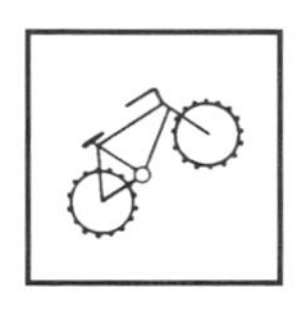

MOUNTAIN BIKE TRAIL

PICNIC SPOT:
May be tables or just a good blanket spot

BIKE TRAIL

DOGS ALLOWED ON LEASH

CAR CAMPING

WALK-IN OR BIKE-IN CAMPING:
Environmental camps

TIDEPOOL ACCESS

HANDICAP ACCESS

RECOMMENDED
FOR FAMILIES

INTERPRETIVE
NATURE TRAIL

TRAIL FOR
EQUESTRIANS

RESTROOMS
AVAILABLE

WATER AVAILABLE

FEE AREA

FISHING ACCESS

NO OIL EXPLORATION
OR DRILLING

5. **WILD THINGS: ANIMAL**. Most of the animal pests of the Humboldt/Del Norte Coast are small, unless a bear goes after your food (keep camp clean and food put safely away) or you get chased by a Roosevelt elk (generally they will not chase you unless you get too close). Watch out for ticks, wasps, mosquitoes, biting spiders, scorpions and rattlesnakes. Human animals are easily the most dangerous, especially in deer hunting season (from mid-August until late September). Always listen for gunfire, especially outside state parks. Never (even in a vehicle) enter an area where logging is in progress.

UNDERWATER ANIMALS: When tidepooling or at the beach, always watch for sea urchins and jellyfish. Both have stinging spines that are painful. Remember that mussels are quarantined each year from May through October (or later); at that time they contain deadly poison.

6. **WILD THINGS: PLANT**. These mean business too, especially poison oak and stinging nettles, which can get you with the slightest touch. Many other plants are poisonous. It is best to not touch any plants unless you know by positive identification that they are safe; this is most important with mushrooms.

7. **POT GARDENS**. Don't even think about messing with one, no matter whose side you are on. If you ever stumble onto a pot patch (not likely if you stay on the trails in this book), leave more quietly than you came. Take only memories.

8. **TRAFFIC**. Coast roads are difficult and often overcrowded. Drive carefully and courteously. Please turn out for faster traffic. You will enjoy the coast more if you do. If you stop, pull safely off the road.

9. **CRIME**. Be sure to lock your car when you leave it at the trailhead. Leave valuables out of sight, or better yet, back at your lodging.

10. **ALWAYS TAKE RESPONSIBILITY FOR YOURSELF AND YOUR PARTY**. This is a trail guide, not a nursery school. The author cannot and will not be responsible for you in the wilds. Information contained in this book is correct to the best of the author's knowledge. Author and publisher assume no liability for damages arising from errors or omissions. **You must take the responsibility for your safety and health while on these trails**. These are wild places. Safety conditions of trails, beaches and tidepools may vary with seasons and tides. Be cautious, heed the above warnings and the warnings for each trail, and always check on local conditions. It is always better to hike with a friend. Know where you can get help in case of emergency.

# THE HISTORY

Native Americans have lived along the Humboldt/Del Norte Coast for at least 5000 years, perhaps as long as 10,000 years or longer. The cultures of the Tolowa, Yurok, Chilula, Wiyot, Mattole and Sinkyone prospered with the coast's abundant natural resources.

Spanish galleons sailed along the coast beginning in the sixteenth century. The first recorded European visitors came in 1775 when Spanish explorers sailed into Trinidad Bay, met the local Yuroks, and erected a cross on Trinidad Head. Their mapping of Trinidad as a safe harbor brought later explorers. In 1806 an American named Jonathan Winship discovered Humboldt Bay as his ship explored the coast for the Russian-American Fur Company. His discovery was forgotten because he deemed the bay unnavigable for large ships.

In the 1820s and 1830s, fur trappers and explorers made the first overland journeys through Humboldt County. .Jedediah Smith, Stephen Meek, Ewing Young, Peter Ogden and three others named McLeod, Mofras and LaFrambois stayed briefly without recording much information about the area.

In July 1848 gold was discovered first on the Trinity River, then on the Klamath. The difficult inland route to these mines provoked the search for safe harbors along the North Coast.

On November 5, 1849, a party of eight explorers left the Trinity mines seeking the Trinidad Bay shown on Spanish maps. They were led by Dr. Josiah Gregg, writer and frontiersman, who made the first extensive record of a visit to Humboldt County. The Indians told Gregg it was an eight-day journey to the coast, so the party set out with enough food for a ten-day trek. Lacking guides, they lost the Indian trail in a snowstorm and struggled through rugged country. The snow turned to rain. By the seventh day they were reduced to eating the flour paste that formed inside their packs. On their journey, they had to cut their way through immense quantities of fallen timber in the vast forests, often progressing only two miles a day. They traveled four and a half weeks to reach the coast.

The starving party arrived at Trinidad Bay on December 7. They traded with the native people for provisions, then headed south. Crossing the Mad River in Indian canoes, they named it for an argument they had there. They found Humboldt Bay the next evening, and by Christmas Day they camped at the future location of Arcata, feasting on elk and clams provided by the friendly Wiyots.

They headed south to tell California of their discoveries. They named the Eel River as they met Indians fishing for eels (actually lampreys). They named the Van Duzen River for one of their members. Then the eight men separated into two groups. Gregg's group sought a route along the coast, but the rugged country forced them to turn inland south of Cape Mendocino. Gregg died of starvation near Clear Lake. The other group, led by L. K. Wood, followed the Eel River south, faring little better. Wood was mauled by grizzly bears and crippled for life. But they reached Sonoma to report their discoveries on February 17, 1850.

Several ships immediately left San Francisco searching for Humboldt and Trinidad Bays. Settlement began at Trinidad in March, at Humboldt Bay in April. By that summer a trail was completed to the Klamath and Trinity mines. In September the first sawmill opened at Eureka. By 1853 nine mills along Humboldt Bay shipped 20 million board feet of lumber to San Francisco. By 1856 the packing business to the northern mines had 5000 mules in service.

The towns of Eureka, Arcata and Trinidad grew and prospered, but not without hostilities from the Indians and natural hardships caused by the wild, rugged country. Eureka became the county seat in May 1856. Humboldt County remained accessible primarily by ship until 1911, when an all-weather road was established to San Francisco.

## THE CLIMATE

The climate of the Humboldt/Del Norte Coast is cool, but mild enough for you to hike year round, if you are prepared for varying conditions. In planning your excursions, keep in mind the following about the seasons along the North Coast: November to March are the rainy months, time to bring rain coats and rubber boots. Still, there are often fine sunny days between storms.

April and May are often windy, with occasional rainstorms. The wind may be gentle, or fierce and unrelenting. The landscape is at its most lush and beautiful. Bring layered clothing and hats.

June, July and August bring sunny summer days, alternating with thick fog. You may be comfortable in shorts, but bring layered clothing in case the fog comes in. Sometimes you can beat the fog by heading a few miles inland. This is the most crowded season, especially July and August.

September and October are a beautiful time. Fog is less common. Though there may be rainstorms, most of the days are calm and warm. The land is dry, the hills golden, and the sunsets often spectacular.

# GET READY, GET SET, HIKE!

You must be chomping at the bit to get out on the trail by now. Here are a few suggestions of what you need to take on your hike: layered clothing—sweater, sweatshirt, hat, windbreaker and/or raincoat; insect repellent; sunscreen; sunglasses; and small first-aid kit including moleskin for blisters. Highly recommended for all but the shortest walks: water container, extra food, pocket knife, flashlight or headlamp and extra batteries, matches and fire starter, map, compass (helps if you know how to use it), and of course your ***Hiker's hip pocket Guide!***

Additional suggestions: spare socks, toilet paper and plastic trowel, binoculars, camera, field guides to birds, wildflowers and/or trees. If you are backpacking, you should consult an equipment list for that purpose.

When you are on the trail, remember to slow down, open your senses and enjoy. Most people hike at a rate of 2 to 3 miles per hour. But beach sand or steep terrain may slow all but the most hardy to as little as one mile per hour. Leave ample time to do the hike you plan at a pleasant pace. Hike not to count the miles, but to enjoy and appreciate nature. Happy trails to you!

# TOLOWA DUNES STATE PARK & LAKE EARL WILDLIFE AREA

*This state park and the adjacent wildlife area (managed by California Department of Fish and Game) together comprise about 10,000 acres of lagoon, marsh and beach surrounded by vegetated dunes with wooded ridges and flowered meadows. Lying between the Smith River delta and Crescent City, the large natural tract offers diverse plant and animal life in a fascinating array of habitats. Up to half of this acreage may be covered with water during the wet season, providing a rich habitat for migratory and resident birds. More than 250 avian species use the area; during migration you might see as many as 100,000 birds here. Wildflowers present spectacular displays from late March through summer. Lakes Earl and Tolowa, joined by the deep, slender channel called the Narrows, were once a part of the Smith River watershed, but the mighty river bypasses them to the east and north today. Lake Earl, fed by Jordan Creek, is mostly freshwater, while Lake Tolowa to the west is somewhat saline. Being joined however; they exist in a fluid shifting balance that supports a striking diversity of fish and aquatic vegetation.*

*You can explore the area on an expanding network of trails. They provide access to this wondrous world of ancient sand dunes and changing bodies of water where a wide variety of ecological communities, each with a varied assortment of flora and fauna, exist in a relatively small area.*

## 1. NORTH TO YONTOCKET & THE MOUTH OF SMITH RIVER

CENTER OF THE TOLOWA WORLD

*When the Tolowa world was new, there was nothing. Then, the first three people, Thunder, Baby Sender and Daylight, and their sweat house came into existence. It was extremely cold in the void. One day Baby Sender got up. That is how the cold was chased out. He thought, "A first place, like this one, shall come into existence."*

*Daylight said, "Yes" and opened the door of the sweat house. In that way, daylight came into existence.*

*Baby Sender then spat downward and the ocean came into being. He parted the waters and underneath he could see earth. "What is it that looks this way? It is a world for people, I suppose," Baby Sender said. "Everything will come forth and bloom."*

NORTH TO YONTOCKET &
THE MOUTH OF SMITH RIVER:

DISTANCE: 5¾-mile loop, plus 6¼-mile option to Smith River mouth; 2⅝ miles to Yontocket.
TIME: Three hours to full day.
TERRAIN: Through gently rolling vegetated dunes to a Tolowa village site near mouth of Smith River, returning past several ponds.
ELEVATION GAIN/LOSS: Loop: 300 feet +/-. One way to Yontocket: 200 feet +/180 feet -; to River: 200 feet + /220 feet -.
BEST TIME: Spring, early summer for wildflowers. Autumn for best weather.
WARNINGS: Watch for poison oak. Portions of trail may be wet in winter and spring.
HOW TO GET THERE: Turn west off Highway 101 at M.31.2 onto Elk Valley Road (.6 mile north of Highway 199 interchange). Turn right on Lake Earl Drive in .9 mile. At 2.9 miles from Highway 101, turn left on Lower Lake Road. At 5.5 miles go left on Kellogg Road for .75 mile to trailhead parking on right.
FURTHER INFO: Tolowa Dunes State Park & Lake Earl Wildlife Area (707)465-7385.
OTHER SUGGESTION: For a SHORTER ROUTE TO YONTOCKET, drive north to the end of Lower Lake Road, then west on Pala Road for one mile to trailhead at a white gate; it is ¼ mile to Yontocket, 3⅛ miles to river mouth.

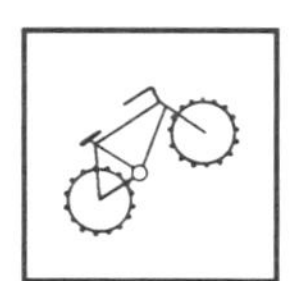

*Historically the Tolowa were a small, prosperous Athabaskan culture, the bridge between the magnificent Athabaskan cultures of the Pacific Northwest coast and tribes of Northern California. Archaeological evidence shows that the Tolowa have inhabited what is now Del Norte County for at least 2300 years. Before the invasion of white people seeking gold in the 1850s, the Tolowa had eight large villages of 100 to 300 people each and several smaller villages. Tolowa culture and religion are similar to those of the Yuroks in many ways, although the Yurok are an Algonkian people. There has been considerable intermarriage between these ethnically different, culturally related groups.*

*The Tolowa and their neighbors considered the Tolowa village of Yontakit, which was located at the north end of this hike, to be the center of the world, the place where the First People created this world. Every year Yurok from the south and Chetco and Tututnu from the north would journey to Yontakit for a ten-day world renewal ceremony believed essential for the continuance of the cycle of life. During one of these ceremonies in 1853, a tragic slaughter occurred at Yontakit. White vigilantes came at the height of the ceremony, setting the village on fire and massacring hundreds of residents and visitors.*

*The Tolowa believed heaven was just behind the sun, somehow fitting for the people who lived in this mist-shrouded world. Sadly, the old environmental camps and the hike/bike/horse camp have been closed and removed.*

Walk through the gate at the north end of the parking area and follow the level double track heading north. You cross grasslands abundant with lupine, yellow mat, knotweed, beach strawberry, sea thrift and coast buckwheat. A willow thicket lies on your left, wooded dunes on the right. Your path winds to the right at 1/8 mile. You pass two side trails on the right. Our described loop returns by the second one.

Head north again by ¼ mile, where yellow Del Norte wallflower grows on nearby dunes, with silverweed and silverleaf phacelia in the grasslands. Around ½ mile you pass through a low area with several tiny seasonal ponds. The trail may be wet here in winter and spring. Your trail skirts a forest where wind-shaped shore pines shelter Oregon grape and the manzanita ground cover known as bearberry or kinnikinnick.

Beyond ¾ mile Sitka spruce dominate the nearby forest as you traverse prairie with clumps of elderberry and huckleberry. Pass the tiny yellow and white flowers of cream cup and johnny tuck around one mile as you climb slightly to top a wooded dune, then descend into a wooded valley.

Beyond 1¼ miles you climb to meet a gravel double track. You can see a large seasonal pond to the east. Follow the gravel track north, rolling over and through dunes as grand fir joins the pines and spruces, with wax myrtle, coyote brush, salmonberry, twinberry, salal, coast silktassel, hairy honeysuckle and red-flowering currant in the understory.

From 1½ miles you follow the crest of a dune. To the west you can see across valley and dune to the Pacific, with St. George Reef Lighthouse seven miles offshore. To the east a large pond is backed by the marshy Smith River delta, the Coast Range rising beyond. Old stumps to five feet in diameter indicate the size of the original forest in this unusual plant community.

Your trail soon descends gently. Ignore a spur on the right, then meet one on the left at 1¾ miles. It heads west

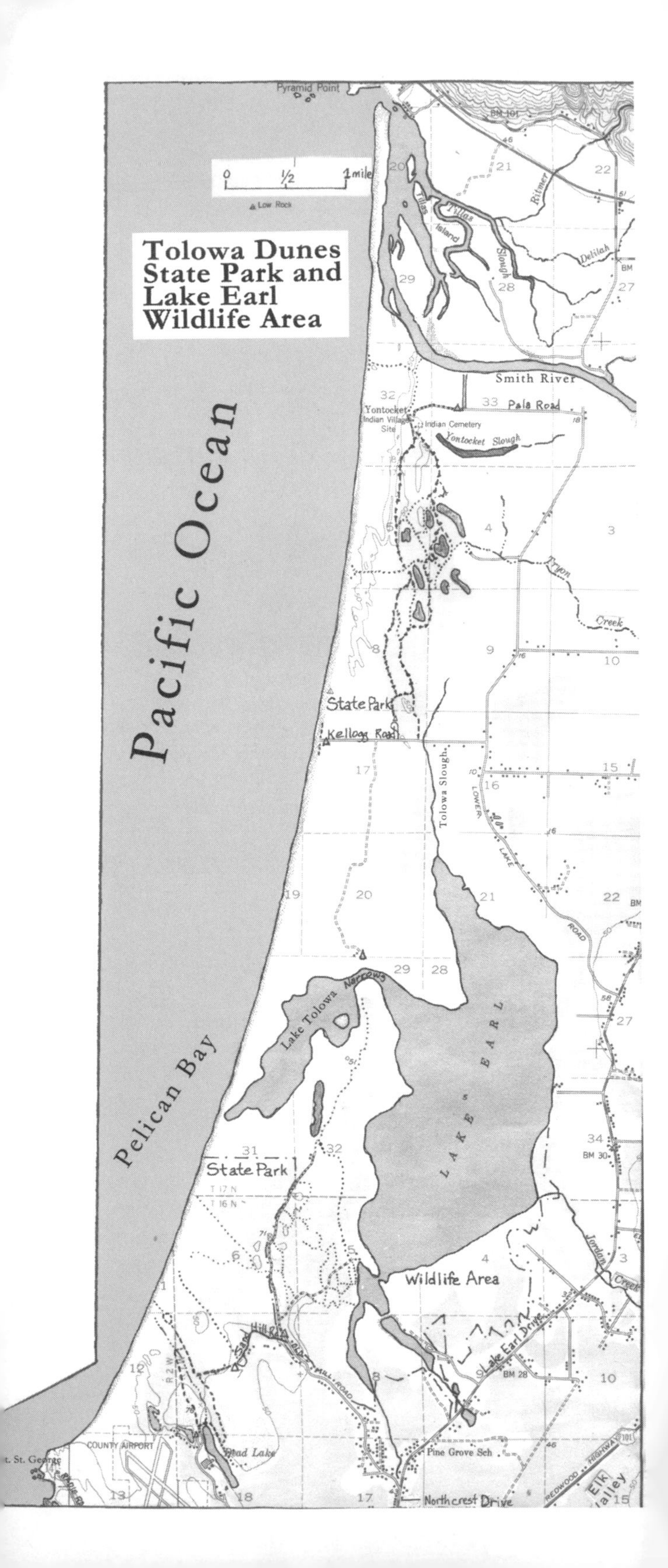

Tolowa Dunes State Park and Lake Earl Wildlife Area
Pacific Ocean
Pelican Bay
Pyramid Point
0 1/2 1 mile
Low Rock
Tillas Island
Tillas Slough
Rilmer
Delilah
Smith River
Pala Road
Yontocket Indian Village Site
Indian Cemetery
Yontocket Slough
Tryon Creek
State Park
Kellogg Road
Tolowa Slough
Lower Lake Road
Lake Tolowa
Narrows
Lake Earl
State Park
Wildlife Area
Jordan Creek
Sand Hill Road
Old Mill Road
Lake Earl Drive
County Airport
Dead Lake
Pine Grove Sch
Northcrest Drive
Redwood Highway
Elk Valley

through dune and marsh, coming to the beach in ½ mile. Descend north on the gravel track, passing checker lilies in spring. By 1⅞ miles your road follows a valley between two vegetated dunes. Common juniper grows as a sprawling ground cover and coastal nemophila offers delicate white flowers in spring.

Beyond 2⅛ miles the track returns to the ridgetop where three-foot-diameter spruce grow. You descend along mossy slopes where calypso orchids and violets thrive in spring, then drop through two grassy valleys lined with conifers.

Ascend gradually for ¼ mile, coming to a junction at the top of a hill at 2⅝ miles. This is Yontocket, anglicized name for the native village of Yon'takit, center of the Tolowa world. The fenced cemetery on the right marks the site of the 1853 massacre of hundreds of Tolowa by vigilante settlers, another tragic cataclysm in the conquering of California. A bench east of the cemetery surveys the magical land where river and ancient dunes meet. Yontocket Slough lies in the flood plain to the east. A picnic table sits nearby.

Our described loop heads southeast from here. (You may also return the way you came for a 5¼-mile round trip.) Before you return however, consider a side trip north to extend your trek.

The double track north descends past pioneer apple, cypress and eucalyptus trees to meet Pala Road (see OTHER SUGGESTION), with an outhouse near the junction. Take the grassy track north, contouring between dunes to another fork at ¼ mile. If you go right, you come to the Smith River at ½ mile. The left fork heads west to the beach at 1⅛ miles. From there it is about 2 miles north to the mouth of Smith River.

Heading south from Yontocket our described loop returns by the left fork. Climb briefly, then descend past spruces with roots like stilts. Around 2¾ miles the grassy double track crosses the edge of the flood plain, where the trail may be flooded in winter. You can detour to the right on a single track along the base of the grassy dune. By 3 miles the trails become one and head southwest through the dunes.

Just beyond 3⅛ miles the old hike/bike/horse camp on

the left has been removed. The main trail, a distinct double track, turns west, then south, passing another spur before 3⅜ miles (Port Orford cedar and Indian plum grow along the spur).

Your double track makes a winding ascent south through forest to a view of a long pond, the most permanent of the seasonal ponds in the area. The trail meanders through grassy hills north, then west of the pond. Before 3½ miles an arrow points right for a single track winding south, but our described loop stays on the double track, soon following a lake shore on your right.

Turn right onto a second arrow-marked track before 3⅝ miles and descend south between two ponds. You follow an enchanting, twisting path that reveals views of the lake on the right, then the one on the left. Watch for head-high poison oak. Iris hunker, entwined with honeysuckle and native blackberry. Melodic bird song and the distant rumble of surf punctuate a pervading quiet.

The path winds, ducks, twists, then hides in verdant tunnels, passing cattails, then foxgloves beside a small lily pond. All too soon your path turns south through grasslands, where hummingbirds dart from one flowering currant to the next in spring.

Meet a graveled double track at 3⅞ miles. Walk 150 feet west on the gravel, then turn left on a single sandy track south through conifer forest. You soon make a winding climb into grasslands for views of a pond on the right. Dense hardwood forest fills a deep depression on your left.

Your sandy track rolls and dips, winding in and out of forest. Beyond 4⅜ miles you have brief glimpses of a second pond on your right, then views of the Smith River flood plain on the left. Climb to a last view of the pond at 4⅝ miles. Then your path turns west to meet a gravel road.

Turn left and wind south to meet another gravel track. Go left again, winding through patchy forest and grasslands. Around 5 miles alders fill a gully on your right. Continue south to a hitching post beside a honey house on the left before 5⅜ miles. In 250 feet a trail on the right is marked horses OK. Take the horse path 400 feet, then go left on the double track, returning to the trailhead at 5¾ miles.

## 2.
# DEAD LAKE LOOP
### SCENE OF THE TOLOWA LEGEND OF THE FALL

*In ancient Tolowa mythology Dead Lake was the scene of the People's fall from grace. After Baby Sender created the world, a numerous tribe dwelt just inland from Tagian-te, what we today call Point St. George. Many summers they lived in peace. The waters abounded with fish, the forests with game, and the peoples' hearts were glad. Then came the time of sorrow. One day in council the chief became angry at one of the elders and struck him to the ground. This blow led to the destruction of the harmony that had existed. Some of the People began to doubt their leaders, others cried for vengeance. While many remained loyal, the discord allowed one dark-hearted person to practice evil. The heavens covered with menacing clouds of terrible darkness and the wind roared over the shifting sands, blinding everyone. Suddenly a deafening sound broke upon the ears of the People. Like the jaws of a dragon, the earth opened beneath their feet and swallowed them. The gaping abyss opened where Dead Lake is today. The storm broke in wild fury and torrents filled the sepulcher. To this day the Tolowa consider the lake bottomless, infested with enormous serpents, and they will not go there.*

*This mysterious lake has no inlet, and yet despite the ceaseless outpouring of Sweetwater Creek from it, retains a constant water level. You might carry angelica root or other protection from evil if you visit Dead Lake today. Or you can steer clear of the lake and head for the miles of open beach to which this trail provides access. It is due to another reason, the sensitive habitat surrounding the lake, that state parks people have closed the area to equestrians. Horseback riders are allowed on the trail to the beach.*

Behind a locked gate, a level double track heads southwest. You cross grasslands surrounded by coastal fir forest. Around 1/8 mile the trail can be very wet in winter and spring. A

DEAD LAKE LOOP:

DISTANCE: 2½-mile loop, plus 2½-mile side trip to beach, where you can go south 1½ miles to Point St. George or north up to 6 miles to Smith River mouth.
TIME: One or 2 hours for loop.
ELEVATION GAIN/LOSS: Loop: 120 feet +/120 feet-.
TERRAIN: Contours through grasslands and wooded dunes, ascends along creek to Dead Lake, then returns.
BEST TIME: Spring, early summer for wildflowers.
WARNINGS: Watch for poison oak.
HOW TO GET THERE: Turn off Highway 101 at M.27.0 (north end of Crescent City) onto Northcrest Drive for 1.3 miles, then go left on Old Mill Road for 1.5 miles, then left on Sand Hill Road .5 mile to its end and the trailhead.
FURTHER INFO: Tolowa Dunes State Park & Lake Earl Wildlife Area (707)465-7385.
OTHER SUGGESTION: CADRE POINT/ MCLAUGHLIN POND LOOP (3¾ miles, fee: $2.50 or current fishing or hunting license) explores the south shore of Lake Earl, then heads north to the pond, where beaver and river otters live. From McLaughlin Pond you can walk 1½ miles north to THE NARROWS, the deep channel connecting Lake Earl with Lake Tolowa. The entire area, accessible from the trailhead at the end of Old Mill Road, provides excellent wildlife viewing. Be aware that hunting is allowed on most of these Department of Fish and Game lands.

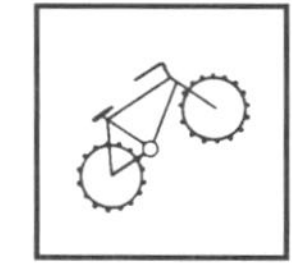

spur on the right leads to a picnic area on an old house site surrounded by cypress trees.

The main trail contours to another picnic table by ¼ mile. Climb a short hill as your path bends left, passing shore pine, wax myrtle, Oregon grape, evergreen huckleberry, coast buckwheat and lupine. Walk sandy tread past Del Norte wallflower in a depression in the dunes on your left.

Your track bends right, coming to a junction at 3/8 mile. The trail on the left, signed "DEAD LAKE" (closed to horses), will be your return path. Go right and head northwest through grasslands, then into forest as Sitka spruce, Douglas fir and grand fir join the pines. Look for false lily of the valley, iris, checker lily and calypso orchid in spring. Red huckleberry and rattlesnake plantain also grow along the route.

At 5/8 mile a faint trail on the left (closed to equestrians) climbs northwest. The main double track (open to horses) continues north-northwest, coming to the beach at 1¼ miles. From there hikers and equestrians can go south 1½ miles to Point St. George, or north up to 6 miles to the mouth of Smith River.

Our described loop goes left on the faint trail at 5/8 mile. It quickly descends into forest, then crosses tiny Sweetwater Creek on one of two logs. (The crossing, particularly in winter; may not be advisable to people with unsure footing.) Shaded by alders, the creek is jammed with skunk cabbage and crowded by tall salmonberry and low waterleaf.

Pick up the faint trail heading south through lush, dense vegetation. At ¾ mile the path climbs above the creek on a mossy roadbed, passing an escaped holly bush on the left. You leave the forest and meet a sandy trail.

Follow the sandy track south-southeast along the crest of a vegetated dune, climbing gradually. Beyond one mile you ascend to a view southwest across expansive dunes to offshore rocks near Point St. George. You can also see Dead Lake to the south.

At 1 1/8 miles your trail drops off the dune's crest to its west face, leaving the conifer forest. Go left as the trail forks, soon heading south through the dunes. The path becomes extremely vague beyond 1¼ miles, but continue south through the dunes until you look out over Dead Lake. The trail reappears, dropping off the dune to approach the lake shore. (The Riverside Street access is to the south.)

Take the trail that heads west along Dead Lake's north shore. Look beyond the alders for pond lilies on the lake. The yellow flowers bloom in spring. Cross Sweetwater Creek on the driftwood logs jammed in the lake's outlet.

Once you cross the creek your trail improves. Around 1 3/8 miles it turns south through the alder forest along the shore. Then climb through grasslands to a junction at 1½ miles. Continue along the lake shore 300 feet to a second junction, where your return trail is on the left. (The shoreline trail continues for 1/8 mile to a large dune area.)

Go left on the path that heads north briefly, then follows the crest of a dune northwest. Pass a side trail, staying on the clearly marked path. At the next junction a spur heads north to Dead Lake Dune in 1/8 mile. Go left for the trailhead, heading northwest on the obvious path through dense vegetation.

At 2 miles the trail bends right and descends east to meet the main double track. Turn right and retrace your steps to the trailhead.

## 3.
# POINT ST. GEORGE LOOP
### EXPLORING DEL NORTE'S WESTERNMOST SHORE

*These 339 acres were for sale and available for commercial development until Del Norte County purchased them for public use in 2002. When added to scattered parcels that were already in public ownership here, the public lands total 370 acres. The Tolowa called it Tagian-te. They and their ancestors inhabited the area since at least 300 B.C. Tolowa people still use it today for fishing and shellfish gathering.*

*Even a visit to the parking lot brings rewards. Point St. George's nature surrounds you, except for the 1926 former Coast Guard facility beside the lot, now a private residence. The surf murmurs or roars from the north. You're likely to see many birds: harriers and other raptors, songbirds, shorebirds, plus ospreys and pelicans in spring, summer and autumn.*

*Castle Rock to the south, a National Wildlife Refuge, is the second most important seabird rookery in California and home to the state's largest breeding colonies of rhinoceros auklets and common murres. It also supports large colonies of Cassin's auklets, fork-tailed and Leach's storm-petrels, pigeon guillemots and tufted puffins. Black oystercatchers, western gulls, and Brandt's and pelagic cormorants also breed here. It's also a pupping ground for harbor seals and a haul-out for sea lions.*

*On clear days you can see north into Oregon to the rounded peaks above the Chetco River and the buildings of Brookings and Harbor. To the east is a vast swath of dark green conifer forest which includes some of the world's tallest trees. The peaks of the Klamath and Siskiyou Mountains rise to pointed rocky heights beyond the green. To the west-northwest, St. George Reef Lighthouse rises seven miles out at sea.*

*Note that there are no official trails at Point St. George. After public acquisition, locals voiced their feelings that the headlands should remain as they were: wild. Our hike is but one way to explore this wild treasure.*

The hike starts at the green gate at road's end. If you descend the gravel path to North Beach, you may be able to walk the tideline of Pelican Bay all the way to the the mouth of the Smith River. See OTHER SUGGESTION. Our described hike meanders northwest through grasslands, heading generally in the direction of St. George Reef Lighthouse, or toward the antenna if the coast is wrapped in fog.

Your level trail forks just before the antenna. Take the right fork, soon coming to a point at bluff's edge at 1/8 mile. Low offshore rocks directly off the point sprawl towards the offshore lighthouse. They are part of St. George Reef, the hazardous marine feature the lighthouse was built to keep

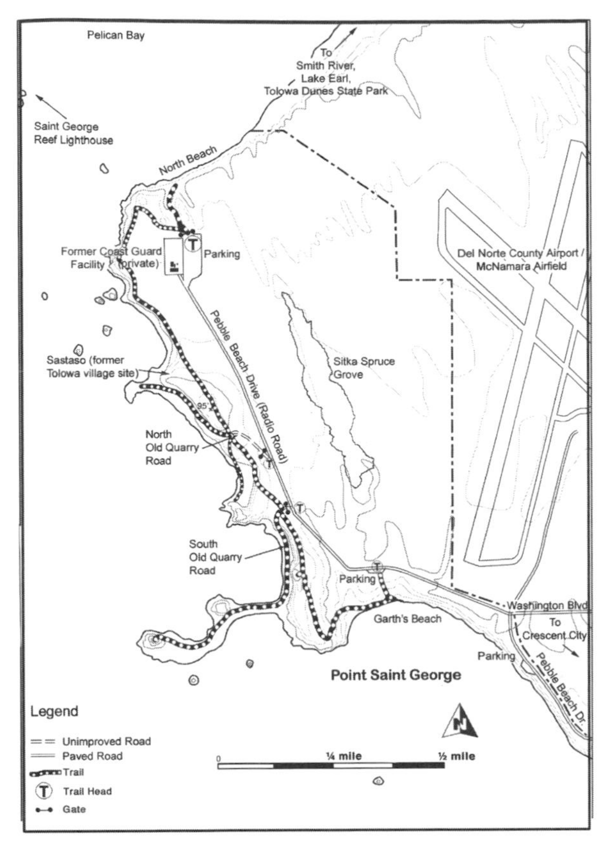


ships away from.

Turn south to follow the grassy track along the bluff, dense with coastal scrub vegetation including gum plant, purple seaside daisy, sea thrift, angelica, yarrow, lupine, beach strawberry, salal and plantain along with invasive Himalayan blackberry and dune grass. Where the grassy track splits about 125 feet south of the point, you can take either one—they soon rejoin. You overlook tall sea stacks, the one white with bird guano known as White Rock. Continue south along the bluff past a larger antenna, beyond which the trail bends right to follow the bluff edge, dipping across an eroded area.

Before ¼ mile you pass a point on your right, the westernmost tip of Point St. George. From here you can see that White Rock has a large arch in it. Just beyond the antenna, a side trail forks left, offering a quick return to the parking lot. Our described hike continues south along the bluff past many irises. You pass the Earth Scope Plate Boundary Observation Station, part of a network of 875 across the western United States observing the Pacific and North American tectonic plates' changing relationship to each other.

By 3/8 mile you pass more large sea stacks on your right, both onshore and offshore. The beach below is heaped with

POINT ST. GEORGE LOOP:

DISTANCE: Roughly a 2½-mile loop, plus optional ½-mile round trip to peninsula at end of North Old Quarry Road and one-mile round trip to tip of peninsula at end of South Old Quarry Road. There are many different possible routes around these wild headlands and down to various pocket beaches.

TIME: One or 2 hours or more.

ELEVATION GAIN/LOSS: Loop: 100 feet +/100 feet-, more if you descend to either quarry.

TERRAIN: Contours through grasslands and vegetated dunes, then climbs to two high points before descending to a rocky beach. Options to descend to tideline at old quarries.

BEST TIME: Spring, early summer for wildflowers.

WARNINGS: Watch for poison oak. On the beaches, watch for sleeper waves and incoming tide; avoid low peninsulas during storm surf.

HOW TO GET THERE: From Highway 101 on the north end of Crescent City, head west on Washington Blvd. (From the north, exit Highway 101 at M.27.0, from south at M.27.54). Follow Washington Blvd. 2.8 miles to stop sign, where Washington Blvd. ends, meeting Pebble Beach Drive. The Point St. George public lands are ahead. Continue 1.1 miles to large parking lot and trailhead at end of Pebble Beach Drive (formerly called Radio Road).

FURTHER INFO: Crescent City/Del Norte Chamber of Commerce (707)464-3174.

OTHER SUGGESTION: You can also walk north along the long, curving BEACH NORTH OF PT. ST. GEORGE. It is about 2 miles to the mouth of Sweetwater Creek, where a trail turns inland toward Dead Lake (see previous trail), 4 miles to the possible winter/spring breach where Lakes Earl and Tolowa sometimes flow into the ocean. If you can pass that point, you can walk north all the way to the mouth of the Smith River.

large bleached driftwood. A steep path descends roughly to the beach. Our described trail veers right to continue along the bluff.

Soon your path veers left to avoid a blackberry thicket. At the next opportunity, veer left again as your path turns rough and overgrown. You soon turn south on the more pronounced trail. Before ½ mile it forges through grasses which are head high in late summer and autumn. The path forks again. Either works, but we stay on the more beaten one. Horsetail and silverweed join the coastal scrub, then wax myrtle, evergreen huckleberry and bracken fern.

Castle Rock and more sea stacks come into view around 5/8 mile. Pass an area of exposed dirt where the trail forks again. Both continue along the bluff edge, but we stay left through an area where Oregon grape, poison hemlock, iris and self-heal thrive. Your trail makes a gentle ascent to the highest point on the property, 95 feet above sea level. The site of the Tolowa village Sastaso was just north of this high point.

Now the trail becomes more traveled and distinct. Where it veers left to descend southeast, that fork is heading for the middle of the three green access gates along Pebble Beach Drive. To continue along the Point St. George headlands, veer right to return to bluff's edge. You descend past purple dog violets, lupines and currants to meet North Old Quarry Road beyond ¾ mile. You can turn right to descend it to a fork. Both forks descend to tideline, but the north fork leads ¼ mile to a low rocky promontory surrounded on three sides by ocean.

We continue southeast along the blufftop for a little more than 1/8 mile to meet South Old Quarry Road, where you have a choice. A left turn leads toward Pebble Beach Drive at the southernmost green gate and to the blufftop route south, detailed in the next paragraph. If you turn right, South Old Quarry Road descends southwest, then south toward the shore, passing beach strawberry, lupine, stonecrop, and an escaped heritage rose. You approach a rocky shore with large and small offshore rocks. In 300 feet the road is washed out, but a trail descends past another old quarry to a rocky beach with a jumble of rocks and driftwood. You should avoid the beach in storm surf, but it was passable in normal surf at a high tide of four feet in spring 2014. If you continue along the beach, by 1/8 mile walking is easier on mostly small, rounded stones. In another 200 feet you reach the long low peninsula immediately north of Castle Rock, probably the best place on land from which to observe the wildlife on Castle Rock. If the tide is not too high and/or the surf too great, you can walk ½ mile from the blufftop junction to the 30-foot-high grassy hill at the tip of the peninsula. From there Castle Rock rises about 5/8 mile south. When you have seen enough, return to the blufftop junction.

From South Old Quarry Road junction, the blufftop route heads for the nearby green gate. About 200 feet before you reach the unmarked gate, turn right on the trail that contours, then ascends south-southeast. The tread soon improves, topping out around 60 feet elevation as Castle Rock looms ahead. In 250 feet, when your path forks again, veer right to head southwest. As your track leaves the coastal scrub, it turns vague, offering two faint trails. The right fork deadends in about 300 feet at a high point with grand coastal vistas north and south, worth a look when the weather is clear. Whether you explore the spur or not, our main route takes the left fork to continue south over the headlands.

In 250 feet the broad path forks. Take the left fork south-southeast, enjoying sweeping vistas of Pebble Beach and, across the bay, to Child's Hill and beyond. Before 1¼ miles both forks converge. Continue south, drawing nearer to Castle Rock.

Before 1³/8 miles, at a point nearest Castle Rock where I stopped to admire it, a huge sea lion plied the swells below. Continue to the southernmost point, where succulents thrive, then turn left to follow the bluff's edge east-northeast, descending. You reach narrow, rocky Garth's Beach at 1½ miles. Follow the beach northeast. Unless you want to continue combing the beach, at the first pronounced gulch at 1⁵/8 miles, climb north on a rough footpath to reach the south parking area. To return to your starting point, you can either retrace some or all of your route, or you can walk the shoulder of Pebble Beach Drive about ⁷/8 mile to its end.

# REDWOOD NATIONAL PARK

*Redwood National Park comprises 133,000 acres of virgin forests, rugged coastal cliffs and beaches, meadows and streams. In its boundaries are three separately administered redwood state parks: Jedediah Smith, Del Norte Coast and Prairie Creek. Redwood National Park stretches for almost 50 miles from Crescent City in the north to Orick in the south. It includes the traditional territories of three Native American groups who have lived here for centuries: the Tolowa, Yurok and Chilula.*

*The virgin forests of the park are among the greatest on earth. The redwoods endure from ancient times: as a species they have survived dinosaurs, several Ice Ages, and the creation of mountain ranges. Today they stand in awesome silence, catching clouds and fog on their sweeping branches and filtering sunlight with stunning effect. Be forewarned: a walk among these ancient beings will have you craving more.*

*Redwood National Park was created in 1968 after 50 years of effort. In 1917 the founders of Save-the-Redwoods League toured the groves along newly opened Highway 101 and began to lobby Congress for a park. In 1920 the House of Representatives passed a bill to create a Redwood National Park. But when the bill was defeated in the Senate, efforts turned to creating California state parks. In 1964 a* **National Geographic** *article rekindled national park efforts after a survey team from the magazine found the world's tallest known tree on private timber land on Redwood Creek. The protracted struggle between logging companies and conservationists ended with the creation of a park of 58,000 acres, the largest national park ever created from privately held lands.*

*The Tall Tree was saved, but logging continued upstream. Resulting erosion threatened the trees in the new parklands. Another bitter battle led to the expansion of Redwood National Park by 48,000 acres in 1978. Since most of those lands had been clearcut, extensive rehabilitation began in the watershed of Redwood Creek. More than 200 miles of roads and 2000 miles of tractor trails are being removed, the natural contours of the land reshaped, extensive acreage replanted.*

*The trail system of the park has been greatly expanded in recent years. We reflect that in new trail reports of Trillium Falls Trail and Berry Glen Trail, as well as new* OTHER SUGGESTIONS.

## JEDEDIAH SMITH REDWOODS STATE PARK

This northernmost of the redwood parks straddles the confluence of Mill Creek and the Smith River. The river, the largest wild and undammed river remaining in California, was named for mountain man Jedediah Strong Smith, who camped here in 1828 while leading an expedition north to Oregon. The Smith River is renowned for its exceptional salmon and steelhead fishing, which peaks during the very rainy period from October through February.

*The park, one of three state-owned units of Redwood National Park, comprises 10,500 rugged wooded acres. Lying a few miles inland from the coast, in summer the park offers some of the sunniest and warmest weather to be found in the northern end of the redwood belt. This inland location also provides hikers the opportunity to observe the transition zone from the immense redwood groves to the Jeffrey pine forests of the upland interior.*

## SMITH RIVER NATIONAL RECREATION AREA

*Bordering Jedediah Smith Redwoods State Park on the east is the Smith River National Recreation Area, a 305,169-acre area with about 70 miles of trails. Conservationists sought national park status for this spectacularly diverse, rugged landscape, but Congress compromised on a multiple-use classification, bowing to pressure from timber companies. Nonetheless, the NRA designation does offer some protection for the 315 pristine miles of the Smith River which drain this wild country.*

*The NRA also encompasses about one fourth of the 183,000-acre Siskiyou Wilderness. Among the state park, the NRA and the wilderness area, hikers can explore a rich and complex series of habitats spanning from near-coastal redwood forest to 7000-foot Coast Range crest.*

## 4. LITTLE BALD HILLS

TRANSITION FROM REDWOODS TO JEFFREY PINES

*This old pack trail begins in climax redwood forest beside the Smith River, then climbs into the very different world of upland Jeffrey pine forest in native grasslands growing on serpen-*

*tine soils, passing through a botanically rich transition zone. A phenomenal variety of plant species occur on Little Bald Hills Ridge, including 70 species endemic to this ridge. In addition to the many species noted in the trail description, the area supports 22 native grasses, five manzanitas and the uncommon deer and huckleberry oaks. More than eleven conifer species and 100 flowering species grow here, including four brodiaeas,*

LITTLE BALD HILLS:

DISTANCE: 9½ miles one way to southern trailhead off South Fork Road, or 9 miles to the alternate trailhead near Sand Camp; $3\frac{1}{8}$ miles to camp, 4½ miles to National Recreation Area boundary.
TIME: Full day or overnight.
TERRAIN: Climbs steeply, then contours through open prairies rimmed by forest before descending to eastern trailhead.
ELEVATION GAIN/LOSS: North-South: 2240 feet+/1800-. To camp: 1600 feet+/100 feet-; to NRA boundary: 1940 feet+/100 feet-.
BEST TIME: Late spring for wildflowers, summer also good.
WARNINGS: Steep trail. Horses have right of way. Mountain bikers use caution, slow to walking speed on curves; announce your presence to hikers and equestrians. Watch for rattlesnakes and poison oak.
HOW TO GET THERE: Exit Highway 101 onto Highway 199 (M.30.6). Go east 7.2 miles, then right on South Fork Road. In .45 mile go right on Douglas Park Road 1.6 miles to main trailhead.
EASTERN TRAILHEAD: Go 7.9 miles on South Fork Road, then right on rough, rocky forest service road for one mile to trailhead at Rock Creek Camp.
FURTHER INFO: Jedediah Smith Redwoods State Park (707)464-9533. Redwood National Park (707)465-7335, Smith River National Recreation Area, Gasquet Ranger District (707)457-3131.
OTHER SUGGESTIONS: Many other trails, both short and long, explore this wonderful state park. STOUT GROVE TRAIL, across the road from Little Bald Hills Trailhead, offers a one mile walk through park's most impressive redwood grove. HIOUCHI TRAIL (2 miles) is an easy hike along the Smith River.

 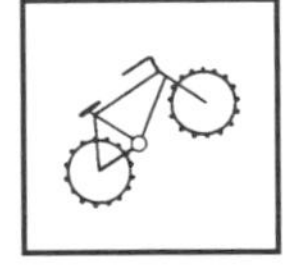  

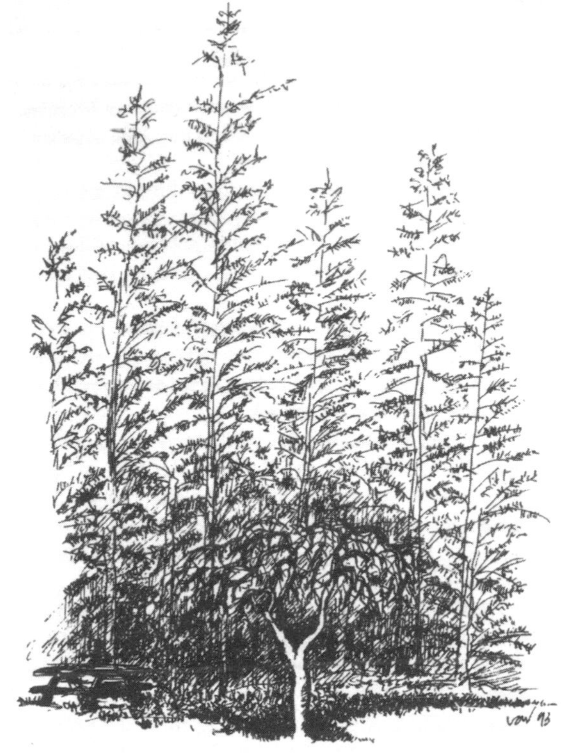

*four violets, the rare ladyslipper orchid, insect-eating pitcher plants, and two uncommon irises. The ridge also offers great opportunities for spotting raptors.*

*The 9½-mile trail begins in Jedediah Smith Redwoods State Park, climbs through Redwood National Park to a trail camp, then enters Smith River National Recreation Area. This is the only trail in Redwood National Park open to hikers, mountain bikers and equestrians. Watch for traffic, especially at blind corners, and please yield to horses. This trail description starts at Howland Hill Road, although you can drive the first 250 feet to more parking.*

Your trail starts in Sitka spruce forest, climbing southwest into a grove of large redwoods where you come to additional parking beside a locked gate. The tread narrows, soon turning south on a gentle climb through typical redwood habitat. The understory consists of sword, lady and deer ferns, evergreen and red huckleberries, rhododendron, salal and redwood sorrel. Beyond 1/8 mile these are joined by thimbleberry, salmonberry, trillium, hazel, bear grass, clintonia and trail plant, as alder, hemlock, tanoak and bay laurel join the forest. Where the path turns southeast beyond ¼ mile, look for vanilla leaf, wood rose, coast lily, evergreen violet, and yerba de selva.

Before ½ mile your trail begins a moderate, winding climb. You begin to see Douglas fir more frequently in the redwood forest, with hazel in the understory. Ascend steeply, then switchback to the right beyond one mile. The forest thins as twisted stalk and Solomon's seal line the path.

Your ascent turns gentle again by 1¼ miles. As you leave state park land for Redwood National Park proper, the original forest has been logged. Young redwoods and alders allow occasional glimpses east over the deep canyons of the Smith River.

From 1½ miles your trail ascends south moderately, passing red-flowering currant, foxglove, inside-out flower and horsetail fern. The path steepens as it crosses several small gullies. You pass a faint spur which heads east past azaleas to a small pond. Cascara sagrada, self-heal and invasive Himalayan blackberry grow on the right.

Your trail climbs gradually beyond the pond. You see abundant Douglas firs around 1¾ miles. The path becomes rocky on a moderate, winding ascent as redwoods become scarce. Your climb eases around 2 miles, where the trail has been rerouted north of the original route.

You encounter the first young Port Orford cedars beside the trail along with ocean spray. You may also see the tiny California lace fern, with lacy foliage on chestnut stalks.

Climb moderately by switchbacks, heading generally east through mixed forest of Douglas fir, tanoak and bay, with occasional Port Orford cedar to two feet in diameter. Rhododendrons and huckleberries abound in the understory.

As you ascend, look for scattered azalea and bear grass in the understory. The first Jeffrey pine grows around 2¼ miles, but this scraggly specimen confirms that the pines are retreating higher up the ridge as the fir/cedar forest grows taller.

Your trail levels briefly around 2½ miles, then resumes its

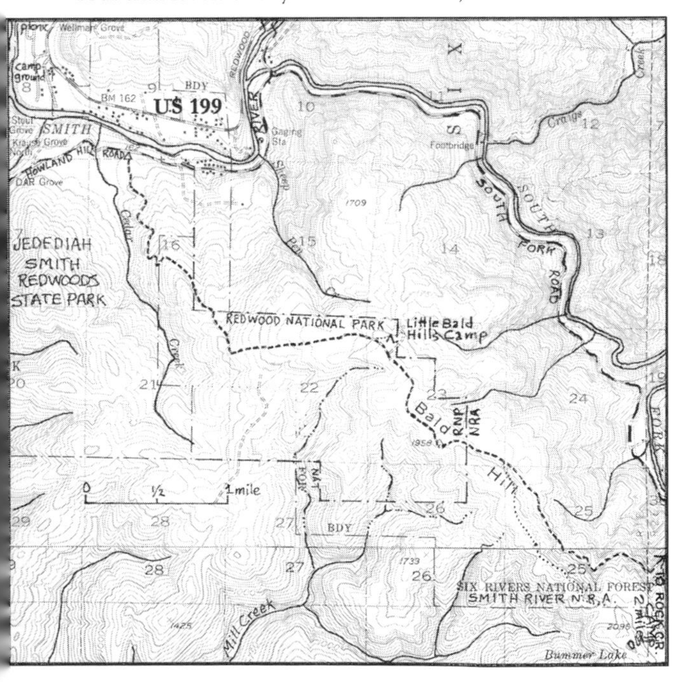

winding ascent northeast through mixed forest. Around 2⁵/8 miles the trail descends briefly as cedars dominate the forest. Your rocky, red-dirt path winds past Douglas firs to six feet in diameter. Calypso orchids thrive here in spring.

By 2¾ miles your trail gains the ridgetop. Turn east on a winding gentle ascent past azaleas, cascara and native bunch grasses. Before 2⁷/8 miles, patchy forest of Douglas fir, Jeffrey and knobcone pine provides plenty of room for the spreading ground covers ceanothus prostratus and pinemat manzanita along with taller manzanita and Oregon grape. You may also see shooting star, fairy bells and crimson columbine in spring and early summer. Return to Douglas fir forest and ascend to a junction before 3¹/8 miles.

The left fork descends for 400 feet to Little Bald Hills Camp. You can camp for free at four sites with tables, fire rings and bear-proof food boxes on a gentle slope at the edge of forest and prairie. The camp also has a corral and piped water that should be purified before drinking. Abundant coffeeberry, brodiaea and berries could be harvested in this glade, as native people undoubtedly did.

Little Bald Hills Trail ascends gradually east from the junction. Snowberry and western wood anemone grow beneath Douglas firs and scattered Jeffrey pines. At 3¼ miles a glade of native grasses beneath large pines offers views south over the canyons of the forks of Mill Creek to 2330-foot Childs Hill. Look for the yellow-white flowers of death camas here in spring. Your trail contours briefly, then climbs moderately along the ridgetop. The ascent turns gentle around 3½ miles, passing through ridgetop grasslands where club mosses thrive nestled amidst the rocks.

You soon return to the old ranch track and contour southeast through more pine-rich prairies. Climb gently south to a ridgetop knob at 4 miles. The tiny scythe-leaved onion grows here. Then your track contours east through more native grasslands along the ridgetop. Ascend moderately to the trail's highest point (1956') at 4¼ miles, where creeping snowberry grows. The trail turns east, contouring along the crest through dense forest, then through scattered forest in native-grass prairies. Leave the ridgetop and descend gradually to the park boundary at 4½ miles. Your trail enters Smith River National Recreation Area, meaning you may camp wherever you like. (A campfire permit is required to have a fire; please be careful if you do.)

Your trail drops over a tank trap, then contours southeast through glades and forest where you encounter deer oak. Dip through a depression where the trail can be wet in spring, then come to a large sprawling clump of common juniper on your left. Knobcone pines grow nearby.

At 4¾ miles you come to another fork. The right fork, signed "BUMMER LAKE WAY," climbs south. Take the left fork to descend southeast away from the ridge. A campsite sits just east of the junction, with a seasonal water source nearby (treat before drinking). The trail begins a winding descent. In spring look for the nodding white and pink flowers of the uncommon creek trillium. Your path descends across several seasonal creeks, dropping through Douglas fir-dominated forest on a north slope. The dense, brushy understory includes rhododendron, bear grass, chinquapin and common juniper. Around 5 miles you have a view southeast to the Siskiyou crest around Sawtooth Mountain (5781').

Little Bald Hills Trail continues its winding descent east and south, descending 1250 feet in 4½ miles to reach Rock Creek Camp and the southern trailhead (elevation 500 feet). Unless you have arranged a car shuttle, it is best to turn back before descending much more.

## 5.
## BOY SCOUT TREE
### GRAND PARADE OF GIANTS

*Boy Scout Tree Trail offers one of the most pristine and rewarding hikes in redwood country. This trail traverses one of the most marvelously dense and diverse block of virgin redwoods remaining on the planet. Bejeweled with immense redwoods, the hike offers a showcase of the world's best redwood scenery. Here you will find redwoods of all sizes, Sitka spruce forest, a lush stream corridor with deciduous woodlands, pleasant Fern Falls, and the marvelous Boy Scout Tree in a quiet off trail setting.*

Follow the signed Boy Scout Tree Trail as it ascends northwest through a forest of large redwoods. Watch for exposed tree roots in the trail that can trip you. A few western hemlocks and tanoaks mingle with the redwoods. Understory plants include Redwood sorrel, salal, false lily of the valley, rhododendron, trail plant, twisted stalk, trillium, both evergreen and red huckleberry, and sword, deer and lady ferns.

Around 1/8 mile you pass three virgin giants with diameters of 11 or 12 feet, even larger than most of their neighbors. Descend to cross a small bridge dwarfed by a burl-encrusted fallen giant. Saxifrage and salmonberry grow beside the small stream. Your trail climbs moderately to ¼ mile, then gradually as redwood violet and inside-out flower join the understory.

Duck under a fallen giant beyond ½ mile as your trail contours, winding through the virgin forest. Resume a gradual ascent as Oregon grape, red clintonia and creek dogwood join the understory. At ¾ mile a redwood giant on your right has a burl that supports elderberry, huckleberry

BOY SCOUT TREE:

DISTANCE: 5 3/8 miles round trip.
TIME: 2 hours to half day.
TERRAIN: Up and down through immense forest to cross Jordan Creek near its headwaters, then more up and down along the canyon of the creek.
ELEVATION GAIN/LOSS: 750 feet+/750 feet-.
BEST TIME: Spring, early summer for wildflowers. On sunny days the forest here sparkles. Delightful even in winter if not too wet, especially when sunny.
WARNINGS: Watch for roots in the trail. Watch for ticks, especially in spring.
HOW TO GET THERE: From Highway 199 1.5 miles east of Hiouchi Information Center, turn right onto paved South Fork Road (also signed for Howland Hill Road). In .5 mile turn right onto Douglas Park Drive. In .6 mile you pass a covered bridge on your right. The road soon narrows, then turns to dirt, becoming Howland Hill Road. In .3 mile Little Bald Hills Trail is on the left. In .8 mile Stout Grove access is on the right. Go 2.2 more miles to the parking and trailhead for Boy Scout Tree Trail on your right.
FURTHER INFO: Redwood National and State Parks (707)465-7335, Jedediah Smith Redwoods State Park (707) 464-9533.
OTHER SUGGESTIONS: MILL CREEK TRAIL has a trailhead .3 mile east of Boy Scout Trailhead. From there it runs east and north for 3¼ miles all the way to the Smith River, across Mill Creek from Stout Grove. MILL CREEK TRAIL also runs south about ¾ mile to end at Nickerson Ranch Trail. NICKERSON RANCH TRAIL has its own trailhead .2 mile west on Howland Hill Road.

and sword fern. You soon contour along a ridge with views left and right over the climax forest.

Around one mile you begin a gentle, winding descent. By 1 1/8 miles your trail contours, still with virgin trees all around and California hazel in the understory. Beyond 1¼ miles you resume a gradual descent. The descent soon steepens past redwood giants to 13 feet in diameter.

Your trail descends its first dozen steps, then winds down to descend more steps to a bridge over Jordan Creek at 1½ miles. Vine maple grows in a short tree form along the small stream. You then climb by rough steps and tread on a winding path beneath hemlocks where red huckleberry bushes grow 15 feet tall.

Soon your trail descends, partially by rough steps as the sound of surf soughs through the forest. After descending to cross a railless bridge, your trail traverses several short dips and rises. Around 1¾ miles a gargantuan redwood on your right flaunts immense candelabra limbs overhead. Cascara sagrada joins the many huckleberry bushes, both evergreen and red, in the understory.

Around 1⅞ miles you encounter the largest redwoods yet, with one giant 15 feet in diameter on your right crowding the trail. Your trail contours through lush undergrowth, with fitful ascents.

Beyond 2 miles you begin a gentle descent. Hemlock trees grow large here, with many buttressed at the base. Descend steeply around 2¼ miles to cross a bridge over a side stream. Bigleaf maples grow large near the bridge, with one about 18 inches in diameter. Soon your trail contours along a straight leg of the trail with Jordan Creek below on your left.

An unmarked side trail forks right. This is the spur to the Boy Scout Tree, worth the detour. It climbs steeply, winding generally east-northeast for about 75 feet. Suddenly an immense behemoth, double-trunked redwood towers overhead. The massive trunk of the Boy Scout Tree splits into two trunks about 80 feet above you. It's likely that the two trees grew together over time, but at the base they appear as one. Boy Scout Tree has a massive average diameter of 31 feet, its oval shaped bole with a circumference of 97 feet! On the steep slope above the tree, a natural gallery with burnished chunks of fallen redwood provides a great vantage point to observe this climax specimen of Sequoia sempervirens. From the natural benches upslope from the tree, the large redwood plank with the tree's name is dwarfed by the tree itself. When I asked park personnel about the Boy Scout Tree's height and circumference, they seemed to dismiss it as a double tree. To me however, this is one of the most impressive trees in a vast park filled with immense trees!

Back on the main trail you descend gradually, soon coming to a clearing in the redwood forest where large bigleaf

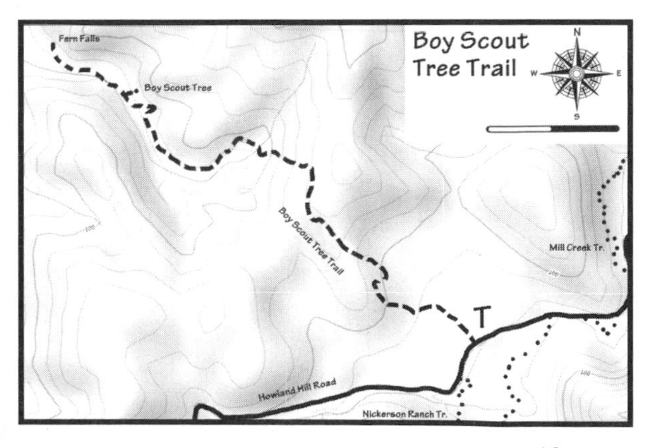

maples, red alders, cascara and elderberry thrive in both sun and fog.

Continue along the level track, with maple- and fern-lined Jordan Creek directly on your left. You cross a railless bridge/boardwalk, then pass skunk cabbage and abundant saxifrage and hedge nettle beneath elderberry, salmonberry and young Sitka spruce. Cross a railed bridge at 2½ miles. In the flat, moist flood plain near the bridge grow vine maple, coast manroot and other moisture-loving plants.

As you descend gently, spruce suddenly dominate the forest, including one seven feet in diameter on your left. A few redwoods mingle with the spruce. Climb briefly around 2⅝ miles to a hillside above the creek where large redwoods again dominate, with scattered spruce. Then wild ginger joins the understory plants as you descend. The descent ends just before 2¾ miles at Fern Falls and trail's end.

The falls are not large, but still impressive as they tumble 40 feet over bedrock at the mouth of the side canyon on your right. The flow was quite small when this author visited in September. Fern Falls are most impressive in spring or after a big storm. A steep volunteer side trail climbs past ferns, redwoods and young maples to the left of the falls. It's a pleasant, cool spot for a break.

When you're rested, retrace your steps to the trailhead.

# 6. ENDERTS BEACH LAST CHANCE SECTION COASTAL TRAIL

## WALK OLD HIGHWAY ABOVE RUGGED COAST

*Enderts Beach Road leaves the west side of Highway 101 about two miles south of Crescent City. Today the quiet side road deadends at the Enderts Beach Trailhead after just 2.3 miles. But this narrow, winding road was once busy Highway 101, the main artery connecting Del Norte County to the rest of California. Enderts Beach Road and most of the Last Chance Section of the Coastal Trail was the main highway until 1935. It was drivable as a scenic route until about 1970. Part of the old road south of Nickel Creek is on the National Register of Historic Places.*

*Enderts Beach Road parallels the broad curve of Crescent Beach, which extends for 4 miles south of Crescent City Harbor. It then climbs to Crescent Beach Overlook, a picnic area with a grand view of the rugged coast. Just beyond the Overlook, the road ends at the start of the Enderts Beach/Last Chance Trail. Use this trail for a one mile round trip to Enderts Beach as a day hike, an easy overnight to Nickel Creek Camp or the longer strenuous hike along the Last Chance Section of the Coastal Trail. The Last Chance Section of the Coastal Trail is now open to bicycles, providing a steep but scenic alternative to busy Highway 101.*

Head south from the trailhead on the now grassy old coast highway, descending gradually. After you pass an old quarry in the cliff to your left, magnificent views appear to the north along Crescent Head and beyond to Crescent City and Point St. George. Beyond 1/8 mile you come to an excellent view south to Enderts Beach.

Rock slides cover portions of the road as you descend south. Just beyond ¼ mile, a side trail on the right descends to Enderts Beach. The surf-scoured, sandy pocket beach is small but pretty. At low tide you can explore tidepools here. Park Service naturalists conduct guided walks in summer.

The Coastal Trail descends southeast on the old road. Dense vegetation grows here where coastal scrub and forest mingle: Douglas fir, Sitka spruce and red alder mix with

ENDERTS BEACH/LAST CHANCE SECTION COASTAL TRAIL:

DISTANCE: One mile round trip to beach or Nickel Creek Camp, 7 3/8 miles one way on Coastal Trail.
TIME: One hour for beach; 3 to 4 hours, whole trail (one way).
TERRAIN: Follows old highway along steep cliffs above coast, then climbs steep hill into virgin forest at headwaters of Damnation Creek.
ELEVATION GAIN/LOSS: To beach: 160 feet+/160 feet-. Coastal Trail, one way 1400 feet+/650 feet-.
BEST TIME: Spring, early summer for wildflowers. When it is not foggy for views.
WARNINGS: Watch for ticks, especially in spring. Trail beyond Nickel Creek is extremely steep. Parking not allowed at southern trailhead (OK at Damnation Creek). Mountain bikers must watch for, yield to hikers.
HOW TO GET THERE: NORTH END: Turn west off Highway 101 at M.23.8 (Del Norte) onto Enderts Beach Road. Drive 2.3 miles to end of road where trail begins. SOUTH END: At M.15.6 (Del Norte) on Highway 101 (no parking allowed; park at Damnation Creek Trailhead and walk south).
FURTHER INFO: Redwood National Park (707)465-7335.
OTHER SUGGESTIONS: CRESCENT BEACH extends for 4 miles from just south of Crescent City to just north of Crescent Beach Overlook. A one mile segment of the COASTAL TRAIL runs between new Interpretive Center on Enderts Beach Road and Crescent Beach Overlook, passing a picnic area in a beautiful spot beside Cushing Creek.

  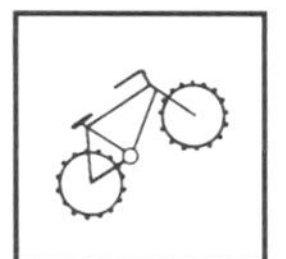 

silktassel, red-flowering currant, Indian plum, coyote brush and berry vines. The trees have been sculptured by the prevailing winds.

Before 3/8 mile, your path bends left and descends into Nickel Creek Canyon. Before you cross the creek, the side trail to the campground heads west to five campsites overlooking Enderts Beach. You must purify water from the stream. Another side trail heads east from the junction, exploring the lush creek canyon.

Beyond the creek your trail leaves the old highway, turning left and climbing southeast above the creek. Pace yourself for a long steep hill. This most strenuous portion of the trail climbs 900 feet in the next 1¼ miles. Your path turns away from the creek at 5/8 mile, continuing the steep climb. Pass the first redwoods around ¾ mile. At 7/8 mile you come to a flat spot at a big west bend. This good picnic spot has views down to Enderts Beach. Then head east, climbing moderately to the one-mile point, with views into Nickel Creek Canyon.

Turn south before 1 1/8 miles, passing ocean spray, Oregon grape, salmonberry, huckleberry and salal, then redwood sorrel, evergreen violet and trillium. Your climb steepens briefly, then becomes moderate again. Rejoin the old highway at 1¼ miles and continue to climb south, following a ridge with steep drops on both sides. Wild ginger, with large, fragrant, heart-shaped leaves, grows along the trail.

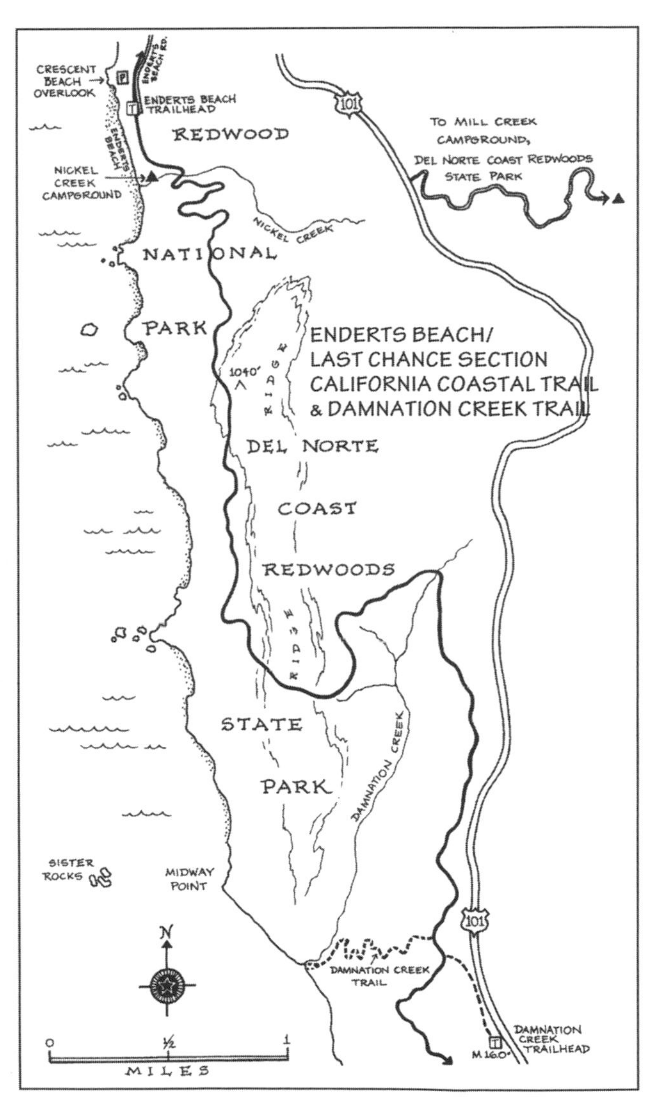

Reach the first summit beyond 1½ miles. A healthy young redwood forest grows in an area logged years ago. Descend briefly before a gentle ascent brings you to a second top at 1⅞ miles, where you may get a glimpse down to the rugged coast. The surf roars from below.

Begin a steady descent south, dropping 400 feet in the next ⅝ mile. Beyond a sign, the trail enters old-growth redwood forest and Del Norte Coast Redwoods State Park around 2⅛ miles. At 2½ miles you can look southwest through alders to the breakers and offshore rocks below. Your trail begins a gradual climb. A fragment of the old highway pavement survives here.

Your ascending trail passes under the power line beyond 2⅞ miles, offering a view north to Lake Earl. Your trail turns east at a spot where the old roadbed survives intact. Your easy climb quickly brings you under the power line again.

At 3 miles an old brass plaque marks Anson Grove. The redwoods grow large as you approach the headwaters of Damnation Creek. Your trail winds south, then east, climbing gradually. By 3¼ miles redwood, fir and spruce grow to ten feet in diameter along the trail.

You quickly come to a sloughing of the roadbed. Here the powerful geologic forces that shape this coast have toyed with the old road. Your trail bends left, entering primeval forest. The trail contours, curving left, then right, to cross a fern-filled gully. Rhododendrons and redwood giants thrive in the moist habitat.

Descend gradually, crossing more gullies and spring-fed streams. Climb briefly around 4 1/8 miles. An immense redwood crowds the road's left shoulder at 4 3/8 miles. The path bends left and descends gently to Damnation Creek at 4½ miles. Where the road is washed out, you once crossed the creek on a slippery log. Now a short bypass crosses a sturdy new bridge.

Rejoin the old road and climb south paralleling the creek to 4¾ miles. Your trail contours through primeval forest, passing several old highway markers. Before 5¼ miles you pass a 14-foot-diameter redwood on your right with a leather fern growing on its south side. You can hear the roar of traffic on Highway 101 less than ¼ mile away. Your path winds somewhat as it contours south.

After a short climb, you meet the Damnation Creek Trail at 6 1/8 miles. It heads west-southwest from a big bend in the old road, descending 1½ miles to the mouth of the creek (see Trail #7). The trail to the Damnation Creek Trailhead is 50 feet beyond, climbing east-southeast. Your trail continues southeast on the old road, descending moderately through a virgin forest of massive trees. At 6¼ miles you can glimpse the ocean through the trees.

Where you reach a big bend at 6½ miles, the roar of the surf and the barking of sea lions rise from the isolated coast below. The road turns southeast for a winding contour. Between 7 and 7 1/8 miles, the forest below the road thins, providing views of the steep, wild coastline.

At 7¼ miles steps lead uphill away from the old road. Take this narrow footpath over a small ridge, coming to Highway 101 at milepost 15.6, 7 3/8 miles from the trailhead. If you continue on the Coastal Trail, be careful crossing the busy road. A "COASTAL TRAIL" sign across the highway marks the DeMartin Section of the Coastal Trail (see Trail #8).

## 7.
## DAMNATION CREEK
### ANCIENT TRAIL TO A HIDDEN COAST

The well-beaten trail climbs northwest into a dense forest of large redwoods and Douglas firs. Ascend gradually for ¼ mile through a lush understory of salal, redwood sorrel, sword and deer ferns, evergreen and red huckleberries, rhododendrons, inside-out flower and wild ginger.

Your trail tops the coastal ridge, then begins a winding descent. At ½ mile, as you descend steeply by three switchbacks, you can see the ocean through the forest. Descend gradually again, paralleling the old highway below to your west. After a short uphill stretch at 5/8 mile, you descend to the old road, now the Last Chance Section of the Coastal Trail (see Trail #6).

The Damnation Creek Trail follows the roadbed north for 50 feet before turning west-southwest at a marked junction. The trail descends gradually west, winding among large, fire-scarred redwoods. Your path levels briefly at ¾ mile, where Douglas firs to eight feet in diameter mix with the giant redwoods.

You then begin a steady but well-graded descent with frequent switchbacks. The sound of the crashing surf rises from below. At 7/8 mile the deep, rugged canyon of Damnation Creek is visible to the northwest. Continue your switchbacking descent into the canyon.

Beyond one mile, as the trail switches sharply right, you get your best glimpse yet of the ocean below. Lady and five-finger fern thrive in this moist habitat, along with gooseberry, ocean spray, fairy bells, bleeding heart, iris and trail plant. Descend steeply to 1¼ miles, then contour briefly before more switchbacks.

At 1½ miles Sitka spruce begin to dominate the forest, with scattered large redwoods. A spruce on the left is eight feet in diameter. Standing beside it, you can look down to the mouth of Damnation Creek Canyon, your destination.

After a short level stretch, you descend by two switchbacks followed by steep steps. As you continue descending by switchbacks, step carefully over the slippery spruce roots in the trail. You come to a stretch of trail disrupted by a small landslide, where saxifrage grows profusely. Watch your footing in this spot.

After three more switchbacks, your trail turns south-southwest, paralleling the creek. You are 1¾ miles from the trailhead. Salmon- and thimbleberries grow in a dense thicket between you and the rushing creek. Red alders are the dominant tree in this moist habitat. You can hear the breakers crashing on the rocky beach below.

Your descent steepens at 17/8 miles. Then your trail bends left and climbs into a side canyon, crossing a small creek on a sturdy bridge. More big spruce roots disrupt the trail bed. Descend gradually through a thicket of alders, willows and berry vines.

At 2 miles you enter a second side canyon, crossing its creek on a bridge below twisted spruce. Pass under a power line as you climb to a bright green one-acre clearing of coastal scrub. As the trail levels, you can see the breakers ahead. The botanically rich wild garden around you includes cow parsnip, angelica, silver beachweed, iris, miterwort, coltsfoot, yarrow, yerba de selva, false lily of the valley, miner's lettuce, bedstraw, false Solomon's seal, giant trillium, and abundant checker lily in spring.

The trail then forks. If you continue straight, you cross over a small natural arch onto a narrow promontory above the beach, where hen and chicks cling to the cliffs. To descend to the mouth of Damnation Creek and the beach, take the right fork before the arch and descend steeply, using caution on the steep drop to the beach.

If you get here at a high tide of +5.0 feet or more, the beach is almost completely submerged. Do not venture onto the beach at such a high tide. If you are trapped by the rising tide on this rugged, isolated coast, there is no escape! If the tide is low enough (+2.0 feet or less) and ebbing, you can walk 200 feet north along the rocky beach and about 1/8 mile south. During a minus tide you can reach rocky tidepools near the mouth of the creek. The Tolowa and Yurok peoples used an earlier version of Damnation Creek Trail to come here to harvest shellfish and seaweed at low tide.

You can find shelter from the harsh wind in the mouth of the rocky creek canyon. Amidst a pile of huge logs jammed into the creek is the rusted piece of an old ship, remnant of one of the many shipwrecks along this wild coast.

From the bluff above the mouth of the creek, you can look northwest to Sister Rocks. To the south are other rocks, including onshore Footsteps Rocks (247') and offshore False Klamath Rock (209'). Gazing at the razor-edged cliffs along the coast, you might marvel that a trail leads to this special place.

Remember to leave adequate time to climb the 2 1/8

| DAMNATION CREEK: |
|---|
| DISTANCE: 4¼ miles round trip.<br>TIME: Two hours minimum.<br>TERRAIN: Descends steeply to beach at mouth of creek, with steep return.<br>ELEVATION GAIN/LOSS: 1100 feet+/1100 feet-.<br>BEST TIME: Low tide, spring, late afternoon.<br>WARNINGS: Steep trail. Take it easy. Do not get trapped on the beach by rising tides.<br>HOW TO GET THERE: On Highway 101, a wide turnout is at M.16.0 (Del Norte), on west side of road. Signed trail leaves from upper end of turnout.<br>FURTHER INFO: Redwood National Park (707)465-7335, Del Norte Coast Redwoods State Park (707)464-9533.<br>OTHER SUGGESTIONS: Del Norte Coast Redwoods State Park has other trails around Mill Creek Campground. Turn east off Highway 101 at M.20.25 (Del Norte). HOBBS WALL TRAIL (3¾ miles, moderate) can be reached just after you turn off the highway. ALDER BASIN and MILL CREEK TRAILS (one mile each, easy) start near the entrance to Mill Creek Campground. |

miles back to the trailhead, an elevation gain of 1100 feet. Fortunately, the trail is well graded. The steepest portions lie in the first mile from the beach.

## 8. DEMARTIN SECTION COASTAL TRAIL

### VIRGIN FORESTS AND GLADES WITH COASTAL VIEWS

*This section of the Coastal Trail was rerouted in early 1998, adding one mile to the distance to DeMartin Camp. The route climbs through virgin forest to gain the east face of the ridge between the rugged coast and the steep canyons of Wilson Creek and its tributaries east of the trail. Where the original route stayed on or near the ridgetop with resultant highway noise, the new route explores virgin redwood groves on the ridge's east face, with far less highway noise and an intimate journey through virgin forest. While the route still never wanders farther than ½ mile from Highway 101, ridge-hugging DeMartin Primitive Campground offers a lovely secluded retreat where the sun often shines even when dense fog shrouds the coast.*

The trail heads east from Highway 101 at M.15.6, where a sign reads "COASTAL TRAIL." Descend through fern-filled forest by steps and switchbacks to a bridge over a skunk-cabbage-filled tributary of Wilson Creek before 1/8 mile. Then climb away from the highway, zigzagging east past redwoods and Sitka spruce to 12 feet in diameter. The trail turns south, ascending through lush forest understory by switchbacks. Before ¼ mile your winding climb becomes gradual, crossing a small railless bridge. Climb past a memorial bench surrounded by wild ginger and redwood sorrel.

Before ½ mile you climb steps, switchbacking right, then climb more steps to switch left. Your ascent continues to the top of the ridge around ¾ mile. Your trail, lined with rhododendrons, bends right and descends gently south, following the ridge on your right, with a steep, verdant canyon on your left. You leave the traffic noise behind. Duck under a large fallen fir nursing a garden, then under a fallen redwood. Follow the winding trail around a gulch at one mile.

The trail passes through a walk-through redwood and winds through another gulch sheltering giant redwoods and firs, the ridgetop visible above. Make a winding descent through another gulch in the virgin forest.

Around 1¼ miles you contour through a gulch with the biggest trees yet, once again with the ridgetop in view

| DEMARTIN SECTION, COASTAL TRAIL: |
|---|
| DISTANCE: 6¼ miles one way.<br>TIME: Three to 4 hours one way, 6 to 8 hours round trip.<br>TERRAIN: Climbs, then descends, then climbs to high point through mixed virgin forest, then descends through coastal prairie with sweeping views. Finally descends into deep Wilson Creek Canyon.<br>ELEVATION GAIN/LOSS: North-South: 870 feet+/1390 feet -.<br>BEST TIME: Spring for wildflowers.<br>WARNINGS: Watch for poison oak.<br>HOW TO GET THERE: NORTH END: On Highway 101 at M.15.6 (Del Norte). Look for signpost marked "COASTAL TRAIL." Additional parking at M.16.0.<br>SOU'I'H END: At M.12.8 (Del Norte) on Highway 101, at north end of DeMartin Bridge over Wilson Creek, east side of highway.<br>FURTHER INFO: Redwood National Park (707)465-7335, Del Norte Redwoods State Park (707)464-9533. |

above. Your trail continues to contour, repeating this pattern through four more redwood-filled gulches by 1⅝ miles. You climb slightly to 1¾ miles. Resume a gentle descent, winding through more gulches. Notice that each gulch has a distinct mix of tree sizes and types.

From 1⅞ miles you climb into another gulch with many immense redwoods and a few firs. Contour through the next gulch beyond 2 miles. Although it is among the steepest drainages, redwoods to 10 feet in diameter thrive here. The next gulch is more gentle, with widely spaced large redwoods. The ridgetop once again rises just above the trail.

Contour to 2¼ miles, then climb into the largest gulch yet. A 12-foot-diameter, fire-scarred redwood on the left side of the trail is loaded with burls. Several other titans are equally large. Climb around another fork of this immense gulch. When you finally leave it at 2½ miles, you have climbed to DeMartin Trail's highest point, 1110 feet. You are rewarded with an ocean view to the south. Dense vegetation at the high point includes abundant huckleberry bushes, rhododendrons, trilliums, wild ginger, cascara, coltsfoot, redwood violets, redwood sorrel, and ferns: sword, lady and deer.

You immediately descend steeply, then moderately. The waxy stemmed, 3- to 7-foot-tall redwood lily grows along the trail here. Consider yourself lucky if you get to see and smell its fragrant flowers. Clintonia and fairy bells also thrive here. A fire, probably lightning caused, burned just east of the trail. You can see the high hills beyond Wilson

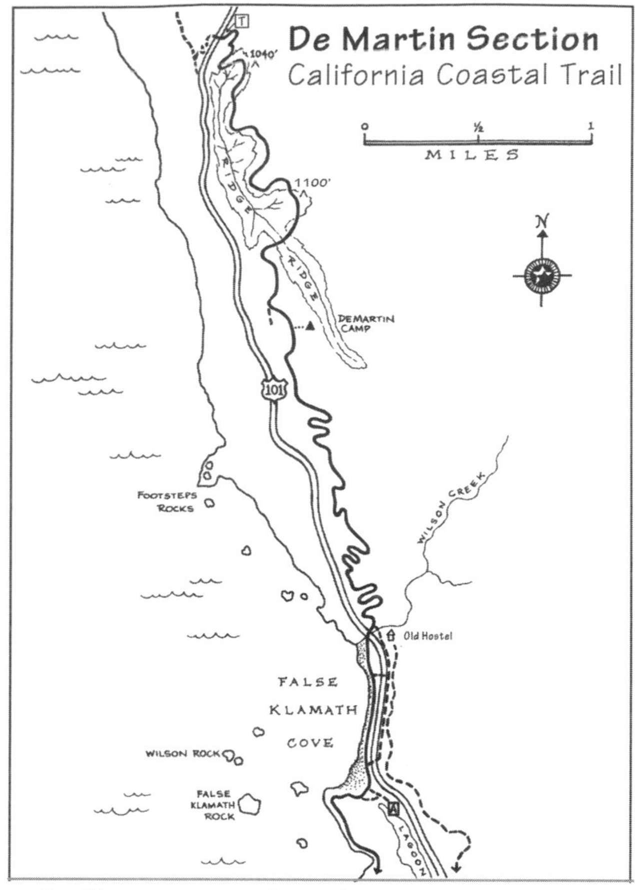


Creek's vast canyon to the southeast.

Beyond 2⅝ miles your descent eases. Then DeMartin Trail contours. By 2¾ miles you resume a gradual climb, once again gaining filtered ocean views as you near the ridgetop, which gets lower to the south, approaching trail level.

Before 2⅞ miles your trail resumes its descent, wrapping around a large spruce and a big, leaning Douglas fir. Then a large Douglas fir on your right is draped in leather ferns and huckleberry. You are leaving the virgin forest for second-growth forest cut long ago. All around you is dense, tall salmonberry and elderberry bushes. No redwoods grow here—it is too exposed to coastal winds. You can hear the surf murmuring 800 feet below.

The next section of trail often gets overgrown with all the lush, dense vegetation. Around 3⅛ miles false lily of the valley lines your path, with bleeding heart also present. By 3¼ miles alders dominate the surrounding forest, with scattered large firs and occasional spruce.

At 3⅜ miles a sign points left to DeMartin Campground. The sign also points left for the Coastal Trail. The path continuing south descends to a service road. Turn left and climb east on DeMartin Coastal Trail, rerouted to pass the edge of the campground. Pass California buckeye and ascend through grasslands scattered with coastal scrub. Beyond 3½ miles you come to a second junction just below the outhouse for DeMartin Campground. From there the Coastal Trail heads southeast on a gradual ascent. The left fork climbs to the camp on the northern edge of DeMartin Prairie, where the remote ambience is punctuated by crashing surf rising on heavy, salt-scented air. The ten sites offer tables, fire rings, bear boxes, and a composting toilet. No open fires are permitted. Sites #1 and 2 are on the left fork, sites 3 through 10 on the right.

The main trail ascends briefly through spruce/alder forest. After passing below campsites 9 and 10, your route descends southeast, soon leaving the forest to cross the heart of DeMartin Prairie, a lush grassland dense with coastal scrub. You pass lupine, canyon gooseberry, coyote brush and clumps of sword ferns. The path bends right to cross an old road lined with alders, then left to descend through more prairie. In winter and spring you may see a seasonal pond below on your right.

At 3⅝ miles you descend south through forest with the prairie on your right. The path descends through the prairie, then through fir/spruce forest. Pass a water tank on your left surrounded by spruce and alder beyond 3¾ miles.

Descend gradually to 3⅞ miles, where you come dramatically upon the edge of steep Wilson Creek Canyon. Though the canyon has been logged, the view is spectacular. The trail switches right and makes a winding descent through forest. A private residence lies below the trail beyond 4⅛ miles.

Your trail descends south by 11 switchbacks for the next ¼ mile. The path levels briefly beyond 4⅜ miles, then switches right and climbs to gain a narrow ridgetop not far from the highway. Climb gradually along this ridgetop, which has broad views of the ocean through the trees around 4⅝ miles.

Your trail switches left and ascends steeply to a magnificent view of Footsteps Rocks on the coast to the northwest. Then two more switchbacks bring you back to the edge of Wilson Creek Canyon beyond 4¾ miles.

Make a winding climb to a level stretch of trail beyond 4⅞ miles where you pass a big rock outcrop on your left. Make a steady descent southeast around 5 miles. Then descend by more switchbacks to 5⅛ miles. Your trail turns south-southeast for a relatively straight stretch through more coastal scrub with scattered alders and large spruces.

As your trail bends sharply right to meet an old road, you might notice claw marks left by bears on alders beside the path. Follow the road northwest for just 150 feet. Then fork right to continue northwest on a footpath through a dense thicket of coastal scrub.

Beyond 5¼ miles your trail switches left and heads southeast, paralleling the power line. Continue your descent through open country, with views of False Klamath and Wilson Rocks offshore. At 5³/8 miles, descend through prairie, cross under the power line and wind through a berry thicket. Descend a series of long switchbacks through the coastal prairie and scrub, Highway 101 not far below.

Enter the forest at 5⁵/8 miles, where your trail levels briefly. After the path bends left, begin a winding descent, crossing eight small boardwalks. The trail levels at 6 miles, coming to an overgrown stretch of old highway and a trail junction. Here you have a decision. In summer you can take the footpath on the far side of the old road. This leads to a bridgeless crossing of Wilson Creek in 1/8 mile, below the highway bridge. But in winter you must turn right and follow the old highway uphill for 500 feet to meet Highway 101 at M.12.8. Then, if you are continuing on the Coastal Trail, use extreme caution as you cross the narrow highway bridge.

# 9. OLD HOSTEL/TREES OF MYSTERY SECTION, COASTAL TRAIL

## COASTAL TRAIL LINK AT TREES OF MYSTERY

*This segment of the Coastal Trail offers through hikers a 2½-mile link between the DeMartin and Hidden Beach sections of the Coastal Trail, an alternative to the old route along the beach of False Klamath Cove. (The alternate route is often impassable in winter when storm waves cover or carry away the sand.) This Coastal Trail segment also offers two pleasant day hikes that can be made from Trees of Mystery: the short, rewarding walk to secluded Hidden Beach, or the longer walk north through the narrowest part of Redwood National Park to the old Redwood Hostel and Wilson Creek. (The latter day hike follows the first two miles of the described hike, but in the opposite direction.)*

*Trees of Mystery is one of those curious California roadside attractions that sprung up in the early days of automotive travel. Owned by the same family since 1940, they gave the old-fashioned tourist stop is current name and built the gargantuan Paul Bunyan and Babe that have become a landmark on Highway 101. Trees of Mystery has its own trail (fee) which meanders for nearly a mile through ancient forest. Most noteworthy is the collection of Native American artifacts in their museum.*

Since the hostel has closed, being too old and decrepit to maintain, you must walk 300 feet down the grassy old road behind the locked gate (**do not block!**) to the bottom steps of the hostel. Walk east 200 feet from the hostel's front steps to find the trail's signed north end. In autumn 2013 this sign was overgrown and easy to miss. Your route climbs moderately west, then south on a gravel road. Your ascent through forest of spruce and alder soon turns gradual. After crossing a seasonal creek at ¼ mile, your winding road offers views north along the coast to onshore Footsteps Rocks, with offshore Sisters Rocks beyond, and west to immense False Klamath Rock.

The road contours beyond 3/8 mile. The lush forest understory includes salal, sword fern, salmonberry, California buckeye, cow parsnip, coltsfoot and angelica. Beyond ½ mile your road becomes less traveled, a winding double track through the forest.

Cross a cascading stream at ¾ mile and wind south, passing a lush patch of saxifrage and skunk cabbage. At one mile a trail sign confirms you are on track. Your road turns east as dense huckleberry bushes tower 15 feet overhead.

Where the winding track descends to cross two creeks, the pristine beauty of the route is marred by a view of the charred clearcut on the steep slope above. This recent cut just beyond the park boundary reminds us that only the virgin forests within park boundaries are protected. Beyond the second creek at 1 1/8 miles, the road becomes a grassy track through lush growth, in sharp contrast to the ugly scar above.

Climb gently to 1 3/8 miles, then contour south, winding away from the clearcut. From 1½ miles your path narrows and descends gently through luxuriant growth, a bit overgrown in 2013. Cross a seasonal creek with abundant skunk cabbage as you near Highway 101. The path contours east to 1¾ miles, then descends to the Trees of Mystery parking lot before 1 7/8 miles. Unless you want to tour Trees of Mystery or visit their gift shop and museum (recommended), walk southeast along the grass strip between the lot and the

## OLD HOSTEL/TREES OF MYSTERY SECTION COASTAL TRAIL:

DISTANCE: 2½ miles one way. From Trees of Mystery: two round trips of 3¾ and 1¼ miles.
TIME: One or two hours.
TERRAIN: Climbs from old hostel into forest, follows mostly level road, then trail, descending to Trees of Mystery; nearly level to beach.
ELEVATION GAIN/LOSS: Entire trail, north-south: 300 feet+/340 feet-. Round trip, Hostel to Trees: 360 feet+/360 feet-; Trees to beach: 280 feet-/280 feet+.
BEST TIME: Spring for wildflowers. Nice anytime.
WARNINGS: Watch for ticks in spring, poison oak year round. When crossing Highway 101, use crosswalk and be careful.
HOW TO GET THERE: NORTH END: Turn east off Highway 101 onto Wilson Creek Road (M.12.53). Park near the locked gate, being careful not to block it. SOUTH END: On Highway 101 at M.10.9 (Del Norte), Trees of Mystery has a gift shop and museum east of highway, motel and restaurant on west. Signed trail to Hidden Beach heads west just north of motel. Trail to hostel climbs east directly across highway.
FURTHER INFO: Redwood National Park(707)465-7335.

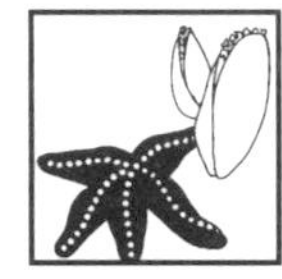

highway. Restrooms are to your left, on the way to the gift shop/museum.

Head south to cautiously cross Highway 101 at the crosswalk, then turn west, paralleling the highway in front of the restaurant and motel. The Coastal Trail continues on a gravel footpath beyond the motel.

Walk 125 feet west from Room #25 of the motel to find the marked trail to Hidden Beach. The gravel path descends southwest through dense young forest of alders and spruce. You cross a bridge over Lagoon Creek, where skunk cabbage and salmonberry are plentiful. Contour across a swampy area, an ancient riverbed carved when the mighty Klamath River emptied into the Pacific where Lagoon Creek does today.

By 1/8 mile you ascend gently to higher ground. The trail soon steepens to climb over a small ridge, then undulates beneath the power line to ¼ mile. Veer west over another small ridge where deer fern grows. A large spruce on your right grows precariously atop a rotting stump.

The trail contours northwest through dense undergrowth beneath mixed forest. Dip across a tributary of Lagoon Creek, then climb to meet the Hidden Beach Section, Coastal Trail at ½ mile (2½ miles from Redwood Hostel).

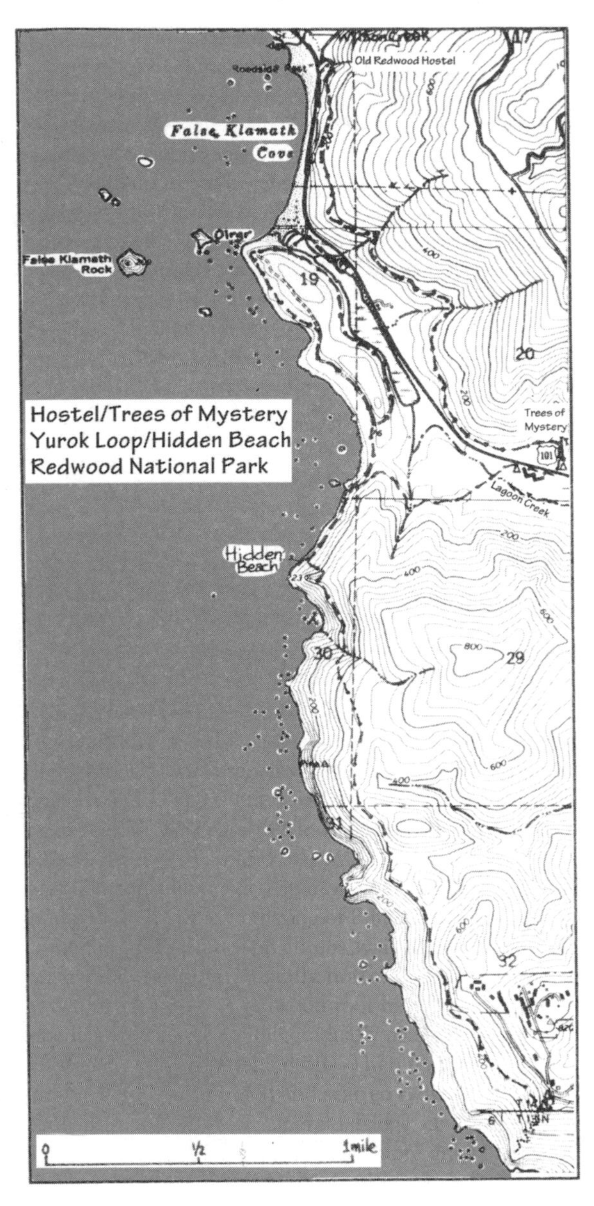


To get to Hidden Beach, go right for 75 feet, then left on the side trail that descends to the jewel of a beach, tucked in the crook of the rocky point to the south.

# 10. YUROK LOOP/HIDDEN BEACH SECTION, COASTAL TRAIL

ENCHANTED COAST NORTH OF KLAMATH

*The Yurok tribe of the Klamath River country has always been one of the largest tribes of Native Americans in Northern California. Their territory stretched from Damnation Creek on the north to Little River (south of Trinidad) on the south, and up the Klamath River to Weitchpec. Before white settlers arrived, the Yurok maintained a continuous trail along the coast of their territory.*

*The Yuroks controlled a land abundant with food along the shore and in the sea and river. This abundance helped them to achieve a complex civilization. They built sturdy houses of split redwood. They carved canoes from whole redwood logs: short agile boats to navigate the rivers; larger vessels with sails for the powerful ocean. The ocean-going canoes were up to 40 feet long and five to ten feet wide. Karok and Hupa peoples traded for the valuable Yurok canoes. The Yurok leaders accumulated property—land, slaves and other wealth. They used a 13-month calendar based on the moon and had a monetary system based on dentalium shells. The Yuroks traded with the Tolowas for these shells, which originated far to the north around Puget Sound.*

*Evidence of Yurok civilization has been traced back at least 5000 years along this coast. They greeted the Spanish galleons that landed at Trinidad in 1775. When fur trapper and mountain man Jedediah Smith explored this country in 1828, his party camped at Wilson Creek and probably received food and other help from the Yuroks. But when hordes of white men arrived in the 1850s, inevitable conflicts occurred, and the Yuroks were displaced. Still, a large number of Yuroks survived by retreating into the heart of their rugged country. In spite of the conflicts, the Yurok tribe retained a viable culture and is currently growing in number. The south end of this hike ends at Klamath Overlook, within the present boundary of Yurok land.*

*The Yurok Loop Trail is a one-mile interpretive trail introducing you to the Yurok culture as it follows an ancient Yurok path along the sea's edge. This short easy loop connects with the Hidden Beach Section of the Coastal Trail.*

*You can follow the Coastal Trail south for 4 miles to an overlook above the mouth of the Klamath River, the lifeblood of Yurok civilization. (The Coastal Trail also leads north for 16 miles. See Trails #6, 8 and 9.)*

The trail heads northwest from the north end of the parking area, following the shore of the freshwater pond on Lagoon

Creek. This pond was enlarged in 1940 as a log pond for a sawmill. Today the pond is stocked with rainbow trout; its surface provides a home for yellow pond lilies and native and migrating birds. Your trail passes through a thicket of alders and willows, then forks. The right fork leads to Wilson Creek Beach and a branch of the Coastal Trail north (see Trail #8). Take the left fork and cross a bridge over Lagoon Creek.

The trail soon heads west, climbing a moderate hill along the edge of the forest. You come to a clearing overlooking the ocean and the mouth of Lagoon Creek. The original Yurok trail south along the bluffs was widened by the U.S. Army in the 1850s. Pioneer settler Peter Louis DeMartin upgraded the trail to a wagon road in 1889.

As you follow the trail along the shore, coastal grasslands alternate with coastal scrub of salal, ferns, lupine, berry vines and ceanothus. At ¼ mile you come to item #4 in the brochure and a grassy clearing. Offshore a jagged rock pinnacle rises 100 feet from the ocean.

The Yuroks referred to it as "the place where bald eagle

YUROK LOOP/HIDDEN BEACH SECTION COASTAL TRAIL:

DISTANCE: One-mile loop; 3⅞ miles one way, 7¾ miles round trip.
TIME: Thirty minutes; 2 to 3 hours.
TERRAIN: Easy loop follows coast and lagoon shore. Easy hike to Hidden Beach, then climbs steeply and descends through forest along rugged coast, coming to steep, grassy headlands above mouth of Klamath River.
ELEVATION GAIN/LOSS: Yurok Loop or Hidden Beach: 150 feet+/150 feet-. Coastal Trail, north to south: 980 feet+/320 feet-.
BEST TIME: Spring, early summer for wildflowers.
WARNINGS: Poison oak along trail. Watch for ticks, especially in spring.
HOW TO GET THERE: NORTH END: Park at the Lagoon Creek Parking Area at M.11.8 (Del Norte) on the west side of Highway 101.
SOUTH END: Turn west off Highway 101 at M.7.1 onto Requa Road. Go 2.5 miles to Klamath Overlook. Trailhead is on south end of parking area.
FURTHER INFO: Redwood National Park (707)465-7335.

rests." With luck you might see a bald eagle somewhere along this hike. Farther offshore is the 209-foot-tall sea stack called False Klamath Rock. To the Yuroks it was *olrgr*, meaning "digging place." Yuroks went there to harvest edible brodiaea bulbs.

A short hill brings you to #6 before 3/8 mile. You then enter a forest of alder and spruce, climbing to a rest bench and #7. The Yuroks considered their trails to be living things that could become resentful if travelers did not treat them with respect. An Indian hiker would ask, "May I come this way again?" Along each major trail the Yuroks designated pleasant spots as special resting places. For travelers to pass such spots without taking off their load to rest showed disrespect for the trail.

The trail soon descends gently, paralleling the shore. False Klamath Rock dwarfs the many other rocks offshore. At ½ mile, the trail forks. To complete the Yurok Loop, go left up a short hill, then descend to the Lagoon Creek pond. As you follow the shore, look for river otters, beavers, herons, egrets and ducks that forage here. Where the trail meets the start of the loop, turn right to return to the parking area.

You take the right fork to get to Hidden Beach or continue south along the Coastal Trail. The trail descends slightly, then levels in dense forest. At 5/8 mile you climb gradually. Leave the forest for a spectacular view of Hidden Beach and the rocky coast. Contour through grasslands at the edge of the forest. Your path tunnels through a stand of young spruce at ¾ mile.

The trail contours along the level, open bluff. Beyond 7/8 mile, the trail returns to forest. At one mile you meet the side trail to Hidden Beach. The spur makes a short descent to the secluded beach.

The Coastal Trail continues southeast, passing the trail to Trees of Mystery (see Trail #9). Go straight, climbing moderately into dense, dark forest. After a view of the coast and False Klamath Rock, start a steep climb around the high, rocky promontory to the south. Climb steeply to 1¼ miles, then moderately. At 13/8 miles you approach the 223-foot-high point on your right.

Your trail climbs sporadically through the forest, with superb views of False Klamath Cove and the rocky coast. Salmon- and huckleberries provide a dense undercover. A silktassel-shrouded rock outcrop on the left has ocean spray growing at its base. You climb again, with the sound of the surf rising from a cove hiding 200 feet below.

At 15/8 miles you pass iris and bleeding heart along rough, slide-prone tread, then climb again. The trail veers east into a wooded gulch, then turns back toward the coast. After a short descent, your trail contours along the steep hillside, where leather ferns grow profusely on the trees.

Climb 18 steep steps to reach the top of the coastal ridge

at 2 1/8 miles. Your trail contours along the ridgetop through a lush patch of false lily of the valley. Only the chattering of birds and the distant roar of surf break the silence of the forest. You descend briefly, then climb to 2 3/8 mile.

Contour through spruce/alder forest on or near the ridgetop to 2½ miles, then descend moderately to a saddle. To the east is the northwest corner boundary of the reservation the Yuroks were left with after the invading settlers took the rest of their land.

Climb steeply through several twists in the trail, then leave the forest for grasslands around 2¾ miles. You are rewarded with a marvelous view. On a clear day you can see Patrick's Point, 30 miles south. The mouth of the Klamath is hidden, but the rest of the rugged coast lies before you. You may hear sea lions barking to the west, 400 feet below. In spring western dog violets grow at your feet.

Your trail contours through grasslands with coastal scrub. Regain the ridgetop briefly at the head of a north-flowing stream. A knot of irises here is surrounded by a whole field of Siberian miner's lettuce, or candyflower. Contour through lush alder forest near the ridgetop, passing a rock outcrop shrouded in scrub. At the head of another stream, a small pond on your left supports lush vegetation.

The trail climbs for 1/8 mile, then contours across lush, steep slopes where red-flowering currant bushes grow to the size of small fruit trees. Ascend to 3¼ miles, where a fence on the left marks the boundary of an old Redwood National Park maintenance center. You quickly come to an overlook with a guard rail and rest bench. The land here is sinking gradually into the Pacific, unlike the coast south of Cape Mendocino, which is still rising from the ocean. You can see the broad mouth of the Klamath River.

Your last stretch of trail contours through steep, scrub-choked grasslands above the mouth of the Klamath, a prime spot for spring and summer wildflowers. Before 3½ miles you pass through a stand of spruce and cross a small creek on a boardwalk. Returning to grasslands, your trail ascends sporadically, angling southeast toward Klamath Overlook Parking Area.

Before 3⁷/₈ miles a bench on the right provides a view of the outlet of the Klamath and the three large sea stacks guarding its mouth. The largest of these is called Oregos after the Yurok spirit who lives there. Yurok legend says that Oregos told the fish when to enter the river and what route to follow upstream.

In another 250 feet, a spur trail on the right winds down to Klamath Overlook in about ½ mile, right above the rock *Oregos* (no ocean access). The main trail climbs to its end at the parking area.

The Coastal Trail continues on the south side of the Klamath, but you need a car to get there, unless you can convince a fisherman with a boat to ferry you across the river. It is 7 miles by road, about 3 miles by the river to Flint Ridge Trailhead.

# 11. FLINT RIDGE SECTION COASTAL TRAIL

## WINDBLOWN VIRGIN FOREST ABOVE THE KLAMATH

*The mighty Klamath River empties into the Pacific just 3 miles downstream from the Douglas Bridge parking area, the eastern trailhead for Flint Ridge. The Klamath, second only to the Sacramento River in size of California rivers, winds 260 miles from southern Oregon to its broad mouth. The Klamath River has the largest runs of salmon and steelhead in the state, making it a popular destination for sport fishermen. In fact, the banks near the mouth of the river have several resorts catering to anglers.*

*The Klamath River is the heart of Yurok culture. Three dozen Yurok villages once lay along the lower 40 miles of the river: The influence of the river was so great upon the culture that the Yurok language expresses directions in terms of upstream and downstream rather than the cardinal points used by most cultures. Today many Yuroks live on the Hoopa Valley Indian Reservation, which lies up the river.*

*After gold was discovered at Gold Bluffs in 1850, prospectors invaded the Klamath, taking much of the Yuroks' land. The forty-niners established the town of Klamath in 1851. The original town, located on the south bank near here, clustered around an iron house that provided protection when angry natives raided the invaders. The town lasted only a year before the gold seekers moved elsewhere.*

*Later another settlement called Klamath grew across the*

*river. A ferry shuttled travelers for a fee until the Douglas Memorial Bridge opened in 1926. The original bridge and the town of Klamath were destroyed by the 1964 flood. The south portal of the old bridge, marked by two golden grizzly bears, is north of the parking area.*

The trail descends northeast into a dense forest of red alders, then turns left to cross Richardson Creek, in a culvert below. Your trail parallels the creek, heading upstream to Marshall Pond. The trail veers right and follows the shore of this old mill pond. Keep an eye out for gnawed logs, a sign of the beavers living in the pond. Sometimes if you sit quietly at the pond's northeast corner (around ¼ mile), you will see a beaver break the surface of the still waters. But be forewarned: it takes patience, silence and luck.

After veering away from the pond, you meet a gravel road. This promptly makes two left turns, coming to a trail sign directing you back toward the pond. Follow the path west along its northern shore. Climb gradually above the shore, passing a piece of old mill machinery at ½ mile.

Just before ¾ mile, your narrowing path suddenly switchbacks right and climbs away from the pond. Ascend into the dense forest, crossing a bridge over a tiny creek. Redwood sorrel, wild ginger, salal, huckleberry, and deer and sword ferns blanket the forest floor. After another bridge, you climb by several switchbacks into a forest of larger redwoods mixed with Douglas firs. The trail steepens at one mile, climbing by many switchbacks toward Flint Ridge. After more bridges and some steps, turn north at 1¼ miles

FLINT RIDGE SECTION, COASTAL TRAIL:

DISTANCE: 4½ miles one way, 9 miles round trip.
TIME: Two and one-half hours each way.
TERRAIN: Follows lake shore, then climbs to a coastal ridge of virgin redwoods, following it to descend near the ocean.
ELEVATION GAIN/LOSS: 880 feet+/460 feet-, east to west. 1340 feet+/- round trip.
BEST TIME: Spring for wildflowers. Any clear day.
HOW TO GET THERE: EAST END: Turn west off Highway 101 at M.3.75 (Del Norte) onto Klamath Beach Road. Go 1.5 miles to Alder Camp Road junction, where there is a parking area. Trailhead is 250 feet west on the north side of Alder Camp Road.
WEST END: See Coastal Drive (next trail).
FURTHER INFO: Redwood National Park (707)465-7335.

and continue a steady but gradual climb through the dense redwood forest.

Just before 2 miles, the trail turns left as it gains the ridgetop. You get a glimpse of the deep Klamath River Canyon to the north. Then climb southwest with the ridge. Redwoods here range to 12 feet in diameter, but most of the trees have broken tops, being exposed to harsh coastal winds that roar in at the mouth of the Klamath.

Your trail winds near the top of the ridge, with short up and down stretches. Beyond 2½ miles a very steep drop lies on your left, with Richardson Creek far below. You stay south of the ridgetop. The trail passes under a big fallen log at 2¾ miles. Descend to 3 miles, passing between a leaning fir and a rock outcrop.

Continue your winding descent to 3¼ miles. Then your trail levels as alders start to mix with the virgin redwood forest. Ascend to a second summit at 3¾ miles. Now alders dominate the forest; the sounds of pounding surf rise from 850 feet below.

At 3⅞ miles your trail switches left and descends by a series of switchbacks toward the coast. The vegetation becomes more lush: buttercup, coltsfoot and yellow skunk cabbage grow along the trail. Lichens droop from the alders.

Your steady descent passes under a power line at 4¼ miles. In 250 feet the side trail to Flint Ridge Campground branches right. Ten sites in a grassy clearing provide tables, metal food lockers and a composting toilet.

Continue your descent north to cross a boardwalk at 4⅜ miles. The trail climbs briefly before it descends and switchbacks left. Cross another bridge and come to a side road at 4½ miles, where a trail sign posts the distances in the opposite direction. Turn right and make a short descent to the western trailhead on the Coastal Drive.

## 12. COASTAL DRIVE AND SHORT TRAILS

### DRIVE/WALK/CYCLE A WILD COAST

*The Coastal Drive hugs a rugged steep section of coast between the Klamath River near its mouth and the north edge of Prairie Creek Redwoods State Park. The road provides the only opportunity (other than by boat) to see this wild stretch of coast. In 2011, after years of maintenance problems on these unstable slopes, the center portion of the Coastal Drive was permanently closed to vehicle traffic. The good news is that the closed portion is being maintained for hikers and bicyclists as part of the California Coastal Trail. The park will eventually*

*complete the conversion of the closed section into a trail, called Te-wo-lew Trail, after the Yurok word for Pacific coast.*

*We describe both the drive and the hike from north to south. You can still drive the northern loop in a passenger car (trailers and RVs prohibited) by following West Klamath Beach Road, Coastal Drive North and Alder Camp Road. The trailhead for the trail portion is just south of where Alder Camp Road meets Coastal Drive North. You can also drive the southern end of Coastal Drive from N.B. Drury Parkway for 1.4 miles to the locked gate.*

*The closed portion of Coastal Drive, also known as Te-wo-lew Trail, is ideal for bicycles, although hikers will see and hear even more.*

## THE DRIVE

Exit Highway 101 onto West Klamath Beach Road, which follows the south bank of the broad river. In 1.5 miles from the highway, you come to Alder Camp Road and the parking area for the Flint Ridge Trail (see Trail #11). Recreational vehicles and vehicles with trailers can turn left on Alder Camp Road to bypass the narrow, steep and winding portion of Klamath Beach Road where they are not allowed. They can follow Alder Camp Road for 2 miles to its end, but the Coastal Drive south from that intersection is permanently closed to motor vehicles. Small RVs may be able to drive north 0.2 miles from there to reach High Bluff Picnic Area.

Continuing along West Klamath Beach Road, you wind along the flat on the south side of the river, passing several seasonal fishing resorts and campgrounds. Immediately after the road starts to climb above the river flat, you come to South Klamath Overlook, 4 miles from Highway 101. From here you have a view of the mouth of the river. You can walk a mile north to the river mouth or, depending on the tide, up to 1½ miles south at the base of steep bluffs.

The gravel road climbs the steep, twisting grade. At 4.5

COASTAL DRIVE AND SHORT TRAILS:

DISTANCE: Road is 10 miles long, but closed permanently to motor vehicles from mile 5.5 to mile 8.6, about 3/8 mile north of Carruthers Cove Trailhead.
Klamath Beach access: One to 5 miles.
Flint Ridge Trail to campground: ½ mile round trip.
Radar station trail: ¼ mile round trip.
High Bluff trail: One mile round trip.
Closed portion of Coastal Drive: Up to 5¾ miles round trip.

TIME: At least one hour. Two to 3 hours to hike closed portion of Coastal Drive.

TERRAIN: Road follows the Klamath River to its mouth, then climbs to high bluffs overlooking a wild and isolated coast. Trail/closed portion of road continue along high bluffs before ending at the still-open southern portion of Coastal Drive a mile before N.B. Drury Parkway.

ELEVATION GAIN/LOSS: Radar station trail: 40 feet-/40 feet+. Flint Ridge Trail to camp: 400 feet+/feet-. High Bluff trail to beach, round trip: 320 feet-/320 feet+. Coastal Drive portion closed to motor vehicles: 900 feet +/900 feet-.

BEST TIME: A clear day; when it's foggy, you do not see much here. Spring for wildflowers.

WARNINGS: Drive carefully on the winding, occasionally steep road and watch for pedestrians and cyclists. No trailers or RVs allowed on Klamath Beach Road west of Alder Camp Road. Do not enter the Alder Camp property; it's a prison. Watch for poison oak and stinging nettles when walking coastal grasslands.

HOW TO GET THERE: Exit Highway 101 onto Klamath Beach Road at M.3.5 (Del Norte) from south, M.3.7 from north.

FURTHER INFO: Redwood National Park (707)465-7335.

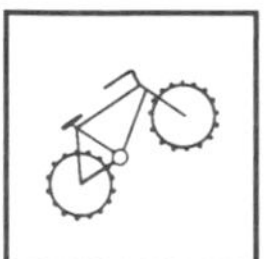

miles from the highway, you come to the parking area for the west end of the Flint Ridge Trail. From here you can look down to the 175-foot pinnacle of Flint Rock Head on the sandy beach below. To the east, a ¼-mile climb leads to Flint Ridge Primitive Campground.

At 4.9 miles on the road, you come to wide spot where a trail descends to a World-War-II-vintage radar station in 1/8 mile. The station was disguised as a typical coastal ranch house to fool possible invaders from the Pacific.

Continuing along the Coastal Drive, at 5.6 miles you come to a short road on your right. The road descends 0.3 mile to High Bluff Picnic Area, with wheelchair-accessible picnic tables and toilet. A short paved path leads to a nearby overlook, where you look down a cliff to the crashing breakers 300 feet below. If it is clear enough, you have one of the best views of the rugged coast to the south, all the way to Patrick's Point 25 miles away. A steep trail winds ½ mile down to the beach.

One mile south stands the massive rock outcrop called Split Rock, sacred to the Yurok people. Composed of metamorphosed volcanic rock called greenstone, it rises 533 feet from the Pacific. Traditional Yurok belief considers rock outcrops the last dwelling places of immortals on this earth. Split Rock has a 100-foot-deep cleft down the middle (not visible from here). Yurok legend says that an ancestral fisherman anchored his net on the rock. When the Spirit of the West Wind filled the net with an enormous catch of salmon, the load split the rock in two.

Just .2 mile beyond the High Bluff access, Klamath Beach Road ends at Alder Camp Road. Motor vehicle access to the next 3 1/8 miles of the Coastal Drive has been closed permanently at the locked gate just south of the intersection. But you can use foot or bicycle to explore the rest of the Coastal Drive. Although I had driven the Coastal Drive many times, walking it revealed hidden treasures: abundant grouse calling from the alder forest west of the road, changing vistas of the immense, elusive dome of Split Rock, and other breathtaking views of coastal landmarks.

## TE-WO-LEW TRAIL

Park near the gate. Do not block it or enter the closed portion of Alder Camp Road above the gate. At the gate, notice the large Sitka spruce towering above you east of the road. While deciduous alders dominate the forest along the trail, spruces also thrive. Near the gate, ceanothus and elderberry grow tall and a pioneer apple tree grows on the right. As you climb gradually south-southeast on the closed road, notice thimbleberry, salmonberry, cow parsnip, poison hemlock, buttercup, sword and lady ferns. and the large palmate leaves of coltsfoot. Most important, watch for stinging nettles, ubiquitous here in all but the dead of winter. They thrive in disturbed areas and are helping to reclaim the old

Requa
Boat Docks
Spruce
Creek
KLAMATH
RIVER
Hatzis
Flat
Klamath
Hoppaw
Klamath South 2
Flint Ridge
Richardson Creek
High Bluff
JEEP TRAIL
Saugep Creek
Alder
Forestry Conservation Camp
Waukell Creek
Split Rock
STATE PARK
Johnson Creek
N.B. Drury Parkway
COASTAL DRIVE
REDWOOD NATIONAL PARK
TRAILS 10,11,12
1/2
1 mile

road as wilderness.

Around 1/8 mile, you pass a construction zone which, in spring 2014, was working to fix a slip-out on the private Alder Camp Road just above. Top a rise, then descend gently past horsetail, yarrow, lupine, native blackberry, coyote brush, manroot, and bee plant. Listen for the thrumming sound of grouse and the zinging of diving hummingbirds. You might also see or hear quail, robins, Wilson's warblers and other songbirds, and raptors.

Resume climbing at ½ mile. Where the pavement resumes, you pass an old turnout on the right with a Pacific view between alders. Alder trees were down across the road around 5/8 mile in May 2014, but you could get by. Soon another old turnout reveals a few offshore rocks far below. Continue your ascent along the old road. At stacks of gravel on the right shoulder, you can see the upper part of Split Rock to the south.

Climb to a high point at one mile. The road descends, narrowing to a single track flanked by nettles. You hit the pavement again briefly at 1 1/8 miles. But as you continue south, mosses, grasses and all the other plants are taking over the pavement, helping it decompose. Animals also strive to reclaim the old road. I saw the scat of bear, coyote and bobcat on my spring hike.

Your old-road trail contours high above the coast from 1 3/8 miles to 1 5/8 miles, where a turnout on the right overlooks the Pacific beyond the thicket of berry plants. As you descend, the trail once again narrows to single track. Your descent steepens around 1 7/8 miles as you traverse a verdant garden. You come to one of the slipouts that led to the decision to close the road to motor vehicles, the lowest point on this hike.

Around 2 miles you climb to a junction with the south end of Alder Camp Road. Stay out! Continue your ascent on this drivable portion of Coastal Drive. Be aware that it is still used by official vehicles. Ascend to an excellent turnout at 2¼ miles, which offers your first view south along Gold Bluffs Beach. When it's clear, the farthest land visible is Patrick's Point near Trinidad. In the foreground Carruthers Cove is barely visible above a ridge draped in alders, with Ossagon Rocks beyond.

Climb past a rock outcrop on your left where stonecrop thrives. After a short respite Coastal Drive trail climbs again, steeply around 2½ miles. Salal and red-flowering currant join the mix of plants.

At 2 5/8 miles Carruthers Cove Overlook is on the right. The Civilian Conservation Corps-built stone wall surveys a cliffy 600-foot drop to the big beached sea stacks at Carruthers Cove just south. An apple tree grows beside the wall. This offers a good and climactic place to turn back unless you want to get to the southern gate.

If you want to continue, descend gradually south along the old road, then dip through another slumping of the old roadbed. Climb briefly to reach the southern gate at 2 7/8 miles. If you have lots of time, the highly recommended Carruthers Cove Trail (no bikes) starts not quite 3/8 mile down the road. Otherwise, retrace your tracks to your starting point.

# PRAIRIE CREEK REDWOODS STATE PARK

*On a moonlit night in Prairie Creek Campground the silhouette of the land takes quintessential wilderness form. The tall forest parades atop the rolling ridges and along the very edge of the glistening, dewy prairie. The distant crashing of waves punctuates the profound silence, joined sometimes by the howl of a coyote, the piercing cry of a night bird, the crackle of a campfire, the soft crunching of elk grazing.*

*Prairie Creek Redwoods State Park comprises 14,523 acres of friendly wilderness (except when the weather turns fierce). The Murrelet State Wilderness now covers about half the park. Somehow nature graced the park with an absence of the bane of hikers, poison oak. Its charms include vast virgin forests, verdant canyons with crystalline streams, herds of magnificent elk, and a wild rugged coast of cliffs, waterfalls, wildflower-dappled dunes and gold-flecked beaches extending for miles. It is one of my favorite places on earth.*

*In 1992 this paradise became even better. The new freeway bypassing the park to the east has alleviated congestion on Newton B. Drury Parkway, making it easier and more pleasant to stop for a walk or look for the majestic elk, even nicer if you camp overnight.*

## 13. CARRUTHERS COVE

SECLUDED BEACH BACKED BY SPECTACULAR ROCKS

*While the Coastal Drive provides spectacular views of the rugged shoreline south of the Klamath River's mouth at almost every turnout, the only trail down to this "Little Lost Coast" is the Carruthers Cove Trail. It leaves the Coastal Drive one mile from the road's south end near the national park boundary sign. The steep, well-graded trail drops nearly 600 feet in ¾ mile to reach a pristine, driftwood-strewn beach with immense rocks at the mouth of Johnson Creek. Unless it is high tide, you can walk south to Ossagon Creek and Gold Bluffs Beach. Though the trail is highly recommended, keep in mind that the steep climb out will be the hardest part.*

The trail drops steeply to a remnant of the old roadbed that you follow to the beach. Head generally west on the old road, descending through mixed Sitka spruce and alder forest with a lush green understory. The forest obscures all views of the coast as your track curves right, then left. You

## CARRUTHERS COVE:

DISTANCE: 1 1/8 miles to rock outcrops at beach (2¼ miles round trip). To West Ridge Trail : 3 1/8 miles one way.
TIME: One hour to all day.
TERRAIN: Descends steeply through alder/spruce forest to small cove on isolated stretch of beach. Coastal Trail south is on sand, may be impassable at high tide.
ELEVATION GAIN/LOSS: Round trip: 560 feet-/560 feet+.
BEST TIME: Low tide. Marvelous for sunsets. Anytime OK.
WARNINGS: Watch for poison oak in the tangle of coastal vegetation near the beach. No camping here. Do not walk south more than ½ mile from the rocks when the tide is rising, or you may be cut off. Watch for oversize waves as you walk on the beach.
HOW TO GET THERE: Turn west off Highway 101 at M.137.45 from south, M.0.3 (Del Norte) from north onto N.B. Drury Parkway. Go south 0.9 mile to Coastal Drive (M.134.2). Trailhead is 1.0 mile from the Parkway, beside the sign marking the entrance to Redwood National Park.
FURTHER INFO: Prairie Creek Redwoods State Park (707)488-2039, (707)465-7354.
OTHER SUGGESTION: Can be used as a portion of the continuous Coastal Trail: after the Flint Ridge Section, walk south along the mostly gravel Coastal Drive. Then take Carruthers Cove Trail (at low tide) to continue the Coastal Trail (see also Trail #19).

descend southwest at ¼ mile.

Continue your steady descent toward the beach, passing iris, fairy bells and bleeding heart. Around ½ mile your trail twists west, then south before returning to a southwest bearing. You get a glimpse of the coastline to the north through the dense forest. Its full grandeur, however, still lies hidden.

Your trail steepens approaching the 5/8-mile point. Swing left for your first good look at the beach below. The path soon bends left again, paralleling the deep canyon of Johnson Creek. Notice how the winds have sculpted the forest.

Descend west above the canyon, heading toward the beach. Your trail comes to a level spot where two cabins stood until the 1970s, marked by bricks and dense clumps of daffodils. Where the path turns sharply right at ¾ mile, you can see the mouth of the creek beyond the bramble thicket below. Pause to absorb your first clear view of the magnificent rock outcrop at the mouth of the creek.

Then you plunge steeply to the beach by a series of short switchbacks. This stretch of trail offers occasionally precarious footing, so proceed with caution. At the base of the switchbacks, make your way over a pile of driftwood. You reach firm footing on the beach sand before 7/8 mile.

It is ¼ mile south across level, sand-filled Carruthers Cove to the base of the spectacular rock outcrops. Sea rocket and salal hunker beneath the imposing cliff. A crevice at the base of these rocks shelters you from the wind. You can snack or picnic here. Previous visitors have built driftwood fires in the shelter of the rock, but camping is not allowed. It is well worth a rest to contemplate the wild isolation of this coast.

To the north and south, the pristine beach stretches along the base of steep cliffs. Less than ¾ mile north, the sandy beach ends at the base of a rocky cliff. Two miles north stands imposing Split Rock, rising 533 feet from the edge of the sea. This greenstone dome has a shape reminiscent of Yosemite's Half Dome when viewed from here.

If the tide is below +3.0 feet and ebbing, you can walk south along the beach to the mouth of Ossagon Creek and beyond. It is 1/8 mile south to the tallest of several offshore rocks, a pointed spire. From the 1 1/8-mile point, the beach gradually narrows. Beyond 1 3/8 miles you pass medium- to large-sized rocks scattered along the tide line. At 1 5/8 miles you come to the crucial narrow spot, impassable at high tide. Here you must scramble around a protruding rock outcrop that is somewhat protected from large waves by the tall rocks offshore. You then hop over a thigh-high rock ledge, after which the beach becomes wider again. At 1¾ miles you pass another narrow spot, but it is nothing compared to the first one.

Continue south on the broadening beach. Tracks of elk, raccoon and occasionally mountain lion may be seen in the

fine sand. Keep an eye out for the herd of elk that grazes Gold Bluffs Beach; they are frequently seen this far north.

At 2¼ miles from your trailhead, you come to the Ossagon Rocks, which are on the beach as well as offshore. Go another ¼ mile and you are west of the place where the Ossagon Trail comes down to the coastal plain. You can head east to find the trail, which is marked by a sign where it rises from the flat beside Ossagon Creek. If you loop back on the Ossagon Trail, be sure to have arranged a car shuttle to return you to the Carruthers Cove Trailhead. If you head south along the Coastal Trail, it is ½ mile to West Ridge Trail, 2¾ miles to Fern Canyon and 3 miles to the end of the dirt road, 4¼ miles to the hike/bike camp at Gold Bluffs Beach.

## 14. OSSAGON

### OLD ROUTE TO HEART OF WILDERNESS BEACH

*This trail follows an old road, now recontoured into a trail, through redwood, spruce and alder forest. Most of the road beyond the crest is now a single-track trail. It makes a steep but short descent to the wildest portion of Gold Bluffs Beach, passing sites of an old homestead and a Yurok village. At the shore it meets the Coastal Trail, which goes south past Butler Creek to Fern Canyon Trailhead. If you time your visit with the tides, you can also walk north to Carruthers Cove. Cyclists can also use the Ossagon Trail, part of a 29.5-mile designated bike loop (see* OTHER SUGGESTION*).*

The trail heads west-northwest from the parkway amidst large redwoods and Sitka spruce. Cross a small bridge, then climb gradually northwest.

Your trail ascends moderately beyond 1/8 mile as the roar of the surf overtakes the sound of road traffic. Climb gradually, descend briefly, then traverse an easy uphill to a rest bench where you join the original trail. Contour to reach the summit at ½ mile.

You now start a steady descent toward the coast. The trail makes a bend to the right, descending moderately. As your track bends back to the left, a stand of immense redwoods lines the path. These quickly give way to a forest of alders as you drop southwest at 5/8 mile. As the trail turns west, you can glimpse the ocean through the trees, though the view is best in winter when the alders have dropped their leaves.

At ¾ mile the trail bends left, then right. Evergreen violets grow in the roadbed. The steady descent wraps around another big bend. At 7/8 mile your trail makes another swing to the right and descends over two boardwalks. Swing sharply

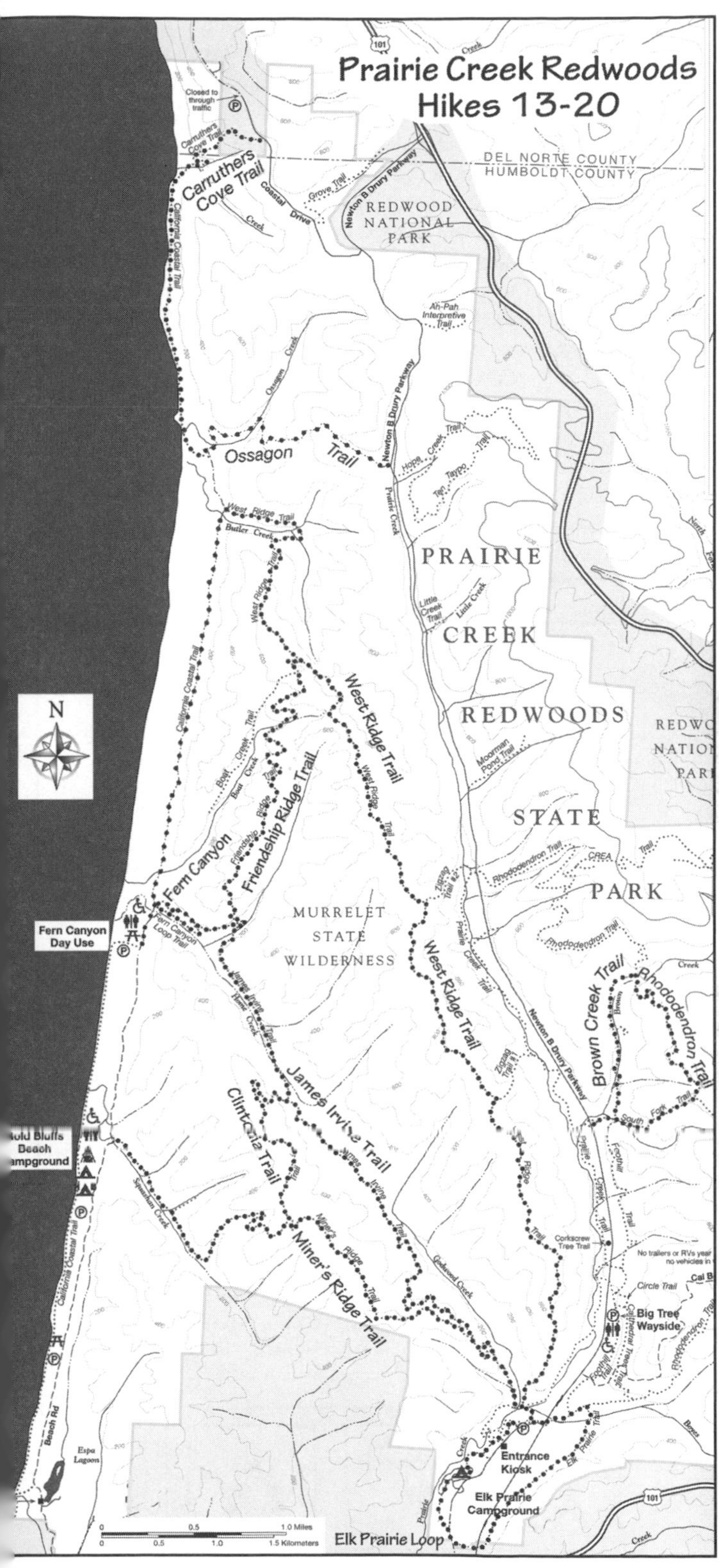

Prairie Creek Redwoods
Hikes 13-20
DEL NORTE COUNTY
HUMBOLDT COUNTY
REDWOOD NATIONAL PARK
Carruthers Cove Trail
Ossagon Trail
West Ridge Trail
Fern Canyon
Friendship Ridge Trail
Fern Canyon Day Use
PRAIRIE CREEK REDWOODS STATE PARK
MURRELET STATE WILDERNESS
James Irvine Trail
Clintonia Trail
Miner's Ridge Trail
Brown Creek Trail
Rhododendron Trail
South Fork Trail
Big Tree Wayside
Entrance Kiosk
Elk Prairie Campground
Elk Prairie Loop
Gold Bluffs Beach Campground
Newton B Drury Parkway
California Coastal Trail
Coastal Drive
Ah-Pah Interpretive Trail
Corkscrew Tree Trail
Circle Trail
Cathedral Trees Trail
Foothill Trail
No trailers or RVs
N
0 0.5 1.0 Miles
0 0.5 1.0 1.5 Kilometers

right before 1 1/8 miles, descending toward Ossagon Creek. Redwoods become scarce, with abundant spruce and alders. A partial clearing on the left is the site of an old homestead. Two large cascara sagrada trees, about 40 feet tall, mark the spot.

Descend to cross the creek on a sturdy bridge, then climb briefly. The trail contours from around 1 3/8 miles. As you descend again, you can see the broad beach ahead. On your right is Ossagon Prairie, once the site of the small Yurok hamlet of Osegen, now very overgrown with berry vines. Faint side trails lead up to the large, steeply sloping prairie with a pleasant southern exposure.

The main trail descends steeply from here. Soon, the old road turns sharply left and makes its last descent to level at a ford of tiny Ossagon Creek, lined with piggyback plant, stinging nettle and lush sword ferns. You are slightly more than 1¾ miles from the trailhead. A sign at the base of the hill marks the trail back to the highway. Although Ossagon Camp has been closed, three picnic tables and a decrepit

| OSSAGON: |
|---|
| DISTANCE: 2 1/8 miles to beach (4¼ miles round trip), 4¾ miles to trailhead at end of Gold Bluffs Beach Road; part of 29½-mile bike loop.<br>TIME: At least 2 hours for trail, half to full day for bike loop.<br>TERRAIN: Climbs briefly, then descends through forest to beach.<br>ELEVATION GAIN/LOSS: To beach: 120 feet+/720 feet-. Round trip: 840 feet+/840 feet-. Bike loop: 1480 feet-/1480 feet+.<br>BEST TIME: Spring for wildflowers, but nice anytime.<br>WARNINGS: Do not approach wild elk on beach. Mountain bikers: please stay on designated route and watch for hikers.<br>HOW TO GET THERE: Exit Highway 101 at M.137.45 from north, M.125.9 from south onto N.B. Drury Parkway. Trail heads west from M.132.74 opposite the Hope Creek Trailhead.<br>FURTHER INFO: Prairie Creek Redwoods State Park (707)488-2039, (707)465-7354.<br>OTHER SUGGESTION: BIKE LOOP (total distance: 29.5 miles) allows two-wheel exploration of the park's backcountry. No other trails at Prairie Creek are open to biking. From park entrance, bike north on N.B. Drury Parkway for 5¾ miles. Go west 1¾ miles on Ossagon Trail to the beach. Take Coastal Trail south 3 miles. Then follow Gold Bluffs Road 4½ miles to its summit, where you meet Streelow Creek Trail. Follow this 1 7/8 miles, then complete loop with 1 5/8 miles on Davison Trail and the campground road. |

 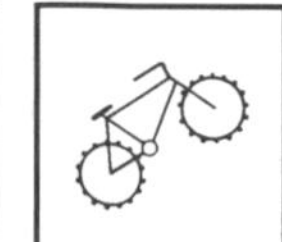  

outhouse still sit beside the creek, a nice spot for a break.

A faint trail leads northwest from this spot, though it quickly becomes overgrown and hard to follow, leading into a swampy area. You should follow the main trail southwest to a signed junction beyond 1⁷/₈ miles. The Coastal Trail leads south to Butler Creek in ³/₈ mile, where it meets the north end of the West Ridge Trail. The parking area at the end of Gold Bluffs Beach Road is 2¾ miles beyond. See Trails #16 and 19.

The Coastal Trail also follows the beach north to Carruthers Cove, passable at a tide of +3.0 feet or lower. It is 1¾ miles to where Carruthers Cove Trail meets the beach (see Trail #13). Keep your eyes open for the herd of elk that frequents this area. You may see elk wallows in the vicinity.

To get to the beach from the junction, take the right fork. The tread turns sandy by 2 miles, as Ossagon Rocks come into view to the north. You come to a bridged creek crossing, this one of Butler Creek. Beyond the creek the trail winds northwest, but quickly turns vague in loose sand. From the old camp via the Ossagon Rocks/Carruthers Cove Trail, it is ³/₈ mile southwest and west to the tide line. Or you can turn north and head for the westernmost of the Ossagon Rocks. If you are heading north, be sure a rising tide does not cut off your return.

Leave ample time before sunset to return to the trailhead.

## 15. BROWN CREEK RHODODENDRON SOUTH FORK LOOP

PRIMEVAL FOREST ON A BABBLING BROOK

*The Brown Creek Trail provides a rewarding break for travelers to stretch their legs before continuing north or south. The trail, built in 1951, is just long enough to stimulate your tight muscles. Its dramatic pristine beauty will stretch your eyes, mind and imagination as well. One of the park's most beautiful hikes at any time of the year; it will reward you in spring with a dazzling array of rhododendrons and other wildflowers.*

*You can stroll up Brown Creek and return by the same trail for an easy 2½-mile (or less) round trip. Or you can follow the loop exactly as described for a steeper 3³/8-mile loop. If you want a longer hike, continue south on the Rhododendron Trail beyond the South Fork Trail. If you have a driver to pick you up where the trail crosses Cal Barrel Road, the hike is about 3¾ miles. If you continue to the end of the Rhododendron Trail and loop back on the Foothill Trail or the Prairie Creek Trail (across the Parkway), the distance is 8 or 8½ miles. Whichever option you take, your entire hike will be in primeval redwood forest.*

Start out on the South Fork Trail, heading east from N.B. Drury Parkway into a forest of immense virgin trees. The path meanders above the south bank of Brown Creek, meeting the Foothill Trail on your right beyond ¹/8 mile.

Your South Fork Trail soon follows the tiny South Fork of Brown Creek. Cross it on a small bridge before ¼ mile, then turn left on the Brown Creek Trail. You head northwest, traversing the base of the ridge separating the two forks of the creek.

The trail turns north past craggy giants beside Brown Creek. Cross the creek on a sturdy bridge before ½ mile, then climb gradually north through primeval forest alongside the

BROWN CREEK/RHODODENDRON
SOUTH FORK LOOP:

DISTANCE: 3⁵/8-mile loop with options for an 8¹/8- or 8¾-mile loop.
TIME: Two to 4 hours.
TERRAIN: Ascends a canyon of primeval redwood forest, climbs to a ridge, then descends the ridge to complete loop.
ELEVATION GAIN/LOSS: 675 feet+/675 feet-.
BEST TIME: Spring for wildflowers, late afternoon for best lighting.
HOW TO GET THERE: On east side of N.B. Drury Parkway at M.129.0, 2 miles north of main park entrance. Parking on either side of highway. (Exit Highway 101 at M.137.45 from north, M.125.9 from south.)
FURTHER INFO: Prairie Creek Redwoods State Park (707)488-2039, (707) 465-7354.
OTHER SUGGESTIONS: You can drive CAL BARREL ROAD to the upper portion of the RHODODENDRON TRAIL. Turn east off N.B. Drury Parkway at M.127.5. At 1.8 miles you cross the Rhododendron Trail. You can hike south 2¼ miles to the Cathedral Trees Trail, or north for 4 miles to its end at the CREA Trail. You can also bike Cal Barrel Road.

creek. Your path soon tunnels under immense fallen logs.

The forest consists of redwoods of varying shapes and sizes. Its understory is jammed with deer and sword ferns, redwood sorrel and salal. In March and April, trilliums and violets abound, and you may see delicate calypso orchids. In May or June, the shocking pink blooms of rhododendrons splash the forest with color.

Your trail winds through the forest, but you never lose the sound of the murmuring stream. Descend briefly before climbing along the creek again. Iris and huckleberry are prolific here. Your path climbs along the base of the canyon wall.

Beyond ¾ mile you come to a spur trail. It crosses Brown Creek and enters the Trees of the Great Grove, dedicated to Carl Schenck, founder of America's first school of forestry. To this forester is attributed a wonderful quote: "Forestry is a great thing but love is better." It took much love and energy (not to mention money) to save the virgin forests of Prairie Creek.

Your trail stays near the creek, climbing gradually to another grove of immense redwood giants. This one is dedicated to Frederick Olmstead, co-founder of the Save-the-Redwoods League and son of the designer of New York's Central Park.

Continue up the canyon. Beyond one mile your trail climbs above the creek to cross two boardwalks. A steep downhill crosses a tributary and brings you back beside the creek at 1¼ miles. Ascend to the junction with the Rhododendron Trail.

Now you must make your decision. For the shortest hike, retrace your steps to the road (2⅝ miles round trip). Either direction you take on the Rhododendron Trail climbs steeply out of Brown Creek Canyon, gaining 300 to 350 feet in elevation in ½ mile. Our described route heads south on the Rhododendron Trail.

Your trail crosses a bridge over Brown Creek, then climbs moderately. At 1⅜ miles the path wraps around an immense redwood with a huge fire scar on its back side. You climb southeast, with views back into the canyon. The ascent steepens around 1⅝ miles. Beyond 1⅞ miles your trail levels briefly, providing a break from the steep climb.

The trail narrows through a brushy area where Douglas firs and hemlocks mingle with the sempervirens. You come to another grove of giant redwoods at 2 miles. Large sword ferns cover every inch of available ground. The distant roar of surf drifts through the silent forest.

Just before 2⅛ miles, you duck under a fallen tree. The mostly level trail winds along the side of a steep hill. Many rhododendrons grow here, as well as abundant huckleberries. Descend to cross two small streams around 2¼ miles, then climb by several short, steep switchbacks to a junction atop a ridge at 2⅜ miles.

For a 3⅝-mile loop, turn right and descend the South Fork

Trail. Those wanting a longer hike can continue south along the Rhododendron Trail. It climbs 120 feet to its 960-foot summit in 5/8 mile. Then it descends to cross Cal Barrel Road (1¼ miles from here) and drops steeply to Boyes Creek, connecting with the Cathedral Trees, Elk Prairie and Foothill Trails.

The South Fork Trail descends along a ridge. Redwoods, rhododendrons, tanoaks, redwood sorrel, trilliums and huckleberries thrive here. Your trail leaves the ridge for its steep, lush north face around 2¾ miles. Descend steeply by numerous short, tight switchbacks.

The trail finally levels at 3 3/8 miles, meeting the Brown Creek Trail. Turn left and cross the small bridge, then retrace your steps on the South Fork Trail, returning to the trailhead at 3 5/8 miles.

# 16. WEST RIDGE TO BUTLER CREEK

## SOLITUDE, FOREST AND SURF

*The West Ridge Trail traverses the backbone of Prairie Creek Redwoods State Park. You can use it for a moderately short but varied day hike by looping back on the ZigZag Trail #1 and Prairie Creek Trail (5 7/8 miles), a longer loop day hike with the Zig Zag #2 and Prairie Creek Trails (8 7/8 miles), or a marathon day of hiking in the virgin forest (14 3/8 miles or more). All these choices offer the solitude and silence of virgin forest.*

Your trail starts at the Visitor Center, where you can inquire about current trail conditions. Follow the Nature Trail across the long bridge over Prairie Creek and head north for just over 1/8 mile. At 3/16 mile, you meet the West Ridge Trail on your right. Take this trail heading north.

Climb steadily by many short switchbacks to gain the ridge before 5/8 mile. The virgin forest stretches in all directions, with large redwoods, ferns, trilliums and evergreen violets crowding the trail. Continue climbing, with occasional switchbacks. Your trail levels briefly at ¾ mile, then begins a more gradual climb. Douglas firs mingle with the redwoods in this drier habitat. Climb steeply again, then descend briefly to one mile. The traffic noise from the nearby road is softened by the forest.

From 1 1/8 miles your trail follows the ridgetop which rolls up and down through the forest. Leather ferns grow on a redwood to the left. You climb intermittently to 1½ miles where the top of the ridge becomes broad and level. Redwoods grow to 16 feet in diameter here.

The ridge soon narrows. Your trail climbs again, reaching

an 800-foot peak on the ridge at 2 miles, the highest point in the first 5 miles. Descend briefly, then contour, winding along the ridgetop. You pass a grove with a rest bench carved from a fallen giant.

Climb by short switchbacks around 2¼ miles, then descend to a low notch in the ridge. At 2½ miles you meet Zig Zag Trail #1, which descends east to Prairie Creek Trail. You can turn right and return to your starting point for a 5⅞-mile loop.

West Ridge Trail heads northwest, quickly coming to the comfortable rest bench of Forever Grove. Look for iris and false Solomon's seal in spring. Descend slightly, then climb with intermittent level stretches, heading northwest. Pass a stand of western hemlock and Douglas fir, then make a short, easy descent to 3 miles. The sound of the surf drifts in from the west.

Contour along the top of the ridge to 3½ miles, with steep slopes to the left and right. Two switchbacks drop you to a low saddle by 3⅝ miles. Climb to 3⅞ miles then descend briefly to the junction with ZigZag Trail #2. Day hikers can turn east here, descending to Prairie Creek Trail in ½ mile and following it south to the trailhead for a 8⅞-mile loop.

After the junction, the West Ridge Trail turns sharply left and heads west, then northwest along the ridge. The trail is mostly level to 4¼ miles. The next section of trail has a series of short, steep ups and downs along the ridgetop. At 4¾ miles

WEST RIDGE TO BUTLER CREEK:

DISTANCE: 7⅜ miles one way, with options for loops of 5⅞, 8⅞, 12½ or 13¼, or round trips of 14¾ or 16¼ miles.
TIME: Full or half day for shorter loops, a long, arduous day of hiking for longer trips.
TERRAIN: Climbs along ridge in virgin redwood forest, then descends along ridge and canyon to Coastal Trail.
ELEVATION GAIN/LOSS: One way to Zig Zag #1: 700 feet+/100 feet-; to Zig Zag #2: 920 feet+/340 feet-; to Friendship Ridge: 1560 feet +/820 feet-: to Coastal Trail: 1560 feet +/1660 feet-.
BEST TIME: Spring.
WARNINGS: No camping in backcountry.
HOW TO GET THERE: Turn west off N.B. Drury Parkway (exit Highway 101 at M.137.45 from north, M.125.9 from south) at M.127.3, the main entrance to Prairie Creek Redwoods State Park. Trail starts from Visitor Center.
FURTHER INFO: Prairie Creek Redwoods State Park (707)488-2039, (707)465-7354.

you climb to a high point that has been marred by a fire.

In 1987 a hiker camped here illegally, then lit a fire inside the goose pen of the scorched redwood on the right. The fire roared to ignite the top of the tree and spread to the surrounding forest. This foolish act cost $100,000 and could have resulted in the tragic devastation of Prairie Creek's virgin forest. But fast-acting firefighters were able to extinguish the blaze without major damage. The charred giants stand as a dramatic reminder to be careful with fire.

Your trail contours north, passing gnarled old redwoods in a forest mixed with Douglas fir and western hemlock. After a short uphill stretch at 4⅞ miles, the trail hugs the ridgetop where it is dense with brush, mostly salal and huckleberry. Then comes an area of dense conifer regeneration with big rotting stumps. Duck under an immense fallen log. Descend through a tunnel of young growth to meet a broad old road that you follow north. Head north along a shady lane, passing a spur trail to Brown Grove on the left. Climb gradually, then steeply through regenerating forest where you may see thimble-, salmon-, elder- and huckleberry plus wild ginger.

At 5⅝ miles the trail forks. The old trail/road on the right no longer goes to Butler Creek. Go left for all points. The trail descends west along a wooded ridge. Climb briefly at 5¾ miles to meet the Friendship Ridge Trail on the left, one of several options for your return hike (see Trail #20). You can descend Friendship Ridge, then return to the trailhead by the Irvine Trail for a 13¼-mile loop. The left fork also meets the old Boat Creek Trail, which no longer goes through to the coast, and the Boat Ridge Trail, a shorter deadend spur through virgin forest.

For the longest hike, contour northwest on the West Ridge Trail, soon returning to virgin forest. Checker lily, false lily of the valley and red clintonia brighten the understory in spring. The ridgetop trail descends gradually around 6 miles. Pass a redwood bench before climbing to one last knob on the ridgetop.

Your trail turns north to descend steadily as the roar of the surf rises through the forest. Many spruce, hemlock and alder trees grow along this ocean-facing ridge. Around 6¼ miles your trail contours through a majestic grove of redwoods. You soon resume a gradual descent, then descend steeply by two switchbacks around 6½ miles.

The path soon leaves the ridge to drop along its west face, passing spruces to eight feet in diameter. Descend steeply again at 6¾ miles. You soon cross a bridge over a tributary of Butler Creek, lush with verdant growth. Descend this canyon to meet the old Butler Creek Trail, then cross Butler Creek on a bridge around 7 miles. Follow the canyon downstream through spruce forest. You descend steep steps and come to the mouth of the canyon, 7⅜ miles from the trailhead. From here fine day hikes can be taken north or south along the beach (see Trails #13, 14 and 20), or you can just lie around and soak up the silence.

There are four great options for your return hike to park headquarters. You can take the Coastal Trail south to Fern Canyon, then follow the James Irvine Trail southeast for a 7-mile return. You can return the way you came, hiking the length of the West Ridge Trail ($7^3/_8$ miles). You can follow West Ridge to Friendship Ridge Trail, then return along the Irvine Trail ($8^7/_8$ miles). Or you can follow the West Ridge Trail to the Zig Zag Trail #2 and complete your return via the latter and the beautiful Prairie Creek Trail, a $7^3/_8$-mile return.

## 17. ELK PRAIRIE LOOP

### STALKING THE MIGHTY ELK

*At least 600 Roosevelt elk (Cervus elaphus roosevelti) now live in and around Prairie Creek Redwoods State Park. The elk is the second largest member of the deer family, smaller than the moose. Males grow up to 1200 pounds, stand four to five feet at the shoulder, and grow antlers five feet long, with a four- to six-foot spread at the tips.*

*Elk once inhabited much of Northern California and the west. They were hunted nearly to extinction for their meat, hides and canine teeth (believed to bring good luck). Now protected from hunting in California, they range north to British Columbia and east to the Rockies.*

*Each March the bulls shed their antlers, growing up to 40 pounds of new antlers by August. As the mating season approaches in September, solitary bulls join the herd. Mature bulls compete for a harem of up to 40 cows. If you visit during mating season, you may hear the bugle-like call of the bull, followed by the clash of antlers as two bulls vie to knock each other to their haunches. Consider yourself lucky if you get to see such a mating joust. Next May or June, some of the cows bear single calves weighing 25 to 40 pounds at birth that will grow to three-quarters of their adult size by fall.*

*Though the elk are primarily peaceful, grazing animals, they should never be approached on foot. Bulls especially may give chase if they feel threatened or cornered, charging at up to 35 miles per hour. They may look tame, but they are wild animals.*

*Our original description of this hike started in Elk Prairie Campground. While campers can still start the Elk Prairie Loop from their campsite, our new description starts from the park's visitor center and circles clockwise around the prairie. Always watch for elk on the trail. If you find them, be sure to make a wide detour around them.*

## ELK PRAIRIE LOOP:

DISTANCE: 2¾-mile loop.
TIME: One or 2 hours.
TERRAIN: Circles the prairie, dipping in and out of forest, then slight ups and downs through forest east of the prairie before mostly contouring to complete the loop.
ELEVATION GAIN/LOSS: 210 feet+/210 feet-.
BEST TIME: Spring for wildflowers. Anytime for elk.
WARNINGS: Elk are wild animals. Never approach them on foot. Use caution crossing road. Trail may be muddy in winter.
HOW TO GET THERE: Turn west off N.B. Drury Parkway (exit Highway 101 at M.137.45 from north, M.125.9 from south) at M.127.3, main entrance to Prairie Creek Redwoods State Park. The hike starts from the Visitor Center.
FEES: Car camping: $33-35/night.
FURTHER INFO: Prairie Creek Redwoods State Park (707)488-2039, (707)465-7354.
OTHER SUGGESTION: REVELATION TRAIL starts south of the Visitor Center, circling through a redwood grove for 1/3 mile. Wood and rope guide rails, tape recorders and signs allow the blind or otherwise disabled visitor to explore the forest independently.

This description circles Boyes Prairie, home to one of the park's herds of elk, letting you view elk habitat first hand. Carry binoculars to observe the elk without getting too close.

From the visitor center, take the Foothill Trail, which starts just wast of the center's entrance. Follow the gravel trail as it parallels the park's entrance road. On your left a thicket of vegetation grows above Prairie Creek: alder, tanoak, bay laurel, cascara sagrada, wood rose, azalea, ferns and berries—huckle-, salmon-, thimble-, and black-. Cross a grassy area and come to a crosswalk at N.B. Drury Parkway. Cross with caution. There is also a walkable tunnel under the parkway at the nearby Boyes Creek bridge just north.

On the east side, follow the gravel path north. Your trail follows Boyes Creek upstream, then crosses it on a bridge and enters the forest. Around ¼ mile you climb a small hill to a trail junction where Foothill Trail goes left. Continue straight on the Cathedral Tree Trail (signed Elk Prairie Trail 0.2 mile). The cotoneaster bush by the sign is non-native, but was planted by early settlers.

Brush by a 12-foot-diameter redwood and come to a rest bench. It has great morning exposure once the sun has cleared the forest. Walk through a grassy clearing, then re-turn to forest. Meet the official start of the Elk Prairie Trail on your right just beyond 3/8 mile. It crosses a bridge over Boyes Creek and heads south through a wooded edge of Boyes Prairie where bigleaf maples, bay and cascara mix with redwoods, Douglas firs and Sitka spruce. Begin a gradual climb around ½ mile, passing abundant berry vines that tower overhead and California hazel. You pass the stumps of redwoods that were cut around 1900 to build the Boyes' houses and barn.

By 5/8 mile your trail has climbed forty feet above the prairie into virgin forest with some of the largest redwoods on this hike. Frequent windows in the forest look out over the prairie. Descend to cross a bridge at ¾ mile.

Your trail contours along the ecotone—the edge between forest and prairie. By 7/8 mile you have nearly unobstructed views of the prairie. Huge apple trees on the right stand near the old Boyes ranch house, a favored spot of some elk.

Follow the ecotone, a good place to spot critters foraging. Large bigleaf maples compete for sunlight here. California bay, wild ginger, huckleberries and sword ferns grow along the trail. Be on the lookout for signs of elk: trees with bark rubbed off by bulls scraping their antlers; droppings and hoof prints along the trail; elk wallows, the depressions dug in the ground by hooves and antlers; munched deer ferns and branches stripped of their bark.

Dip through a low, wet spot where skunk cabbage grows, then climb gently. By 1¼ miles you have climbed high above the prairie, offering a good overview, and perhaps a sighting of elk. Start a gradual descent, passing several gigantic redwoods, one with a 16-foot-diameter base. Soon the prairie is just below. If the bridges here look a bit worn, they get crossed by many half-ton elk.

By 1½ miles you are nearly down to the level of the prairie. The trees here are favorite scratching posts for elk. Spruce and hemlock trees mingle with the redwoods. Your trail descends to cross a boardwalk, then comes to the parkway. Cautiously cross the road and find the signed trail just south.

Follow it west across the south end of Boyes Prairie, enjoying the changing vistas of meadow and virgin forest. By 1¾ miles you come to a T junction. Turn right onto unsigned Davison Trail, following the western edge of this corner of the prairie.

In 350 feet our described hike veers left onto the signed Elk Prairie Trail. (You can also stay on Davison Trail, especially if the elk are nearby.) Elk Prairie Trail dips into forest to overlook Prairie Creek on your left. At 1⅞ miles a spur trail on your left offers easy access to the creek. There once was a bridge here connecting with the south end of the Nature Trail on the creek's west side. Now the bridge is long gone, and the tangle of vegetation across the creek shows no sign of a trail. Elk Prairie Trail parallels the creek through mixed forest.

The track ends at the campground road at 2 1/16 miles, opposite campsite 62. From here you have a choice to make. If you want to continue through forest near Prairie Creek, turn left on the road and follow it west, north and northeast. Near campsite 34, find the trail to the Campfire Center. You can follow that and the Revelation Trail back to the visitor center. Because this hike is about looking for elk, our described route turns right on the campground road to head north. After you pass the restrooms and campground registration station, you return to the edge of Boyes Prairie around 2¼ miles. Scan the grasslands for elk; they can appear at a moment's notice.

Cross to the east side of the campground road as you leave the campground. There you can walk a grassy path along the prairie's edge, watching for elk and other wildlife. (Davison Trail also leads here.) You pass two observation benches facing the prairie by 2⅜ miles. Iris blades here are munched short by grazing elk. Continue along the grassy track paralleling the park road. You pass a pleasant picnic area on the far side of the road, with a trail that connects to the Campfire Center. Pass another rest bench, then the entrance kiosk around 2½ miles. Pass eight more observation benches before you return to the parking lot near the visitor center at 2¾ miles.

# 18.
# JAMES IRVINE MINERS RIDGE LOOP
## ROUTE OF 1851 GOLD SEEKERS

*This fantastic loop has changed considerably since our previous description of it. The original James Irvine Trail had become so popular that silt from the foot traffic was flowing into Godwood Creek and collecting as sediment, making it harder for anadromous fish to swim upstream to spawn successfully. So the first half of the Irvine Trail was rerouted away from the creek, moved up onto the first part of Miner's Ridge, then along its north face. We all miss the original historic start of the Irvine Trail, which had its own magical intimacy with Godwood Creek and its canyon, but the fish are responding favorably. And happily the new route of Irvine Trail reveals many redwood giants that were once hidden from hikers. James Irvine Trail still reaches the headwaters of Godwood Creek; it just takes a while longer to get there.*

*Clintonia Trail has also been rerouted, revealing many immense trees that were once hidden away from the trail. The old Clintonia Trail climbed steeply up a ridge, while the new trail is well graded and much more enjoyable even though 5/8 mile longer.*

*The amazing history of the Irvine Trail has not changed. In spring 1850, five frustrated prospectors left the Klamath mines and headed for the coast. At the mouth of the Klamath River they turned south. Though always keeping their eyes open for gold they perhaps were more enticed by stories of new settlements at Trinidad and Humboldt Bays south on the coast, places where one could find such rare amenities as hot baths, beds, women and fresh food. But after trekking another ten rugged miles through virgin forests and steep terrain, their dreams of comfort were postponed. Near the mouth of Home Creek, Hermann Ehrenberg found fine gold dust mixed with coarse, dark sand on the beach. The prospectors hastily gathered samples, marked their claim, then continued south.*

*After another 25 miles of hard travel, they reached the boomtown of Trinidad. That same year they organized the Pacific Mining Company and began to develop their claim at what came to be called Gold Bluffs and Gold Bluff Beach.*

*The gold was abundant when first found, though in the form of the tiniest gold flakes imaginable. The principals of the Pacific Mining Company, optimistic after their initial excavations, predicted a return of 43 million dollars for each member of the company.*

*Word quickly spread among the settlers at Trinidad and Humboldt Bay. Only the arrival of harsh winter storms kept them from setting out immediately. But in the spring of 1851,*

| JAMES IRVINE/MINERS RIDGE LOOP: |
| --- |

DISTANCE: James Irvine Trail: $5\frac{3}{8}$ miles, one way. Miners Ridge Trail: $3\frac{5}{8}$ miles, one way. Clintonia Trail: $1\frac{5}{8}$ miles, one way. Combined loop as described, with or without Fern Canyon: $11\frac{3}{8}$ miles. Shorter loop without west end of Irvine Trail: $7\frac{3}{8}$ miles.
TIME: Minimum 4 hours. Best as full day with lunch.
TERRAIN: Climbs moderately through virgin forest to a summit, descends to headwaters of Godwood Creek, then along Home Creek to mouth of Fern Canyon. Return trail climbs through more virgin forest to and along Miners Ridge, then descends to starting point.
ELEVATION GAIN/LOSS: Full loop: 1350 feet+/1350 feet-. James Irvine Trail east to west: 580 feet+/700 feet-. Round trip: 1280 feet+/1280 feet-. Short loop: 900 feet+/900 feet-.
BEST TIME: Spring for wildflowers. June to September for footbridges in Fern Canyon. Still recommended: March through October.
WARNINGS: May be wet and muddy November to February after big storms.
HOW TO GET THERE: Turn west off N.B. Drury Parkway (exit Highway 101 at M. 137.45 from north, M. 125.9 from south) at the main entrance to Prairie Creek Redwoods at M.127.3. Trail starts near Visitor Center.
FEES: Car camping: $33-35/night.
FURTHER INFO: Prairie Creek Redwoods State Park (707)488-2039, (707)465-7354.
OTHER SUGGESTION: A DIFFERENT LOOP can be made by walking the Irvine Trail to its west end, then following the beach south one mile to the western Miners Ridge Trailhead and returning the full length of that trail. The first portion of the latter follows an old corduroy logging road. Distance: $11\frac{5}{8}$ miles.

*thousands headed north to the Gold Bluffs. They left the recently established trail to the Klamath mines at Madison Prairie and headed west on a narrow track, the original James Irvine Trail. Arriving at Gold Bluffs, they rapidly built a tent city in a clearing above the beach.*

*The boom was short-lived, however. Retrieving the gold required labor- and machine-intensive methods only a few were patient and resourceful enough to pursue. Although thousands of dollars in gold were eventually recovered, the boom tent city quickly dwindled to a small company mining camp. Still the Irvine Trail remained the main route to the gold fields, being used extensively during the Civil War when gold was at a premium, and again in the 1870s, as two other companies tried to succeed. In the end Gold Bluffs mining may have produced more debts than gold.*

*Today the explorers come for different reasons: to see the magnificent virgin forest, to revel in nature's quiet, and to explore the non-negotiable treasure of Fern Canyon.*

Your hike starts at the Visitor Center, where you can ask about current trail conditions. Follow the Nature Trail across the long bridge over Prairie Creek and head north for just over 1/8 mile, passing through a grove of some of the most impressive redwoods in the park. You soon meet the West Ridge Trail on your right. Go left, descending to cross a bridge over maple-lined Godwood Creek. You quickly come to a junction where the Nature Trail continues west. You want to turn right on the combined James Irvine/Miners Ridge Trail.

Follow the trail north on a winding gradual climb. Descend to cross a bridge over a side stream at 3/8 mile, then resume your ascent through climax virgin forest. You overlook Godwood Creek on your right, which the original Irvine Trail followed more closely. Deer ferns, yerba de selva and trilliums mix with abundant sword ferns beneath the giant forest. Cross two small bridges before 5/8 mile. Your trail ascends moderately, switchbacking away from Godwood Creek. Soon you are on the west side of a ridge that hides the creek.

At 7/8 mile Miners Ridge Trail forks left to climb along the ridgetop. Stay right on James Irvine Trail, which contours along the ridge's east face, then climbs gently as Godwood Creek comes back into view, now far below. Although larger redwoods grow down in the canyon, both redwoods and Douglas firs grow to ten feet in diameter on this steep slope.

Irvine Trail descends briefly, winding through three steep gullies. Around 1¼ miles, after a short climb your trail bends left to traverse the two biggest gullies yet. Pass a 12-foot-diameter redwood on your right. The pattern continues, passing more redwood giants as you wind through more big gullies, all of which flow into Godwood Creek. Cross three railless bridges around 1 5/8 miles, then a railed bridge. They mark the 520-foot summit of the Irvine Trail. The scarred giant below you has a diameter of 15 feet.

Descend moderately through the forest of giants. At 2 miles you traverse a boardwalk and continue your descent, passing under the flank of an oddly shaped redwood. After crossing two more bridges, notice on your right that the floor of Godwood Creek canyon is no longer far below. The creek may be as much as forty feet below you, but you are es-

sentially on the canyon floor, approaching the creek's headwaters. The trail bends left to cross a bridge over a gentle tributary of Godwood Creek. Resume climbing briefly, then descend past a memorial rest bench in a pleasant spot. This is where you rejoin the original Irvine Trail. Imagine the 1850s miners with their loaded pack animals traipsing west along this trail heading for Gold Bluffs Beach.

As the miners did long ago, continue west on the James Irvine Trail. Cross another small boardwalk over a seasonal stream. Around 2½ miles, where you cross two tiny boardwalks, you can hear Godwood Creek burbling on your right. The creek's flood plain is nearly level between the steep canyon walls. Godwood Creek actually starts in the steep side canyon that is on your right, so the trail leaves it here. Notice how much more lush it is here on the flood plain than it was up on the steep slope. Understory vegetation is nearly everywhere, with fungi and abundant ferns cloaking the ground and giant spruce standing beside immense redwoods. You can feel the moisture in the air.

Your trail continues its ascent to almost 2¾ miles, but well before that the canyon bottom begins sloping gently west toward the Pacific. You can hear the roaring surf quite clearly now. Duck under a large fallen fir, then descend past a gargantuan redwood 16 feet in diameter on your right.

Contour through the forest of immense virgin trees. Beyond 3⅛ miles your trail passes through a cut, fallen giant eight feet in diameter. Climb briefly, wrapping around another immense redwood, this one draped with huckleberry bushes growing 40 feet up its leaning trunk. This scarred behemoth has a base more than 20 feet in diameter. Descend steps to cross a small boardwalk over a side stream at 3¼ miles, then climb to the junction with the Clintonia Trail. The junction marks a secondary summit of the Irvine Trail.

You are still 300 feet above sea level.

Now you have a decision to make. James Irvine Trail descends along the canyon of Home Creek, meeting Friendship Ridge Trail in 1 3/8 miles, the mouth of Fern Canyon in 2 miles. If you don't have time or energy to hike down to the mouth of Fern Canyon and return, consider a shorter 7½-mile loop, which climbs from here on the Clintonia Trail, then returns to your starting point via Miners Ridge Trail, described in the return portion of this hike.

The Irvine Trail descends gradually, then more rapidly. Beyond 3 5/8 miles you cross a bridge over the headwaters of Home Creek. The trail then levels before a series of short ups and downs brings you to a bridge over a side canyon at 3 7/8 miles.

The vegetation becomes more dense as you approach the coast. Deer ferns, red and evergreen huckleberries and delicate redwood violets thrive here. Follow the sound of a waterfall down to another bridge, this one over a 50-foot-deep canyon lush with ferns. After the bridge a short spur trail forks right to a grove.

From 4 miles you meander up and down the slope above Home Creek, crossing more corduroy bridges. At 4 3/8 miles a very large spruce sits on the left, on the edge of upper Fern Canyon. The trail contours before descending to cross a beautiful canyon at 4½ miles. Baldwin Bridge has two seats overlooking the gorge.

You soon pass the junction with the Friendship Ridge Trail (see Trail #20). After crossing a small bridge at 4 5/8 miles you again approach Fern Canyon. But you must hike another ½ mile before meeting the trail into the canyon. On this fairly level stretch, notice a spruce on your left growing atop a fallen redwood.

About 5¾ miles from the trailhead, you meet the upper end of the Fern Canyon Trail. You may descend into the canyon here, or walk the Irvine Trail to the beach and return by way of Fern Canyon. Our description follows the Irvine Trail to its end. The trail descends steps through alder forest. On your left is the Alexander Lincoln Prairie, the site of the Gold Bluffs tent city of the 1850s, now with no hint of its strange history. Descend more steps, follow a 100-foot boardwalk, then drop to the beach just north of the mouth of Fern Canyon.

For a total loop of 11 miles, you can walk south 1 3/8 miles on trail and beach or road, then return the full length of the Miners Ridge Trail.

Our described loop follows Trail #19 through marvelous Fern Canyon to its junction with the Irvine Trail. Then retrace your steps east to the junction with the Clintonia Trail (2 miles from the beach). If you want the shortest route back, continue to retrace your steps on the Irvine Trail.

If you are still game for new country, follow the Clintonia/Miners Ridge Loop described below. It requires only an extra mile and an extra 200 feet in elevation gain and loss. Like James Irvine Trail, Clintonia Trail has been rerouted since our previous edition. In fact, the Clintonia Trail is much improved over its steep old route which climbed straight up a ridge.

The new Clintonia Trail climbs north briefly, then northwest, but on a much gentler grade than before. You soon encounter more redwood giants. Here they are interspersed with many giant redwood snags (dead standing trees), remnants of an even more ancient forest, as well as with living large Douglas firs, hemlocks and spruces. Dense huckleberries, thimbleberries, salal, cascara sagrada, and sword and deer ferns jam the understory.

Make a sharp bend left to climb south. At ¼ mile the tread turns briefly to sandstone. Around 3/8 mile your trail makes a long winding contour through giant forest. Resume a gradual ascent by ½ mile, soon passing a faint spur trail that heads west for about ¼ mile to explore more giants. While the trees tend to be smaller on this west facing slope, they are still abundant and impressive.

Climb briefly east, then turn south to contour along the ridgetop around 5/8 mile. Resume a gentle meandering climb on or near the ridgetop. Beyond ¾ mile trail and ridge descend gently, but you resume climbing by 7/8 mile. You pass through an area well stocked with young redwoods, many less than a foot in diameter. Still, the ridgetop also has widely spaced redwood giants.

Contour along the ridgetop where trilliums, redwood violets, redwood sorrel, iris, starflower, twisted stalk, and trail plant are abundant, along with some cascara and false lily of the valley. In spring, watch for the bright red flowers of clintonia on long stalks. In summer they bear dark-blue, inedible berries. Contour south along the ridgetop around 1¼ miles. Soon a rest bench sits on the left side of the trail. Clintonia Trail continues its contour south, but by 1 3/8 miles the ridgetop rises above you on the left.

Descend briefly before 1½ miles to meet a side trail on your right. It descends gently west for about 1/8 mile along a side ridge where giants 12 to 16 feet in diameter grow. The spur ends near a massive stump with springboard cuts, possibly cut by early settlers since it's the only stump around.

From the spur, Clintonia Trail makes a short climb that leads to another descent, ending at Miners Ridge Trail before 1 5/8 miles. Turn left to climb east on Miners Ridge. A sign claims "PARK HEADQUARTERS 2.2 MILES" but it is actually 2 5/8 miles.

Climb moderately, then fitfully to a ridgetop knob. Descend then climb past huge fire-scarred redwoods and abundant Douglas firs to the first of two 600-foot elevation high points on Miners Ridge at 2 miles. Descend, then contour along the ridge, with grand views of virgin forest in every direction. Your trail undulates along the ridgetop past abundant trilliums, redwood violets, redwood sorrel, twisted stalk and star Solomon's seal amidst ferns and huckleberry bushes beneath the immense forest.

From 2¼ miles your trail contours along the ridgetop. One 12-foot-diameter redwood on your left has a trunk encrusted with burls. Climb to the high point on the ridgetop around 2½ miles where you might see irises and redwood lilies. Your trail bends left to head east. Notice the lack of big trees to the south. Here it is less than 300 feet to the park boundary. Though now national parkland beyond, it was clearcut in the 1960s.

Beyond 2⅝ miles you start to descend, gradually, then steeply, but still with a few uphill stretches. Your trail still follows the descending ridgetop, very narrow here with steep sides. Descend past Oregon grape and red clintonia beneath virgin forest. Descend steeply to a rest bench beyond 2¾ miles. From here you can see the Irvine Trail not far below.

Descend steeply then climb slightly to a last level stretch of ridgetop around 2⅞ miles. Descend steeply through the grand forest only to climb once again around 3 miles. Then make a winding, steady descent to return to the junction with the Irvine Trail at the 3¼ miles. Retrace your steps down the Irvine Trail, returning to the trailhead at 4¼ miles.

## 19. FERN CANYON LOOP

FIFTY-FOOT WALLS OF FERNS

*Known as the jewel of Prairie Creek Redwoods State Park, Fern Canyon nestles in the heart of Gold Bluffs Beach. Though its name is common along the fog-enshrouded North Coast, this one stands alone for its geology, history and singular beauty.*

*About four million years ago, the Klamath River emptied into the sea here. The river deposited gravels from the Klamath Mountains 40 miles to the east. Rough ocean waves washed and eroded these gravels for thousands of years until they were laid out in flat uniform deposits. In more recent geologic times, Home Creek carved its way through these layers of gravel to create the canyon you see today. Its nearly level floor differs from the steep slopes of most North Coast streams.*

*The ancestral Klamath River also deposited the fine particles of gold that brought prospectors to the area from 1850 to the 1920s. The gold was so fine that much of it could not be separated from the tons of dark sand and gravel mixed with it. Mining activities peaked in the 1880s, when 300 people lived near Fern Canyon to work the gold deposits. Most of them lived on the Lincoln Prairie, a grassy clearing north of Fern Canyon.*

*Today the signs of past mining and logging have vanished.*

*Coastal fog and an annual rainfall of 80 inches help to create the verdant, fern-filled habitat of Fern Canyon. The most common fern here is the five-linger fern, a relative of the maidenhair. The Yuroks gathered these ferns for the black stems with which they wove designs into their beautiful baskets. Other ferns grow in the canyon in less abundance: sword, lady, deer, woodwardia, California wood, and leather: Less common but found occasionally are bladder, bracken and licorice ferns, nine species in all. Other moisture-loving plants grow here: saxifrage, common and tooth-leaved monkeyflower, coast manroot, fairy lantern and twisted stalk. One of the most lethal plants in North America grows here, California water hemlock. As little as one centimeter of the plant can be fatal. The oenanthe is another poisonous plant commonly found in the canyon. Edible plants include salmonberry and thimbleberry.*

*Many water-loving animals call Fern Canyon home. The coastal giant salamander lives in the still pools of Home Creek, feeding on banana slugs, snails, insects and mice. It is one of the largest North American salamanders, up to 14 inches*

| FERN CANYON LOOP: |
| --- |
| DISTANCE: 1 1/8-mile loop.<br>TIME: Thirty minutes, but it is worth taking more time or planning a picnic.<br>TERRAIN: Follows nearly level canyon floor upstream beneath fifty-foot-high, fern-covered walls, then climbing out of the canyon into virgin forest and descending back to its mouth.<br>ELEVATION GAIN/LOSS: 180 feet+/180 feet-.<br>BEST TIME: Bridges to keep feet dry June to September. Otherwise, any time the creek is not flooding.<br>WARNINGS: Wet stream crossings in winter and spring.<br>HOW TO GET GET THERE: Turn west off Highway 101 at M.123.9 onto unpaved, steep and winding Davison Road (no trailers). Go 6.9 miles to the Fern Canyon parking area at road's end.<br>FEES: Day use/parking: $8/vehicle ($4 for seniors). Car camping: $33-35/night. Hike/bike camp: $5/person/night.<br>FURTHER INFO: Prairie Creek Redwoods State Park (707) 488-2039,(707) 465-7354. |

*long. Other amphibians include the rare tailed frog, the Olympic salamander and the more abundant western red-legged frog. The American dipper or water ouzel is a bird that hunts insects in the stream. It actually flies underwater to catch its prey. Winter wrens are the only other birds living in the canyon, though others may visit, like the majestic great blue heron. Mink, river otter, coastal cutthroat and steelhead trout round out the community.*

*The loop trail through Fern Canyon is less than ¾ mile long. It has temporary bridges from June through September. If you visit during other times of the year, you may get your feet wet but you will not have to contend with the crowds of summer. Fern Canyon provides a rewarding short walk during any season.*

Your trail begins at the Fern Canyon picnic area at the end of Gold Bluffs Beach Road. Follow the trail north along the base of the bluff. Before ¼ mile, it descends to Home Creek. Take the trail that forks right, quickly entering the mouth of the steep-walled canyon. You cross Home Creek at least twice more before 3/8 mile; the position of the creek changes from one season to the next. Take your time and observe the lush riparian community of plants thriving here.

Beyond ½ mile the steep canyon walls get higher. The north wall rises vertically for over 60 feet at one point. Five-finger ferns grow nearly everywhere on the sheer walls. The trail passes under a large fallen log, also covered with ferns, mosses and lichens. Saxifrage grows along the canyon floor. The canyon winds as you cross the stream several more times.

The canyon broadens by 5/8 mile. A side trail branches right, climbing a narrow side canyon to its boxed end where a small waterfall tumbles down in winter and spring.

The main trail continues up Fern Canyon for 250 feet beyond the side trail. There a sign proclaims the end of Fern Canyon. The loop trail climbs the canyon's north wall. You ascend by uneven steps, switchbacking out of the canyon and into Sitka spruce forest. Meet the James Irvine Trail before 7/8 mile. Go left to return to the trailhead. You cross a small bridge and head northwest above the edge of the Alexander Lincoln Prairie, the site of the mining town of Gold Bluffs.

Cross a long boardwalk, then descend many steps through alder forest to return to the mouth of Fern Canyon. Energetic hikers will find many other trails in the area. See Trails #18 and 20. When your explorations are done, walk south on the Coastal Trail to return to the trailhead.

# 20. FRIENDSHIP RIDGE COASTAL LOOP

## THROUGH VIRGIN FOREST TO WILDERNESS BEACH

*This route provides a marvelously varied day hike. In less than 8 miles you encounter steep-walled canyons, virgin forests, high ridges, and an expansive wilderness beach where a herd of wild elk roam at the base of waterfall-draped cliffs.*

The Coastal Trail (formerly called Beach Trail) heads north from the trailhead at road's end. Before ¼ mile, you ford Home Creek at the mouth of Fern Canyon, then come to a trail that forks right. Turn right for Friendship Ridge Trail (also for Fern Canyon and James Irvine Trails). After you head east for 150 feet, fork left on the Irvine Trail, leaving the mouth of Fern Canyon to climb by rough steps. You ascend into Sitka spruce forest to ½ mile, then contour past the Lincoln Prairie on your right, meeting the top end of the Fern Canyon Trail around 5/8 mile. Continue on James Irvine Trail, climbing to cross a bridge over a small stream at ¾ mile. In 150 feet you turn left on the Friendship Ridge Trail.

Friendship Ridge Trail climbs north, then west through a lush understory with many deer ferns beneath spruce forest. Redwoods dominate the forest by 7/8 mile as you ascend northwest. A switchbacking climb brings you to Friendship Ridge around one mile. Ascend along the ridgetop through virgin forest with plentiful salal, huckleberry, evergreen violet, sword fern and trillium in the understory.

Your trail ascends sporadically along the ridgetop, with views into pristine forest in every direction. Redwoods and firs grow to six feet in diameter, with Oregon grape joining the understory. Descend briefly around 1¾ miles, then contour just west of the ridgetop as western hemlock joins the forest.

The path makes a gradual winding descent to 2 miles, where you cross a small seasonal creek. Contour north, winding through several more side canyons, tributaries of Boat Creek to your west. Pass redwoods to ten feet in diameter. Beyond 2¼ miles your mostly level path makes several brief ascents. Cross a large side canyon jammed with fallen logs at 2⅝ miles.

Resume a winding, gradual climb to cross a seasonal creek around 2¾ miles. Your trail almost regains the ridgetop by 3 miles, but continues its winding ascent along the ridge's west face, passing redwoods of diverse sizes.

Ascend to a junction at 3¼ miles. The deadend trail on the left descends west, then southwest into rugged Boat Creek Canyon for 1¾ miles. Lady fern and red huckleberry grow at the junction. Friendship Ridge Trail climbs moderately northwest to another spur on the left. The Boat Ridge Trail explores virgin groves along a descending ridge, about ⅝ mile round trip. Friendship Ridge Trail climbs past Wheeler Grove, ascending by several short switchbacks to meet West Ridge Trail on the ridgetop at 3⅝ miles.

Turn left on West Ridge Trail and follow the undulating ridgetop northwest, then north (see Trail #16 for more about West Ridge Trail). From 4¾ miles the trail descends steeply,

FRIENDSHIP RIDGE/COASTAL LOOP:

DISTANCE: 7¾-mile loop.
TIME: Four hours or more.
TERRAIN: Climbs up and along one ridge, then down another, descends canyon to beach, contours along the beach below coastal bluffs.
ELEVATION GAIN/LOSS: 960 feet+/960 feet-.
BEST TIME: Spring for wildflowers. Fall also nice.
WARNINGS: Do not approach the elk. Give them plenty of room.
HOW TO GET THERE: Turn west off Highway 101 at M.123.9 onto unpaved, steep and winding Davison Road (no trailers). Go 6.9 miles to Fern Canyon parking area at end of road.
FEES: Day use/parking: $8/vehicle ($4 for seniors). Car camping: $33-35/night.
FURTHER INFO: Prairie Creek Redwoods State Park (707) 488-2039, (707) 465-7354.

leaving the ridgetop to drop along its lush west face. You cross a bridge over Butler Creek around 4 7/8 miles, then descend along the creek to the mouth of the canyon at 5¼ miles. Water from the creek must be purified before drinking. The Coastal Trail continues north about 3/8 mile to the Ossagon Creek Trail, 2 1/8 miles to Carruthers Cove (see Trails #13 and 14).

Our described loop turns left to head south on the Coastal Trail, paralleling the cliffs known as Gold Bluffs on your left and the shore on your right. Watch for the elk that live here; you may have to detour to stay out of their way. In summer and fall you can follow the level, easy track that leaves the alder forest and heads south through grasslands near the base of the bluffs. During a wet winter or spring, this section of trail may be flooded, impassable in anything but shin-high rubber boots (The author got swamped here in late April 1993.) When the trail is flooded, detour west about ¼ mile to walk the dunes or beach south for 7/8 mile, then turn east to return to the trail.

Presuming the trail is not flooded, your path follows the base of the bluffs south, passing a large spruce snag around 5½ miles, then climbing over a small rise. Pass a gravelly slide and veer right around some alders around 5¾ miles, where you have a view north to Ossagon Rocks. Your trail skirts the edge of spruce forest along the base of the wooded bluffs. The roar of the surf echoes loudly from the cliff face above you.

Before 6 1/8 miles a spur trail forks left into spruce/alder forest to the base of an 80-foot waterfall. In 300 feet another short spur on the left leads to a rest bench below Gold Dust Falls, where a small stream plunges 100 feet to disappear in the sandy soil beneath the spruce forest. A third waterfall in alder forest beyond 6¼ miles flows in the wet season.

Your trail skirts alder/spruce forest at the base of the steep bluffs. Lupine thrives in the grasslands. At 6 5/8 miles you round a point to look south to the alder thicket marking the mouth of Boat Creek. Follow dry, gravelly tread past a stand of dead trees. Around 6 7/8 miles sandstone rocks on both sides of the trail are crowned with beach strawberry. Wind through the alders to ford Boat Creek where it emerges from its heavily wooded canyon at 7 1/8 miles. Continue south through grasslands, then into alder forest. You meet the Irvine Trail at 7½ miles to complete the loop. Ford Home Creek and continue south to the trailhead before 7¾ miles.

# 21. TRILLIUM FALLS LOOP

## PAST A WATERFALL TO VIRGIN GIANTS

*Elk Meadow Trailhead sits in a large grassy clearing surrounded by forest. The National Park Service restored this area more than ten years ago, tearing down a defunct sawmill and restoring its surroundings to a more natural state, a great example of natural restoration of an industrial area. The plan was to create an area off the busy highway where people could stop to observe the magnificent Roosevelt elk that inhabit the park. Unfortunately the elk usually congregate elsewhere, often near the highway where they often slow or stop traffic, creating a traffic hazard and endangering the elk. But it has proved fruitless to argue with these half ton grazers. They may sometimes be seen across Davison Road just east of Elk Meadow, closer to the the highway where the elk seem to consider the grass tastier, if not greener. Trillium Falls Loop explores a remnant swath of virgin forest, with prime trees that wondrously survived despite being within hearing distance of the once screaming saw blades.*

Follow the paved trail near the restroom that heads west, then southwest through grasslands. In 250 feet at a double junction, veer left then right on the paved Davison Trail. In another 200 feet veer right on the signed, narrow dirt Trillium Falls Trail. You soon leave the grassland to ascend through virgin forest, quickly passing 12-foot-diameter virgin redwoods.

By ¼ mile you can hear the creek burbling below. Switchback right and climb by three more switchbacks. Climb past a large Sitka spruce on your left and a fallen redwood's roots on your right. Pass the first of many memorial groves around 3/8 mile. Your trail descends, passing beneath a fallen redwood. Redwood sorrel and ferns grow nearly everywhere.

Cross a small wooden bridge and descend by two switchbacks to Trillium Falls at ½ mile, where a long metal bridge overlooks the small falls. Large bigleaf maples tower above the creek surrounded by virgin forest of redwoods and spruce, with many giant snags confirming the ancient origins of this forest.

Climb briefly past monkeyflowers to a small ridge with a

| TRILLIUM FALLS LOOP: |
| --- |
| DISTANCE: 2¾ mile loop.<br>TIME: One or 2 hours.<br>TERRAIN: Descends through grasslands, then ascends and descends through virgin forest to a dirt road along the edge of forest, creek and meadow. After the road turns paved you return to grasslands.<br>ELEVATION GAIN/LOSS: 450 feet-/450 feet -.<br>BEST TIME: Spring, early summer for wildflowers. Late summer, early autumn for berries. Nice anytime.<br>WARNINGS: Keep your eyes and ears open for elk.<br>HOW TO GET THERE: Turn west off Highway 101 north of Orick at M.123.9 onto Davison Road. Go 0.6 miles, then left for trailhead parking. Trail starts near restrooms.<br>FURTHER INFO: Redwood National Park (707)465-7335. |

few giant redwoods, then contour through forest of smaller trees, crossing another small wooden bridge around 5/8 mile. Your trail undulates, with views down to grassy meadows beyond this small enclave of forest.

From ¾ mile you ascend moderately through forest, switchbacking right. Climb by three short switchbacks, then ascend to a bench in a memorial grove around 7/8 mile. A short climb soon leads to fire-scarred old redwood giants.

Your trail contours through more giant forest, then climbs to its high point beyond one mile. Descend through a jungle of huckleberry, salal and fern. Skunk cabbage grows beside the two small wooden bridges around 1 1/8 miles. Descend gradually then steeply to cross an old dirt logging road at 1¼ miles.

Beyond the road, your trail passes the largest and most impressive redwoods on the loop. Contour past two memorial groves. You pass a bench in a peaceful spot around 1 3/8 miles. Contour through grand forest, passing two more rest benches beyond 1½ miles as you start to descend. Tunnel beneath a grand huckleberry bush and come to another bench near a fine goose pen redwood.

Descend to a big bend left, the westernmost and southernmost limit of this loop. Your trail descends east, then switchbacks right as rhododendrons join the understory. A rest bench offers a break in gorgeous grove of giants.

At 1 7/8 miles your trail dips into a steep, small canyon and crosses a railed bridge. Descend by two switchbacks past abundant starflowers to cross a similar bridge around 2 miles. The highway noise is more noticeable on this lower part of the loop.

Soon the forest parts for views of the alder-lined flood plain on your right, with more tall forest rising beyond. Your trail climbs briefly up a rocky slope in the forest. Pass under a fallen giant, then rise past maple and hazel. Descend from 2¼ miles to trail's end. Turn right and follow the dirt road, descending back to Davison Trail. On the right Davison Trail crosses a long wooden bridge to cross Highway 101 and meet the bottom of the Berry Glen Trail (see Trail #25).

You want to turn left on Davison Trail. Follow it on a gradual climb, with forest on your left and alder-lined Prairie Creek on your right, with grasslands beyond where elk sometimes graze. Follow Davison Trail past elk clover, elderberry, piggyback plant and young redwoods for ¼ mile to meet the north end of Trillium Falls Trail just beyond where Davison Trail turns paved. Complete the loop by continu-

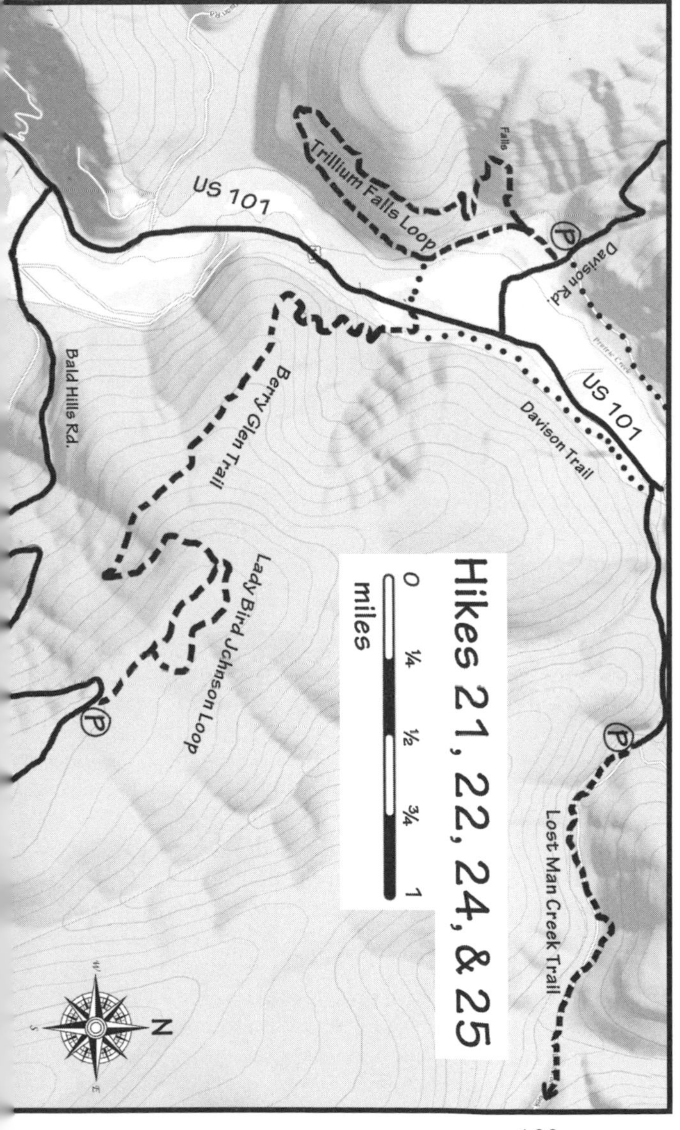

ing on Davison Trail to cross a small creek, then go left on the paved path to return to the trailhead.

# 22. LOST MAN CREEK

## OLD ROAD THROUGH VIRGIN FOREST TO VIEWS

*One of the least used trails in Redwood National Park, Lost Man Creek Trail lies one mile east of Highway 101 on a gravel road. It provides easy access to a beautiful redwood grove beside the pristine pools and rapids of the creek. Photographers love its combination of forest clearings and creek. People in wheelchairs can reach the picnic area, restrooms and first portion of trail.*

*In 1982 a special dedication ceremony took place here. Redwood National Park was designated a World Heritage Site by UNESCO, the United Nations Educational, Scientific and Cultural Organization. About 960 international sites have been chosen as World Heritage Sites because of natural and cultural properties of outstanding universal value to the human race.*

*The short, easy trail becomes arduous if you continue beyond the third bridge. The trail steepens and soon enters lands that were logged.*

*Lost Man Creek Trail offers mountain bikers a rugged but thrilling 20½-mile loop: 11 miles of motor-vehicle-free riding on Lost Man Creek/Holter Ridge Trail followed by a 6-mile descent on paved Bald Hills Road, then returning on Highway 101 (for 1.3 miles, the most hazardous part) and Lost Man Creek's gravel access road. The safer choice is the 22-mile out and back ride free of motor vehicles.*

The parking area is a clearing beside Lost Man Creek. Pass through a stile (broad enough for wheelchairs) and immediately come to several picnic tables beneath immense redwoods in a pleasantly shady spot above the creek. Head southeast on the graveled Lost Man Creek Trail, climbing gradually through the forest. At ¼ mile you cross a bridge over Lost Man Creek. From the bridge you have fine views of the rocky pools upstream.

Your climb steepens after the bridge. The trail recrosses the creek in 200 feet and continues climbing moderately, the creek again on your right. After a level stretch around ½ mile, the path climbs gently, offering views of the creek tumbling around boulders below. Young hemlock and Sitka spruce struggle for light beneath towering redwoods. The understory includes sword, lady, five-finger and deer ferns, iris, salal, redwood sorrel, wild ginger and inside-out flower. In spring trilliums grow beneath salmon-, thimble- and huckleberry.

At ¾ mile your trail levels again, drawing alongside the creek. Then climb gradually again as the path angles away from the stream. Pass a logged area on the left at one mile. You cross a creek (your third bridge) that enters Lost Man Creek from the north.

Then the old road begins to climb a long, steep hill, with views of the cascading creek on your right. You re-enter virgin forest as you begin to climb high above the creek. Those preferring an easy hike should turn back before climbing far up the hill. By 1½ miles you are 100 feet above Lost Man Creek. Below to the south the creek splits. The main fork flows down from far to the south. Geneva Road climbs steeply up a side drainage coming from the east.

The road steepens at 1½ miles. Beyond 1¾ miles the forest starts to thin as the habitat becomes drier. Your path turns briefly north before 2 miles, where the road almost levels, providing relief from the steady climb. The climb steepens again as you turn east, then northeast. Beyond 2¼ miles the forest has been logged. You have occasional views down to the virgin forest of Lost Man Creek.

By 2½ miles you have climbed 1000 feet from the trailhead.

| LOST MAN CREEK: |
| --- |
| DISTANCE: 2 miles, round trip; 11 miles, one way to Bald Hills Road, up to 22 miles round trip; or 20½-mile mountain bike loop.<br>TIME: One hour or all day.<br>TERRAIN: Climbs gradually through picturesque virgin forest alongside creek, then steeply through logged area up and along a high ridge; bikers can descend on paved road to complete loop.<br>ELEVATION GAIN/LOSS: First mile: 160 feet+/-, round trip. To Holter Ridge: 1600 feet+/1600 feet-, round trip. To Bald Hills Road: 3740 feet+/1100 feet-. Bike Loop: 4040 feet+/4040 feet-.<br>BEST TIME: Spring for wildflowers, but nice anytime.<br>WARNINGS: Very steep after the first 1½ miles. Bikers use caution returning on roads with traffic.<br>HOW TO GET THERE: Turn east off Highway 101 at M.124.4 and follow gravel road .9 miles to picnic area at its end.<br>FURTHER INFO: Redwood National Park (707)465-7335. |

  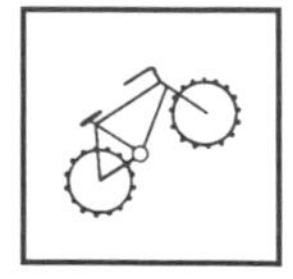 

The road continues to climb without relief until you level at 3¾ miles and come to a fork in the road. You are on the eastern park boundary at 1500-foot elevation. To continue, turn right onto Holter Ridge, where Lost Man Creek Trail continues. It generally follows the ridge and the park boundary south to meet Bald Hills Road in about 6 more miles, climbing to an elevation of 2300 feet. You meet Bald Hills Road in its sixth mile, about a mile north of Tall Trees Access Road.

While hikers do best to return on the designated trail they ascended, mountain bikers can complete the 20½-mile loop on paved Bald Hills Road, Highway 101 and the gravel Lost Man Creek access road. Watch for traffic!

## 23. SKUNK CABBAGE CREEK SECTION COASTAL TRAIL

### SPECTACULAR APPROACH TO COAST

*This trail was built in 1987 as a segment of the Coastal Trail. We describe the trail from south to north, the most dramatic approach to the wilderness beach. You may also hike it from the north end starting at the Gold Bluffs Beach entrance kiosk. The Coastal Trail is still not marked where it leaves Davison Road. From there you must climb over driftwood to head south on the beach to reach the west end of the Skunk Cabbage Creek Trail.*

Your trail starts at the parking area near Johnson Creek, about ½ mile west of the old southern trailhead. The trail heads west beneath young alders, descending briefly to cross Johnson Creek. Climb past several ancient redwoods, remnants of the the virgin forest that once covered most of these canyons. The understory has plentiful salmonberry, lady, deer and sword ferns, Siberian miner's lettuce, giant skunk cabbage and tiny club moss. Contour north past huckleberry and evergreen violet.

By ¼ mile you climb gradually northwest, leaving the redwoods for a dense second-growth forest of young alder and Sitka spruce with scattered Port Orford cedar, western redcedar and hemlock. Descend to a bridge over a tiny side stream where red elderberry thrives. Your path then descends through lush growth, crossing a boardwalk over another stream.

At ½ mile you pass through spruce forest with a luxuriant understory of skunk cabbage, fairy bells, twisted stalk and false lily of the valley. Mushrooms and other fungi thrive in this damp environment. Contour along an old road, crossing several boardwalks over tiny creeks and seeps. You soon pass spruce two feet in diameter growing in the road bed.

The broad bed of Skunk Cabbage Creek on your right supports an abundance of its namesake plant beneath spruce forest. The boggy soil there is too wet for redwoods.

Your easy path crosses a feeder creek at ¾ mile, then two more around ⅞ mile, where a few large redwoods mix with the spruce forest. Continue contouring to 1⅛ miles, beyond which only a few redwoods grow. Your trail climbs gradually, winding to cross a small creek.

Around 1¼ miles the path turns northeast to cross a bridge over Skunk Cabbage Creek. The creek splits into two forks just above the crossing. Ascend past healthy young spruce and redwoods with bleeding heart in the understory. As your trail turns northwest you can hear the surf roaring to the west.

At 1½ miles you climb past young redwoods with their bark scraped off by elk. An immense snag is nearby. Standing dead trees provide habitat for birds and other animals of the forest. Ascend along the North Fork of Skunk Cabbage Creek, soon crossing it twice by bridges. Red huckleberry mingles with its evergreen kin. Salal, yerba de selva and bedstraw join the understory.

Beyond 1¾ miles you descend briefly to level ground beside the creek. Spruce and alder dominate the forest, punctuated by the rotting remnants of immense redwood stumps. Your trail contours, then climbs along the creek.

You soon cross one more bridge over the headwaters of

| SKUNK CABBAGE CREEK: |
|---|
| DISTANCE: 8-mile round trip to beach. One way to Davison Road: 5⅜ miles.<br>TIME: Three to 5 hours.<br>TERRAIN: Climbs gently along wooded canyon, then up to and along coastal ridge before descending to beach.<br>ELEVATION GAIN/LOSS: One way to beach: 600 feet+/640 feet-, round trip: 1240 feet+/1240 feet-.<br>BEST TIME: Spring or summer, but nice anytime.<br>WARNINGS: Watch for rogue waves at the beach.<br>HOW TO GET THERE: SOUTH END: Turn west off Highway 101 at M.122.7 onto side road. Where road bends left at 0.1 mile, take the gravel road on the right for 0.65 mile to trailhead parking.<br>NORTH END: Turn west off Highway 101 at M.123.9 onto unpaved, steep Davison Road (no trailers). Go 5 miles and park opposite entrance kiosk.<br>FEES: Day use/parking at Gold Bluffs Beach: $8/vehicle ($4 for seniors). No fee at eastern trailhead.<br>FURTHER INFO: Redwood National Park (707)465-7335. |

Skunk Cabbage Creek. Look for saxifrage and watercress at the crossing. The trail ascends along the west bank of the south-flowing creek. Switchback twice at 2 miles to climb above the creek, then ascend a switchback with steps, heading away from the creek.

After one more switchback, your trail contours around 2¼ miles. Then climb to a gap at the very head of the creek before 2½ miles. The trail splits here. The left fork leads 50 feet west to a grand view through alder forest to the wild beach below (best when the alders have dropped their leaves).

Our described route takes the right fork, climbing east, then southeast on the trail as cow parsnip, foxglove and manroot thrive beneath alders. You soon begin a steep, switchbacking ascent through redwood forest on the east side of the ridge.

Beyond 2⅝ miles you pick up an old road grade to climb northwest and north to coastal views. Your trail veers left around 2¾ miles to make a winding descent north along the ridgetop. Pass an immense, blackened redwood stump around 3 miles, then continue a gradual descent along the ridgetop, with glimpses of the Pacific to the west.

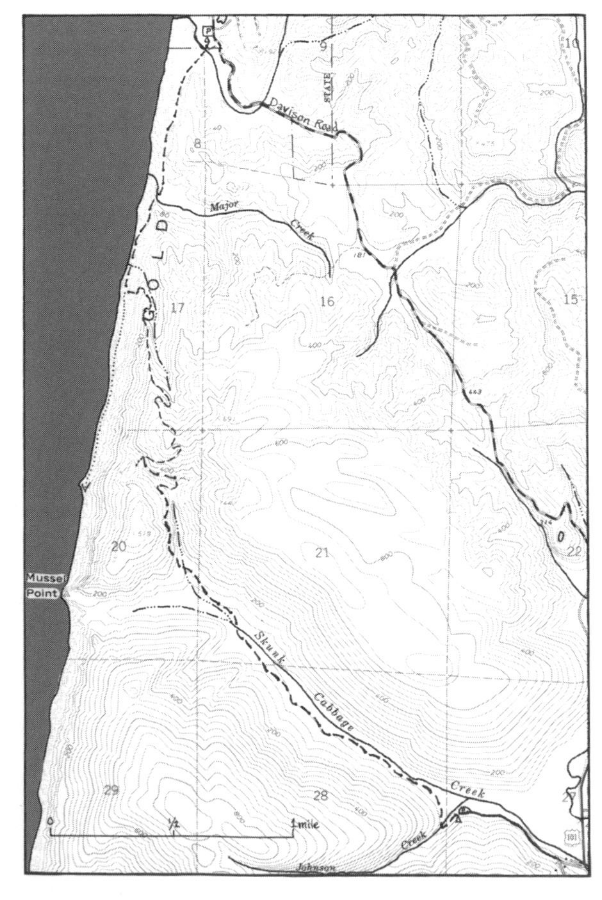

At 3¼ miles you cross a small boardwalk over a wet gully, then continue on a winding descent. Views of the breakers alternate with glimpses east into a fern-choked canyon. By 3¾ miles the trail steepens for a switchbacking descent to the mouth of an unnamed creek. At 3⅞ miles California polypody grows on an alder leaning over the trail. Descend along a magical stretch of creek, where osprey nests decorate twisted Sitka spruce trees.

Pass lupines in a dense thicket of coastal scrub and break through to a view of the beach. On a clear day you can see all the way north to Midway Point on the Del Norte coast. Five miles offshore sits Redding Rock, a breeding ground for seabirds. Your trail drops to the beach, coming to the high tide line at 4 miles, just south of the mouth of the seasonal creek along which you descended. (It is almost 1⅜ miles north along the beach, the designated Coastal Trail, to Davison Road and the Gold Bluffs entrance kiosk.) Retrace your steps back up to the ridge, then down the canyon of Skunk Cabbage Creek to return the trailhead at 8 miles.

# 24.
# LADY BIRD JOHNSON GROVE LOOP
## LUSH HIGHLAND VIRGIN FOREST

*When she was First Lady, Lady Bird Johnson spoke out for the creation of Redwood National Park. Her stand helped break a deadlock in Congress over establishment of the controversial park, and the acquisition funds were allocated. Appropriately she came to dedicate the park in 1968. The ceremony occurred in what is today called Lady Bird Johnson Grove.*

*A short easy loop trail, 1³/₈ miles in length, explores the virgin grove, located on a high ridge. People in wheelchairs can follow the trail with little or no assistance.*

*The master plan for trail development in Redwood National Park has long included plans for a trail to connect the coast with the east side of the Redwood Creek basin. The Berry Glen Trail (see Trail #25), 2¾ miles in length, now descends west from the northwest end of the Grove Loop to Highway 101, crossing it and continuing to Elk Meadow Day Use Area.*

The trail leaves the parking area and crosses Bald Hills Road on a pedestrian bridge. In 300 feet a dispenser provides pamphlets for the self-guiding nature trail. The trail heads northwest through virgin forest of redwood, Douglas fir, grand fir and hemlock. This high-elevation forest differs

| LADY BIRD JOHNSON GROVE LOOP: |
|---|
| DISTANCE: 1³/₈-mile loop.<br>TIME: Thirty to 60 minutes.<br>TERRAIN: Gentle loop along high ridge through virgin forest.<br>ELEVATION GAIN/LOSS: 150 feet+/150 feet-.<br>BEST TIME: Spring for wildflowers. Nice anytime.<br>WARNINGS: Steep winding road to trailhead not advisable for trailers.<br>HOW TO GET THERE: Turn east off Highway 101 at M.122.3 onto Bald Hills Road. Go 2.6 miles to the Lady Bird Johnson parking area on the right.<br>FURTHER INFO: Redwood National Park (707)465-7335.<br>MAP: See page 103. |

from the coastal forests of redwood and Sitka spruce and the drier forests farther inland.

The trail climbs gently along the north end of Bald Hills Ridge. Numerous rest benches provide stopping places. The lush understory growth is dominated by salal, sword fern, red and evergreen huckleberry, salmonberry and red-flowering currant. Other understory plants include tanoak, wild rose, redwood sorrel, coltsfoot, redwood violet, rhododendron, Oregon grape and blue flag iris. On clear days you might glimpse the ocean beyond the trees on the left.

At ¼ mile a rest bench sits at the spot where the return trail enters on the right. The trail climbs gradually, then starts a gentle descent. Salmonberries grow to ten feet tall here, with hairy honeysuckle vines twining through the understory.

The easy descent continues to ½ mile, where a plaque on the right marks the spot of the 1968 dedication of Redwood National Park by Lady Bird Johnson. The redwoods here have broad, thick-barked trunks but do not grow as tall as the trees sheltered in the deep, protected canyons. The maximum heights are generally less than 250 feet. Just beyond the plaque at 5/8 mile the new Berry Glen Trail forks left to descend west along a ridge ( see Trail #25).

Soon the Pacific Ocean peeks through the trees as you near the edge of a clearcut. Most of the land between here and the coast is now protected in state and national parks. The trail bends right at the edge of the clearcut, then starts a gentle climb.

About ¾ mile from the trailhead, your trail bends right again and heads southeast. On your left the forest drops steeply toward Little Lost Man Creek, ½ mile away and 700 feet below. Your trail levels before 7/8 mile. Giant rhododendron shrubs grow on the left with trunks four inches in diameter.

The level path continues through a forest of big trees with a lush understory. In spring trilliums and redwood sorrel present white and purple flowers. Tiny calypso and coral root orchids may also grow along the trail. Licorice ferns grow on the bark of trees. Native Americans mixed them with the tobacco they grew to sweeten the smoke.

At one mile a rest bench sits beside the edge of the steep drop to Little Lost Man Creek. The trail climbs a short hill, then descends gradually to meet the return trail at 1 1/8 miles. Turn left and descend ¼ mile to the parking area.

# 25.
# BERRY GLEN

## REDWOOD GIANTS PARADING DOWN A RIDGE

*One of Redwood National Park's newest hikes, Berry Glen Trail had been on the drawing board since about 1990, but only opened in autumn 2010 after the California Conservation Corps completed it. While you can start the trail from the Elk Meadow Day Use Area near Highway 101, that offers a long, steep climb. I prefer to start from the trail's top end on the Lady Bird Johnson Loop (see Trail #24). If you have two vehicles, or if someone in your party chooses not to do the hike, a car shuttle allows you to hike downhill nearly the entire way, Another choice is to hike from the top end to about the half way point and return, which allows you to see most of the large redwoods it surveys with much less elevation change. On the top half of the trail, you also will not hear much traffic noise.*

Start your hike on the Lady Bird Johnson Grove Loop. Where the trail forks at ¼ mile, take the left fork for the shortest route. Around ½ mile you pass a plaque marking the spot where the trail's dedication ceremony was held in 1968. Not far beyond, the Berry Glen Trail forks left. Berry Glen Trail heads west to descend along a ridge. Deciduous red huckleberry bushes join the evergreen huckleberries and salmonberries so abundant in Lady Bird Johnson Grove. As your trail bends left to descend south, you enter a grove of immense redwoods. On this tall, steep-sided ridge, views stretch to the horizon beyond the nearby giants. The understory is lush with sword and deer ferns, along with salal, yerba de selva and redwood sorrel, joined by trilliums, honeysuckle, bedstraw, milkmaids, and inside-out flower in spring.

After your trail bends left and right, at ¾ mile it straightens out to descend south through virgin forest. Soon a steep drop on your right reveals a forest of mostly smaller redwoods and scattered firs.

Big trees thrive on the ridge as your trail makes a big bend left to leave the ridgetop for a steep side hill. You pass the heart-shaped leaves of wild ginger. Around one mile your trail makes an even bigger bend to the right, continuing to descend through virgin forest. By 1⅛ miles you reach relatively level ground with big clearings dense with ferns.

After your steady descent resumes, around 1¼ miles a spring on your right flows from beneath a huge fallen log, apparently originating from a wetland just above, where abundant sedges grow. Descend to ford a stream where seep-spring mimulus grows, then walk a rare level stretch of trail between giants.

Your trail contours to 1¼ miles, where an immense huckleberry bush on the left has a four-inch-diameter base. Pass another seep on your right with wild ginger, Siberian miner's lettuce, trail plant, piggyback plant along with bracken fern. This seep disappears beneath gravel. Drop into a significant stand of Douglas firs, with the largest on your left. Contour past coffeeberry and hedge nettle on a southwest-facing slope.

You soon resume a gradual descent, meandering through a forest of giants. The main ridgetop towers on your right. Vistas open up on your left across a canyon to wooded hills beyond.

Beyond 1½ miles you pass a few cut stumps, perhaps taken before the advent of chainsaws. Most of the virgin trees were left standing. Resume a fitful descent, still traversing some level stretches.

By 1¾ miles the steady descent resumes, still dancing through the giant forest. As your trail bends to the right and draws near the ridgetop, you encounter an immense fallen redwood. This rotting nurse log has sprouted young Sitka spruce, western hemlock, salal, red and evergreen huckleberries, salmonberries, and sword and lady ferns. This is one good turnaround point if you don't have a shuttle vehicle waiting for you at the lower trailhead.

If you are continuing to the bottom, beyond the nurse log the trail bends left to descend steadily by five switchbacks to 1⅞ miles. Plenty of big trees still lie ahead. Your path winds among giants, both standing tall and fallen to nurse new trees.

| BERRY GLEN: |
|---|
| DISTANCE: 3⅞ miles one way, 7¾ miles for full round trip.<br>TIME: Two to 4 hours.<br>TERRAIN: Descends along a ridge through virgin forest, then through second-growth forest to level ground and meadows along Prairie Creek.<br>ELEVATION GAIN/LOSS: 1270 feet-/1270 feet+.<br>BEST TIME: Spring for wildflowers. Nice anytime.<br>WARNINGS: Steep winding road to trailhead not advisable for trailers.<br>HOW TO GET THERE, TOP END: Turn east off Highway 101 at M.122.3 onto Bald Hills Road. Go 2.6 miles to the Lady Bird Johnson parking area on the right. Berry Glen Trail leaves Lady Bird Johnson Loop at ⅝ mile.<br>HOW TO GET THERE, BOTTOM END: Turn west off Highway 101 north of Orick at M.123.9 onto Davison Road. Go .6 miles, then left for trailhead parking. Trail starts near restrooms.<br>FURTHER INFO: Redwood National Park (707)465-7335.<br>MAP: See page 103. |

Before 2⅛ miles your trail makes the steepest descent of all, winding down by six short switchbacks. Then your trail levels briefly before descending fitfully. At 2¼ miles you are surrounded by redwood giants to 12 feet in diameter. The trail climbs briefly to gain the nearby ridgetop. Here you are on the boundary between virgin forest south of the ridge and cutover former timber lands here on the ridge and to the north. Having descended slightly more than half the elevation of this hike, here is your last best chance to turn back if no shuttle awaits at the bottom end. Plenty more virgin redwoods lie ahead, but mostly not as impressive as the ones you passed above. Notice how alders and spruce thrive where the big redwoods have been removed. Other species in the cut area include coffeeberry, abundant huckleberry and even some grasses.

Continuing down the ridge, virgin redwoods again claim the ridgetop at 2½ miles, but the forest is still sparse north of here. Traffic noise increases from here to the bottom. As you descend, virgin forest drapes both sides of the ridge before 2⅝ miles.

Your trail switches right to leave the ridge on a moderate, switchbacking descent. You may even get a glimpse of Elk Meadow 400 feet below from the first switchback. Descend steeply by eight switchbacks in the next ⅛ mile, passing many giant huckleberry bushes. Continue your steady winding descent through virgin forest.

By 2⅞ miles, where you encounter a stand of spruce, you leave the virgin forest for former commercial timber lands. Continue your steady winding descent. Pass a big old redwood stump wrapped in the roots of a young spruce. Spruce then alder dominate the regrowing forest as coast manroot and false lily of the valley appear.

By 3⅛ miles the highway is close by—you can glimpse speeding vehicles through the trees. You come to relatively level ground as the trail turns right to join an old road. Pass an escaped domestic fuchsia, elk clover, skunk cabbage and Himalayan blackberry. You can see a house below on the left, then encounter remnants of road pavement. Your path merges with the paved Davison Trail just beyond 3¼ miles.

Come to Highway 101 at 3⅜ miles. Cross cautiously and follow the broad, level trail heading west. You cross a long wooden bridge. It protects the wetlands of lower Elk Meadow on your right, then crosses alder-lined Prairie Creek near its west end.

Beyond the bridge you meet the south end of Trillium Falls Loop (see Trail #21) on your left at 3½ miles. Veer right to head north-northwest, with forest on your left and Elk Meadow beyond Prairie Creek on your right. You pass young redwoods used as scratching posts by the elk. After Davison Trail turns paved, you meet the north end of Trillium Falls Loop on your left at 3¾ miles. Cross a small creek, then turn left on the paved trail, coming to Elk Meadow Trail before 3⁷/₈ miles.

If you have arranged a car shuttle, you're all set. Otherwise, retrace your steps back up the ridge on Berry Glen Trail. When you get to the Lady Bird Johnson Loop, you can go either left or right to complete your hike. Taking the left turn takes an extra 1/8 mile to return to the parking lot, but it's worth it if you are not short of daylight.

## 26. REDWOOD CREEK

### EASY BACKPACK TO TALL TREES

*Two trails reach the Tall Trees Grove of Redwood National Park. Both routes have seasonal limitations; hikers must heed the warnings about offseason travel on both the Redwood Creek and Tall Trees Trails. To ignore them could mean disaster at the worst, or a ruined trip or cold night in the woods. Redwood Creek Trail is the longer route into Tall Trees Grove. This easy, rather long trek avoids the steep terrain surrounding Redwood Creek by following the creek's gradual canyon upstream. The problem for offseason travelers lies in the trail's two crossings of the creek. In summer (generally June to September, inquire at Kuchel Information Center) temporary bridges are installed at the crossings. In late spring and early fall when the bridges have been removed you can usually ford the creek (inquire!) to find solitude at Tall Trees Grove. But as waters rise with the rains, you cannot get beyond the first ford.*

*Redwood Creek Trail offers a pleasant 3¼-mile round trip to the first ford or longer trips farther up the creek. The 15 3/8-mile round trip to Tall Trees Grove makes for a long day hike, especially if you have to ford the creek twice in each direction when the summer bridges are not in place, and even without the additional 7/8 mile loop through the grove. For arduous hikers it can be done as a marathon day hike, but at least one night camping along the gravel bars of the creek make a more pleasant trip, even if you must carry a backpack. With a free permit, camping is permitted anywhere beyond the first ford except within 0.3 mile of Tall Trees Grove. Adding another night or two provides enough time to explore side trails and further explore the creek and its surroundings.*

*Redwood Creek was the domain of the Chilula people, an Athabaskan group related to and allied with the Hupa to the east. The Chilula had about 20 small villages, mostly on sunny south slopes east of Redwood Creek, from McArthur Creek upstream to Minor Creek, near where Highway 299 is today. In summer they would leave their creekside homes to camp in the Bald Hills to the west, where they were consummate at snaring game. They also gathered abundant seeds and bulbs. Fish from Redwood Creek provided the balance of their sustenance. They had virtually no contact with European immigrants until the Trinidad Trail to the Klamath and Trinity mines came through their territory in the 1850s. This led to twelve years of hostilities, after which the few Chilula survivors were removed to the Hupa Reservation.*

From the parking area, the Redwood Creek Trail heads southeast, promptly crossing an 80-foot bridge over an unnamed creek. The level, graveled trail, which may be wheelchair accessible for the first portion, passes through a streamside forest of alders, bays and willows. You pass your first redwood before 1/8 mile. Then a young tree on your right is dwarfed by a huge old redwood stump with spring board cuts on the left. These notches indicate that this area was logged long ago, before the advent of chain saws.

Your trail soon comes to the bank of Redwood Creek. From here you have your most expansive view up the creek, with big redwoods along both sides.

Continue southeast beyond ¼ mile, where you cross a bridge over Hayes Creek, then turn south, crossing another small bridge. At ½ mile you come to a big meadow between the trail and Redwood Creek. Blackberries thrive in the sunny clearing. Pass a wildlife observation booth on your left where you can record any sightings.

You come to a second meadow at 5/8 mile. Your trail bends right and brings you alongside the creek again at ¾ mile. An osprey nest sits atop a tall tree about 200 feet east of the meadow. Continue across two small bridges into an area of lush riparian vegetation. Sitka spruce, alder, salmonberry, water hemlock and saxifrage grow here.

Pass through a third meadow at 1 1/8 miles, right beside the gravel bed of the creek. A riot of wildflowers grows here in the spring. After the meadow comes an immense berry patch, then an area where stinging nettles crowd the trail in late spring and summer. The next meadow stretches along the trail for ¼ mile. At its end you pass through a tunnel of vegetation, then drop onto the gravel bar of the creek bed at 1 3/8 miles.

In summer you cross the creek on a temporary bridge. But in the off-season you must ford the creek. The gravel crossing 200 feet upstream from where the trail meets the creek usually provides the best ford. To find the trail south, look for the two red diamonds on the opposite bank, south-southwest from where you meet the creek. When the author hiked here one autumn, two mergansers floated downstream, perturbed by my intrusion.

On the west bank duck under a fallen maple and enter more riparian forest. On your right a giant maple stands against a fern-covered cliff. The path drops to a crossing

REDWOOD CREEK:

DISTANCE: 7¼ miles one way. 15 3/8 miles round trip with ¾-mile Tall Trees Grove Loop.
TIME: Four to 5 hours, one way.
TERRAIN: Follows meandering, nearly level canyon of Redwood Creek.
ELEVATION GAIN/LOSS: One way: 500 feet+/440 feet-. Round trip: 940 feet+/940 feet-.
BEST TIME: Late spring or fall for solitude. June to September 15 for bridges.
WARNINGS: Creek fords are usually treacherous to impassable during rainy season (October-April); inquire before you go. Watch for poison oak and stinging nettles. Permit required for overnight camping, available at Redwood National Park visitor centers.
HOW TO GET THERE: Turn east off Highway 101 at M.122.3 onto Bald Hills Road. Go .4 mile to turnoff on right, then .5 mile to trailhead parking.
FURTHER INFO: Redwood National Park (707)465-7335.
OTHER SUGGESTIONS: A NETWORK OF HORSE TRAILS starts at the Orick Rodeo grounds east of town. About 34 miles of trail, with two free camps, loop through clearcut areas and some old growth forest west of Redwood Creek.
FOR GUIDED HORSE TRIPS in Redwood National Park, contact Redwood Creek Buckarettes (707) 499-2943.
CROSS COUNTRY HIKING: In summer the most rewarding backcountry experience comes to the hiker who walks the gravel bars of Redwood Creek. The creek repeatedly swings across the route, forcing the hiker to ford knee-deep water. You can go about 14 miles before the steep, narrow gorge of Rocky Gap bars progress. You can camp anywhere on the gravel bars, except within 0.3 mile of the Tall Trees crossing.

of McArthur Creek beyond 1¾ miles. Your trail then runs along the base of the steep canyon wall until you descend onto the gravel bed of Redwood Creek at 2 miles. On the canyon wall grow five-finger and sword ferns and many saxifrage plants. Bracken and deer ferns grow a bit farther along the trail. At 2¼ miles pass a large redwood on your left, then climb a short, steep hill. This is followed by three short up and down stretches.

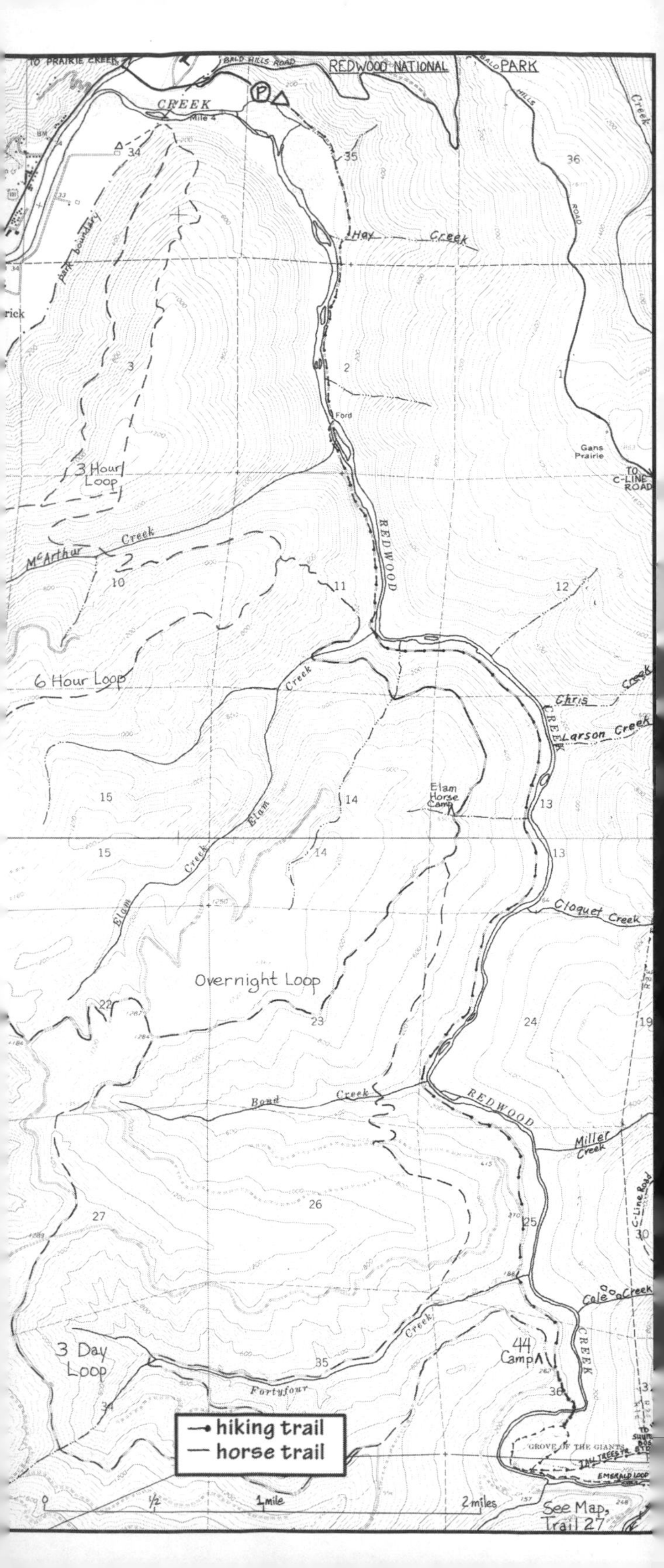

TO PRAIRIE CREEK
BALD HILLS ROAD
REDWOOD NATIONAL PARK
CREEK
Mile 4
Hay Creek
Ford
Gans Prairie
TO C-LINE ROAD
3 Hour Loop
McArthur Creek
REDWOOD
6 Hour Loop
Creek
Chris Creek
Larson Creek
Elam Horse Camp
Elam Creek
Cloquet Creek
Overnight Loop
Bond Creek
REDWOOD
Miller Creek
C-Line Road
Cole Creek
CREEK
3 Day Loop
44 Camp
Fortyfour Creek
hiking trail
horse trail
GROVE OF THE GIANTS
TALL TREES TR.
EMERALD LOOP
0
1/2
1 mile
2 miles
See Map, Trail 27

Shortly before you drop to a bridge over Elam Creek at 2⅝ miles, the unsigned Elam Creek Trail forks right, leading to a horse camp and outhouse. Beyond the outhouse the spur climbs north into virgin forest. Our described route crosses the Elam Creek bridge and continues up Redwood Creek. The canyon becomes very broad here. Cross a small seasonal creek and head due east at 2⅞ miles, passing under large maples draped with lichen.

Your level trail stays near Redwood Creek, making a big, slow bend to the right. Drop back beside the creek at 3½ miles, heading south. Pass some big redwoods before the trail veers onto the gravel bar of Redwood Creek at 3⅝ miles.

You are soon back under the alders. At 3¾ miles the steep slope of the canyon is right beside the trail. The trail passes under a huge, still-growing fallen redwood. After crossing a small stream, you come to a broad spot in the trail at 4 miles, a pleasant rest spot with dry ground and a good view of Redwood Creek Canyon.

The trail contours upstream following the creek. Beyond 4¼ miles you enter a logged area. Only a few small- to medium- sized redwoods remain. Make a gradual climb to 4½ miles, then cross a bridge high over an unnamed creek. Cross two more bridges over nameless creeks in the next ¼ mile, then descend alongside Redwood Creek again at 5 miles.

After large redwood stumps at 5¼ miles, you start another gradual climb. By 5½ miles you are about 100 feet above big pools in Redwood Creek. You drop quickly to a bridge over Bond Creek, then angle left at 5¾ miles and climb gradually, heading southeast. This is the biggest climb on your way to Tall Trees Grove; you gain 200 feet in the next ¾ mile. You pass a stand of virgin redwoods but most of the remainder of the trail passes through an area clearcut before this became a national park. A young alder forest has grown quickly to cover the scars and provide shade along most of your route. The shade of alders also helps the light-sensitive young redwoods get established.

A wooden post marks the 6-mile point of your hike. Continue your climb, passing another stand of virgin redwoods below the trail. You come to a sunny rest bench at the top of the hill. Then you descend gradually to cross a rustic bridge over cascading Forty-Four Creek.

Begin another gradual ascent, gaining 100 feet in a mile to reach the highest elevation on the trail, 250 feet above sea level, at 7⅛ miles. Your broad trail follows what was once a major logging road. Ruffed grouse nest along this section of the trail. One might spook with a noisy flurry of wings.

The road narrows and levels. If you hiked here in the 1990s, you'll be relieved to known that the route to Tall Trees Grove has been shortened by nearly one mile. It no longer circles the grove to approach it from the south. Now the trail descends a ridge southeast, passing through an

industrially logged redwood grove.

You reach the bottom of the hill and a trail register. Sign in here, like fellow visitors from around the world. A sign indicates that camping is not allowed within .3 mile of the Tall Trees crossing. Pause here once more to appreciate the heights of the trees across the creek. Once you are in the grove you will be too close to get any sense of their height.

It is 500 feet across the creek and into the grove. A temporary footbridge crosses the creek from June to September. In other months you will have to get your feet wet (or it may be impassable). A ¾-mile loop trail circles through the Tall Trees Grove. It passes under immense bigleaf maples, then leads to the tallest trees around, up to 366 feet. It also passes a brine vat used by an early settler to salt the fish he caught in the creek.

If you are camping on Redwood Creek, put on your old tennis shoes and shorts and hike upstream or downstream along the gravel bars. As the creek wanders from one side of the canyon to the other, you must ford the azure stream many times. But you are rewarded with solitude, as well as a chance to sight herons, ducks, hawks, perhaps even a golden eagle, black bear, mountain lion or fox. Or perhaps you can spot their tracks in sand along the creek.

It is 1½ miles upstream to the Emerald Ridge Trail (see Trail #27). You can continue about two more miles before you encounter Rocky Gap, a narrow, steep-walled jumble of huge boulders that blocks further progress. Only hikers with adequate rock climbing experience and a minimum party size of three should attempt to get beyond Rocky Gap.

If you camp on the gravel bars of Redwood Creek, treat your drinking water, hang food beyond the reach of bears, bury body waste at least 150 feet from the water, do not wash or let even biodegradable soap get into the streams, and use only dead, downed wood for fires. Of course hikers should carry out all their trash at all times.

# 27. TALL TREES EMERALD RIDGE LOOP

EASY WALK TO TALL TREES, STEEP WALK OUT

*You can now once again get a permit to drive your private vehicle (motor homes and RVs prohibited) to the Tall Trees Trailhead. Up to 50 free permits are issued daily between 8 a.m. and 2 p.m. at Kuchel Information Center one mile south of Orick on Highway 101. Come early, especially in summer since permits are limited to 50 per day. Please note that all day hikers must be outside the locked gate at Bald Hills Road by 7 p.m.*

*If you have a driver drop you off, you may also bring a backpack, camp along Redwood Creek, then hike out on the Redwood Creek Trail (see Trail #26) for the full tour. From Tall Trees Grove in winter you will not be able to cross swift-flowing Redwood Creek when you get there, requiring that you return the way you went in.*

After passing through the clearcuts along graveled C-Line Road for six miles, you come to the Tall Trees Trailhead. The trail descends south, quickly passing two shady picnic spots with tables. The ridge to the west of the trail was saved from logging, making this a pleasantly shaded hike. A forest of redwoods and Douglas firs to four feet in diameter provides shade for you and the lush understory plants: rhododendron, evergreen violet, huckleberry, ceanothus, salal, yerba de selva, chinquapin and tanoak. These are soon joined by western hemlocks, lichen-draped maples and occasional Port Orford cedars.

You soon come to a junction; the Emerald Ridge Trail on the left heads southeast, while the main trail turns west. Descending toward the grove, the habitat grows more moist and the trees are larger. Rest benches sit along the trail.

You turn northwest around ¼ mile and draw closer to the ridge. The trail zigzags, descending across a small stream cascading down the steep hillside. Cross another small creek at

5/8 mile, where deer and sword ferns thrive. Continue your descent, passing more rest benches.

Your trail levels at an alluvial flat deposited by Redwood Creek eons ago, before it had cut as deep a canyon as it follows today. The gold-rush-era Trinidad Trail came through here on its way to the Trinity mines.

Descend once again, coming to a restroom at 1 1/8 miles. Then you drop quickly to the floor of Tall Trees Grove, passing a redwood with a goose pen on the right. In 250 feet you meet one of the world's tallest trees. The twin trunks of the 600-year-old Tall Tree (AKA Libby Tree) now rise 362.8 feet, having lost five feet of top since it was the champion, dethroned by taller finds in 1994. It's now the 34th tallest known tree. Also in this grove is the Paul Zahl Tree, currently #17 at 366.4 feet). The Redwood Creek watershed currently has six of the 18 tallest known trees.

Be sure to take time to walk the ¾-mile loop trail that winds through the grove. If you want a longer hike but do

| TALL TREES/EMERALD RIDGE LOOP: |
|---|
| DISTANCE: 1¼+ miles, one way; 2 5/8 miles, round trip (plus ¾-mile Tall Trees Loop); or 4¼-mile loop (5 miles with Tall Trees Loop).<br>TIME: To Tall Trees: 30 minutes.<br>Return to bus stop: 45 minutes to an hour.<br>Emerald Loop: Two to 3 hours.<br>TERRAIN: Descends steeply to some of the world's tallest trees in a big bend of Redwood Creek. Loop follows creek upstream, then climbs ridge to trailhead.<br>ELEVATION GAIN/LOSS: Round trip to Grove: 680 feet-/680 feet+. With Emerald Loop: 720 feet-/720 feet+.<br>BEST TIME: Off season visit offers solitude and serenity; you must always get a permit at Kuchel Information Center first.<br>WARNINGS: Redwood Creek cannot be forded in winter, early spring. Steep trail on return hike. Watch for poison oak.<br>HOW TO GET THERE: Get permit first. Turn east off Highway 101 onto Bald Hills Road at M.122.3. Go 7.1 miles to Tall Trees Access Road on right, open and close gate, then drive 6.1 miles on winding, gravel road.<br>FURTHER INFO: Redwood National Park (707)465-7335. |

not want to hike 7⅝ miles on the Redwood Creek Trail, you can make the Emerald Ridge Loop described below.

You can only hike upstream along Redwood Creek during the time of low water, generally from May until October Even then you must make several knee-deep crossings of the creek. Head upstream from the Redwood Creek Trail crossing, just south of Tall Trees Grove. You head east for ½ mile. Then the creek and canyon make a big bend right. You turn south about ¾ mile, then head south-southeast as the creek bed broadens to wide gravel bars. An old road meets the west side of Redwood Creek just after one mile. The creek bends left until you are heading southeast. About 1¼ miles, creek and canyon again bend to the left.

Soon a stream with a small waterfall enters Redwood Creek on your right, beside some lichen-covered rocks. A pleasant swimming hole is here in summer. The Emerald Ridge Trail is about 200 feet beyond. It heads north from the southernmost bend in this section of Redwood Creek. If you miss the trail, you will come to Emerald Creek on your left within ¼ mile. IF YOU COME TO EMERALD CREEK YOU HAVE PASSED THE TRAIL. (You can follow Redwood Creek for 2 more miles to Rocky Gap, where you can go no farther.)

The Emerald Ridge Trail climbs away from Redwood Creek, passing a huge circle of redwoods on the right. Climb through moss-draped forest with eight-foot diameter redwoods and Douglas firs, with glimpses of Emerald Creek canyon below. You pass the lower end of Dolason Prairie Trail (see Trail #28) around 1⅞ miles. If you want to extend your hike, consider a side trip along that trail. It is ⅜ mile round trip to the pretty crossing of Emerald Creek.

Emerald Ridge Trail soon climbs away from the creek into drier habitat, heading generally northwest. Descend briefly just before 2¼ miles. A redwood root ball of fine geometric shape lies on the left. Climb gradually again before leveling amidst many large rhododendrons. Then resume your climb, winding around a shattered and scarred redwood giant.

You gain the crest of Emerald Ridge at 2½ miles and wind along it, climbing steeply, then more gradually. Climb northeast with several switchbacks through a forest of fire-scarred redwoods, scattered hemlocks and Douglas firs. The trail climbs and winds through the forest, leaving the ridge and heading north after 2⅝ miles. Then you turn west and climb more steeply. After two more turns you meet the Tall Trees Trail a few hundred feet from the parking area. Turn right and climb back to the trailhead. The entire loop is 4¼ miles, 5 miles with the loop through Tall Trees Grove.

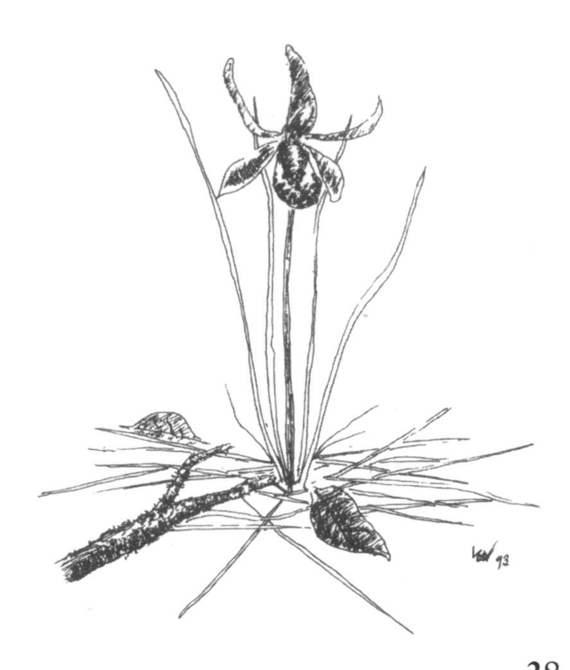

# 28. DOLASON PRAIRIE

STEEP PRAIRIES AND VIRGIN FORESTS

*This delightful trail explores the "balds" or prairies, large grassland clearings in the forest offering dramatic sweeping views of Redwood Creek's watershed. It then drops into virgin forests upstream from Tall Trees Grove. Dropping through steep terrain, the trail requires a moderately strenuous 9 3/8-mile round-trip effort with a steep climb out. During peak season (mid-May to mid-September), you can reduce the effort required to explore this trail by arranging to meet a second vehicle at the Tall Trees Trailhead at the bottom end, reducing the hike from the 9 3/8 miles round trip to a 5¾-mile one-way shuttle. Or you can limit your hike to the easy 2 3/8 miles round trip to the Dolason Barn for the grand views of Redwood Creek basin.*

*The large prairies of this area were so important to the Chilula people native to the area that their name originates from the Yurok term meaning "people of the Bald Hills." The Chilula dwelt in the upper reaches of these prairies during the summer, gathering abundant seeds and bulbs and snaring game. In the 1850s they came into conflict with the goldseekers who crossed the area while journeying from the coast to the Trinity and Klamath mining districts.*

*In the 1860s the Lyons family started a cattle ranch in the area, switching to sheep in the 1870s. Lyons Ranch won a prize for their wool at a Paris exhibition, bringing them in-*

*ternational acclaim. Redwood National Park inherited three barns from their spread, one of which is along this trail.*

The trail descends south from the shaded trailhead and picnic area on Bald Hills Road. You quickly turn southeast, descending through grasslands at the edge of Douglas fir forest. These grasslands have been invaded by Scotch broom and foxglove, non-native plants. By 1/8 mile your trail descends steadily through second-growth forest that burned in the last 20 years. You soon switchback to the right and descend west on an old road.

You veer right to descend a narrow path through the forest, then return to grasslands. At 3/8 mile you meet a broad gravel road. Turn right and follow it for ¼ mile, then veer left to descend a trail into the forest. Your path makes a moderate, winding descent, passing bay laurel, Indian plum and red-flowering currant. Switchback left to descend steadily south on another old road, then wind right and descend across two seasonal streams where gooseberry grows. Beyond the second creek you get a glimpse of the barn ahead.

Your descending path passes the barn beyond 1 1/8 miles. The nineteenth century barn has an intriguing steep-roofed design. Enjoy the sweeping views up Redwood Creek to the high peaks at the headwaters, snow-covered in winter and early spring.

The trail continues, descending across the large expanse of Dolason Prairie, brightly sprinkled with poppies, lupines and other wildflowers in spring. Your descent steepens by 1½ miles, where you drop along a ridge, ducking in and out of Douglas fir forest. Iris and wild strawberry thrive in the grasslands, while the forest understory has evergreen and red huckleberry, Oregon grape, clintonia, trail plant, trillium and evergreen violet. You will likely see the scat of some of the many wild animals that inhabit the area: elk, coyote, bobcat, perhaps bear or mountain lion.

Your route continues winding down the crest of the ridge, passing Douglas firs to eight feet in diameter. At 1 7/8 miles you leave the forest and the old ranch, entering a logged area on the north side of the ridge where you see the first redwoods along the trail. In spring the modest blue-violet flowers of snow queen bloom here, as do showy calypso orchids. Look northwest for a view of the tall virgin forest near Tall Trees Trailhead.

Continue your descent into the deep canyon below. The trail winds through long switchbacks, offering views up the canyon of Redwood Creek. By 2¼ miles you again descend through forest along the ridge. Look for slink pod, vanilla leaf, redwood sorrel and wood rose. Large redwoods soon dominate the forest, with scattered Douglas fir, hemlock, grand fir, madrone, tanoak and bay.

Your switchbacking trail drops along the north face of

DOLASON PRAIRIE:

DISTANCE: 9 3/8 miles round trip; 2 3/8 miles round trip to barn, 10¼ miles round trip to Redwood Creek.
TIME: Full day.
TERRAIN: Descends moderately through forest to prairie, then steeply down a ridge to cross Emerald Creek, then climbs to meet Emerald Ridge Trail.
ELEVATION GAIN/LOSS: One way to Dolason Barn: 540 feet-; to Emerald Ridge: 2280 feet-/240 feet+. Round trip to Redwood Creek: 2800 feet-/2800 feet+.
BEST TIME: Late spring, early fall. Can be hot in summer.
WARNINGS: Steep trail, recommended for fit hikers. Watch for poison oak and rattlesnakes. No overnight parking at trailhead. No bikes or horses.
HOW TO GET THERE: Turn east off Highway 101 (M.122.3) onto Bald Hills Road. Go 11.5 miles to trailhead on right.
FURTHER INFO: Redwood National Park (707)465-7335.
OTHER SUGGESTION: LYONS RANCH TRAIL, 6 miles farther up mostly unpaved Bald Hills Road from Dolason Trailhead, descends to Home Place at the heart of the Lyons family's 19th-century sheep and cattle ranch, 3 5/8 miles round trip. While the original house is gone, Home Place still has two bunkhouses and a barn, giving a vivid glimpse of life on a remote homestead. You can use Ranch Road, which forks east about two-thirds of the way down, to expand the trek to a 4½-mile loop past an old sheep shed. The views over Redwood Creek are even more dramatic than from Dolason Prairie Trail.

the ridge. At 2 7/8 miles a big redwood with a deep fire scar in its swollen base stands on the left. The path soon levels beside a rock outcrop. You can hear Emerald Creek murmuring to the north. Climb briefly past false Solomon's seal and rhododendron.

From 3 miles you descend west along a ridge for ¼ mile. Then descend by two long switchbacks, returning to the ridge briefly at 3½ miles. Descend along a steep northwest-facing slope, dropping gently to 3¾ miles, then moderately as you pass redwoods and Douglas firs to ten feet in diameter, with chinquapin in the understory.

At 4 miles your trail turns north to ascend briefly, then resumes its winding descent. Descend north again at 4¼ miles, where a redwood on your right has a 17-foot diameter base and leans like the Tower of Pisa. Wind down to a beautiful redwood suspension bridge spanning the deep canyon of Emerald Creek at 4½ miles, a pleasant spot for a break.

The creek's beryl waters tumble from pool to pool below.

Your trail winds steeply up the far bank to 4⅝ miles, then gradually up to its junction with the Emerald Ridge Trail (see Trail #27). If you turn right, the trail ascends ⅞ mile to Tall Trees Trail, one mile to Tall Trees Trailhead and the Tall Trees parking area. If you turn left on Emerald Ridge Trail you descend to Redwood Creek in just over ½ mile.

Unless you have arranged for a pick up at Tall Trees Trailhead, be sure to leave enough time and energy for the steep climb back to Dolason Trailhead.

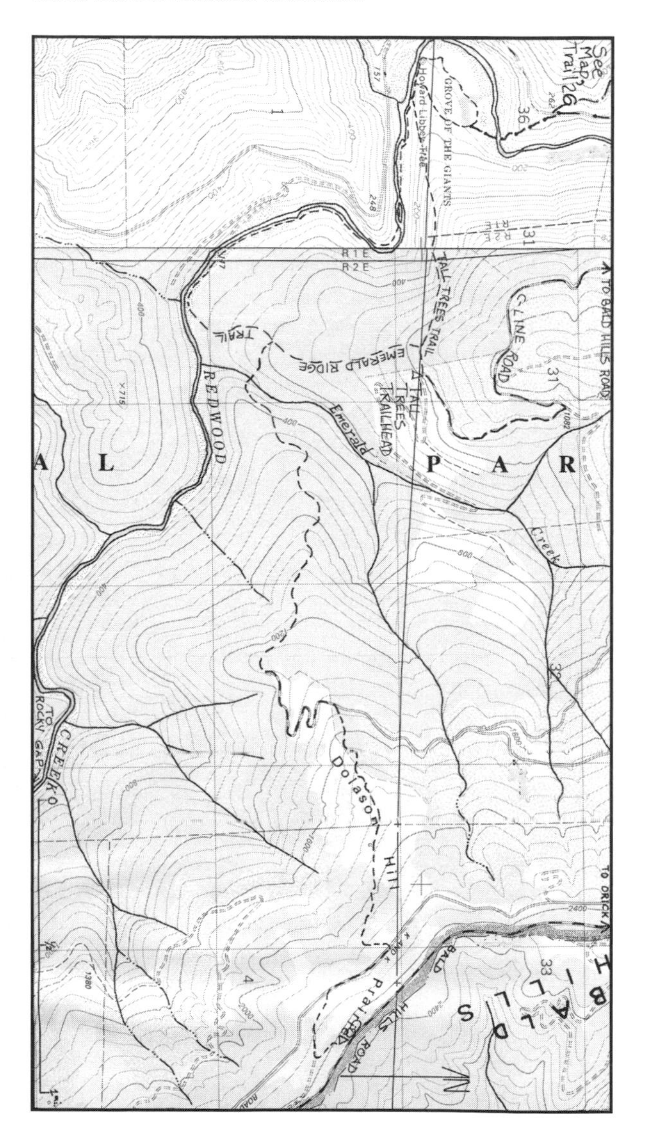

# 29.
# DRY LAGOON TO BIG LAGOON BEACH

BARRIER BEACH ALONG LAGOON SHORE

*In 1931 the Department of Parks and Recreation acquired the Gillis Ranch and made it a state park. Today Humboldt Lagoons State Park encompasses 2256 acres. The hike along the barrier beach of Big Lagoon has a wilderness feeling. In winter or at extreme high tides, it may be impassable as high water breaches the barrier. When the author hiked here in spring 1993, the beach was impassable at a tide of +1.0 foot or more. But this figure varies from one season to another. If you arrive at high tide, you can picnic at the tables surrounding the parking area while you wait for the tide to recede.*

*The second most populous Yurok village on the coast was Opyuweg or Oketo (meaning lake), located at the southwest corner of Big Lagoon. Four smaller villages were on the eastern shore. The Yuroks would take their redwood dugout canoes out onto the 1470-acre lagoon to fish. Prospectors came through here after the 1849 gold strikes on the Klamath and Trinity Rivers. Following the Gold Bluffs excitement, some prospectors worked Big Lagoon's barrier beach in the 1850s, but with little success. Ranchers settled the area in the 1870s. Timber firms acquired the forests to the east about the same time, although no logging occurred here until after World War II.*

*The Coastal Trail leads north from here to Stone Lagoon, winding east to a walk-in camp on the west shore of Stone Lagoon, then following the shore to the Stone Lagoon Picnic Area.*

To get to the barrier beach of Big Lagoon, go left from the parking area and follow the beach, which runs south-southwest from here. The high, wooded bluff on your left is the site of the Dry Lagoon Environmental Camps, currently closed.

Walking the beach of salt-and-pepper pebbly sand, you come to the first of several large rocks at tide line after 1/8 mile. Around ¼ mile a landslide on the bluff has made the beach very narrow at high tide. Consult your tide table before proceeding. If the tide is higher than +1.0 feet for your hike, you may not be able to pass this point on your return. These bluffs have slide activity for the next 3/8 mile.

More rocks are scattered along the tide line, including a very large one before 3/8 mile. If the surf is large on the day of your hike, watch out for waves that surge through the gaps in the shoreline rocks. At 3/8 mile another slide has narrowed the beach (in 2013), so make sure you can get by on your return. Then the beach broadens. Beyond the landslide at 5/8 mile, you can see Big Lagoon ahead.

You reach the north end of the lagoon at ¾ mile. At the

flood channel here, Big Lagoon may drain into the Pacific after breaching. At extreme high tides, waves may dump their salt water into the lagoon here as well. If you can cross the flood channel, climb to the high barrier beach beyond.

DRY LAGOON TO BIG LAGOON BEACH:

DISTANCE: Round trip as described: 6 miles (can go 8½ miles or more).
TIME: Two to 4 hours.
TERRAIN: Narrow beach at base of steep bluffs, then broad barrier beach between ocean and Big Lagoon.
BEST TIME: Medium to low tide.
WARNINGS: Beach may be impassable at tide of +0.5 foot or more. Do not get cut off by the rising tide. In winter, the lagoon breaches its barrier and the beach walk may be impassable. Watch for rogue waves as you walk on the beach.
HOW TO GET THERE: NORTH END: Turn west off Highway 101 at M.114.4. Go one mile to end of road and beach parking area.
SOUTH END: Turn west off Highway 101 at M.108.4 onto Roundhouse Creek Road. Go .3 mile, then turn right on Big Lagoon Park Road. Go .5 mile to day use parking area.
FEES: NORTH END: None. SOUTH END: Day use parking: $2/vehicle.
FURTHER INFO: Information: (707) 488-2171. Big Lagoon County Park: (707) 445-7652.
OTHER SUGGESTIONS: At STONE LAGOON (M.117.4), a similar hike starts at the southwest corner of the picnic area, following the barrier beach (2 miles round trip, may be impassable November to April). From there A SEGMENT OF COASTAL TRAIL heads southeast to a walk-in and boat-in camp; then continues over Sharp Point to Dry Lagoon (4 miles total). At DRY LAGOON, a one-mile loop trail leads through the old environmental camps and follows a portion of old highway. From Dry Lagoon Beach parking area, you can also walk the BEACH NORTH to Sharp Point, less than one mile. From June to September (and sometimes beyond, especially weekends), HUMBOLDT LAGOONS VISITOR CENTER (M.115.) offers interpretive exhibits and kayak rentals. SOUTH END: You can also walk Big Lagoon's barrier beach north from Big Lagoon County Park. See HOW TO GET THERE.

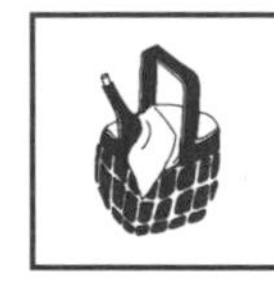

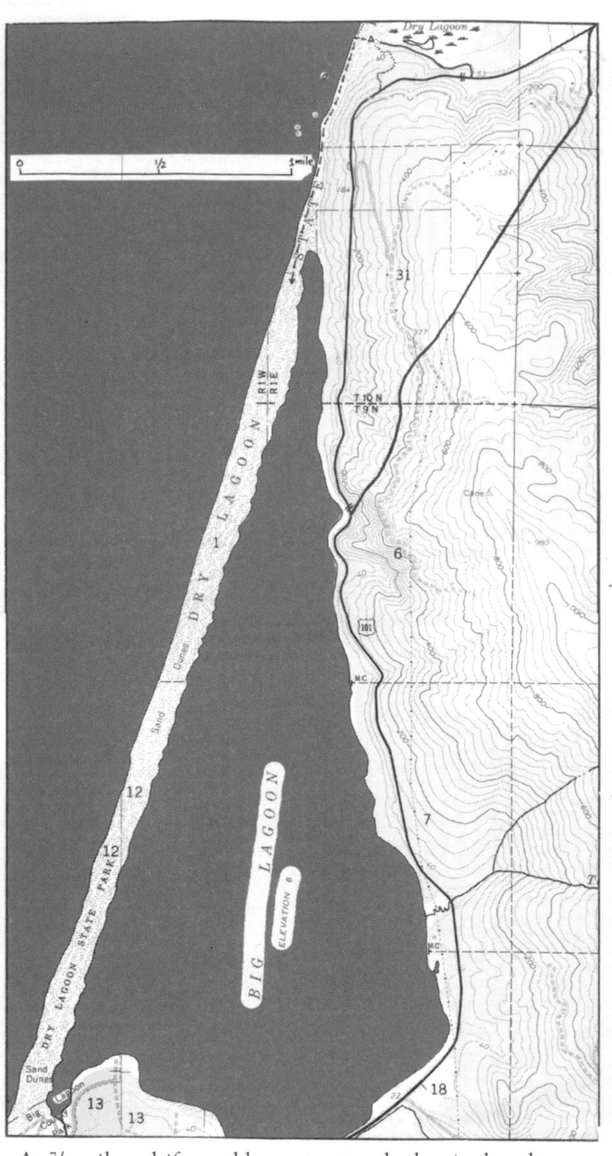


At 7/8 mile a driftwood log rests atop the barrier beach, providing a bench overlooking lagoon and channel. Big Lagoon stretches south for more than 3 miles.

Walk the crest of the barrier beach, heading toward Patrick's Point. At one mile you encounter scattered pockets of coastal strand vegetation; yellow-flowered northern dune tansy and sand verbena dominate.

The barrier beach broadens at 1 1/8 miles and stays very broad for ½ mile. Low dunes provide shelter for salt-tolerant plants. Sea rocket and sea fig join the dune tansy and sand verbena. Denser vegetation grows along the lagoon's shore. Big Lagoon is an important stop on the Pacific Flyway. Thousands of birds rest and feed here in winter. Year-round residents include members of the heron family, egrets and various shore birds.

Beyond 1⅝ miles the barrier beach gradually narrows as Big Lagoon increases in width. Dense patches of dune and cord grass grow near the lagoon's shore, providing nesting cover for shore birds. At 2⅛ miles, you come to one of several low spots in the beach. At extremely high tides, the breakers carry over the top of the sand spit, adding seawater to the brackish waters of the lagoon. About 30 species of fish inhabit the lagoon, as well as Dungeness crab, soft-shelled clams and bay mussels.

Continuing along the crest of the barrier beach, you encounter beach strawberry and seaside daisy growing with the other coastal-strand plants. Two more high-tide breaches lie around 2½ miles. The sand along the crest gets softer and looser here. You might want to veer west to the hard-packed sand near tide line. If you do, watch out for the large, churning waves that break quickly and run up the beach. An extremely violent undertow lies offshore as well. You can also veer east to the lagoon's shore.

At 2⅞ miles a log atop the beach crest is posted "STATE PARK PROPERTY." At 3 miles Big Lagoon is over a mile across. Highway 101 runs along the east shore. A dense forest of windblown redwood, Sitka spruce and grand fir grows there. On the barrier beach, large driftwood logs provide seating and some shelter for a picnic and/or bird watching.

It is 1¼ miles farther to Big Lagoon County Park on the south shore. Beach-walk fanatics can continue another 2 miles along Agate Beach to Patrick's Point State Park.

Most hikers will want to turn back by the 3-mile point, for a 6-mile round trip. Before you do, notice the spectacular view of the rugged coastline of Agate Beach and Patrick's Point. You may want to walk closer to the lagoon's shore on your return, watching for birds as you go. But try to stay above the dense patches of grass along the shore so as not to disturb the birds and other small native creatures living there. Plan 1½ hours for your return and always keep the tide in mind.

## PATRICK'S POINT STATE PARK

*This 652-acre state park sits upon a level promontory surrounded on three sides by the rugged Pacific Ocean. Long ago the level headland was beneath the Pacific before sea level receded. Ceremonial Rock and Lookout Rock now stand high above the headland. When the headland was flooded they were sea stacks, like the ones offshore today.*

*The park was named for Patrick Beegan who homesteaded the area in 1851. Patrick's Point became a state park in 1929. The Yurok had a seasonal village called Sumeg at Patrick's*

*Point. It has been reconstructed so that you can get an idea of the setting of ancient Yurok life (see* OTHER SUGGESTION, *Trail #31).*

*The annual rainfall averages 65 inches, most of it falling between October and April. Coastal fog can shroud the headland almost year-round. It occasionally lingers for days at a time, especially in summer. But spring and fall often bring crystal-clear days, making those seasons the best time to visit. On the clearest days you can stand atop Ceremonial Rock and see the mouth of the Klamath River 30 miles north. From the top of Wedding Rock you may be able to see Cape Mendocino, 50 miles south.*

# 30. AGATE BEACH

## CLIFFS ABOVE THE CRESCENT SHORE

From the northeast corner of the parking lot, your trail heads northeast, then east, descending quickly to the best view of Agate Beach, 160 feet below. Beyond the beach lie Big Lagoon and Sharp Point. Descend through Sitka spruce forest where understory plants include dense salal up to five feet deep, coltsfoot, azalea, salmonberry, twinberry, false lily of the valley, fairy bells, and yellow skunk cabbage.

At 1/8 mile a memorial rest bench on the right has a fine view of Agate Beach. Your trail descends north along a narrow ridge, then along a ravine where the forest gives way to dense coastal scrub of salal, bush lupine, coastal manroot, yarrow, elderberry, blackberry and red-flowering currant.

As you descend toward the beach, you have an excellent view of the evenly tilted sandstone strata in the cliff above

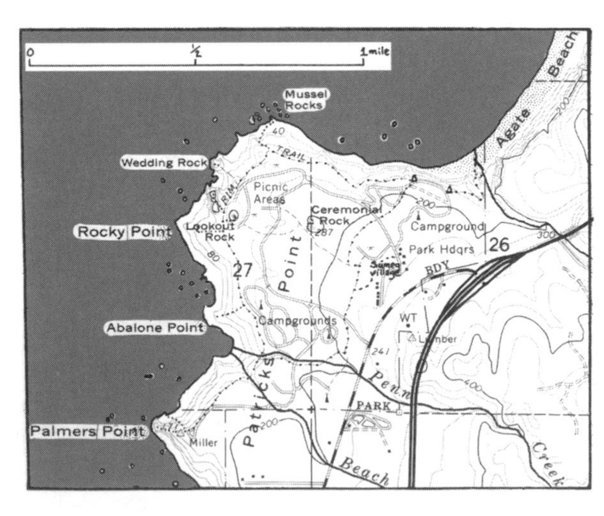

AGATE BEACH:

DISTANCE: ½ mile round trip to beach, up to 4½ miles round trip.
TIME: Thirty minutes or more.
TERRAIN: Short, steep descent to beach backed by high cliffs. Don't forget the steep climb back to trailhead.
ELEVATION GAIN/LOSS: 180 feet+/180 feet-.
BEST TIME: Spring for wildflowers. Low tide for greatest beach access. After winter storms for agate and jade collecting.
WARNINGS: Dangerous undertow here. It is unsafe to wade or swim.
HOW TO GET THERE: Exit Highway 101 onto Patrick's Point Drive (M.106.6 from north, M.105.9 from south). Go .5 mile to park entrance, where you turn right. Go past entrance station and follow signs to Agate Beach. The parking area is one mile from the park entrance.
FEES: Day use/parking: $8/vehicle. Car camping: $35-45/night. Hike/bike camping: $5/person/night.
FURTHER INFO: Patrick's Point State Park (707)677-3570.
OTHER SUGGESTIONS: CEREMONIAL ROCK is reached by several trails of about ¼ mile in length. You climb 94 steps to the top of the 287-foot-high ancient sea stack. It was used for ceremonies by the Yurok people.

the beach. Your trail bends to the left and descends steeply to the beach at ¼ mile.

The beach ends at a cliff 300 feet west of the trail. It extends northeast, then north for 7 miles. It is 2 miles to the south end of Big Lagoon. The broad beach then continues north to Sharp Point.

From the stairway at the bottom of the trail, walk northeast for 75 feet to cross a small creek. The mouth of the creek has layers of dark graywacke sandstone, backed by towering cliffs of light yellow sandstone (unfortunately defaced by carvings of names and initials). Continuing along the beach, at 3/8 mile you are beyond the steepest portion of the sandstone cliff. The beach curves north in a gentle crescent.

At ½ mile lupine covers the face of the cliff, providing a spectacular display of color at the peak of bloom from April to June. At ¾ mile a steep gully cuts through the cliff. Just beyond the gully, the magnificent cliffs reach their highest point, rising almost vertically for 400 feet.

By now you may have seen people scurrying along the beach with collecting bags. Rockhounds frequent Agate Beach to collect small pieces of agate and black jade polished by the waves and cast upon the beach.

Continue along the beach as long as you wish, leaving time to return to the trailhead before sunset. Beyond the one-mile point, you will have improving views back to the spectacular, rocky coastline of Patrick's Point.

After your return walk along the beach, you end your hike by climbing steeply to the trailhead.

# 31. RIM LOOP

## STAIRS, SEA STACKS AND BEACHES

*The Rim Trail follows an old Yurok path along the edge of the park headlands. This easy, mostly level trail provides access to six steep spur trails that lead to promontories with breathtaking views. You can approach most of these spur trails by car, but the Rim Trail provides an intimate look at the wild side of Patrick's Point.*

*The described trail begins at Agate Beach Trailhead and parking area, then circles the shore in a counter-clockwise direction. It circles back through the center of the park to your starting point. The trail is 3 1/8 miles long without any of the spur trails, 4½ miles long if you take them all.*

Head west from the Agate Beach Trailhead, walking the paved path past the restrooms. The old dirt path along the obtrusive chain link fence has been abandoned, forcing hikers to walk the road shoulder for the first 3/16 mile. The fence prevents foolish people from risking life and limb on the steep 200-foot bluff that drops to the ocean.

The proper trail begins opposite campsite 86, heading north to bluff's edge and an excellent view of Agate Beach. Spruce rise above a dense understory of salal, blackberry, twinberry, ferns, angelica and azalea. Red alders, cascara sagrada and shore pines join the forest. Tall salmon-, elder- and thimbleberries shade the path where old apple trees also grow.

Enter dense forest again at ¼ mile. Tiny Beaver Creek gurgles on your left. Follow the edge of the bluff, meandering through lush mixed forest to another overlook. Pass through a dense tunnel of foliage and come to a spur trail on your right. It leads in 150 feet to bluff's edge. Turn left to cross a bridge over a tiny creek and descend through forest to meet the Mussel Rocks Trail on your right beyond ½ mile.

If you turn right, the path descends steeply to the rocks, with a fantastic view of Agate Beach stretching north to Big Lagoon. It is 1/8 mile to the end of the spur, where you can fish or look. Climb 146 steps to return to the Rim Trail.

The Rim Trail climbs a bit, then contours before climbing south. Pass between two big rocks, then descend stone steps to a convenient picnic spot around 5/8 mile.

Your trail heads west to another view of the coast. You pass another picnic spot (with a water spigot). As you approach the Wedding Rock parking area, take the first right fork at ¾ mile to avoid the congestion at the popular day-use area. You soon meet the Wedding Rock spur trail.

The Wedding Rock spur descends rough steps, then climbs to the top of Wedding Rock at 1/8 mile. From the top of the 120-foot-high ancient sea stack, you have a spectacular view of the coast to the south. This is also a great spot for whale watching and storm watching.

Returning to the Rim Trail, head south. You climb steps to join a mostly level path, then meet the Patrick's Point spur trail before 7/8 mile. The Patrick's Point trail branches right. The path descends through a tunnel of vegetation to a picture-postcard view of Wedding Rock and the surrounding coast. The detour to Patrick's Point and back totals ¼ mile.

The Rim Trail wraps around the base of Lookout Rock on your left to meet the Lookout Rock spur in just 150 feet. (It is 1/8 mile round trip to the top of the ancient sea stack.)

Then the Rim Trail descends gradually through spruce forest. Descend steps to cross tiny Ickie Ughie Creek, then climb to the Rocky Point side trail around one mile. (Turn right to walk down to Rocky Point, a 1/8-mile round trip.)

Beyond the Rocky Point spur, the Rim Trail climbs a hill to meet an unsigned trail to the hike/bike camps. Note that, at press time, there is a steep, rough slip out not far ahead. State Parks expects to fix it in winter 2014-15. While game hikers can navigate the slip out and continue along the Rim Trail, those wanting an easier hike should take the trail to the hike/bike camps, then loop back to the starting point.

If you continue along the Rim Trail, follow it south through alder forest. The relatively open forest provides glimpses of the rugged coast. Pass a large cypress that stands between the trail and the sea. You continue through forest, coming to the slip out at 1 1/8 miles. Be careful if you try it; you do not need to return this way. If you choose to continue, the trail continues through forest and coastal scrub along the western edge of Abalone Campground. Before 1 3/8 miles you meet the side trail to Abalone Point, where the Yurok tribe once had a seasonal village. (The steep spur descends to oceanside fishing and diving access—1/8 mile round trip.)

The Rim Trail turns southeast. Follow the wooded bluff, soon crossing a small bridge. At 1 3/8 miles you meet a trail from Abalone Campground. Turn right onto the trail and

| RIM LOOP: |
| --- |
| DISTANCE: 3⅛- to 4½-mile loop or 1¼ miles shorter for short return via hike/bike camp.<br>TIME: Two to 3 hours.<br>TERRAIN: Follows a convoluted shore through dense vegetation, with access to rocky points and beaches. Loops back through the center of the park.<br>ELEVATION GAIN/LOSS: Rim Loop: 180 feet+/180 feet-. To Mussel Rock, Wedding Rock and Abalone Point: add 320 feet+/320 feet-.<br>BEST TIME: Spring and fall.<br>WARNINGS: Stay back from edge of steep cliffs. Watch for poison oak. On the shore, never turn your back on the ocean; watch for rogue waves.<br>HOW TO GET THERE: Exit Highway 101 onto Patrick's Point Drive at M.106.6 (north) or M.105.9 (south). Go .5 mile to park entrance and turn right. Follow signs to Agate Beach parking area, about one mile.<br>FEES: Day use/parking: $8/vehicle. Car camping: $35-45/night. Hike/bike camping: $5/person/night.<br>FURTHER INFO: Patrick's Point State Park (707)677-3570.<br>OTHER SUGGESTIONS: A WHEELCHAIR ACCESSIBLE PATH explores PATRICK'S POINT, about ⅜ mile round trip. A short trail explores the reconstructed YUROK VILLAGE OF SUMEG, where there are now eight traditional Yurok buildings, a native plant garden and a picnic area; park at the lot by the entrance kiosk for a ¼-mile round trip, or at park headquarters for a ⅛-mile round trip. |

cross a bridge over Penn Creek, coming to the junction of three trails. On your left is the return path to the trailhead. The middle trail continues to the Campfire Center. Unless your time or energy is running short, take the right fork to one last magnificent viewpoint: Palmer's Point.

You follow Penn Creek to a bench and overlook, then veer left. Turn right at a junction. At 1½ miles you cross a bridge over Beach Creek and head northwest. The trail passes through dense forest of spruce, shore pine and Bishop pine. The trail bed ends before 1¾ miles at the paved road to Palmer's Point. Walk the road shoulder for ⅛ mile to its end where a picnic area has a wonderful view up and down the coast. One spur trail leads west to the end of Palmer's

Point. Another forks north to descend to rocky Cannonball Beach, a popular tidepooling spot.

Now retrace your steps back to the Penn Creek bridge. Do not cross the bridge, but instead take the trail that leads east, heading upstream with the creek on your left. Soon you cross a paved road. At 2 3/8 miles you cross Penn Creek and come to a fork. Bear left to return to the trailhead.

The trail climbs gradually through dense spruce forest, turning north as it crosses six small bridges. You meet the park entrance road just east of the entrance station. Walk northwest on the road shoulder for 250 feet. Turn northeast before the entrance kiosk, passing the Visitor Center (at 2 5/8 miles if you've done the whole hike) and taking the paved trail leaving the parking lot on the right side of the Visitor Center. You pass a Yurok dugout canoe and head northeast. In 150 feet veer left on a gravel path (the paved trail continues to the reconstructed Yurok village—see OTHER SUGGESTION).

Descend north to cross a tiny creek and meet another fork at 2 7/8 miles. You can take the right fork to Park Headquarters, then walk the road back to your trailhead. I prefer to take the left fork. Veer left again on the trail to Ceremonial Rock. At an unmarked junction a left turn leads to Ceremonial Rock, a 3/8 mile round trip. Our described hike turns right to head north then northeast. You soon cross a paved road where a sign confirms this is the way to Agate Beach Trailhead. Your trail dips to cross tiny Beaver Creek, then ascends to a restroom near site #95 in Agate Beach Campground. Head northeast on the campground road and follow it about 1/8 mile to Agate Beach Trailhead parking.

## TRINIDAD STATE BEACH

*The town of Trinidad is the oldest on the California coast north of San Francisco and, with a population of about 365, one of the smallest incorporated cities in the state. The history of habitation here goes back much farther. The Yurok village of Tsurai, their largest coastal village, was located on the north shore of Trinidad Bay. Archaeological evidence shows it was inhabited continuously for over 5000 years, perhaps even longer. This southernmost village of the Yuroks was occupied until 1916.*

*Spanish explorers entered the bay on Trinity Sunday in 1775, naming it and claiming it for Spain. Russian fur trappers visited several years later. The Josiah Gregg party stopped here on December 7, 1849, carving the latitude and date into a tree. They named it Gregg's Point, unaware of the previous Spanish discovery.*

*As gold fever grew in California, ships left San Francisco searching for the protected harbor described by Gregg's party. Three schooners finally succeeded in March 1850. A month later streets were laid out, temporary buildings erected and 140 people voted in the first election. By July Trinidad boasted 300 residents and opened a trail to the Klamath and Trinity mines. A sawmill opened in 1852. But as Eureka and Arcata grew, Trinidad's star faded. Still, a lighthouse was established in 1871 and the town boomed briefly again as a whaling port in the 1920s. Today the sleepy little city on a marine terrace caters mostly to tourists and fishermen, not miners and whalers. The charm of Trinidad State Beach lies in its wildness. Although its 159 acres are within and adjacent to town, the short easy trails transport you to a rugged and wild shoreline with spectacular views.*

## 32.
## ELK HEAD/COLLEGE COVE
### WILD GARDEN AND SHORE

The Elk Head Trail leaves from the north end of the unpaved north parking area. The trail heads northwest through coastal scrub and grasslands, quickly turning west onto the broad promontory of Elk Head. The tall shrub cotoneaster grows here with its attractive red berries, as do Sitka spruce, red alder, wood rose, red-flowering currant, wild ginger and the endangered Eureka lily. The Columbia lily and black crowberry reach their southern limit here. Your trail descends gradually, approaching the southern shore of the headland. At 1/8 mile a side trail on the left descends by many steps to the north end of the beach at College Cove. The Elk Head

Trail continues west on the flat-topped promontory. This is a marine terrace, ancient ocean floor uplifted by the geological forces which continue to shape this coast. Dense clumps of salmon-, elder- and thimbleberry grow along the trail.

At ¼ mile bear left as the trail forks. The coastal scrub opens up on your left. Take a few steps to the edge of the bluff for a spectacular view of College Cove, Pewetole Island and Trinidad Head. After your trail turns southwest, you leave the scrub for grasslands with scattered pockets of scrub.

Your trail leads to bluff's edge before 3/8 mile. Below you is jagged Omenoku Point. A brushy fisherman's trail leads down to the point. Your trail bends right, heading northwest past many western dog violets to scrub-covered Elk Head and Megwil Point.

Just before ½ mile, the trail makes a big right bend. Here, near the tip of Elk Head, another side trail on your left heads west, then north for 1/8 mile to the tip of Megwil Point (last section too steep for wheelchairs), where you can see the coast to the north. Offshore sits Green Rock, with one of

ELK HEAD/COLLEGE COVE:

DISTANCE: 7/8 mile or 1½ mile semi-loop.
TIME: One hour.
TERRAIN: Level headland to grass- and scrub-covered promontory. Possible tidepooling and walk on beach.
ELEVATION GAIN/LOSS: Less than 100 feet to Elk Head. To College Cove: 100 feet-/100 feet+.
BEST TIME: Spring, early summer. Medium to low tide for beach.
WARNINGS: Watch for poison oak. Stay back from edge of cliffs.
HOW TO GET THERE: Exit Highway 101 at Trinidad, M.100.9 from north, M.100.1 from south. Go west on Main Street, then right on Trinity Street (which becomes Stagecoach Road) for .7 mile and turn left into unpaved parking lot. Trail leaves from north end.
FURTHER INFO: Trinidad Chamber of Commerce (707) 677-1610.
OTHER SUGGESTIONS: A HORSE TRAIL leaves from west end of parking area and winds south to Mill Creek and Trinidad Beach. WHEELCHAIR ACCESS follows Elk Head Trail to Megwil Point.

the state's largest colonies of common murres, 16-inch tall, black and white seabirds of the auk family. The population of Green Rock is estimated at 55,000 murres! To the southwest is Flatiron Rock, home to 24,000 more murres and five other bird species, as well as seals and sea lions. At low tide you can descend to excellent tidepools at Megwil and Omenoku Points. Be careful!

The main trail turns east, making a short loop. Pass shore pine, spruce and cypress, then scattered pockets of heather. At 5/8 mile you rejoin the main trail. Continue east ¼ mile to your car.

You may prolong your hike with a walk on College Cove Beach. To do this, take the side trail 1/8 mile from the trailhead. It descends by 100 rough steps to the north end of the beach. You can walk southeast on the beach for ¼ mile, although at high tide you must scramble over a pile of boulders. South of the rockpile, the sandy beach continues. A beautiful, large specimen of coast silktassel grows just above the beach. A small waterfall lies just beyond. Return by the same route to your trailhead.

## 33.
## MILL CREEK TO BEACH
### TO THE FOOT OF PEWETOLE ISLAND

The paved southern parking area lies within the city limits of Trinidad. A pleasant picnic area with restrooms and piped water is on a lawn-covered hillside. The Mill Creek Trail to Trinidad Beach starts here.

The trail heads north, passing to the right of the restrooms. Descend by switchbacks into forest of Sitka spruce, grand fir and red alder. You descend above the creek, crossing a boardwalk before coming to a rest bench with a pleasant view of Mill Creek Canyon. The lush understory includes sword, deer and lady ferns, redwood sorrel, miterwort, bleeding heart, fairy bells and skunk cabbage.

At 1/8 mile a giant evergreen huckleberry towers over the trail. Continue a gradual descent, paralleling the creek. The forest soon gives way to coastal scrub with blackberry, bush lupine, twinberry and coltsfoot. You come to an expansive view of the beach and wooded Pewetole Island just offshore.

The trail turns right and descends steps to a junction with a horse trail. (If you turn right, it is ¾ mile to the northern parking area. See Trail #32.) Go left at the junction and drop to the beach at the mouth of Mill Creek, ¼ mile from the trailhead. You can walk the broad beach south for 3/8 mile to the base of Trinidad Head, where you can turn east and walk city streets back into town if you wish. Or you can return the way you came.

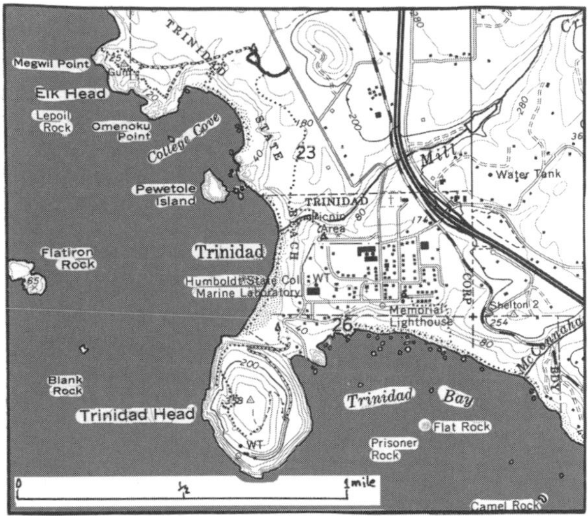


The beach north of the creek's mouth is best at low tide. At a tide of -1.0 foot or better, you can walk west about 400 feet, then walk northwest to the base of Pewetole Island. This steep rock island has a heavily forested top. Black oystercatchers nest there. This 17-inch-high black bird has a long red bill for prying shellfish from the rocks. If you are here at low tide, be careful that the rising tide does not block your return.

| MILL CREEK TO BEACH: |
|---|
| DISTANCE: ½ mile, round trip to beach. Full hike: 1 3/8 miles, round trip.<br>TIME: One hour.<br>TERRAIN: Descends along Mill Creek to Trinidad Beach. Beach walking to south, tidepooling to north.<br>ELEVATION GAIN/LOSS: 160 feet-/160 feet+, round trip.<br>BEST TIME: Low tide. Spring.<br>WARNINGS: Do not get trapped by the rising tide. Watch for rogue waves on beach.<br>HOW TO GET THERE: Exit Highway 101 at Trinidad, M.100.9 from the north, M.100.1 from the south. Go west on Main Street, then right on Trinity Street, where first left leads to the paved parking area.<br>FURTHER INFO: Trinidad Chamber of Commerce (707) 677-1610. |

# MORE TRINIDAD TRAILS

*The Trinidad area is a paradise for the hiker who likes short and scenic seaside trails. In addition to the trails of Patrick's Point State Park and Trinidad State Beach, the trails described below provide access to the spectacularly rugged coast and beaches.*

## 34. TSURAI LOOP ON TRINIDAD HEAD

CLIMB HIGH ABOVE THE PACIFIC

*Trinidad Head rises prominently above this dramatic shoreline because it is composed of a huge block of altered volcanic rock known as metagabbro. Like the rest of the Franciscan complex of rocks that comprise most of the Northern California coast, it was scraped off the ocean floor as the Pacific plate burrowed beneath the North American plate about 100 million years ago. Trinidad Head stands high above the surrounding coast because of its hardness compared to the rocks that formerly surrounded it. The Head is now federal property housing activities of the Coast Guard and the National Oceanic and Atmospheric Administration. Though often shrouded in fog, when Trinidad Head is beneath clear skies, it offers some of the best whale watching in Humboldt County.*

Park your car at the beach parking lot at the west end of Edwards Street. Walk 200 feet south, where a sign marks the start of the Trinidad Head trails (day use—no vehicles except Coast Guard beyond that point). The trail starts as a narrow path that climbs steeply for 150 feet. Then climb west on a narrow paved road, entering the Coast Guard Reservation.

After the gate, the road climbs through dense coastal scrub as the hill steepens. At ¼ mile, as you come to a big bend left, a dirt trail leaves the road heading west. Benches at the start of the path provide views north to Trinidad Beach, Pewetole Island and Elk Head. Take the dirt trail, climbing to more benches with grand views. Just beyond those benches, a side trail forks right. It descends in 500 feet to more view benches at the base of a rock outcrop.

Beyond the fork the main trail climbs southeast. You pass many berry vines that flower in March and April and bear fruit from June through September. The moderately steep trail switchbacks left, then to the right before 3/8 mile. You level and come to more benches; this is a good whale-watching spot when gray whales are migrating, December

through April. Look beyond the buoy for their spouts.

Your trail climbs again, heading south. Ahead you see your destination, a high rocky point. Climb through a thicket of silktassel to another rest bench at ½ mile. Unless it is very windy or foggy, take the side trail on the right. The short spur climbs steps to the top of the rock outcrop on the western edge of Trinidad Head. You are 300 feet above the Pacific, with views in every direction. Although you are about 60 feet below the summit of Trinidad Head, the view from here is more expansive than the view from the top. Pilot Rock, due south of here, was used by early explorers to locate and navigate the entrance to Trinidad Bay.

When you get enough of the view, descend to the main

TSURAI LOOP ON TRINIDAD HEAD:

DISTANCE: 1½-mile loop.
TIME: One hour.
TERRAIN: Climbs from sea level through coastal scrub on the promontory of Trinidad Head to a rock outcrop 300 feet above the Pacific, then loops back to starting point.
ELEVATION GAIN/LOSS: 300 feet+/300 feet-.
BEST TIME: Spring. Any clear day.
WARNINGS: Watch for traffic on paved road. Watch for poison oak on trail.
HOW TO GET THERE: Exit Highway 101 at Trinidad, M.100.9 from north, M.100.1 from south. Go west on Main Street, then left on Trinity Street to its end. Go right on Edwards Street and descend to beach parking area. Signed trail starts to the south.
FURTHER INFO: Trinidad Chamber of Commerce (707) 677-1610.

trail and head south through a pocket of lush vegetation where cow parsnip abounds. Soon, another short spur on the right leads to a view down the steep southwest face. The main trail switches left and climbs again, switching right in 150 feet. You pass through tall coastal scrub dominated by wax myrtle. Another view bench looks south at 5/8 mile. On a clear day you can see Cape Mendocino.

Your trail contours past a mountain beaver den, then through more tall scrub. You quickly come to a large granite cross marking where the Spanish explorers placed a wooden cross during their visit in 1775. Two benches overlook the coast and a grove of large spruce growing on the south face below. A side trail south leads to a small viewing platform, from which the real Trinidad Lighthouse is visible below.

Now head north toward the microwave station at the summit. At ¾ mile you come to a gravel road. Turn right on the road and descend toward town. You can see boats anchored in Trinidad Bay below. To the east lie Houda Point and Little River Rock.

At 7/8 mile you pass another bench and switchback right. You wind back to the left at one mile and meet the paved road. Go left on the pavement, making a gradual descent past several rest benches with fine views of Prisoner Rock just offshore, Trinidad Harbor, Little Head and Indian Beach.

At 1¼ miles your descent steepens. The road bends right, completing your loop as you pass the dirt trail on the left. Descend to your car, a total hike of 1½ miles.

## 35. INDIAN BEACH

### TRAIL TO SECLUDED BEACH

*One of Trinidad's oldest trails has been rebuilt. The "Hogback Trail" follows a rocky ridge hidden in coastal scrub between town and Indian Beach on Trinidad Bay. The trail marked "INDIAN BEACH TRAILS" descends by steps or wheelchair-accessible concrete ramp to the memorial lighthouse, a replica of the still working 1871 lighthouse that hides from view on the west face of Trinidad Head beyond the small harbor on your right.*

Hikers want to take the gravel track signed "AXEL LINDGREN MEMORIAL TRAIL." It descends with views of the sea-stack-studded Trinidad Bay. Descend 65 steps through a jungle of coastal scrub with coyote brush, blackberry, thimbleberry, alder, coffeeberry, cow parsnip, bee plant and coastal manroot, coming to a bench with a view of Trinidad Head.

Descend steeply by 144 more steps, passing an immense bay tree on your right, then another bench on your left, coming to a view of Indian Beach just ahead. The trail

## INDIAN BEACH:

DISTANCE: ¼ mile round trip to beach. Total hike is 1 1/8 miles.
TIME: One hour.
TERRAIN: Descends to secluded beach right below town for beach walk and tidepooling.
ELEVATION GAIN/LOSS: 160 feet+/ 160 feet-.
BEST TIME: Medium to low tide.
WARNINGS: Use caution on the steep stairs.
HOW TO GET THERE: Exit Highway 101 at Trinidad, M.100.9 from north, M.100.6 from south. Go west on Main Street, then left on Trinity Street to its end. Turn right on Edwards Street and immediately turn left into the small parking area near the lighthouse.
FURTHER INFO: Trinidad Chamber of Commerce (707) 677-1610.

winds past one more bench, then descends 26 more steps to reach Indian Beach just beside a tiny creek before 1/8 mile. Use caution on the final steep, sometimes loose steps.

From the stairway, you can walk west about 3/8 mile, passing twinberry and willow on the bluffs above the beach. At its west end, the beach meets a promontory of jumbled rocks.

From the stairs, you can also walk Indian Beach east for almost 3/8 mile. You cross a creek about 1/8 mile from the stairs. In a site above the beach densely overgrown today, the Yurok village of Tsurai (pronounced Cher-ai') saw at least 5000 years of continuous use until 1916. A sea stack called Split Rock lies in the surf zone. Continue east along the beach, crossing another creek. After passing beneath a cliff where sticky monkeyflower grows, you meet a beached sea stack with a grassy top around ¼ mile. Large spruce grow on the bluffs above. Around 300 feet beyond the grassy rock outcrop, Indian Beach ends. Unless it's high tide, you can scramble over rocks to a rocky tidepool area, ideal at low tide. Stretching east is the pebbly beach of He'Woli-Wroi Cove which you can walk to the cliff at its east end. As you do, the many offshore rocks provide spectacularly changing vistas of the rugged coast.

Return to the trail and climb the steps back to the lighthouse. If you walked to both ends of the beach and back, you hiked 1 1/8 miles.

# 36.
# OTHER TRINIDAD TRAILS
SHORT HIKES TO RUGGED COAST

*The other Trinidad area trails leave from Scenic Drive, the picturesque old portion of Highway 101 which follows the coast south from the main Trinidad exit. They are listed from north to south.*

The BAKER BEACH TRAIL leaves the road about .2 mile south of Baker Beach Road. The trail leaves from the north end of the parking area, descending steeply through alder and spruce forest to reach the beach in 350 feet. The beach stretches north for 3/8 mile. After you come to a rocky point, good rocky tidepools lie offshore from the pebbly beach.

The LUFFENHOLTZ BEACH TRAIL leaves from the north end of the large paved parking area for Luffenholtz County Park. It descends steeply west to reach the sandy beach in 300 feet. Another trail from the southwest portion of the parking area leads out onto narrow, scrub-covered Tepona Point, ending in 1/8 mile.

The HOUDA POINT TRAIL leaves from a cypress grove, descending stone steps. In 150 feet the trail forks. The left fork leads to Houda Point, with a spur descending steeply south by steps to a pocket beach. The right fork descends in another 300 feet to a popular surfing beach beside Little River Rock. The flat beach is broad at low tide, narrow to

OTHER TRINIDAD TRAILS:

DISTANCE: ¼ mile to 1 mile round trip each. At Moonstone you can walk as far as you want.
TIME: Less than one hour.
TERRAIN: Steep trails to small pocket beaches.
ELEVATION GAIN/LOSS: 100 feet-/100 feet+, each.
BEST TIME: Medium to low tide.
WARNINGS: Watch for oversize waves on beach. Do not trespass on adjacent private property. Watch for poison oak along trails to beach.
HOW TO GET THERE: Exit Highway 101 at Trinidad, M.100.9 from north, M.100.1 from south. At four-way stop, go south on Scenic Drive. It is 1.5 miles to Baker Beach Trail, 2 miles to Luffenholtz, 2.3 miles to Houda Point, 3 miles to Moonstone Road, where you go right.
FURTHER INFO: Trinidad Chamber of Commerce (707) 677-1610.

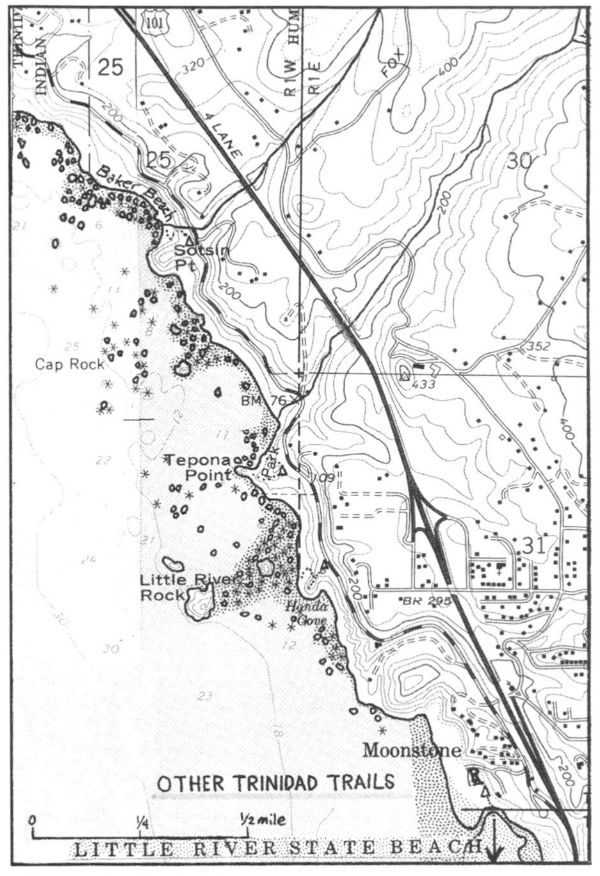


submerged at high tide.

MOONSTONE COUNTY PARK is reached by a side road on the right, descending to a parking area at the beach. There is no developed trail here, just access to the beach. You can walk south along the beach for miles, though you must ford Little River to do it (easy ford in summer and fall, may be deep in winter and spring).

## 37.
## HAMMOND SECTION, COASTAL TRAIL

### MULTIPLE-USE LINK IN COASTAL TRAIL SERVES COMMUNITY

*The community loves and uses its Hammond Trail, a key link in the California Coastal Trail. Here you will see hikers, joggers, dog walkers, families with babies in strollers, and families on bikes out to enjoy nature and take in the bracingly fresh air that is one of the treasures of the North Coast. The trail is wildly popular in good weather, but well used year-round whether sunny or foggy, calm or windy, wet or dry.*

*When I first hiked the Hammond Trail in 1997, it was already popular despite the obstacle of crossing Widow White Creek which could then be quite a challenge. Today the trail is complete, realization of a vision that began nearly thirty years ago. Still, efforts to extend the trail both north and south are in the works. If you are from out of the area, Clam Beach County Park at the northern trailhead has camping.*

Our described hike (or bike ride) starts at the trail's northern terminus at Clam Beach County Park South Day Use

| HAMMOND SECTION, COASTAL TRAIL: |
|---|
| DISTANCE: 10½ miles round trip, plus a 3/8-mile nature trail.<br>TIME: Two or 3 hours for cyclists, up to a half day or more for hikers.<br>TERRAIN: Contours through low dunes, then climbs to views of the coast. Descends paved road to a fork, where Nature Trail goes right, paved trail veers left, then descends Murray Road's shoulder to dedicated trail along Mad River shore. Contour through a neighborhood, then woodlands to Hiller Park. After more contouring past residences, trail descends to Mad River flood plain, then crosses bridge over Mad River.<br>ELEVATION GAIN/LOSS: 250 feet+/250 feet- each way, 500 feet+/500feet- round trip.<br>BEST TIME: Spring for wildflowers, any day that is not foggy for views.<br>WARNINGS: Watch for traffic at street crossings and on portions shared with vehicle traffic. Cyclists must yield to those on foot. Pedestrians and cyclists must yield to horses.<br>HOW TO GET THERE: NORTH END: Take the Clam Beach exit off Highway 101 at M.95.8 from north, M.95.5 from south. Trail heads south from parking area.<br>MIDDLE: Exit Highway 101 at Murray Road or School Road.<br>SOUTH END: Exit Highway 101 onto Janes Road at M.89.05 from north, M.88.6 from south. Go west on Janes Road, then right on Heindon Road for .4 mile. Go left on Miller Lane for .7 mile. Then go right on Mad River Road, coming to Hammond Bridge in 1.7 miles. Park to the right of bridge entrance, off the road.<br>FEES: Car camping at Clam Beach: $15/night.<br>FURTHER INFO: County Parks (707) 445-7652. |

 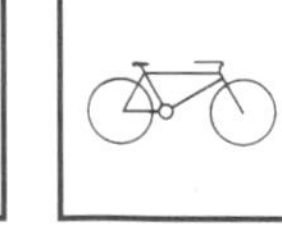  

Area. The paved level trail heads south, crossing a small bridge over Strawberry Creek. Although Your track parallels Highway 101, its location at least 100 feet from the highway provides breathing room, allowing the roar of surf to mingle with the roar of traffic. The tangle of vegetation on your right includes yellow bush lupine, willow, mustard, native blackberry, coast manroot, twinberry, coyote brush, cow parsnip, poison hemlock, foxglove, yarrow, bracken fern and occasional shore pines.

By ½ mile the vegetation grows on low, rolling dunes as your trail undulates, with little elevation gain. Beyond 5/8 mile, the pavement gives way to gravel. As the highway climbs on your left, your view opens up on the right to the tide line and breakers. Look behind you for a view of Trinidad Head.

Beyond one mile your trail climbs a moderate grade, still paralleling the highway. As you near the top of the hill, look ahead on your right to see the mouth of Mad River. After the highway vista point directly left of the trail, wind-shaped Sitka spruce and alder join the shore pines.

At Hammond Trail's high point beyond 1 3/8 mile, the pavement resumes. Cross a small bridge beneath cypress trees at 1 5/8 miles and come to the Airport Road parking area. Coffeeberry and red-flowering currant grow along the trail.

The next section of Hammond Trail uses sleepy Letz Avenue for its route. Keep your eyes and ears open to motorized traffic, especially after the Airport Road intersection. Descend along the edge of the two-lane pavement. By 2 1/8 miles the Hammond Trail again has a dedicated no-vehicle route. Continue a gentle descent along the paved trail. More trees line your route here, mostly pines and alders with some spruce. Elderberry, salmonberry, huckleberry, elk clover and salal form a dense understory.

Before 2 3/8 miles Hammond Trail splits into two routes. The left, paved multiple-use fork continues parallel to Highway 101 until Murray Road. The right fork becomes a narrow dirt path, passing through a stile to keep bikes out, then bends sharply right to descend west. This is the Hammond Interpretive Trail. Even if you are riding a bike, I recommend locking your bike near the junction and exploring the short nature trail.

Walk the verdant path west, descending through gorgeous lichen-draped forest of grand fir and Sitka spruce. The lush understory harbors abundant sword and lady ferns, elderberry, currant, buttercup, coast manroot, false lily of the valley, and Siberian miner's lettuce (AKA candyflower). The terrain on your left drops steeply to Widow White Creek. Around 1/8 mile the forest thins as you veer away from the creek through dense coastal chaparral. Wind past California poppy and abundant wild strawberry as grasslands joins the rich vegetative mix. As you draw near the creek, a rest bench overlooks it, with an escaped garden fuchsia running

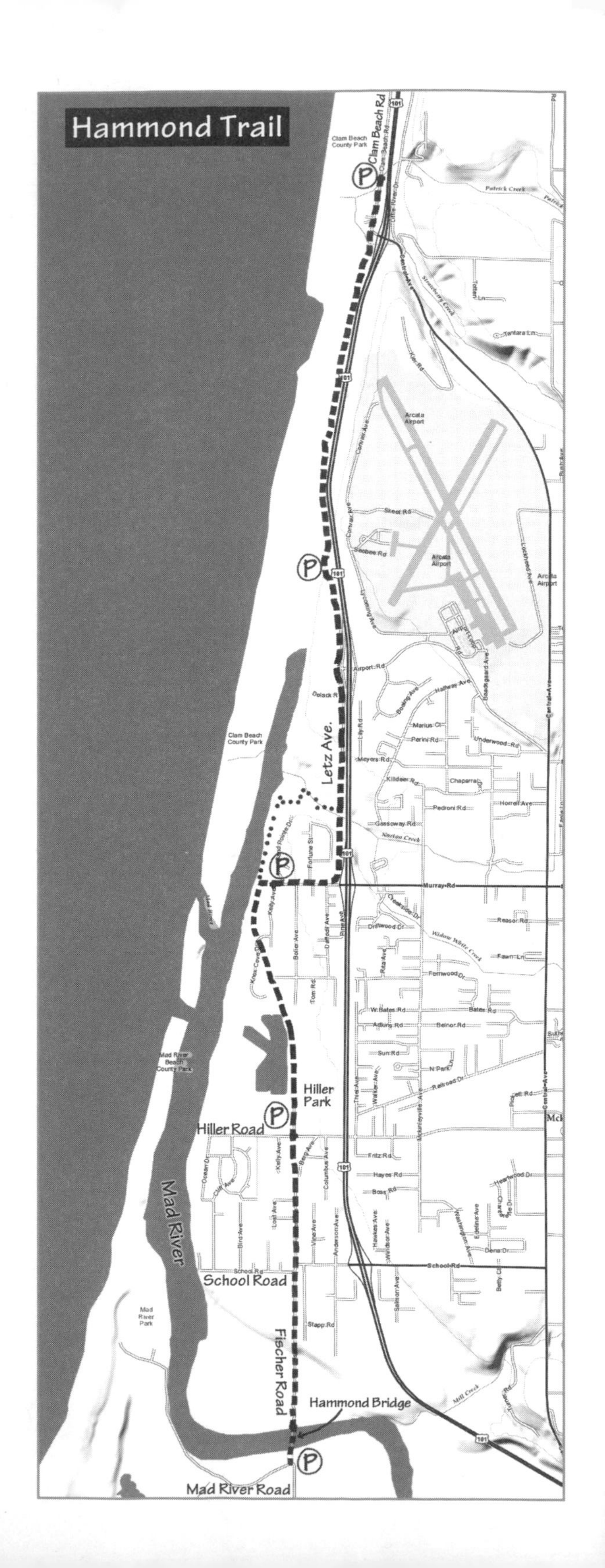

Hammond Trail
Clam Beach Rd
Clam Beach County Park
Letz Ave.
Arcata Airport
Airport Rd
Murray Rd
Hiller Park
Hiller Road
Mad River
School Road
Fischer Road
Hammond Bridge
Mad River Road
Mad River Beach County Park
Mad River Park
Patrick Creek
Widow White Creek
Norton Creek
Mill Creek
School Rd

wild nearby. The bench offers a great place to take a break, enjoying the lush vegetation and watching and listening for birds that frequent this forest: Swainson's thrush, Wilson's warblers. black phoebes, belted kingfishers and more.

After crossing the creek, your trail ascends steps around ¼ mile. At the top you can see down the verdant creek canyon to the beach and breakers. To the east you can see the ridge line at the top of the Widow White watershed. Climb more steps past iris and abundant huckleberry bushes to pass through another stile and come to a rather confusing junction. The left fork soon ends in a residential neighborhood. The right fork is the dirt/gravel Hammond Trail, once again multi-use. (If you turn back at this second stile, the round trip on the Interpretive Trail is about 5/8 mile.) For those who continue on this leg of the Hammond Trail, it climbs a short hill where strawberries grow beneath coast silktassel and huckleberry. By 3/8 mile it comes to the top of a steep hill with a grand view of Mad River. If you descend the steep hill, a view opens to the north beyond the river to Clam Beach, with Trinidad Bay and Trinidad Head beyond. Where the trail switchbacks to the left, it meets a spur signed "COASTAL ACCESS." The spur actually descends to the shore of broad Mad River. The left fork heads south, tunneling beneath alders to rejoin the southern portion of the Hammond Trail.

Back at the junction on the paved trail, contour south on the paved trail, once again paralleling the highway. It veers away from the highway around 2¾ miles, then parallels Murray Road briefly before ending, forcing you onto the bike lane or the shoulder of Murray Road. Follow the busy road west to its end at 3 1/8 miles. This alternate trailhead has parking, picnic tables and benches.

At the T intersection, turn left to follow the level, paved path south. (A right turn would follow the dirt/gravel track north, coming to the "COASTAL ACCESS" fork in just over ¼ mile.) Hammond Trail south follows a corridor with a dense wall of vegetation on the left and occasional river views on the right. You pass an immense stone house on the left at 3 3/8 miles. Just beyond, use caution as your trail crosses Knox Cove Avenue.

You suddenly leave the residences behind as you contour south on the paved trail. Hammond Trail negotiates a corridor through lush vegetation, crossing a bridge around 3¾ miles. The paved trail continues south through verdant woodlands. Soon you can see the wastewater treatment plant through breaks in the forest on your right.

Hammond Trail comes to Hiller Park at 3 7/8 miles, a nice spot for a break. This city park has restrooms, drinking water, picnic tables, and a playground as well as ball fields. A loop trail of about one mile explores the western part of the park, providing access to the shore of Mad River.

Hammond Trail continues south, following sleepy, nature-lined Fischer Road, essentially the access road for the park here. You pass a few houses on the left. then come to Hiller Road. Cross cautiously and find the Hammond Trail, which at 4¼ miles continues south as a separate paved path paralleling residential Fischer Road. Vehicle traffic is light until Fischer Road meets busy School Road at 4½ miles.

Where you meet School Road, it jogs south on Fischer Road briefly. Use caution on this short busy stretch. School Road promptly heads west along with the School Road Multi-Use Trail, which follows School Road to its end on the shore of Mad River. On your right at the southern School Road intersection, Roger's Market offers a chance to grab a snack or drink.

Hammond Trail shares the lightly traveled, unstriped pavement of Fischer Road as it heads south. At 4¾ miles trail and road descend a fairly steep hill down to the Mad River flood plain. The pavement narrows as it passes through agricultural fields.

At 5⅛ miles Fischer Road ends, but the Hammond Trail climbs to cross the big green bridge over Mad River. Despite the intrusive chain-link fence, the bridge offers views up and down the river, a good place to spot shore birds. As the dedicated portion of Hammond Trail descends from the bridge's south end, it comes to its end at Mad River Road at 5¼ miles. A rest bench and bike rack here offers a break.

Mad River Beach County Park (see next trail) is one mile west along Mad River Road. You can also ride rural roads into the city of Arcata. To do so, follow Mad River Road south. When it ends, go left on Upper Bay Road which heads east to the city limits. From there, you'll want to know where in Arcata you want to go.

When you've had a break, retrace your route back to your starting point.

# 38.
# MAD RIVER BEACH AND DUNES

## NINETEEN MILES OF UNBROKEN BEACH

*The steep and rocky shores running from Del Norte County to Trinidad change abruptly at the mouth of Little River. From there a continuous beach stretches south-southwest for 19 miles to the mouth of Humboldt Bay. Most of it is backed by high and low sand dunes that provide a wild and varied habitat for the adventurous hiker, not to mention shelter for the coastal-strand community of plants.*

*An ambitious hiker could start south from Moonstone*

*County Park, ford Little River and hike the entire beach. The major obstacle is the crossing of Mad River. This major stream can be easy to ford in late summer or early fall. During the rest of the year, however, one must head east to the Hammond Trail (see Trail #37), cross the river on Hammond Bridge and return to the beach at Mad River County Park. No obstacles lie from there to the jetty at the mouth of Humboldt Bay.*

*The hike described here explores the beach and dunes around Mad River County Park. The park includes 150 acres south of the river mouth. It provides access to river and ocean fishing, clamming, hiking, horseback riding and (unfortunately) four-wheeling. No developed trail is here, just acres of beach and dunes to explore; you can keep walking along the beach for as long as time and motivation will permit.*

MAD RIVER BEACH AND DUNES:

DISTANCE: 4-mile loop or open-ended beach walk.
TIME: At least 2 hours.
TERRAIN: Long, unbroken beach backed by high dunes.
ELEVATION GAIN/LOSS: 125 feet+/125 feet-.
BEST TIME: Spring for wildflowers, any day that is not foggy for views.
WARNINGS: Watch for killer waves on beach. You may share the beach and dunes with motorized vehicles. Be aware of them. Poison oak may be found in the dune vegetation.
HOW TO GET THERE: Exit Highway 101 onto Janes Road at M.89.05 from north, M.88.6 from south. Go west on Janes Road, then right on Heindon Road for .4 mile. Go left on Miller Lane for .7 mile. Then go right on Mad River Road, coming to Hammond Bridge and the south end of the Hammond Trail in 1.7 miles. The road turns west to reach the parking area and trailhead in 1.1 miles (4 miles from Highway 101).
OTHER ACCESS TO 19 MILE BEACH: Moonstone County Park: Exit Highway 101 at M.98.5.
Little River State Beach: Exit Highway 101 at M.97.4.
Clam Beach County Park: Exit Highway 101 at M.95.8 from north, M.95.5 from south.
Also off Highway 255 near Manila and Samoa.
FURTHER INFO: County Parks (707) 445-7652.
OTHER SUGGESTION: MOUTH OF MAD RIVER is 2 miles north. The estuary is used by hundreds of migratory waterfowl and shorebirds. Snowy plovers nest south of the river mouth. You may also see bald eagles, prairie falcons and Aleutian Canada geese.

From the parking area follow a jeep trail west-northwest through low dunes. You come to the tide line in about 1/8 mile. Head south along the firm sand just beyond the reach of the waves. By ½ mile the beach becomes broader, and the dunes east of the beach are taller. From the one-mile point, much large driftwood lies along the beach. Sandpipers, sanderlings and curlews feed along the water line.

At 1½ miles a pole stands atop the dune nearest the beach; you can use it as a landmark. You can walk south along the beach for another 11 miles, but the described hike follows the beach for 1/8 mile beyond the pole. Where two large driftwood stumps lie at tide line, a double track heads east into the dunes. Follow this to the top of the first dune. From there you can see a high dune to your east with a top covered with Sitka spruce.

Look southeast for the tallest dune in that direction. Your route heads cross-country through the dunes for the top of that 75-foot-tall sand hill. As you walk through an area lush with coastal-strand plants, please try not to trample them. Along with dune grass grow yellow bush lupine, sea rocket,

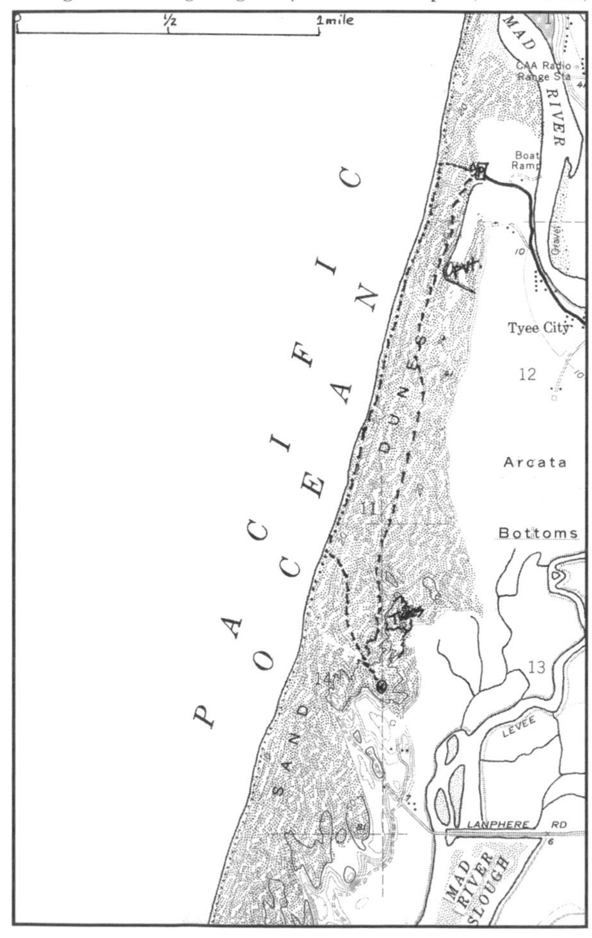

beach strawberry and yarrow.

At 2 miles you are heading up the last incline to the top of the high dune. You reach the top before 2 1/8 miles. It provides fine views (unless you are fogbound). An old ranch sits in a lush green valley to the south. Beyond it is the Nature Conservancy's Lanphere-Christensen Dune Preserve. East of that is Mad River Slough, the ancient mouth of Mad River when it emptied into Humboldt Bay. Beyond the slough lies the north arm of Humboldt Bay. The town of Arcata spreads along its shore. To the east lie the farmlands of the Arcata Bottoms, the Trinity Mountains rising beyond. When it is very clear you can see Trinidad Head to the north.

Your return route goes cross-country through the dunes, heading generally north. Before you leave the high dune, study your route: stay west of the tree-covered dune to the north, and head generally toward the left side of a distant stand of trees near the mouth of Mad River.

Descending the high dune, aim for the west side of the spruce-covered dune, which you reach at 2½ miles. Then head for the trees near the river mouth (15 degrees NNE if you have a compass). At 3 miles is a hollow where bush lupine and beach strawberry thrive. Continuing toward the far stand of trees, you encounter dense vegetation. You might want to detour left to find bare sand for easier walking.

At 3¾ miles a big barn lies to your east. Steer wide of it, because it is surrounded by an electric fence. Continue past the left side of the trees and come to the parking lot at 4 miles.

# 39. ARCATA'S COMMUNITY FOREST

## MODEL FORESTRY SUPPORTS RECREATION

*Few city parks have enough trails to be included in hiking guides, but this is no ordinary city park. Redwood Park and Community Forest, now include 790 acres on the north slope of Fickle Hill, prime redwood-growing land. The City of Arcata acquired the land through several purchases, starting in 1905. In 1955 it was dedicated—the first municipally owned forest in California.*

*Today Redwood Park and Community Forest include 11 miles of trails, many of which are available to equestrians and mountain bikers (see map). Trails are open except when logging occurs in a particular area. In that case the closure is posted. The trails are well used by the residents of Arcata, being no more than a ten-minute walk from downtown or Humboldt State University. When the Arcata Ridge Trail (see Trail #40) is completed, it will cross the Community Forest on a roughly southeast-to-northwest route, using parts of Ridge Loop Trail, Janes Creek Road and Vista Trail.*

*The city is striving to create a model forest. All logging is done to strict environmental standards. Low-impact, balloon-tired vehicles are used. Sustained-yield timber harvesting is the law here. The enhancement of wildlife, watershed and aesthetic values of the forest is a primary goal. Proceeds from logging support recreational facilities in the city.*

*The loop described below samples the best of the trail system in the park. Since bikers and equestrians are not allowed on the first ¾ mile of trail, they should use the Meadow Trailhead, where 14th Street enters the park.*

The parking area is at the end of 13th Street, where a grassy field has picnic tables, a playground and restrooms. Look across the field to a sign, "COMMUNITY FOREST NATURE TRAIL" Climb the steps by the sign and enter a forest of redwood and Sitka spruce. Your trail climbs past huckleberry bushes beneath the forest. By 1/8 mile you encounter the first

ARCATA'S COMMUNITY FOREST

DISTANCE: 6¼ mile loop.
TIME: Two to 4 hours.
TERRAIN: Up and down steep canyons of a north-slope redwood forest.
ELEVATION GAIN/LOSS: 1200 feet+/1200 feet-. Add 80 feet/80 feet- from Meadow Trailhead.
BEST TIME: Anytime.
WARNINGS: Bikes and horses restricted (see map).
HOW TO GET THERE: Exit Highway 101 at Arcata, on north at Sunset Avenue (M.87.2), on south at Samoa exit (M.85.5). Go east on 11th Street (hikers) or 14th Street (bikers: Meadow Trailhead), following signs to Redwood Park. Main parking area is at end of road.
FURTHER INFO: City of Arcata Environmental Services (707) 822-8184. Find a downloadable trail map at www.cityofarcata.org
OTHER SUGGESTION: AZALEA STATE RESERVE provides a mile of trails through dense stands of fragrant azalea in spring. Exit McKinleyville South at M.89.8 from south, M.90.1 from north, and go east on North Bank Road.

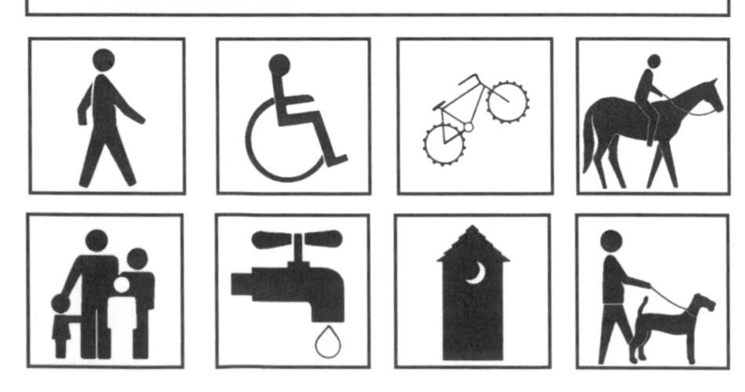

of many big stumps left from the logging activities of the late 1800s. In 200 feet, a canyon lies on the left. The trail climbs along its edge.

In 300 feet the unsigned Short Trail forks right. You return by it at the end of the described hike. Now go left on the Nature Trail. Descend across a small bridge, then veer left on a bridge over tiny Campbell Creek, climbing steps on the other side.

Jog left to descend again, passing a huge stump at ⅜ mile. Descend by trail and steps to cross a side canyon. The trail descends along Campbell Creek. Cross a bridge over another side canyon and come to a boardwalk at ½ mile. Cross a third side canyon bridge and come to a junction.

The end of the Nature Trail goes left, but our described hike goes straight on the Sitka Trail. It roller coasters over boardwalks, steps and bridges. You can no longer see the old skid, or corduroy, road in the creek bed, but imagine a dozen oxen pulling a giant log down the creek. The trail climbs gradually to a rest bench at ⅝ mile. Descend to meet the Meadow Trail. People on horses or bikes should come up the hill to meet the trail here, just ⅛ mile from 14th Street.

Logging in Mendocino, 1870 — Packard

From the junction, climb the steep hill to the ¾-mile point, where you go right to continue on Meadow Trail, climbing moderately. You are heading east along the north boundary of Redwood Park. The trail steepens, then continues its steady climb. The trail levels briefly in a clearing where redwood violets, redwood sorrel and self-heal grow. You climb gradually to the next junction.

At 1⅛ miles you meet two dirt roads. The second one is Fickle Hill Grade. (You can turn right for a shorter hike of 2 miles.) Go left and head north, passing the Big Rock Trail before 1¼ miles. Follow Fickle Hill Grade as it veers right and heads east, descending slightly. Red-flowering currant, trillium, coltsfoot and iris grow along the trail. Berries include elder-, salmon- and thimbleberries. You climb gradually again from 1⅜ miles.

At 1½ miles you cross a fork of Jolly Giant Creek, then climb quickly to a junction. Fickle Hill Grade ends here, but you continue on the same road surface, now called Community Forest Loop Road. You pass under the power line and climb through an area planted with young trees. Descend to meet the new Powerline Trail on your left, then cross Jolly Giant Creek.

After the creek you climb north. The trail levels at a junction with Ridge Road around 1¾ miles. (You can go left on Community Forest Loop for a shorter hike of 4½ miles.) Our described route goes right on Ridge Road and climbs, passing Ridge Loop Trail on the right, then Lower Janes Creek Trail on the left at 2 miles. After a steep hill, you meet the Upper Janes Creek Trail on the left, which you follow. (You can go right for a loop one mile longer or to connect with the south end of the new Arcata Ridge Trail.)

The Upper Janes Creek Trail climbs for 250 feet, then levels. Look for starflower and red clintonia beneath abundant sword, lady and deer ferns. Descend through a swampy area where skunk cabbage thrive. After a brief climb, you descend toward Janes Creek at 2¼ miles, promptly crossing tiny Janes Creek on a bridge. The trail switches left and climbs above the creek. Wild ginger and deer fern thrive in the moist habitat. Around 2³/8 miles you switchback right

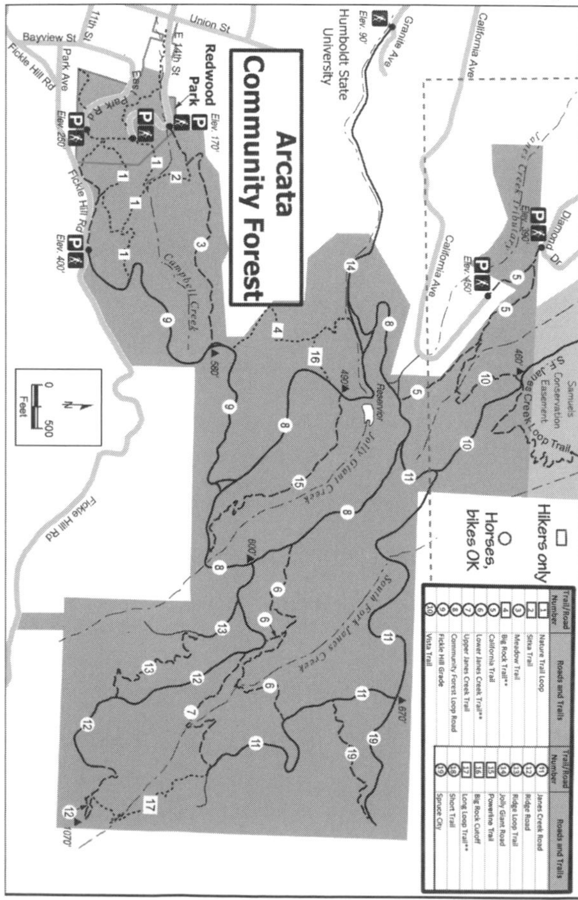

and climb steeply through healthy second-growth forest.

Meet Janes Creek Road before 2½ miles. Turn left and climb through an area planted with redwood and Douglas fir seedlings. In 250 feet you reach the summit of your hike, 900 feet in elevation. If you are tired, it might please you to know that most of the return hike is downhill. Descend generally north. Violets, irises, trilliums and red and evergreen huckleberry bushes brighten the path in spring.

You pass several small clearcut areas, then pass the top end of Lower Janes Creek Trail on your left. Pass the upper end of Spruce City Trail on your right, then descend to its lower end before 3 1/8 miles. Your trail descends generally west, with views of the coast north of Arcata. The sunny clearings along the road provide an ample harvest of berries in summer: red and black huckleberries, blackberries, thimbleberries, salmonberries, elderberries, salal berries, currants and Oregon grapes.

You meet the power line cut around 3½ miles. Descend a steep hill. After you cross Janes Creek, your trail leaves the clearing, crosses a feeder creek, and climbs for 1/8 mile. The trail levels and meets Vista Trail at 3¾ miles. Go left on Janes Creek Road and descend a steep hill. (Vista Trail and this part of Janes Creek Road will become part of Arcata Ridge Trail.) The road then climbs briefly to end at Community Forest Loop Road.

You head straight (west). After passing a large water tank at 4 miles, the road descends past the California Trail on your right. Continue a gradual descent, with private houses on the right. On your left is the canyon of Jolly Giant Creek. Your track bends left beyond 4¼ miles and descends into the canyon. At an unmarked junction you veer left and head east. (The right fork leads to the HSU campus.)

The trail climbs along Jolly Giant Creek for 1/8 mile, then crosses the earth-fill dam of Jolly Giant Reservoir at 4½ miles, where a picnic table offers a break. Ascend through the forest to the new Powerline Trail on your left, then to the Big Rock Cutoff Trail at 4 5/8 miles (hikers can go right for a shorter but steeper route). The Community Forest Loop Road climbs for over ¼ mile before it tops a hill and descends to Fickle Hill Grade at 5 miles.

Turn right and retrace your steps of the early part of the hike, descending to the Meadow Trail at 5 3/8 miles. Bikers and equestrians should descend the Meadow Trail to the starting point. Hikers stay on Fickle Hill Grade, climbing for 150 feet before descending in a big loop around the lush headwaters of Campbell Creek.

The descent steepens at 5½ miles. At 5 5/8 miles you descend gradually around a big bend left, where grand fir mixes with the redwoods. At 5¾ miles you climb briefly, coming to a water tank, then to Fickle Hill Road. Immediately veer right onto Short Trail and descend through the forest.

You join the Nature Trail Loop at 6 miles. Go left, returning to the parking area at 6¼ miles.

## 40.
## ARCATA RIDGE TRAIL

### NEW MULTI-USE TRAIL WILL TRAVERSE ARCATA SOUTH TO NORTH

*A work in progress, slated to open fall 2014 for north half, fall 2015 for south half. When complete Arcata Ridge Trail will traverse Sunny Brae Forest, Arcata Community Forest, and the Samuels conservation easement to the north.*

For now Arcata Ridge Trail climbs the 18 concrete steps from the bend on Margaret Lane, entering the Sunny Brae Community Forest. By late 2015, a parking area and a more bike-friendly start to the trail will be built to the east. Pass a large green water tank, then climb northeast through second-growth forest of redwood, Douglas fir. Sitka spruce and hardwoods. Understory plants include huckleberry, rhododendron and tanoak.

You meet the Beith Creek Loop on the right. Arcata Ridge Trail switchbacks left around 1/8 mile, climbing moderately west, then northwest. Beyond ¼ mile a power line is on your left. Wrap right around the site of a new water tank on your right to climb gently east. At 3/8 mile your trail branches right from the old skid trail it was following.

At ½ mile your trail switchbacks left to climb north, soon crossing the same old skid trail. Climb gradually then contour through the forest.

Beyond 5/8 mile you come to The Hub where you again meet the skid trail and also the Directional Trail on your right. The latter, signed "CHALLENGING STEEP TERRAIN," descends to meet the Beith Creek Loop near where it meets the Arcata Ridge Trail below.

Arcata Ridge Trail switchbacks left to head north on a gentle ascent. Soon you switchback right to climb moderately southeast. Around ¾ mile you meet the Schmidbauer, an old logging road that has been improved. It runs generally northwest to southeast. A right turn would descend to Beith Creek Loop.

Turn left on a gradual climb. By 7/8 mile your trail bends left on a gentle descent. Before one mile you cross a 70-foot railroad flatcar bridge over East Fork Grotzman Creek, lined with wildflowers in spring.

You come to a level spot just beyond one mile, from which Schmidbauer Road descends west leading to a dead-end in about ½ mile. From here, Arcata Ridge Trail will ascend steeply northeast and north to cross Fickle Hill Road around 1 3/8 miles. The crossing, possibly through an underground culvert, will be above Boynton Prairie Road in the upper 1700 block. From there it will descend into Arcata Community Forest on new tread, crossing Jolly Giant Creek near its headwaters.

ART will descend, then contour across another fork of Jolly Giant Creek before descending to meet, then follow Ridge Loop Trail, descending through the forest.

When Ridge Loop Trail ends at Ridge Road around 2 miles, turn left to descend Ridge Road to its end at Community Forest Loop Road beyond 2 1/8 miles. Turn right and descend the latter past Lower Janes Creek Trail on the right, then under the power line. Community Forest Loop Road descends a ridge. After a steep descent, turn right on Janes Creek Road before 2 5/8 miles, rounding the teadwaters of a seasonal creek.

At the next junction you want to turn left on Vista Trail. It descends along a ridgetop, approaching the Community Forest's north boundary. As the Vista Trail turns sharply left, Arcata Ridge Trail continues northwest, soon coming to the Community Forest's northern boundary at 3 miles, with the Samuels Conservation easement beyond. Eventually ART will continue down the same ridge, heading generally north-

### ARCATA RIDGE TRAIL

DISTANCE: 9 3/8 miles round trip when trail is complete. For Sunny Brae Forest 2 1/8 miles round trip. For South Fork Janes Creek Loop: 2-mile loop.
TIME: Two to 4 hours.
TERRAIN: Climbs through forest to the ridge, descends through forest to north end at West End Road.
ELEVATION GAIN/LOSS: Sunny Brae Forest: 485 feet+/485 feet-. South Fork Janes Creek Loop: 320 feet-/ 320 feet+. Total elevation change for Arcata Ridge Trail still undetermined.
BEST TIME: Anytime.
WARNINGS: Cyclists and hikers must watch for and yield to equestrians
HOW TO GET THERE: Exit Highway 101 at M.86.2 from north, M.85.5 from south onto Samoa Blvd. Go east on Samoa Blvd., then left on Buttermilk Lane. Then go left on Margaret Lane to parking.
For South Fork Janes Creek Loop: Follow California Avenue (north of Sunset Avenue) to its east end. Also a trailhead on Diamond Drive.
FURTHER INFO: City of Arcata Environmental Services (707) 822-8184.

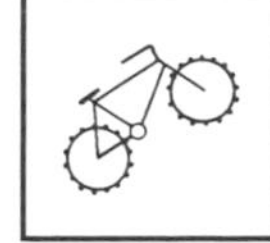

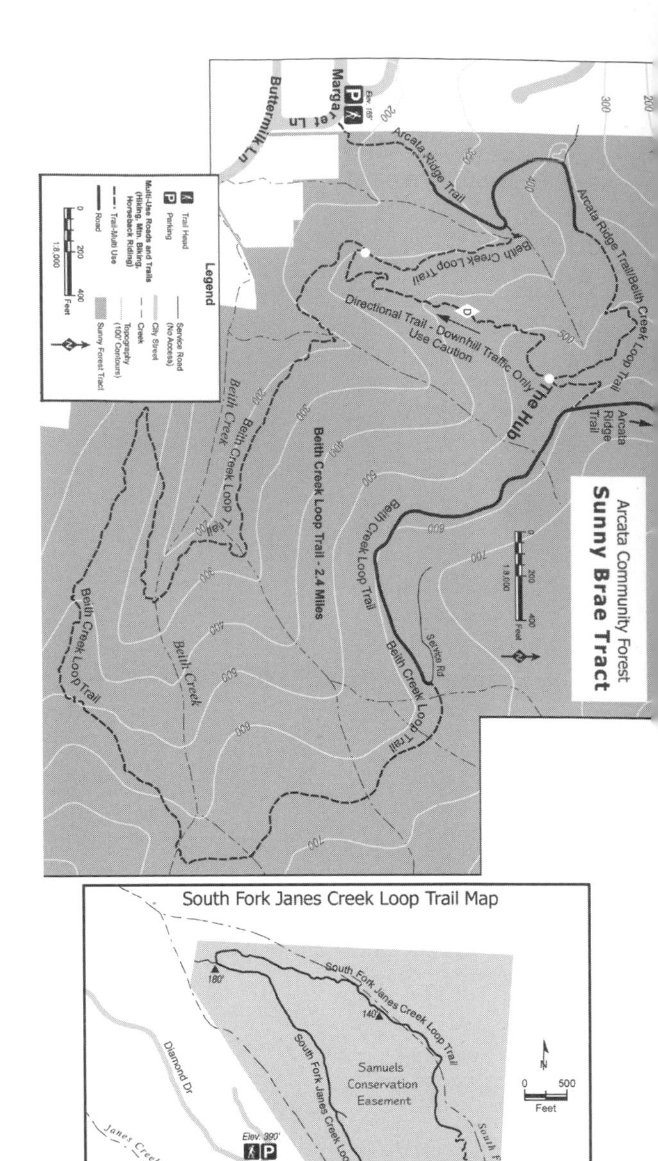


west to end at West End Road at 4¾ miles, just beyond the northwest corner of Humboldt State University. At press time the new South Fork Janes Creek Loop Trail had just opened, leaving Vista Trail near the northern boundary of the Community Forest. The right fork of the new loop starts with about ½ mile of single track, closed to horses until the new trail is seasoned, descending 320 feet along South Fork Janes Creek before climbing along the ridge on a gravel road to return to Vista Trail at 2 miles.

# 41. ARCATA MARSH AND WILDLIFE SANCTUARY

## RESTORED WETLANDS PROVIDE FINE BIRDING

*Having first hiked here in 1987, I'm excited to see how the habitats at Arcata Marsh have matured, with the vegetation grown in and the web of life well established, though still constantly evolving. Because the Arcata Marsh Interpretive Center offers such valuable enhancement to the complex story at work here, we now start our trail report at the Center. Of course you can still start your hike from the foot of I Street if you prefer. There are currently 5 3/8 miles of walking and biking paths here.*

*In 1979 the City of Arcata created its Marsh and Wildlife Sanctuary, reclaiming the area along South I Street that had become an industrial wasteland left over from the post-World War II logging boom. The Sanctuary, considered a model wetlands restoration project, serves as an integral part of Arcata's wastewater treatment system.*

*The city first built three freshwater marshes and a lake at the site. They planted the marshes with sedge, sago pondweed and ditch grass, and stocked the lake with rainbow trout. Today the 307 acres of wetlands, double the original acreage, are a haven for some 300 bird species. Salmon and trout raised in the wetlands are used to stock local creeks. The complex was expanded with restored salt marsh and several new ponds. Amateur birders will find the 8:30 a.m. Saturday morning walks led by local Audubon Society members a wonderful introduction to the birds of the Sanctuary. They leave from the end of I Street.*

*The Arcata Marsh Interpretive Center, wheelchair accessible, open daily, provides detailed educational displays about the environments of the marshes and the systems at work there. In addition, marsh tours are offered every Saturday at*

*2 p.m., rain or shine, from the Interpretive Center. Each year about 150,000 visitors enjoy the many aspects of nature in the Arcata Marsh and Wildlife Sanctuary by birdwatching, walking, jogging, fishing, boating and picnicking—all within seven blocks of downtown Arcata.*

Enjoy the 250-foot path from the parking lot to the Interpretive Center, landscaped with native plants. Stop into the Center to view its excellent exhibits and the dramatic views from inside. Even when the Center is closed, the pleasant wraparound deck offers fine views of the salt marsh trails on the site of an old plywood mill.

From the center follow the path 150 feet, then go left at the first fork, start of the Log Pond Loop (officially the Butcher's Slough Trail). You pass Sitka spruce, western

ARCATA MARSH AND WILDLIFE SANCTUARY:

DISTANCE: 2¾-mile loop, plus optional 1¾-mile semi-loop in southeast corner.
TIME: At least one hour. It is easy to spend hours here when the birdwatching is good.
TERRAIN: Mostly level around fresh- and salt-water marshlands.
BEST TIME: Audubon-led walks every Saturday at 8:30 a.m. Low tides in spring and fall best for birding. Friends of Arcata Marsh lead hikes every Saturday at 2 p.m.
WARNINGS: Open sunrise to sunset. Be quiet along the trail, or you may be the target of a bird watcher's wrath. Quiet dogs on leash only please.
HOW TO GET THERE: Exit Highway 101 at M.86.2 from north, M.85.5 from south onto Samoa Blvd/Highway 255 going west for .9 mile. Turn left on G Street. Go .4 mile to Marsh Interpretive Center parking on right.
FURTHER INFO: Arcata Marsh Interpretive Center (707)826-2359. Audubon Society (707)822-6918. City of Arcata: (707)822-5951.
OTHER SUGGESTIONS: ARCATA ARCHITECTURAL TOUR: A morning of birding might well be followed by an afternoon of touring fine old Victorian buildings. Maps of the self-guided tour are available at the Chamber of Commerce, 1635 Heindon Road, (707) 822-3619.

redcedar, and shore pines, with willows most abundant. The understory includes wild radish, mustard, bedstraw, plantain, wild geranium and poison hemlock. Soon red-flowering currant, a favorite of hummingbirds, grows fifteen feet tall on your right.

In 250 feet you reach a viewing platform with comfy benches. It overlooks the south end of the former log pond, jammed with cattails. (If cattails grow there, the water is fresh.) Follow the trail north, with the log pond on your right and Butcher's Slough, the tidal portion of Jolly Giant Creek, mostly hidden by the vegetation on your left: coyote brush and blackberries, both California native and invasive Himalayan.

Beyond 1/8 mile you pass another rest bench as open water shows in the middle of the pond. It's a good place to spot black-crowned night herons in winter when they roost in willows around the pond. Continue to an old concrete fish ladder at ¼ mile, which has been taken over by red-legged frogs, duckweed and pennywort.

In 250 feet your trail forks. For a short hike, you can go right to reach the parking area in 1/8 mile or complete the Butcher's Slough Loop (5/8 mile total). Our described hike goes left, crossing a bridge oner Butcher's Slough. Your trail veers left to head southwest paralleling I Street, following the rails of an old railroad spur. Beyond 3/8 mile you cross a more obvious railroad track and come to I Street. Turn left and walk the road shoulder briefly.

Look for a trail across the street on your right. Our described hike cautiously crosses I Street and heads north on that path. (If you are pressed for time, you can continue straight on the path along the left shoulder of I Street.) The trail heads north along the relatively recent brackish pond on your left, paralleling the railroad tracks beyond a smaller pond on your right. The brackish pond was built with three islands that break up its open water, creating more habitat for birds and other wildlife.

Before 5/8 mile the trail veers left, following the shore of the brackish pond. Cattails grow on the right and teasels, lupine and mustard line the path. When the path veers left again, you pass a bird blind, then come to a spur that forks right. The spur heads northwest past another pond to the northern extreme of marsh property.

We head south with the brackish pond on the left. On your right a grassland is evolving into a salt marsh as bay waters now flood it during high tides. Egrets sometimes hunt there. Beyond 3/8 mile you leave the brackish pond and follow the shore of Gearheart Marsh (signed "WASTEWATER—NO DIRECT CONTACT)," also dotted with islands. Both it and Allen Marsh to the east were named for two local professors who helped establish the marsh project.

At one mile your trail ends at lower I Street. Our described hike turns right on a trail that parallels I Street briefly, then

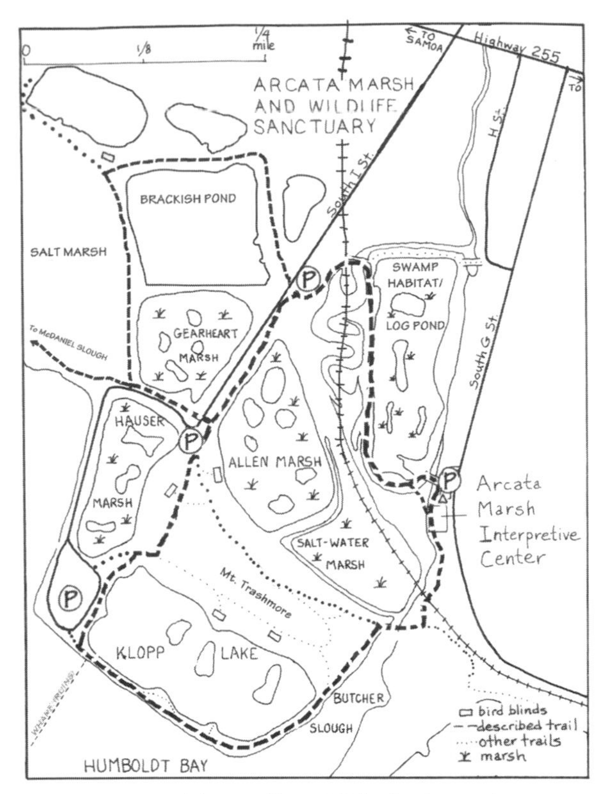


continues west with a well established salt marsh on your left and the grasslands evolving to salt marsh on your right. Where the path bends right, two well placed benches provide a sweeping view of Humboldt Bay.

Follow the trail to its end in about 300 feet to overlook McDaniel Slough at the spot where it was recently opened up by heavy equipment to allow greater tidal flow into and out of the evolving salt marsh to your north. Thanks to the recent breaching, you will often see a large flow of fast-moving water here. Before the breach the flow had been barely more than a trickle. This is one of the ways the Arcata Marsh lands are managed to create better habitat, both for birds and for the natural wetlands cycles that are being recreated.

Retrace your steps to the southwest corner of Gearheart Marsh, then continue along the shoulder of I Street to the middle parking area at 1⅝ miles. Allen Marsh is straight ahead. Unlike Gearheart Marsh which is fairly open, Allen Marsh is densely bordered by alders and willows, with willow and cattail islands breaking up the open water. Still, seen here in one day were mallard, pintail, cinnamon teal, shoveler and bufflehead. In late March 2014 an Anna's hummingbird nest was visible in a willow tree over the edge of the marsh. In just two weeks from hatching, the young fledge and go out on their own!

Our described hike heads southwest. If you are running

short of time, turning left on the trail that heads southeast along Allen Marsh allows a ½ mile return to the Interpretive Center and parking lot. On the trail southwest, at first tall Bishop pines and spruce hide Hauser Marsh on your right. Elderberry bushes grow there too. Soon a bench on the right offers a view over Hauser Marsh to the Arcata Bottoms.

Continuing southwest you meet a trail on the left that explores Mount Trashmore. At 40 feet above sea level, the hill is the highest point in the Arcata Marsh and Wildlife Sanctuary, created when the county landfill was closed and sealed in 1973. Continue southwest past another bench. Descend slightly then veer left to overlook expansive Klopp Lake. Continue along Klopp's shore. As Hauser Marsh ends on the right, you pass the parking area and a vault toilet at the foot of I Street. Tall Bishop pines shelter picnic tables in this pleasant spot.

Veer left and climb steps to join the main trail from the nearby lot at 2 miles. As it heads southeast on the rise between Klopp Lake and Humboldt Bay, you can see the rotting pilings of the Arcata Wharf, built in 1855, which extended over two miles into Humboldt Bay. At high tide the mudflats are submerged, but at low tide they are busy with feeding curlews, dowitchers, godwits, willets, egrets, herons, sanderlings and sandpipers. On the lake float surf scoters, cormorants, coots and various gulls (seven or more species) and ducks. Pass benches on your left facing the lake, with stationary binoculars just beyond. River otters are often seen here as well.

At 2¼ miles your path bends left. The mouth of Butcher Slough lies on your right, with the wastewater treatment plant in the background. Pass another observation bench, then lupine and a squat apple tree. The first fork is at 2³/8 miles. The path on the left leads to Mt. Trashmore overlooking the lake. You continue on the main path past No Name Pond, then past another bench to a "Y" intersection at 2½ mile. A tree in the salt marsh before you is a common place to spot black-shouldered kites. Marsh wrens also live in the marsh.

Turn right and head east, crossing a bridge over Butcher's Slough, a great place to spot egrets and other birds at low tide. You quickly come to a fork. If you want to extend your hike, go straight to explore a salt marsh and oxidation ponds at the south end of the marsh complex. That semi-loop adds 1¾ miles to the total. Our described hike goes left at the fork, crossing the railroad tracks and meandering toward the Interpretive Center. This part of Butcher's Slough is a good place to spot river otters or their sign. Otters are at the top of the Humboldt Bay watershed's food chain.

The pilings between here and the Center once supported a plywood mill that closed in 1969. What a magnificent transformation has occurred since! Continue up the path along the slough. You come to the parking lot and Interpretive Center paved trail at 2¾ miles.

# 42.
# HIKSHARI' MULTI-USE

## FIRST LEG OF EUREKA'S WATERFRONT TRAIL

*From a humble beginning in 1984, when the City of Eureka created the 104-acres Elk River Wildlife Sanctuary and 5/8 mile of trail near its wastewater treatment plant, the newly dubbed Hikshari' Trail now runs 1½ miles along Eureka's western waterfront. Incorporating the old Elk River Wildlife Sanctuary Trail off Hilfiker Lane, the Hikshari' Trail runs from Herrick Avenue in the south to Truesdale Avenue in the north. Eureka will expand this trail north and east to create the 6½-mile Waterfront Trail, running on or near the city's entire waterfront and ending at Tydd Street in Myrtletown. While completing the entire trail will take some time, all the planning has been done and a significant amount of funding obtained. The next section, from Truesdale Avenue to West Del Norte Street will likely begin construction in 2016. The Eureka Boardwalk from C Street to about G Street is already in place.*

*Hikshari' Multi-use Trail provides a great start to that ambitious plan and offers an enjoyable stretch of nature along the shores of Elk River and Humboldt Bay. Elk River, Humboldt Bay's largest tributary, empties into Humboldt Bay near the Hilfiker Lane access. With help from the undeveloped sand spit west of Elk River, the new trail offers sweeping views over Humboldt Bay to its mouth and pockets of natural habitat where you might least expect to find them. The Wiyot people native to the Humboldt Bay area called the village area near the Elk River estuary Hikshari'.*

*While you can start your excursion from any one of the three access points, I prefer the way the scenery unfurls from south to north, like the Elk River it follows.*

From the parking lot head northeast on the paved path. In 200 feet it swings left away from the freeway to meet a paved road at a dark green gate. Follow it west past yarrow, coyote brush, silverweed, plantain, rushes, blackberry, mustard, and invasive periwinkle and pampas grass. Beyond 1/8 mile you cross a ditch lined with ceanothus, twinberry and poison hemlock. Continue west past wax myrtle and horsetail. You come to a pond lined with cattails behind a chain link fence on your right, where you might see ducks.

Stay left at a fork, passing rest benches and an information kiosk. A salt marsh lies on your left. The Wiyot people native to this area still use the area and consider it sacred. Please pass through here with a sense of stewardship. Starting in 1886 the Bucksport and Elk River Railroad passed through here, hauling timber cut upriver around the town of Falk (see Trail #43). The railroad shut down in 1952.

HIKSHARI' MULTI-USE

DISTANCE: 3 miles round trip, 3½ with side trip to Elk River railroad bridge.
TIME: One to two hours.
TERRAIN: Level ground surrounded by marsh and estuary.
BEST TIME: Spring and early summer for wildflowers. Anytime is good.
NOTE: Wheelchair access is best at the northern trailhead, but possible at the others.
WARNINGS: Do not trespass on adjacent private lands. No firearms, vehicles or camping. Pets on leash only.
HOW TO GET THERE: HERRICK AVENUE ACCESS: Exit Highway 101 at M.75.0 from north, M.74.9 from south onto Herrick Avenue. Parking is directly west of the freeway in the Park & Ride lot.
HILFIKER LANE ACCESS: Turn west off Highway 101 onto Hilfiker Lane (south end of Eureka at M.76.0). Go .5 mile to parking area to right of entrance to Wastewater Treatment Plant.
TRUESDALE AVENUE ACCESS: Turn west off Highway 101 at M.76.4 onto Truesdale Avenue (south of Mall). Trailhead at end of street.
FURTHER INFO: City of Eureka (707) 441-4184.
OTHER SUGGESTIONS: OTHER PARTS OF THE WATERFRONT TRAIL can be found between C (drive to the foot of C Street in Old Town) and G streets on the EUREKA BOARDWALK and at EUREKA OR PALCO MARSH (turn west off Highway 101 onto Del Norte Street at M.76.8 and go .4 mile to parking on left), will link with Hikshari' Trail in the next construction phase. At press time, a ¼-mile loop explores the bay shore; a longer trail just east of the railroad tracks explores the edge of a freshwater marsh. Local Audubon-led BIRD WALKS occur here third Sunday of each month, 9 a.m. FORT HUMBOLDT STATE HISTORIC PARK, ¼ mile north of Hilfiker Lane on east side of Highway 101, was established in 1853 to control raids by local Indians. Today it has a small museum, picnic area and-accessible restrooms. Call (707) 445-6567.

Continue west on the broad track, passing two Sitka spruce and a Bishop pine on your right at ¼ mile. Your paved trail crosses railroad tracks (inactive), then veers right. A gravel track parallels the tracks heading south, described at the end of this report.

Follow the paved trail onto a small bridge over a side slough, from which you have a good view of Elk River watershed to the south-southeast. Soon the Elk River and its sloughs appear on the left of your trail, with Humboldt Bay beyond. Much bird life can be seen here, including ducks, egrets and herons in the estuary. Lupine grows beside the trail. An interpretive panel shows the pattern of folds and faults (buckles and fractures) that created the local landscape. The view south to Humboldt Hill and southwest to Table Bluff shows that the accordion-like shape of Humboldt Bay is a result of this folding and faulting.

Hikshari' Trail meanders north, with Elk River Slough and shell middens in low dunes on the left, a willow and wax myrtle thicket on the right. The sounds of surf increase, although freeway noise can still be heard.

Around 3/8 mile an interpretive panel describes wildflowers in the area: yellow sand verbena, Humboldt Bay wallflower, beach morning glory, beach strawberry, dune goldenrod, dune sedge, slough sedge, dune rush, beach pea, beach layia and native dune grass. Continue past a small bench overlooking the slough.

At ½ mile, lupine and the low-growing yellow and white flower johnny tuck grow in low dunes on your left. Your trail passes through dense vegetation where alder, coffeeberry, evergreen and red huckleberry, rock rose, coast buckwheat, and low-growing ceanothus join the mix of vegetation. Osprey, kites, hawks and northern harriers often hunt overhead. River otters are also sometimes seen. Around 5/8 mile a volunteer spur trail on the right popular with birders explores the woodlands and wetlands. An interpretive panel on the paved trail describes birds that live in and visit the area. Pass another volunteer path on the left which goes to the shore of Mad River Slough. Sitka spruce and invasive cotoneaster join the dense thicket of vegetation.

Beyond ¾ mile you meet the graveled south end of the Elk River Loop Trail on your left. Beyond it you can see the red-roofed Coast Guard building on Samoa Peninsula on the horizon west-northwest. Your paved trail continues north, now with the wastewater plant on the right peeking through the vegetation. Wild fennel and native geranium join the plant mix.

Pass the north end of the Elk River Loop Trail, then come to the parking lot at the end of Hilfiker Lane at one mile, where picnic tables, benches and a bike rack cluster around an interpretive sign. Bishop and shore pines grow nearby.

Paved Hikshari' Trail continues north, with Hilfiker Lane on the right. Marsh restoration is in progress on the left. Arrowgrass, pickleweed and salt grass have been planted in the tidal zone, and gum plant and sea lavender above the tide line. You soon follow a chain link fence on your left. The fence ends by 1 1/8 miles. Continue north along the shore with a strip of wild fennel and coyote brush on your left. Around 1¼ miles you pass the remnants of an old railroad trestle that once ran out the sand spit. Just beyond, Elk River Slough empties into Humboldt Bay.

On your right, just beyond where Hilfiker Lane turns east toward the highway, you pass more trail parking, this lot graveled and with more picnic tables. On your left a short

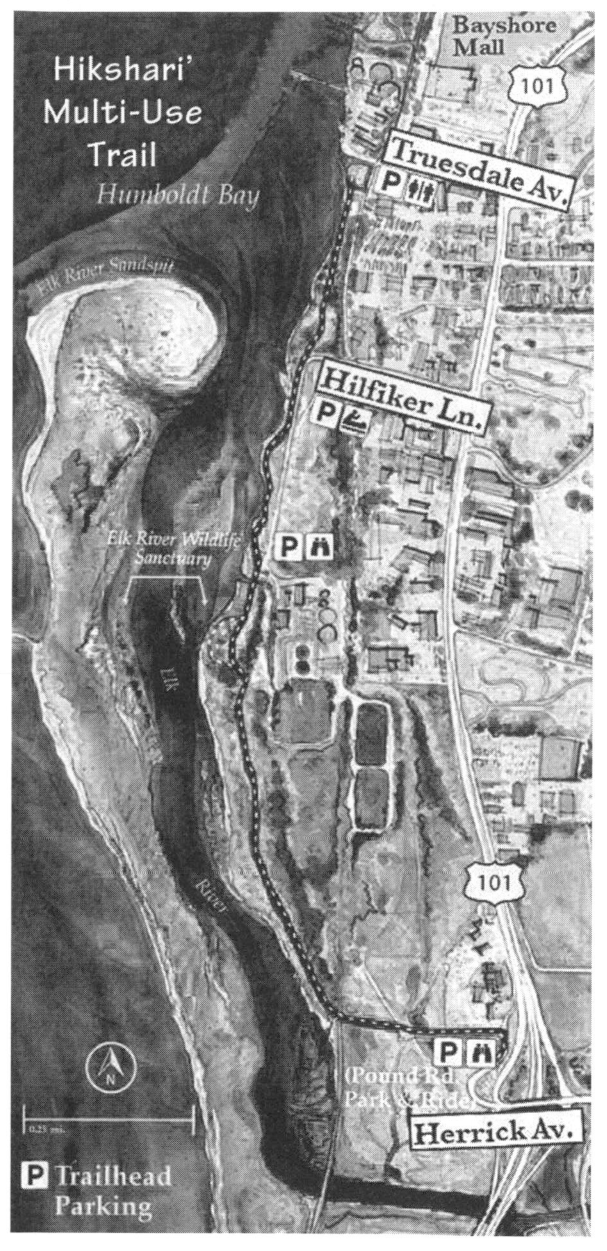

trail leads to the shore near the old railroad bridge. Hikshari' Trail continues north, in 300 feet coming to Bishop pines growing on your left along the edge of the Humboldt Bay. A rest bench there offers a good spot to contemplate a relatively wild span of the bay.

The trail continues north near the shore. At 1½ miles you meet the first of several picnic tables in a crushed gravel strip beside the bay. A restroom is on the right, beside the parking lot. This was the site of Bucksport in the 1850s and '60s, founded by David Buck, a member of the 1849 Josiah Gregg-L.K. Wood party who were among the first Euro-Americans to walk to Humboldt Bay. The next stretch of trail to be built to the north will be among the most challenging parts of the Waterfront Trail to complete because of the extensive industrial and commercial area it will traverse. But look at the extensive progress already created by the Hikshari' Trail!

When you are ready, retrace your steps south along the trail. After you pass the paved parking lot near the wastewater treatment plant, consider taking the signed Elk River Loop Trail that soon forks right. That gravel path heads southwest toward the Coast Guard Headquarters, promptly veering left past shore pines, willows and coyote brush. It meanders south along the estuary shore with woodlands on the left. You pass decaying conifer stumps, probably Sitka spruce, cut long ago. Soon a small bench on your right overlooks the estuary and Humboldt Bay beyond. Coast silk-tassel grows in the woodlands nearby. Beyond 1/8 mile the gravel trail veers left away from the shore, passing lupine and tall coyote brush. Before ¼ mile the gravel loop ends at the paved trail. Turn right to head south on the paved path.

When you get to the railroad tracks, consider one more side trip. You can follow a gravel trail south along either side of the overgrown railroad tracks. The path on the west side of the tracks is best. It is slightly less than ¼ mile to the Elk River railroad bridge. While the river is still tidal here, you can look upstream and ponder its journey from the hills to the east. West of the bridge, Elk River makes a big bend right to head north to its estuary and mouth. The volunteer trail continues south along the tracks, but we return to Hikshari' Trail and follow it east to the Herrick Road parking lot.

# 43.
# ELK RIVER TO HEADWATERS FOREST
## THROUGH FALK GHOST TOWN TO VIRGIN STANDS

*Visit a corner of the old-growth forest that was the centerpiece of more than 14 years of protests, civil disobediance and controversy, beginning in 1986 and running full tilt into 1999, with repercussions continuing for another decade. You may have heard of Julia "Butterfly" Hill, who gained fame by living for two years and a week perched 180 feet up in an old-growth redwood she dubbed Luna. That was here. Hill was just the most famous, and one of the most articulate, of many tree sitters occupying ancient trees in the Headwater Forest owned by Pacific Lumber Company (PALCO), which had long been Humboldt County's largest employer.*

*That venerable Humboldt County company, which had managed its vast timber holdings sustainably, was the object of a hostile take over by Texas financier Charles Hurwitz, who sold millions of dollars in junk bonds to purchase the privately held, greatly undervalued corporation. Sustainability went out the window when Hurwitz took over as PALCO doubled the annual harvest, trying to cut timber fast enough to pay off the vast debts incurred to buy it. It was that rapid acceleration of the harvest of old growth that led to the years of protests. The civil disobediance culminated in a 1996 protest of 6000 people where 1000 were arrested, and a 1997 protest of 9000 souls where only two were arrested. It was not until 2009 that the last two tree sitters were convinced to come down.*

*We are glad that 3088 acres of the ancient forests were saved, but the back room political dealing that made it happen was extremely controversial and smells quite rotten. After conservation groups urged that the state of California purchase the virgin forests, the political maneuvering and deal making began. Hurwitz claimed he had no intention of selling, but engaged in off and on negotiations and grandstanding that ultimately guaranteed him the princely sum of $480 million for 7472 acres of the Headwater Forest, only about 40% of which was truly old growth. In a truly just society, the virgin forests would have been seized from Hurwitz as compensation for the $1.6 billion government bailout of his failed United Savings and Loan, the largest government bail out of a savings and loan to that time. In 2009 Hurwitz was sued for fraud in the Headwaters buy-out deal. The plaintiffs wanted $380 million, but ended up with a settlement of $4 million that did little more than cover their court costs and let Hurwitz off the hook for running Humboldt County's most venerable company into bankruptcy.*

*Since it's all history now, you may as well visit the only public trail into the Headwaters Forest. While it doesn't reach the biggest, most intact stands of ancient groves, it still offers a pleasant hike that eventually leads to some large redwoods. You can see more of the ancient groves if you sign up for one of BLM's guided hikes into Headwaters Forest via the Salmon Pass Trailhead.*

*Speaking of history, the most accessible portion of the Elk River Trail passes through the logging ghost town of Falk about a mile from the trailhead. Falk was established in 1884, quickly growing to a company milltown of 400. Lumber cut at the Falk mill was hauled to Eureka on the Bucksport and Elk River Railroad, then loaded onto ships. By 1937 most of the nearby timber had been cut, and the mill closed. A few residents remained in Falk into the 1940s. After the land was bought by PALCO, insurance liability concerns prompted them to bulldoze and burn most of Falk's remaining buildings in 1979. Still, the few remnants remaining add interest and intrigue to this hike.*

ELK RIVER TO HEADWATERS FOREST:

DISTANCE: Up to 10½ miles round trip, or 2¼ miles round trip to Falk townsite.
TIME: Four or 5 hours, one hour round trip to Falk.
TERRAIN: Lush second-growth river canyon, then ascends steeply into virgin forest.
ELEVATION GAIN/LOSS: 1440 feet+/1440 feet-
BEST TIME: Spring for wildflowers. Offers a good trek year-round, although the upper end often has slippery mud after rains.
WARNINGS: Lock your car and leave no valuables. Break-ins have occurred at trailhead. Watch for nettles. Dogs allowed only to end of road. No fishing, swimming, fires, horses, nor guns.
HOW TO GET THERE: Exit Highway 101 at M.75.0 from north, M.74.9 from south at Elk River Road. Turn right and go 6 miles on Elk River Road to its end and trailhead parking.
FURTHER INFO: Bureau of Land Management (707)825-2300.
OTHER SUGGESTIONS: On the drive to the trailhead, look for TWO COVERED BRIDGES across the river below the road. You can also get to HEADWATERS FOREST RESERVE on guided hikes from the southern Salmon Pass Trailhead near Fortuna. Call BLM to sign up for a guided hike.

The Elk River Trail, a paved road at start, descends gently east from the trailhead, following the South Fork Elk River canyon upstream. You pass beneath alders, bigleaf maples and willows surrounded by twinberry, wax myrtle, coyote brush, manroot, ceanothus, sword ferns, native blackberry and buttercup. Soon a young forest of redwoods and firs rises above the deciduous streamside species. Watch for stinging nettles crowding the trail. Several interpretive signs describe area history. The paved trail undulates but doesn't get steep until it crosses the river.

Around ¼ mile your trail descends briefly as grand fir, Sitka spruce and elderberry join the mix, then cow parsnip, rhododendrons and elk clover. Around 3/8 mile watch on your right for a concrete path and porches with yews and heather planted long ago plus an old shed, first signs of the townsite of Falk. A rest bench overlooks the river.

Continue along the paved path. Around ½ mile you come to an old train barn on your left, moved here and restored as an interpretive center, open weekends and holidays. Beside the barn, a railroad sand shack has a few railroad remnants.

The undulating trail descends as the vegetation becomes more open. Coffeeberry and both evergreen and red huckleberry join the mix of plants. Ascend to ¾ mile where a picnic table on your right overlooks the burbling stream. Horsetail, coltsfoot and sedges join the tangle of plants.

Descend to cross a small side stream. You climb again, with many large stumps with springboard cuts. Your trail dips accross another small side stream, then passes another picnic table on your right. Climb to two interpretive signs at the old sawmill site, now a wide and pretty natural spot on South Fork Elk River beneath sprawling maples. Steps descend to the river bank.

Continue along the pavement through what was once the downtown of Falk, marked by a large clearing now filling with alders and willows. Beyond one mile the pavement ends as a side trail forks left. Hidden in the vegetation are a few vague relics of the town. Easier to find are escaped domestic plants like cherry, quince and plum trees, lilacs, roses, and holly.

The Elk River Trail, now well packed gravel, continues past the site of old bachelor quarters on the right that were in a stump beneath a spruce, burned in a mysterious 2011 fire. The trail's undulations increase as you pass foxglove. Beyond 1 1/8 miles you climb a short, steep hill to get past a slipout. You pass lupine, starflower, trail plant, slink pod, hedge nettle and bedstraw, with a sunny clearing on your left. Descend moderately, then resume climbing gently.

Before 1½ miles, your trail narrows and bends left, crossing a tiny sidestream then climbing around another slipout. Cyclists should walk their bikes over this rise, which has steps on both the uphill and downhill sides. You pass thimbleberry, poison hemlock, Siberian miner's lettuce and redwood violet.

Beyond the slipout the gravel track resumes. Continue up the canyon across another sidestream, then past a picnic table on your right. Beyond 1⅞ miles you dip to cross a bridge over a tributary that tumbles down gray clay and rock to a small waterfall. Climb a short, steep hill where five-finger ferns grow beneath Redwoods and huckleberry, then dip slightly to cross a seasonal sidestream.

Your trail winds up the canyon, roughly following the bends of the river. You might notice a wrecked yellow van down near the river, a victim of the 1990s logging protests.

Around 3 miles the trail makes a big bend right to descend to the river. Near the top of the bend, the original logging road forks left. The original trail went that way too, but that area is now closed. Descend to cross a broad steel bridge over South Fork Elk River. You might want to take the volunteer path down to the river's edge, where maidenhair and other ferns thrive, to cool off or filter water before tackling the big hill ahead.

Beyond the bridge you come to a gate. No dogs or bikes are allowed on the Little South Fork Elk River Trail that climbs to the virgin redwoods. From here a single-track path climbs moderately southwest, then south, following an old roadbed at the start. Climb through second-growth forest with monkeyflower, ferns and berry vines in the understory.

Around 3¼ miles your ascent eases at a broad bend. In 250 feet you leave the old road bed where it turns sharply right. Ascend moderately on true single track with occasional steps, soon switchbacking right. By 3⅜ miles the climb eases. You pass large stumps both old and recent and second growth to three feet in diameter. Look for redwood sorrel, Siberian miner's lettuce, bee plant and thimbleberry, then wild ginger, twisted stalk, trillium, redwood violets and starflower. You soon switch right, climb more steps, then switch left on a gradual climb.

Around 3½ miles you switchback right, then left to climb southeast along a ridge. Switch left to climb steps, then ascend along the east side of the ridge. Climb by more switchbacks and steps. The ascent varies but seldom relents.

By 3⅞ miles the ridgetop has risen high above you. Ascend along the ridge's east face by more switchbacks and steps to gain the ridgetop by 4 miles. Climb fitfully along the ridgetop past slink pod, then abundant huckleberry bushes and ferns. After contouring briefly, resume climbing along the steep sided ridgetop. Pass a sign claiming the 4-mile-point; we think it's actually 4¼ miles. Contour along or near the ridgetop, soon crossing a small wooden bridge.

Even though you resume a steady ascent, by 4⅝ miles the ridgetop has once again risen well above your trail. Climb along its east face to 4¾ miles, then contour, crossing another small bridge. Contour through a clearing in the forest, probably logged by a cable logging operation. Resume climbing with the large clearing now below you.

Around 5 miles you meet the loop junction. Although the sign says to go right, we prefer to go left, returning by the right fork. Your trail descends briefly then bends left as you meet the first virgin trees towering upslope. Pass red clintonia, then duck under a fallen redwood.

Around 5 1/8 miles you enter the first grove of virgins scattered in a deep gully. Giants sprawl from below on your left up the steep slope on your right. Your trail winds through the lower grove, with giants eight to 12 feet in diameter towering above. Climb through this remnant virgin redwood stand with ferns, salmonberry and redwood sorrel carpeting the ground.

Around 5¼ miles you climb along the edge of a gully filled with giants, then dip to cross to its other side. Your trail then contours across the steep slope. Around 5 3/8 miles your trail veers left to overlook another gully filled with giants. Pass a seep with bedrock exposed. Climb briefly, then contour across a steep slope before descending to loop's end at the junction at 5½ miles. Retrace your steps down to the bridge, then back down South Fork Elk River Canyon to the trailhead.

## 44. TABLE BLUFF COUNTY PARK

### BEACH/DUNE WALK TO MOUTH OF EEL RIVER

*The Wiyot tribe inhabited the coastal lowlands from Mad River on the north to the tidelands of Eel River on the south. The tribe came from the Algonkian family, the dominant linguistic group of eastern and central North American native peoples. But their customs followed the Yurok pattern in houses, baskets, canoes and the use of dentalium money.*

*The Wiyots had two settlements at Table Bluff on the south end of Humboldt Bay—Legetku and Yachwanawach. Legetku was located near the trailhead of this hike. In these villages salt-water fishing and clam digging provided the main food sources. Hunting was of little consequence. Today an Wiyot rancheria is located on Table Bluff.*

*In the 1850s settlers, attracted by the rich soil of the bluff, established a small agricultural community, and farming continues today. A lighthouse built on Table Bluff in 1892 served ships entering Humboldt Bay until 1972. From atop Table Bluff on a clear day one has fine vistas north to Humboldt Bay and south to the Eel River delta. The persistent winds make the 170-foot cliff at Table Bluff a popular spot for hang gliding.*

*There is no trail for this hike, just a 4¼ -mile-long sand spit between the ocean and the tidal marsh lands of the Eel River. The easiest walking is generally on the hard damp sand near the tide line. But the most interesting part of the area lies in the low dunes east of the beach, near McNulty Slough and North Bay. This is the Eel River Wildlife Area. The described hike follows the beach south and returns through the dunes. You can vary the hike as you prefer.*

From the base of Table Bluff, jeep trails lead south through the dunes. Follow the main jeep track for 1/8 mile to the westernmost point of the bluff. Then veer toward the beach on a narrower track that drops to the beach at ¼ mile. The best walking is on the hard sand near the tide line.

Follow the dark sand beach south for at least 2 miles to get to the bays, sloughs and estuaries, the best features here. Beyond 2 miles large stacks of driftwood are along the high tide line. It is just over 4 miles to the mouth of the Eel River. A colony of harbor seals lives on the beach at the river's mouth. The Eel is a reasonable destination for a full-day hike. But keep in mind that walking in soft sand is tiring and that your return hike will probably be against the wind.

Whether you go 2, 3 or 4 miles on the sand spit, head east to explore the low dunes and the shore of North Bay. The dunes shelter beach strawberry, yellow sand verbena, northern dune tansy, sea rocket, bush lupine, purple seaside

TABLE BLUFF COUNTY PARK;

DISTANCE: Up to 9 miles round trip.
TIME: Plan on 1½ to 2 miles per hour.
TERRAIN: Straight beach backed by low, rolling dunes.
BEST TIME: Spring for wildflowers. Medium to low tide for best walking conditions.
WARNINGS: You may share the beach with off-road vehicles. Not recommended during hunting season.
HOW TO GET THERE: Exit Highway 101 at M.68.0 onto Hookton Road. Follow it west 5 miles to Table Bluff County Park. Follow road .5 mile more to base of Table Bluff, where parking is on left at big bend.
FURTHER INFO: County Parks (707) 445-7652.
OTHER SUGGESTIONS: SOUTH SPIT: You can also walk north along the beach, if you do not mind paralleling a paved road. It is about 5 miles to the South jetty. CRAB COUNTY PARK provides access to more dunes northeast of the Eel River mouth. To get there, turn west off Highway 101 at M.66.3 onto Cannibal Road and go to its end, about 5 miles.

daisy, silky beach pea, and beach morning glory.

Hike back just east of the ridge of the tallest dune where you can find some protection from the wind. Even without a trail, the route provides good walking on mostly hard-packed sand. A four-wheel-drive track winds through the dunes to your east. Its generally loose sand makes poor walking.

One mile north of the river, the mouth of Mosley Slough lies to the east. In another mile you reach the north end of North Bay. It breaks into McNulty and Hawk Sloughs, which swing to the northeast and east, respectively. As you walk through the dunes, you may scare out a black-tailed jack rabbit, the most abundant mammal in Eel River Wildlife Area.

In the 2 miles before Table Bluff, the route along the sand ridge becomes vague. Take your choice of dune, beach or four-wheel track. As long as you head for the left side of Table Bluff, you cannot go wrong.

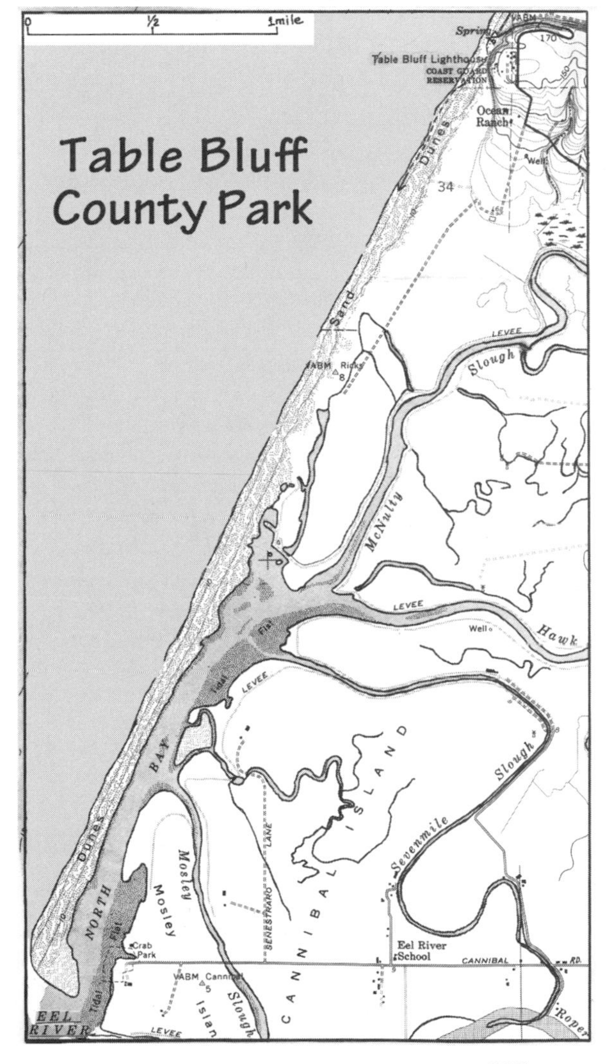

## CENTERVILLE BEACH

*Five miles west of Ferndale is four-acre Centerville Beach County Park, providing access to 9 miles of ocean beach. You can walk north to the mouth of the Eel River or south toward False Cape. Dairy farms back the wild beach in the north, steep cliffs in the south. The original stagecoach road from Ferndale to Petrolia, completed in 1871, went through Centerville, followed the beach south before climbing steeply along Oil Creek Ridge, then descended to Capetown.*

*Centerville Beach was open to four-wheel-drive vehicles in 1993 when we did our second edition. Then it was closed to off-road vehicles for several years. Now somebody's bad decision has reopened all-terrain-vehicle access to the beach. Although they are supposed to stay on the wave slope, no one seems to enforce the rule. So you may have to share the beach and dunes with smelly and whining gas-powered vehicles. Still, the wild beach can absorb many people before feeling crowded. Judging by the changed look here after 20 years, big ocean surf and extreme high tides occasionally scrub the beach and parking area clean.*

## 45. CENTERVILLE BEACH NORTH

### MORE DUNES AND ESTUARIES BY THE EEL

For walking north along the broad beach from the county park, the best path lies along the firm, moist sand near the tide line. East of the steep wave slope is a flat expanse of soft sand backed by low dunes. Judging by my visit in spring

2014, high tides and storm surf sometimes scrub the trail-head clean and rearrange things a bit.

As you walk north, you might pass driftwood sculptures around ¾ mile. At one mile the beach broadens. From 1½ to 1¾ miles, the lower part of the beach is so steep you cannot see the dunes for the sand bank.

Beyond 2 miles a more gradual slope lies between tide line and dunes. Sandpipers scurry along the water's edge. Cormorants, gulls and pelicans glide above the surf. Harbor seals may peer curiously from the breakers. On a clear day you can see the abrupt rise of Table Bluff to the north.

The beach cuts in to the east at 3 miles, then cuts in even farther at 3¾ miles, where the westernmost dune is only 200 feet from the surf. The dunes stretch north to Table Bluff.

CENTERVILLE BEACH—NORTH AND SOUTH:

DISTANCE: North: up to 11¼ miles round trip.
South: up to 6¾ miles round trip, depending on tide and recent landslides.
TIME: North: full day. South: Up to 6 hours.
TERRAIN: Mostly level beach and dune walking.
BEST TIME: Low to medium tide. Spring for wildflowers.
WARNINGS: Heed tide warnings on south hike; do not get trapped by the rising tide. Watch and be prepared for rogue waves as you walk the beach.
HOW TO GET THERE: Leave Highway 101 at Ferndale exit M.64.5 on north, M.62.9 on south. Cross Fernbridge and go west 5 miles through town. At south end of Main Street turn right and go 5 miles to Centerville Beach parking lot.
FURTHER INFO: County Parks (707) 445-7652.
OTHER SUGGESTIONS: Both the FLEENER CREEK TRAIL and the GUTHRIE CREEK TRAIL provide access to the beach south of Centerville without walking the tide line. FLEENER CREEK TRAIL, one mile south of Centerville Beach descends 320 feet in ½ mile to the mouth of Fleener Creek. Three miles south of Centerville Beach, GUTHRIE CREEK TRAIL descends 420 feet in one mile to the mouth of Guthrie Creek.

Centerville Beach North:

Centerville Beach South:

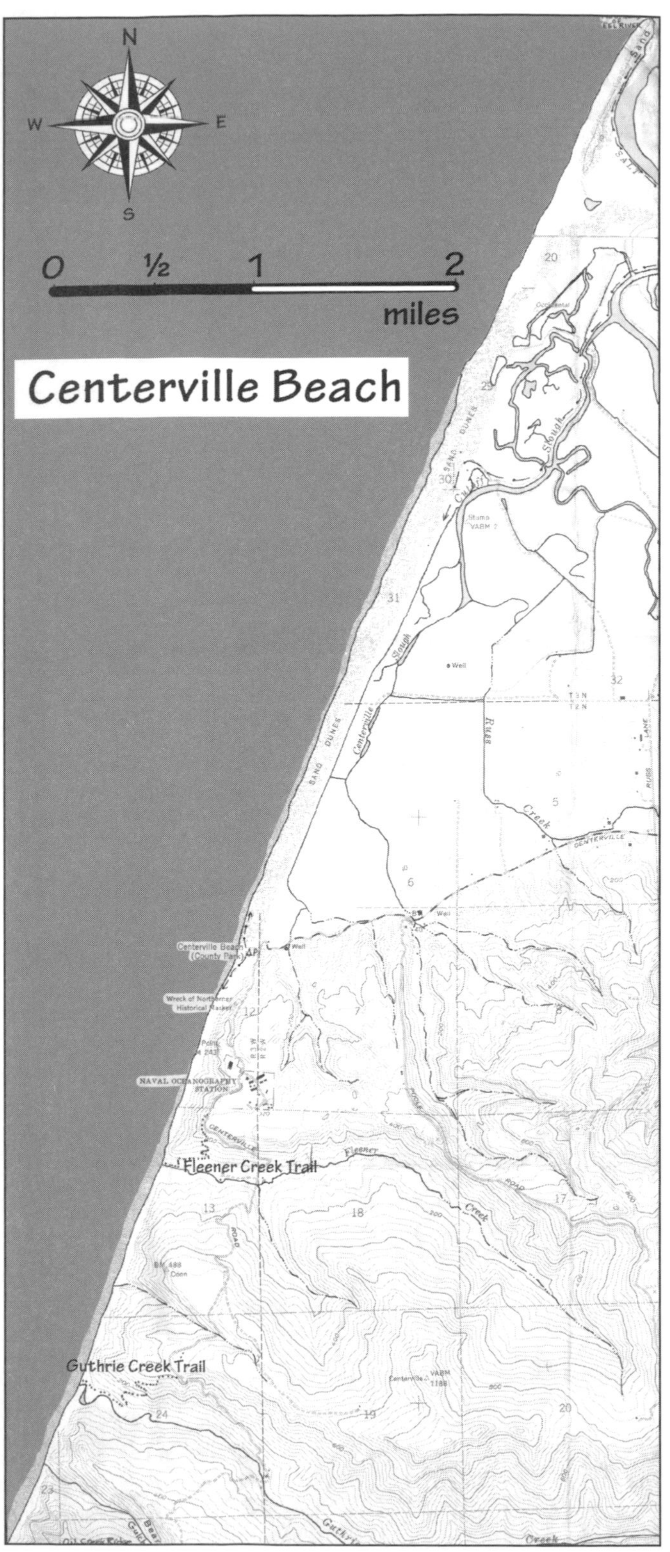
N
W
E
S
0
½
1
2
miles
Centerville Beach
Fleener Creek Trail
Guthrie Creek Trail

A vast wild area of grasslands and marshes lies to the east. To the northeast is the Eel River, with farms along its shore.

The dunes east of the beach are lower after 4 miles. At 4⅝ miles the last high dune lies to the east. Around 5½ miles you come to the mouth of the Eel River, which moves seasonally. Fresh water surges into the ocean here. At high tide, the flow may be reversed. A colony of harbor seals living on the sand bank at the mouth are in prime position to feed on the salmon and steelhead that enter the Eel to spawn.

For the return hike, follow the shore of the Eel River to its confluence with the Salt River in ¼ mile. Then follow the Salt River south, passing the high dune at ⅞ mile. As you walk upriver, the extent and variety of vegetation increases. Beach morning glory and dune grass dominate.

At one mile from the mouth of the Eel, you come to two redwood stumps on the shore of the Salt River, the larger stump being about eight feet in diameter. Imagine virgin redwood forest extending this close to the mouth of the Eel. In fact, when the first settlers came to Ferndale in 1852, redwood forest covered much of the delta. Some trees were said to be over 400 feet tall. Most of the trees were cut by the 1870s. Barnacles growing on the base of the redwood stump indicate that this land is too wet and brackish to grow redwoods today, suggesting that either this land has sunk since the trees were alive or the river level has risen.

At 1⅛ miles the Salt River estuary splits. Follow the right fork (Cutoff Slough) for ⅛ mile until it splits. Then follow a jeep track along the dry (except at high tide and after heavy rains) channel veering right. At 1½ miles the road splits; take the right fork. It gets sandy, then veers left through loose sand to join a broader track at 1⅝ miles. This heads southwest, then veers back toward Centerville Bluff at 1¾ miles. Dune tansy, beach morning glory, yellow sand verbena and other flowers line your route.

At 2 miles a sign to your east marks a gun club. Egrets and great blue herons congregate beyond the sign. In winter many tundra swans live in these wetlands. From 2¼ miles your route follows an arm of Cutoff Slough. Before 2½ miles your path splits; stay left unless you want to return to the beach. At 2⅝ miles you come to a level, grassy area, then climb onto a levee near a high dune. Head west from here through the dunes to avoid private property surrounding the barn ahead.

After you pass the barn, 3 miles from the Eel River mouth, you can continue on the beach or return to the east edge of the dunes, staying west of private property signs. Pacific silverweed, with bright yellow flowers, and lupine grow along the base of the dunes. You approach another barn at 4 miles. Stay west of the barn and fence at 4⅜ miles.

At 4½ miles your path veers right. Trudge through loose sand near the top of the first dune. You may want to return to the beach here because the last mile through the dunes leads through loose sand ¾ mile from the parking area. Come to the parking lot at the county park 5¾ miles from the mouth of the Eel.

## 46.
# CENTERVILLE BEACH SOUTH
### TOWARD FALSE CAPE

You can walk the beach south from Centerville Beach County Park as well as north. This hike is recommended at a low tide of -1.0 foot or lower.

Head south along a beach of pebbly salt-and-pepper sand. From ¼ mile, sandstone cliffs rise to the high bluffs. A stone cross at ⅜ mile memorializes the wreck of the steam schooner *Northerner*, sunk in 1869, en route to the Columbia River. It hit an uncharted rock off Cape Mendocino, attempting to reach Humboldt Bay, sinking off Centerville Beach. Though hundreds of local people came to Centerville to help in the rescue efforts, 38 of the 108 passengers were lost in the stormy seas.

At ½ mile the cliffs rise 240 feet above the beach. Beyond ⅝ mile, layers of gray and orange sandstone protrude to the surf. You must have a minus tide in order to continue. There are two more narrow spots on the beach at the base of soft cliffs of gray sandstone between ¾ and ⅞ mile. Come to the mouth of Fleener Creek at 1⅛ miles. Fleener Creek Trail climbs up the canyon from the mouth of the creek. Cattle graze above the beach.

Walking south you need a tide of less than +1.0 feet to continue. Follow the base of more sculpted gray cliffs. At 1½ miles they reach their highest point, towering nearly 500 feet above the beach. A small waterfall drops 20 feet to the beach at 1¾ miles. Then the beach broadens at the base of a slide area.

Before 2¼ miles you come to a protruding high point, where progress south is blocked at tides higher than -1.0 foot. Do not pass this point unless the tide is low enough and is still ebbing, or else you will not be able to get back around it on your return trip. You may get wet feet even if you wait for a break in the waves. The high cliffs taper to 2⅜ miles where you come to Guthrie Creek and the new Guthrie Creek Trail.

The mouth of the creek is jammed with driftwood. You can find a sheltered spot for a picnic among the logs. A small lagoon lies between the cliffs at the mouth of the creek. Upstream Guthrie Creek is mostly wooded, unlike the pastures of Fleener Creek.

Just ¼ mile beyond Guthrie Creek, another shelf of gray sandstone protrudes to the surf. You must climb over slippery rocks to proceed. At a tide of -1 .0 foot you may be able to walk ¾ mile beyond Guthrie Creek. Even that involves scrambling over several areas of slippery rock.

The route south beyond 3⅜ miles is safely passable only at the lowest tides of the year: -1 .5 feet or lower. The mouth of Oil Creek is 4⅜ miles from the trailhead. Beyond it, the steep promontory of False Cape rises 600 feet. Offshore lie False Cape Rocks, a rookery for several thousand common murres, pigeon guillemots, Brandt's cormorants and western gulls.

On your return hike, be sure to leave time to get around the protruding rocks 2¼ miles from the county park before the tide comes in.

## 47. RUSS PARK

### VERDANT WILDERNESS IN A CITY PARK

*Ferndale (founded 1852, population 1372) has remained remarkably unchanged since the 1890s. Dozens of well-preserved Victorian buildings can be found around town. This haven for artists has many galleries and craft shops along Main Street.*

*Russ Park lies within the city limits. The 110-acre primitive park has over 50 species of plants and 65 species of birds during various times of the year: The park's 3¾ miles of trails lead through dense vegetation on the steep terrain. It feels more like a wildlife and plant sanctuary than a typical city park.*

*Zipporah Patrick Russ, an early settler, donated Russ Park to the city in 1920 "as a park . . . and a refuge and breeding place for birds."*

From the parking area, the Lytel Ridge Trail climbs south

into the forest. In 200 feet you come to a wooden trail map. A picnic table sits on the right. Continue steeply uphill through dense vegetation with abundant sword and lady ferns, passing large Sitka spruce and bigleaf maples. Salmonberry and red elderberry tower overhead, with bleeding heart, nettles, cow parsnip, manroot and elk clover also in the understory. Ascend gradually as your trail bends left, often tunneling through the dense growth. Salal, twisted stalk, coltsfoot, Siberian miner's lettuce, inside-out flower, hedge nettle and bedstraw carpet the ground.

By ¼ mile you climb steadily south again. A rest bench offers a break. Huckleberry, honeysuckle and western redcedar join the mix. Then your climb eases, passing through dense thimbleberry thickets. The path levels briefly as you pass red huckleberry and California bay. Wind past another bench, climbing again at 3/8 mile. In 300 feet go left at a fork. (Take the right fork for a shorter hike to Zipporah's Pond.)

You climb to ½ mile, where the trail tops a ridge and forks into three paths. The right fork leads to Zipporah's Pond and the Bluff Creek Trail. You can follow it now if you prefer a shorter loop of 1 3/8 miles. The described trail takes the left

RUSS PARK:

DISTANCE: 2 1/8-mile double loop, plus optional side trails.
TIME: At least 2 hours.
TERRAIN: Climbs a steep, lush coastal ridge from bottom to top, then returns.
ELEVATION GAIN/LOSS: Full double loop: 700 ft+/700 ft-. Lytel Ridge/Bluff Loop only: 460 feet+/460 feet-.
BEST TIME: Spring is heavenly. Summer, autumn good too.
WARNINGS: No motor vehicles or bikes allowed. Open 6 a.m. to dusk. Watch for poison oak and nettles. Trails are slippery and muddy after rain. Steep terrain; take it easy.
HOW TO GET THERE: Exit Highway 101 at Ferndale (M.64.5 from north, 62.9 from south). Cross Fernbridge and go west 5 miles through town. At the south end of Main Street go left on Ocean Street. It is .6 mile to Russ Park. Dirt parking on right.)
FURTHER INFO: City of Ferndale (707) 786-4224.
OTHER SUGGESTIONS: At Russ Park, you can also explore the VILLAGE TRAIL (aka PACIFIC VIEW TRAIL) on the park's west side. FERNDALE ARCHITECTURAL WALKING TOUR is a self-guided tour of the city's fine Queen Anne, Eastlake, Gothic Revival and Italianate style buildings. Get a map at the Ferndale Museum, 515 Shaw Ave. (707) 786-4466.

fork to make the ¾-mile Francis Creek Loop, which will return to this point by the center path.

The left fork contours southeast along a ridge. On your right is a steep, wooded canyon. Along the trail is false lily of the valley, slink pod, cascara sagrada, ocean spray and Douglas iris. Your trail bends to the right and climbs steeply. At 5/8 mile you veer right again and the climb eases.

The trail forks in 300 feet. The left fork climbs 100 feet to the highest point in the park, a grassy knob in its southeast corner (elevation 660 feet) with views across the flood plain of the Eel River. A bench nearby looks southwest over a wild, wooded canyon.

The main trail is the right fork. It contours along the ridge, then descends along it, descending gradually to ¾ mile, then more steeply past Oregon grape. The trail switches north, then returns to the ridge briefly as you descend by several more switchbacks. By 7/8 mile you leave the ridge for good, descending north, then switchbacking south. Watch

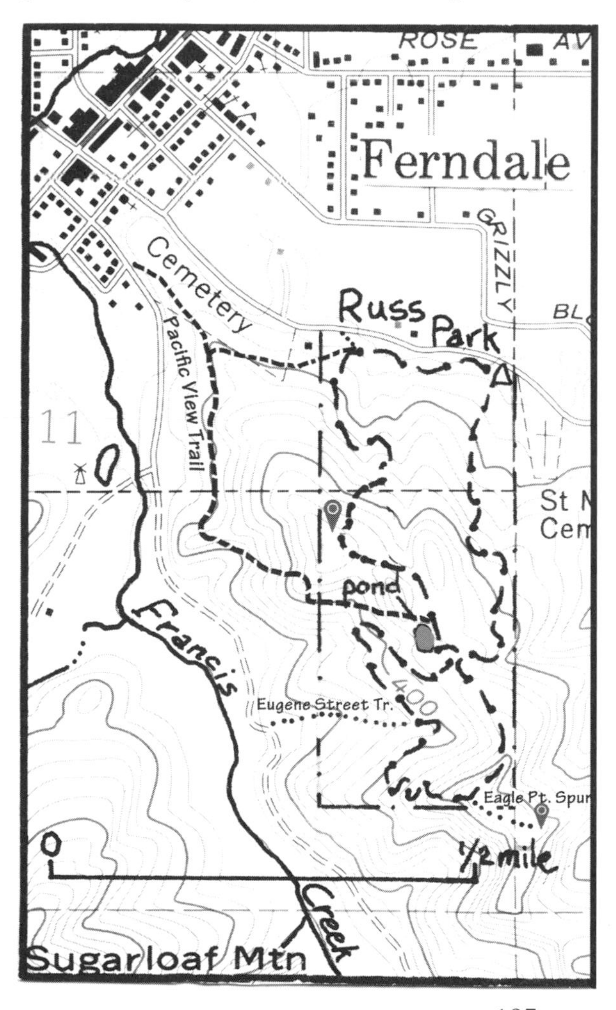

out for uneven footing on this section.

At one mile you are descending into a shady canyon. You pass many large Sitka spruce plus trilliums, fairy bells and five-finger ferns. Then switchback left on a fern-shrouded section of trail. As you turn left again, the path heads down the center of the canyon. In just 100 feet you come to a fork. Straight ahead, Skunk Cabbage Trail descends steeply 1/10 mile to a gate. You can descend to Eugene Street not far beyond, then follow it ½ mile to Main Street.

Take the right fork at the junction, climbing gradually northwest. Watch for poison oak here. The trail switchbacks to the right before 1 1/8 miles, climbing through sword ferns by several more switchbacks. At one of these bends grows a western redcedar over two feet in diameter. This represents the southern reach of its range. In Washington, where it is a major forest tree, it reaches heights of 200 feet. Climb more switchbacks past wild ginger to complete the Francis Creek Loop at 1¼ miles.

Now take the fork on your left. The trail climbs to overlook green Zipporah's Pond. The trail bends right and descends to the shore in 100 feet. You may smell the giant skunk cabbage at the pond before you see them.

The pond nestles in a hollow in the Sitka spruce forest. Skunk cabbage grows in the shallows. The entire surface of the pond is covered with duckweed. This is a special spot, very tranquil, with only the chirp and buzz of birds and insects. Sedge, ferns, manroot, morning glory and alder line the shore. Berries include evergreen and red huckleberry, thimbleberry, salmonberry and red elderberry.

At a junction above the pond, take the right fork (left fork is the Village Trail, an alternate way down) heading north along the shore of the pond. On the north shore is William Crane Grove. The grand fir, spruce and alder are native; the redwoods were planted as seedlings and watered by hand for years. The grove makes a wonderful picnic spot. Please keep it clean!

The trail continues north, climbing a hill and passing cascara and elderberry. The path leads to a point with a picnic table where the village of Ferndale lies 500 feet below like a storybook town, with the mouth of the Eel River and the Pacific Ocean beyond. The trail soon descends steeply. Watch for rough spots in the trail. At 1½ miles the descent eases briefly. Star Solomon seal and holly grow along the trail. You soon come to a vista on your right of the steep drop into Bluff Creek Canyon.

The trail descends moderately steeply, winding through dense salal and sword ferns. It descends a ridgetop, then makes a side hill descent into the canyon. Watch out for nettles growing tall along this section of trail. Watch your step, too; the dense vegetation may obscure uneven tread on this steep descent. Pass California wax myrtle, then descend steeply through lush growth, passing a six-foot-diameter grand fir around 1¾ miles. Native California hazel bushes arch gracefully overhead. Elderberry, thimbleberry, elk clover and nettle also tower above you in season. Ripe salmonberries may be found as early as March, as late as September.

The trail winds left, then right, as it becomes steep and slippery. Beyond 1⅞ miles a trail on the left leads to the lower end of the Village Trail and the road, but not the parking area. (You can exit the park here if you walked from town.) The main trail veers right, descending through a moist area and back into spruce forest at 2 miles. Descend through another salmonberry patch, then level in spruce forest again. Descend slippery tread, sometimes steeply.

As your trail levels, you enter lush grasslands. Watch for poison oak here. Another spur forks left toward town. You stay right, climbing through a tunnel of salmonberry bushes. A final rest bench sits in a small grove of three large redwoods. Climb into another grove of spruce, with houses across the road below. Descend across a steep slope, then descend to the trail map junction before descending 200 feet to the parking area beyond 2⅛ miles.

## 48. CAPE MENDOCINO

DRIVE AND BEACH WALK

*Cape Mendocino rises dramatically from the Pacific to its 1200-foot summit in less than a mile. The sparsely settled, windblown cape is the westernmost point of land in California. (A widely believed untruth says it is the westernmost point in the continental US., but Cape Flattery in Washington extends ten miles farther west) The prominent cape and its hazardous, rock-strewn coast were first charted in 1543 by the crew of the Manila galleons of Cabrillo's expedition, returning from the Philippines to Mexico with silk and other oriental treasures. Appropriately, they dubbed it Cabo de Fortunas—Stormy Cape or Cape of Perils. It was given its present name in the 1580s in honor of the viceroy of New Spain, Lorenzo Suarez de Mendoza.*

*The rugged cape has been a major landmark for coastal navigators ever since. The wind-whipped waters off the cape are among the most dangerous in the Pacific Ocean, with rocks, reefs and shoals often shrouded in dense fog. Although a lighthouse was established on Cape Mendocino in 1868, more than 200 shipwrecks off its shore took dozens of lives from 1850 to 1950. The Japanese Navy torpedoed an American steamship off the cape in 1941, claiming five lives.*

*Nearly all the steep, rolling grasslands of Cape Mendocino are privately owned, but a paved public road leaves from Ferndale on the north (or Honeydew on the south) to explore the remote ridges, valleys and coastline. The 28 miles from Ferndale to Petrolia lack towns, lodgings or gas stations; they provide some of the most lovely pastoral scenes in California. You have the bonus of access to a wild four miles of beach south of Cape Mendocino.*

*Just south of the hamlet of Petrolia, this route provides hiking access to the north end of 25 miles of wilderness beach, the Lost Coast of King Range Wilderness Area (see Trail #53).*

The Mattole Road heads south from the charming Victorian village of Ferndale. It climbs steeply above the flat Eel River delta. In 6 miles you come to "Malfunction Junction," where Bear River Ridge Road forks left. You have climbed to 1800 feet. Follow Mattole Road as it winds along the ridge, passing ranches and barns. A clearing at 7 miles affords views north to Humboldt Bay and Trinidad Head.

After 13 miles of winding through forest and glade, your road makes a winding descent into Bear River Valley. The rolling hills have the look of the Scottish Highlands. Capetown Ranch, before the river crossing, was once a stagecoach stop. Beyond Bear River the road climbs Cape Ridge, passing a huge lily pond west of the road.

The Mattole Road tops Cape Ridge at 980 feet, then descends steeply, with wonderful views of the cape and the coast. You approach sea level at the mouth of Singley Creek, ½ mile south of the cape, 18 miles from Ferndale.

The road follows the level coast for 6 miles. For hikers, the best all-tide access is 6 miles south at McNutt Gulch. If your visit coincides with a low tide, the northern half of the beach may be passable. You can reach it from the unnamed creek one mile south of Singley Creek. Park at the north end of the bridge and walk 200 feet down the steep creek to the beach. At low tide you can walk north 1¼ miles to the foot of the cape, or south to Devil's Gate.

You can also reach the beach from three parking spots at Devil's Gate, 20 miles from Ferndale, but you need a medium tide to walk north or a low tide to go far south. Excellent tidepools in this area were rich with marine life until the April 25, 1992 earthquake. The temblor uplifted the entire coast from Cape Mendocino south to Punta Gorda up to four feet. Now the tidepools at Devil's Gate are barren, except for a few sea vegetables and turban snails. Scientists are studying how long it takes for various species to repopulate the pools.

You cross three more creeks as you drive south from Devil's Gate. The third is McNutt Gulch, where the road turns inland to climb the gulch on its way to Petrolia. At M.23.3 (24.5 miles from Ferndale) a path leads through the fence to the dunes and beach. You can walk north for 4 miles along the beach, with inspiring views of the rugged Cape and 323-foot Sugarloaf Island. Steamboat Rock, Hell Gate and hundreds of lesser rocks provide breeding areas for seabirds and Steller sea lions. From the McNutt Gulch trail, you can also walk south for up to 3 miles, depending on the tide.

Continuing on Mattole Road, you enter Petrolia in 5 miles. A store and cafe offer provisions, while a steepled church and an old wooden schoolhouse add charm to this pastoral hamlet named for California's first oil boom. Occurring in the 1860s, the boom died after little success.

One mile beyond the store you cross the Mattole River and come to Lighthouse Road, which provides access to the Lost Coast's 25 miles of wilderness beach (see Trail #53).

| CAPE MENDOCINO: |
| --- |
| DISTANCE: Drive: 66 miles Ferndale to Petrolia to South Fork.<br>Beach hike: 8 miles or more round trip.<br>TIME: Drive: Plan 4 hours minimum. Beach hike: up to 5 hours.<br>TERRAIN: Steep winding drive with access to a wild, windswept beach.<br>BEST TIME: Spring; autumn is next best.<br>WARNINGS: Drive slowly and enjoy the scenery. Walking on the beach, watch for oversized waves and do not get cut off by the rising tide. Do not trespass on adjacent private property.<br>HOW TO GET THERE: Take Ferndale Exit from Highway 101 (M.64.5 from north, M.62.9 from south). Follow signs across Fernbridge and go 5 miles to south end of Main Street. Go right on Ocean Street, then left on Mattole Road. Description starts there. |

Mattole Road turns east along the river for which it is named. In 6 miles, A. W. Way County Park lies on the right on a big bend of the river. The park is truly AWAY from the cares of the world. It provides swimming and fishing in the Mattole and picnic and camp spots for reasonable fees.

If you follow Mattole Road 8 more miles, you come to the Honeydew Store, where Mattole Road and Wilder Ridge Road meet. The store, a popular local hangout, is open 9 to 5, Monday through Saturday. It is 23 miles farther on the Mattole Road to reach Highway 101 at South Fork, in the heart of Humboldt Redwoods State Park. The steep, winding road takes one hour. Or you can drive south along Wilder Ridge Road for more access to the King Range Wilderness Area (see Trails #53 through 58).

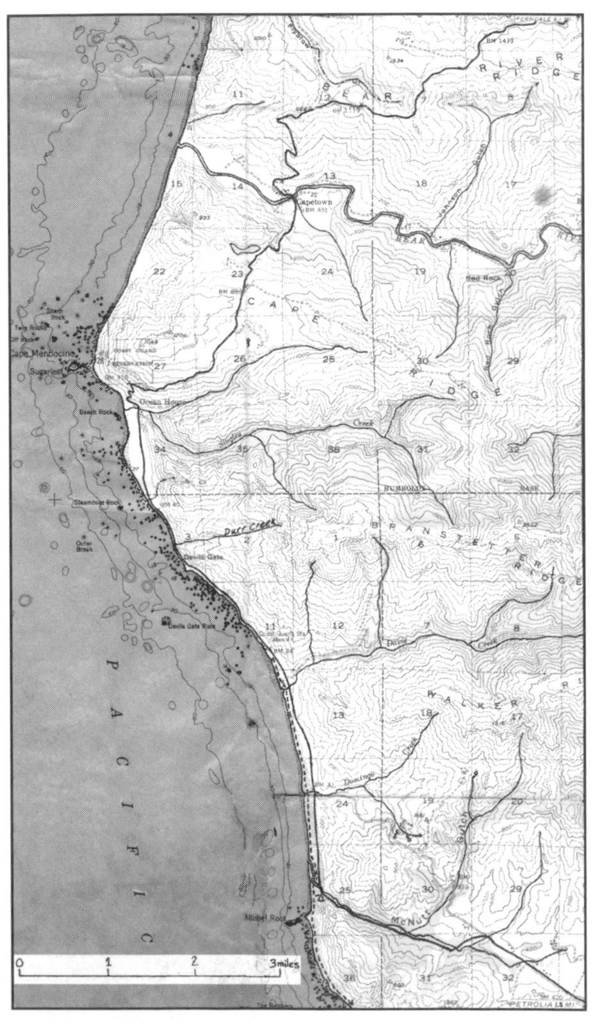

## HUMBOLDT REDWOODS STATE PARK

*California's largest state park north of San Francisco Bay (more than 53,000 acres, third largest of all California state parks) stretches along Highway 101 for 40 miles, from south of Scotia on the north, to Phillipsville on the south. Virgin redwood forests comprise about 17,000 acres of the park, including the largest contiguous stands of virgin redwoods remaining on the planet. While coast redwoods come in a huge variety of shapes and sizes, Humboldt Redwoods State Park shelters nearly 70 percent of redwoods known to be taller than 350 feet (specifically 153 of the 220 redwoods over 350 feet). Many of the park's spectacular redwood groves are accessible by car or short walks. The 33-mile-long Avenue of the Giants brings visitors through grove after grove of virgin giants. This world-famous scenic drive is highly recommended, but to experience the essence of these primeval forests, hike into the backcountry away from Highway 101. The more zealous hiker can take a full day to loop through the Rockefeller Forest along Bull Creek Flats or to climb to Johnson Camp and even beyond to the top of Grasshopper Peak. You can even get a permit to sleep overnight in the backcountry at one of five trail camps in the Bull Creek basin.*

## 49. HIKER'S GUIDE TO THE AVENUE OF THE GIANTS

*Every year three-quarter million visitors from around the world come to see the Avenue of the Giants, but many never venture more than ¼ mile from their cars. Although they see many beautiful redwoods, they never experience the grandeur and solitude of a redwood grove away from the sounds of roaring traffic. Yet numerous trails beckon along Avenue of the Giants. For further information about these trails, refer to* Humboldt Redwoods State Park Trail Guide (revised 2012), *available at the park's Visitor Center for $10.*

On the north, the Avenue of the Giants begins at the Pepperwood exit from Highway 101, at M.46.1 (if you are following the Avenue from the south, read the listings from bottom to top). Stop and pick up a free Auto Tour brochure. Pass through the tiny town of Pepperwood. Leaving town you come to the following features at the markers indicated:

M.43.8. Drury-Chaney Trail on the west side of the road.

The 2¼-mile semi-loop leads through virgin forest with a lush understory of lady fern, oxalis, star Solomon seal, hazel and poison oak. May be wheelchair accessible.

M.43.6. Grieg-French-Bell Loop Trail on west side of road. The ½-mile loop leads to dedicated groves and a picnic table.

M.43.3. Freeway access.

M.40.0. The tiny town of Redcrest.

M.39.65. Freeway access. Then the milepost markers jump to M.24.

M.22.8. High Rock River Trail provides the park's only access to the main stem of the Eel River, running along the river for 2¼ miles and providing access for vistas, swimming and, in winter, fishing. Also accessible from M.22.3, M.22.1, and M.21.9. Between M.22.3 and M.22.1, a spur trail offers a short walk to High Rock Overlook for a dramatic river view.

M.22.12. Five Allens Trail on west side of road. In its 2⅝-mile round trip, the trail passes through a tunnel under the freeway and climbs 1000 feet to reach a lush and magical redwood grove. The trail through mixed forest provides an abundant huckleberry harvest in September.

M.20.8. Junction with Mattole Road, which provides access to Trails #50-56, including the tremendous Rockefeller Forest on Bull Creek Flats (see Trail #50). Freeway access going south.

M.20.5. Go east .1 mile to the Founder's Grove Loop

HIKER'S GUIDE TO AVENUE OF THE GIANTS:

DISTANCE: Various trails from ½ mile to 6 miles in length.
TIME: Thirty minutes to all day.
TERRAIN: Varies from level to steep, all in virgin forest.
BEST TIME: Spring for wildflowers. Summer for swimming and seasonal bridges. Fall for autumn colors.
WARNINGS: Watch for poison oak, which grows extensively in Humboldt Redwoods State Park. Drive carefully and use turnouts.
HOW TO GET THERE: Avenue of the Giants leaves Highway 101 at Pepperwood (M.46.1) on the north, at Phillipsville (M.17.5) on the south. Various freeway access points in between.
FEES: $35/night for car camping, $20/night for environmental camps, $5/person/night for trail camps.
FURTHER INFO: Humboldt Redwoods State Park (707) 946-2263, 445-6547.

Trail, one of the prettiest, most popular hikes in the park, with a restroom at the parking area. The first part of the 1¼-mile double loop is level enough for wheelchairs, although it gets uneven on the second half. The Dyerville Giant was, at 370 feet, the tallest known tree in Humboldt Redwoods State Park before it fell in 1991. Its prone remains still impress. Today we know that the park has three taller trees. Freeway access going north. Avenue of the Giants then crosses to the west side of the freeway.

M. 19.6. Road on west leads to California Federation of Women's Clubs Grove, with a short trail and a picnic area. In summer a bridge crosses the river to Lower Bull Creek Flats.

M.18.4. Gravel trail on west leads into Marin Garden Club Grove, location of a group campground.

M.18.0. Road on east leads to town of Weott (no services) and to freeway.

M.17.5. Parking on west for Gould Bar—fishing and swimming.

M.16.6. Burlington Campground (year-round) to the east. Between campsites 24 and 25 the Burlington-Weott Trail follows Robinson Creek to reach the river in ¼ mile. You can fish in season (with a license) or spot wildlife at dawn or dusk. In summer the swimming is great, and a low-water bridge leads to River Trail and miles of other trails west of the river. Branching left off the Beach Trail is the wheelchair-accessible Gould Grove Trail, which parallels the river for 5/8 mile and includes a self-guiding nature loop.

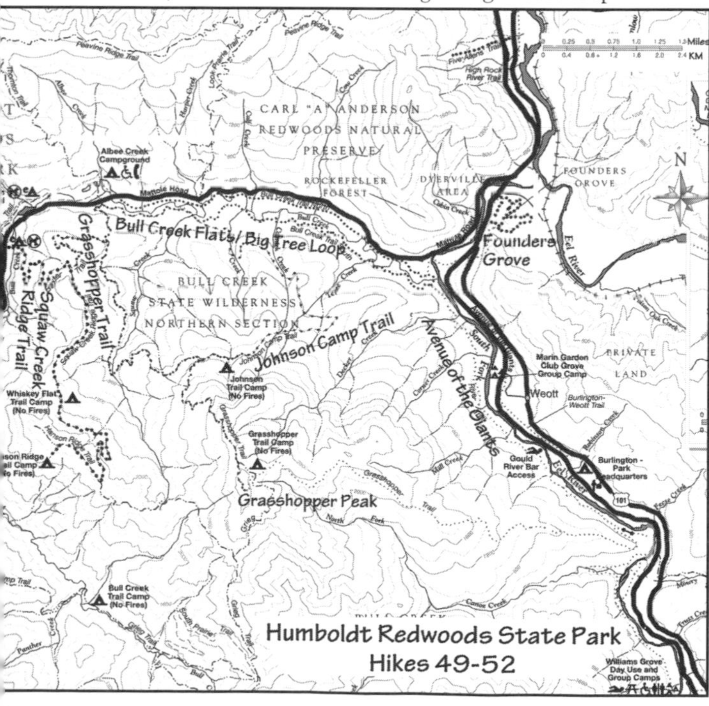

Burlington-Weott Trail continues north to Weott.

M.16.5. Humboldt Redwoods State Park Visitor Center includes a fine natural history museum and a store with postcards and a great selection of nature guidebooks. Open year-round.

M.15.0. Kent-Mather Loop Trail on west side of road makes a one-mile loop through virgin forest, passing William Kent Grove and coming to an overlook of the South Fork, a good place to spot birds.

M.14.73. Road on west leads to Garden Club of America Grove, with picnic tables and restrooms. In summer (May through September), a low-water bridge crosses the river, providing access to the beautiful Canoe Creek Trail, a 2-mile loop through virgin redwood forest in a steep stream canyon rich with wildlife. On the west side of the river, the River Trail north parallels the river to Bull Creek Flats (5¼ miles). The River Trail also runs south. Just north of Canoe Creek Loop, Grasshopper Trail heads west. This scenic hike climbs to Grasshopper Peak in 6 miles.

M.13.5. Road on west leads into Williams Grove, which has picnic tables, restrooms and river access. In summer only, a bridge crosses the South Fork of the Eel and connects with the Children's Forest Loop Trail, a 1¾-mile round trip with a loop through old-growth forests. East of the Avenue, a trail leads to Hidden Springs Campground, 1¾ miles to south end, 2 miles to north end.

In one mile the Avenue of the Giants passes through the town of Myers Flat. There is access to the freeway as you pass under Highway 101 and head east.

M.11.7. Hidden Springs Campground on left (open May to September). A trail leaves from the campground and goes west to Williams Grove, 1¾ or 2 miles, depending on route. A short trail to Hidden Springs Beach is opposite the campground entrance.

M.10.5. Bolling Grove, dedicated in 1921, was the first grove purchased for the park. Across Elk Creek, a short trail follows the stream.

M.6.96. Stephens Grove Loop Trail offers a ¾-mile loop through a virgin redwood grove that had a campground before the 1964 flood. One large tree was cut because it threatened to fall on Avenue of the Giants. A fire charred the grove in 2001.

M.6.80. Town of Miranda.

M.4.83. Freeway access.

M.2.27. Franklin Lane Grove marks the southern end of Humboldt Redwoods State Park. A 3/8-mile loop trail leads through the grove, where there is a picnic area.

In one mile the road passes through Phillipsville, then passes the Chimney Tree and Hobbittown before joining Highway 101.

## 50.
# BULL CREEK FLATS/BIG TREE LOOP
### THROUGH HEART OF IMMENSE FOREST

*Bull Creek acquired its name in the 1860s as the hinterlands of Humboldt County opened to settlement. A settler who lived on South Fork Eel River became one of the first white men to explore Bull Creek when one of his bulls wandered from the herd. He named the pristine creek hidden among immense redwoods after the animal that led him there. Bull Creek was settled in the next decade but the settlers had difficulty with raids by Indians, mountain lions and grizzly bears.*

*In the summer of 1917 three prominent conservationists, Madison Grant, Henry Osborn and John Merriam, drove the new Redwood Highway through Humboldt County. Camping at Bull Creek, they heard the sounds of logging filtering through the immense redwoods around them. They returned home determined to preserve the tall trees in parklands. In 1918 they established the Save-the-Redwoods League. In 1921 the League purchased its first grove, now a part of Humboldt Redwoods State Park.*

*John D. Rockefeller Jr. brought his family to see Bull Creek Flats in 1930. Rockefeller's two-million dollar donation to the League in 1931, matched with state funds, purchased 9000 acres at Bull Creek.*

*As logging accelerated after World War II, the headwaters of Bull Creek were heavily logged.*

*With the record rains of 1955, the creek became a raging silt- and gravel-filled torrent 300 feet wide, washing away 50 acres of Bull Creek Flats and toppling 525 trees. Such dire effects of upstream logging led to state acquisition of virtually the entire Bull Creek Basin, bringing Humboldt Redwoods State Park near its present size. Though upper Bull Creek still shows logging scars, the forest slowly recovers, aided by reforestation and stream restoration.*

*The following trail explores the virgin forests along Bull Creek, where at least 15 of the world's tallest 100 known trees reside. Another 20 of the 100 tallest stand within a mile of this loop. Most of the hike traverses Bull Creek State Wilderness. It provides a cool, shady respite from the heat of summer: In winter, however, the virgin forest can be like an refrigerator, though no less beautiful. Whenever you hike it bring a sweater or heavier protection.*

*This description starts at Big Trees Day Use Area. An alternate trailhead is at the trail's west end .2 mile west of the turnoff for Albee Creek Campground.*

*You may join the hike at its 2¼-mile point by going over the summer bridge (or during the rest of the year, by fording if water is low enough) across the creek at the Big Tree Area.) In summer a low-water bridge provides access to the east end of the trail from Lower Bull Creek Flats (Rockefeller Loop), allowing you to start there or make a loop with the north shore trail.*

From the Big Trees Day Use Are, follow the Big Tree Trail west beneath redwood giants. In 100 feet turn right on the short Tall Trees Loop. In 150 feet it leads to the Tall Tree, also known as the Rockefeller Tree. It was recently measured as 371 feet tall, one of the six tallest-known trees in the world. Take a moment to ponder this leviathan, which exceeds 15 feet in diameter. The Tall Trees Loop quickly returns to Big Tree Trail. Turn right and follow it as it swings back toward Bull Creek, crossing a small bridge.

Contour through primeval forest with an understory of redwood sorrel, evergreen violet, salal, iris, wood rose, trail plant, tanoak and ferns, with tiny calypso orchids in spring. Some trees support healthy vines winding around their

BULL CREEK FLATS/BIG TREE LOOP:

DISTANCE: 9¾ mile loop, or shorter round trip options.
TIME: One to 5 hours.
TERRAIN: Begins mostly level through forest of immense redwoods. South of Bull Creek the trail has many short climbs and descents through virgin forest, then descends to seasonal bridge/ford of Bull Creek. After you cross creek, head west through more virgin forest along north bank flood plain with many short ups and downs and a short road walk before returning to virgin forest to complete loop.
ELEVATION GAIN/LOSS: 340 feet+/340 feet-, mostly on south side of creek.
BEST TIME: Spring for wildflowers. Nice anytime.
WARNINGS: Watch for poison oak. Use caution if fords are required.
HOW TO GET THERE: Leave Highway 101 at South Fork/Honeydew exit (M.36.1 from north, M.35.5 from south). Go west on Mattole Road 4.5 miles to Big Tree Road on left. Alternate Trailhead: On Grasshopper Road, on left at 5.4 miles. Trail on left side of Grasshopper Road 250 feet from pavement.
FURTHER INFO: Humboldt Redwoods State Park (707) 946-2263, 445-6547.
OTHER SUGGESTION: If you don't have time to hike all or part of this loop, visit ROCKEFELLER LOOP TRAIL, a 5/8 mile, nearly level loop around Lower Bull Creek Flat with an impressive ancient grove of redwoods with three trees over 360 feet tall. Find it 1.5 miles west of Highway 101 on left side of Mattole Road.

trunks—most of them are poison oak: beware! The taller-than-head-high shrub with the soft, light green serrated leaves is California hazel. After nearing a creek overlook, your path winds away from Bull Creek to cross two small bridges around ¼ mile. Continue past California bay beneath the giants.

Before ½ mile your trail nears Bull Creek again. Redwoods are everywhere you look. Note the scarcity of Douglas firs on this flood plain, prime sempervirens habitat. Cross a railed bridge over a seasonal stream. By 5/8 mile the forest understory is more dense, with abundant huckleberry bushes and less open ground.

By ¾ mile a few young Douglas firs have found enough light filtering through the redwood canopy to gain a foothold. Cross a small boardwalk and come to a grassy clearing surrounded by virgin forest. Here coyote brush and ceanothus thrive, along with some invasive Scotch broom.

Before 7/8 mile your path ends at paved Mattole Road. If you have seen enough, retrace your steps to the trailhead. Most hikers will want to continue; the best parts of this hike are on the other side of Bull Creek. To do so, turn left to walk the road shoulder across the bridge over Bull Creek, passing bigleaf maple and wild fennel. Just 75 feet beyond the bridge, veer left on the unsigned path to head south through virgin forest, crossing two small bridges before one mile.

Just before the flood plain meets the steep slope, you encounter another unmarked junction. A right turn would lead to Grasshopper Multi-use Trail in about 1/8 mile (alternate trailhead). Our described hike goes left to head east on Bull Creek Flats Trail, which follows the base of the sidehill along the upper edge of the flood plain. Native California blackberry joins the understory.

At 1 1/8 miles you cross a small bridge over a seasonal stream. As your trail climbs gradually up the sidehill, notice that giant redwoods grow on both flood plain and slope, but that Douglas firs grow mostly on the slope. Your trail winds up a side canyon lush with huckleberry, red clintonia, trillium, inside-out flower, starflower, and thimbleberry. Climb gradually east, winding across the sidehill and crossing more seasonal streams.

Around 1 5/8 miles you pass under the base of a large redwood leaning against another. You have climbed about 80 feet above the flood plain. Begin a gradual winding descent, crossing another seasonal stream. The flood plain comes back into view. Your trail switchbacks sharply left to descend to it. Cross a short boardwalk and contour east among giants.

Just beyond 2 miles you come to a junction. The left fork leads to the seasonal bridge/ford of Bull Creek at Big Trees Day Use Area. If the bridge is in place or the ford is shallow, you can shorten your hike by going that way. Our described hike turns right to follow the hiking/horse trail signed "JOHNSON TRAIL CAMPS." Duck between a living behemoth and the dead base of another redwood to head northeast across the flood plain. This area has a jumble of fallen redwoods brought down by wind and age among the many standing giants. Seeing them prone underscores their immensity. You pass the fallen Flatiron Tree, which fell in a 1995 storm.

At 2¼ miles your trail meets another spur on the left that also leads to the seasonal bridge/ford. Even closer on that spur, the impressive Giant Tree stands 354 feet tall, among the tallest trees in the park, and massive with its diameter of nearly 17 feet. Bull Creek Flats Trail continues east through the forest of giants. You cross a bridge over Squaw Creek just above its confluence with Bull Creek. In late summer and fall, it usually looks tiny here; most of its water flows underground through layers of gravel.

At 2½ miles you meet the Johnson Camp Trail, where equestrians must go right (See next trail). Continue on Bull Creek Flats Trail, winding generally east among giants. At 2⅝ miles you pass the base of a fallen giant, then climb slightly along the base of the sidehill above the flood plain. You shortly return to the flood plain, meandering east.

Your trail winds toward Bull Creek, passing more immense redwoods, both standing and prone. A small sunny clearing is jammed with iris, bracken fern and a raspberry bush, uncommon in climax redwood forest. Continue through a lush understory around 2⅞ miles, with iris, oxalis, twisted stalk, hedge nettle, coltsfoot, wood rose, thimbleberry, native California blackberry and head-high sword ferns. Watch for poison oak too! Your trail bends right to pass a redwood with a burl as large as a refrigerator. A fire-scarred giant on your right has a diameter of more than 20 feet.

Beyond 3 miles you can see the light green corridor along Bull Creek about 100 yards on your left, but you don't see the creek itself for a while. Watch on your right for a classic corkscrew redwood; such trees usually have gorgeous wood. Before 3¼ miles you cross a bridge over tiny Miller Creek. Wind by the base of the steep slope at the top edge of the flood plain, then wind back toward Bull Creek, where a short volunteer path on the left leads to an overlook of the stream. Bull Creek Flats Trail gets no closer to it before its end.

Your trail quickly returns to the base of the sidehill in this narrowest part of the Bull Creek flood plain. By 3⅜ miles the flood plain again becomes broad as you trail bisects it. Less understory vegetation grows here.

You soon cross a wide swath of grassland that extends far away from the creek. This natural clearing was created where two old bends of Bull Creek have been bypassed by the present creek bed. The spot makes a pleasant rest stop. The break in the virgin forest allows bigleaf maple, madrone, coyote brush, honeysuckle, rushes, raspberry, thimbleberry, even wild strawberry. The trail follows the cutbank of Bull Creek before plunging back into dense forest of large redwoods.

Cross a bridge over Connick Creek before 3⅝ miles. Your trail bends right to follow the base of the sidehill, encountering a different blend of understory plants. Yerba de selva, redwood violet, and starflower abound here along with Douglas fir and grand fir seedlings.

Contour along the base of the slope until 4 miles, then climb gradually until the flood plain is 120 feet below. Then descend gradually, with plenty of large redwoods and firs on this slope. When you cross a seasonal creek at 4¼ miles, the gently sloping flood plain is directly on your left. Your trail continues along the slope with a few more short ascents.

At 4⅞ miles your trail bends right to descend, crossing a small bridge over a side stream. Descend along Tepee Creek, passing a side trail to a redwood grove on the left, then crossing the creek on a bridge before 5 miles. Descend to a rest bench at the upper edge of the flood plain.

Soon your trail bends sharply right around the base of a fallen giant, then climbs up a side canyon. Climb steadily up the canyon until you switchback left to continue your ascent on the sidehill. The ascent continues to 5⅝ miles, clearly the biggest climb on this hike. Contour along this steep slope, enjoying a bird's-eye view of the monster redwoods on the flood plain 160 to 200 feet below. Of course their tops still tower overhead.

You pass five-finger ferns right before you descend to a junction. The trail straight ahead leads to the River Trail, but that trail only connects to Avenue of the Giants south of here when summer bridges are in place. If you know that the seasonal bridges are not in place and that Bull Creek cannot be forded, you may as well turn back here.

If the bridges are in place or you know that Bull Creek is fordable, turn left on a winding descent to the flood plain, then follow the trail down the cutback to Bull Creek at 6 miles. Ford if it is safe, or cross the seasonal bridge if it's in place, then climb steeply to the flood plain on the north side of Bull Creek. Just 75 feet from the creek you reach a signed junction. A right turn leads quickly to the Rockefeller Loop (see OTHER SUGGESTION).

Our described hike turns left on Big Tree Trail (signed 3.7 miles to Big Tree). It leads generally northwest, staying near the top of the cutbank for the first ⅛ mile, then winding away from Bull Creek only to soon draw near again. By ¼ mile the creek is right below on your left and Mattole Road is just above on your right. Around ½ mile the flood plain broadens. Big Tree Trail soon nears the creek again, but you are still in virgin forest on a small flood plain.

Cross a small double bridge at ⅝ mile, then wind left. Climb two small hills around ¾ mile on a narrow trail intimate with the surrounding nature. Descend to the flood plain, watching out for the occasionally exposed iron pipe this trail seems to follow. Around one mile you pop over another rise, then dip to a broader flood plain well stocked with virgin trees. On your left the creek murmurs, sometimes sending bright shafts of green light into the dark forest.

Suddenly you are again at the top of the cutbank. Look for poison oak and elk clover beneath bigleaf maples. Traverse a fine rock ford of a seasonal stream and continue across the broad flood plain, where woodwardia fern and elk clover grow tall beside your trail. Around 1½ miles a giant double-trunked redwood guards the path, its one-arm-bandit like lower limb with gun drawn.

Soon your trail veers left onto an old road bed right above the river, then returns to virgin forest. Beyond 1⅝ miles you cross a bridge over the broad, gravelly bed of Cow Creek. Rejoin the old road briefly, then return to virgin forest. Pass some fire-scarred giants until 1⅞ miles where you join a broad grassy track that appears to have been two lanes wide here.

Return to virgin forest by 2 miles, with more redwood giants to 12 feet in diameter. Ford a small gully/seasonal creek at 2⅛ miles, then continue through virgin forest with many fallen giants. By 2¼ miles you pop out of the forest, following the old road along the cutback one last time.

You return to deep forest at 2⅜ miles as your trail makes a sharp bend right at a big bend of Bull Creek. Head north, then northwest, winding through the forest and passing under a fallen redwood. After crossing tiny, seasonal Calf Creek, continue through virgin forest.

By 2⅝ miles you once again overlook Bull Creek, with the virgin forest extending right to the cutbank. Follow the bank through forest, crossing a short boardwalk at 2¾ miles. Return briefly to a grassy track where irises thrive, then climb to Mattole Road, where your narrow path parallels the road above Bull Creek. Watch for poison oak as you quickly drop below road level.

At 2⅞ miles you briefly follow rocky tread right above Bull Creek, then climb back up to the road shoulder. You soon veer away from the road to follow a grassy track, then climb a small bank to return to virgin forest, the flood plain broader here.

Before 3⅛ miles you climb to Mattole Road's shoulder again, the trail signed here, with redwood giants on your right. Follow the road shoulder for ⅛ mile, sometimes on a dedicated path, sometimes not.

Around 3¼ miles you reach Blue Slide Picnic Area. Follow the trail south away from the road, soon returning to virgin forest. After your path contours west along the top of the cutbank, you cross a bridge over Harper Creek. Make one final traverse through flood-plain virgin forest, with many giants 12 feet in diameter and one goose-pen behemoth on your right pushing 16 feet. Cross a railless bridge and contour past a few more giants, coming to paved Big Tree parking area at 3¾ miles.

# 51. GRASSHOPPER PEAK VIA JOHNSON CAMP

TREES, TIE HACKS AND VISTAS

*This report follows the Johnson Camp Trail from Big Tree Area to the rustic cabins of Johnson Camp, then joins Grasshopper Road to climb Grasshopper Peak, at 3379 feet the highest point in Humboldt Redwoods State Park. Once the shortest (and steepest), most direct route to the peak, Johnson Camp Trail was reworked recently. It no longer follows the steep old logging road, but rather makes a well graded climb through impressive groves of virgin redwoods. Once open only to hikers, Johnson Camp Trail now accommodates equestrians as well. If you want to ride mountain bikes to the summit, follow Grasshopper Road (starts one mile to the west) for the entire trip, the shortest route. A third route, the most scenic way to the peak, is accessible only in summer. Grasshopper Trail leaves from Garden Club of America Grove (see Trail #49).*

*To reach the peak on a day hike, leave early and take lunch and plenty of water. Plan seven to ten hours round trip for the long hike. An overnight trip, whether you camp at Johnson or Grasshopper Camp, gives you time to linger at the summit and explore the surrounding countryside.*

Park at the Big Trees Day Use Area. Johnson Camp Trail starts on the north (opposite) side of Bull Creek. In summer a seasonal bridge provides a dry-foot crossing. During the rest of the year you need to ford the stream. You may still be able to keep your feet dry at low water. (If rain is falling or imminent, consider that the ford might be impassable on your return. In that case, you can walk west on Bull Creek Flats Trail for 1¼ miles to Mattole Road, then walk Mattole Road or Big Tree Trail about a mile back to Big Trees parking area.)

On the north side of Bull Creek, turn left to follow the Bull Creek Flats Trail east, soon leaving creekside. Pass the Giant Tree and head south briefly, then east again, coming to the Johnson Camp Trail junction at 3/8 mile. (The mileages given at the junction are correct, not those at Bull Creek.)

Take the right fork south, starting to climb in 200 feet. You will gain 1400 feet in elevation in the 5¼ miles to Johnson Camp, so the climb is steady, but well graded. At first you head generally east, but by ¾ mile your trail climbs southeast to cross a bridge over tiny Miller Creek. The virgin forest continues almost to the camp, but the redwoods are mostly under eight feet in diameter, sharing the forest canopy with madrone and Douglas fir.

Your trail levels briefly, then climbs gradually from one mile. You may hear the sound of Miller Creek on your right or Connick Creek on your left. Around 1¼ miles you can briefly see the steep face of Grasshopper Peak ahead to the south. Continue your steady climb until $2\frac{1}{8}$ miles. A brief downhill stretch leads to a bridge over Connick Creek beyond $2\frac{1}{4}$ miles. This pleasant spot has tree-like vine maple and tanoak beneath redwoods and Douglas firs to eight feet in diameter. On the forest floor grow salal, huckleberry, inside-out flower and sword ferns.

Beyond the bridge your trail twists and turns, then climbs gradually north. You soon encounter virgin forest of redwoods to six feet in diameter and smaller firs. From $2\frac{3}{8}$ miles your trail contours along a somewhat rocky ridge as madrones join

| GRASSHOPPER PEAK VIA JOHNSON CAMP: |
|---|
| DISTANCE: 16 miles round trip to peak, $10\frac{1}{2}$ miles to Johnson Camp round trip from Big Trees Area. $13\frac{3}{8}$ miles round trip via Grasshopper Road (hikers, mountain bikers and equestrians). Hikers and equestrians can make a $10\frac{5}{8}$-mile loop of Grasshopper Road, Johnson Camp Trail and the $1\frac{1}{4}$-mile connector on Bull Creek Flats Trail (park at Grasshopper Trailhead.) Add the climb to Grasshopper Peak for a $15\frac{5}{8}$-mile trek.<br>TIME: Long, full day or overnight.<br>TERRAIN: Contours through virgin forest, then makes a long winding climb through more virgin forest to Johnson Camp, then old road to top of peak.<br>ELEVATION GAIN/LOSS: Round trip to Johnson Camp: 1360 feet+/1360 feet-; to Grasshopper Peak: 3340 feet+/3340 feet-.<br>BEST TIME: Spring is ideal, but any clear day is good.<br>WARNINGS: Watch for extensive poison oak. Long, steep trail. If climbing peak as a day hike, leave early, take water and lunch. Permit required to camp at Johnson or other backcountry camps.<br>HOW TO GET THERE: Leave Highway 101 at South Fork/Honeydew exit (M.36.1 from north, M.35.5 from south). Go west on Mattole Road 4.5 miles to Big Tree Road on left. Mountain bikers and equestrians must use Grasshopper Road, on left at 5.4 miles.<br>FEES: Johnson Camp and other backcountry camps: $5/person/night.<br>FURTHER INFO: Humboldt Redwoods State Park (707) 946-2263, 445-6547. |

For Grasshopper Road only:

the forest. Resume a fitful ascent, winding northeast.

As you gain the ridgetop, your climb eases. Contour south past scattered large redwoods and abundant mature madrones. Resume a gradual ascent around 2¾ miles, soon passing through an abundant mix of large redwoods, Douglas firs, madrones and tanoaks.

Beyond 3 miles your trail bends left as the ascent steepens. Beyond 3⅛ miles you encounter the largest redwood since the flood plain along Bull Creek. Beyond 3¼ miles redwood giants abound as you cross the multiple forks of the headwaters of Tepee Creek. Iris grow beside the path in a forest of various sized firs and redwoods, some 14 feet in diameter.

Your trail winds generally east, mostly contouring as you approach the headwaters of East Fork Tepee Creek around 3⅝ miles. Resume a winding ascent. Switchback sharply right beyond 3¾ miles to climb west. You recross the headwaters of Tepee Creek, less obvious on generally steeper slopes than below. Climb fitfully through intermittently rocky terrain, well stocked with virgin redwoods and firs and pockets of immense trees.

At 4¼ miles your trail winds through a gully with a stand of large, straight redwoods. Make a winding climb into a larger gully with even larger redwood giants, unusually large for redwoods above 1300 feet elevation. Beside the flowing stream around 4³/8 miles grow wild ginger, redwood sorrel, saxifrage, and woodwardia ferns among the ubiquitous sword ferns and salal. Your trail climbs moderately.

Around 4⁵/8 miles you descend to cross Connick Creek in its steep, rocky canyon. On these steep slopes the tops of the virgin trees appear closer, although they still tower overhead. Climb out of the steep canyon, then contour as daylight increases on your left, the result of a cutover strip of formerly private timberlands near Johnson Camp. Your trail turns southwest, climbing fitfully around 5 miles, then winding west across the headwaters of Miller Creek. You meet a recontoured old road, route of the original trail here.

Your trail descends southwest and west to Johnson Cabin Camp at 5¼ miles. It has an outhouse, bench, spring, water trough, and metal bear locker near the rickety remains of two rustic cabins from the old tie cutters camp. Twenty years ago there were four cabins. The two remaining look like they are not long for this world, with caved-in floors and daylight pouring through the walls and roofs. The small second-growth redwoods here underscore the immensity of the virgin forest you just walked past. This shady spot housed "tie hacks," men who split redwoods into railroad ties and fence rails. It was active from about 1920 into the 1950s. Mosquitoes thrive in this pleasant spot, so be sure to bring plenty of repellent!

From the camp, your trail continues west, descending to cross a fork of Squaw Creek where elk clover grows, then contouring past red huckleberries to meet Grasshopper Road at 5½ miles. (It is 4.2 miles back to Bull Creek Flats Road if you go right.)

If you have enough time and/or are camping in the backcountry, turn left onto the broad road and climb. At 5¾ miles you climb steeply, but most of the grade is moderate. You are halfway to the top of Grasshopper Peak in elevation, about 70% in miles). Views open up to the west. Just beyond 6 miles, you cross another small stream that flows in winter and spring.

At 6³/8 miles your trail turns sharply left and heads northeast. Climb steadily by long switchbacks through young forest. At 6¾ miles you pass a redwood stump at least 16 feet in diameter. This and other giants here were cut 80 to 100 years ago; on some stumps you can see the springboard cuts where the fallers put planks to stand on.

Beyond 7¹/8 miles a stand of virgin redwoods is alongside the road, somehow missed by the ax men. The large redwoods here are remarkable mostly for the fact that they are growing around 2500 feet elevation, about the highest that coast redwoods grow. At 7³/8 miles the steadily climbing road bends right and heads straight toward the summit.

At 7¼ miles you come to the best view yet. Kings Peak

(4088') is to the southwest. From here to the summit the soils consist of small, fractured light-color rock, just like the soils of the Kings Crest.

About 7¾ miles from the trailhead you meet the turnoff to Grasshopper Camp. Bear left to the camp, right to climb the peak. It is less than ¼ mile of level walking to the camp, on the border between forest and meadow. The Grasshopper Trail from Canoe Creek meets the road near the camp. (The bridge across the Eel River on that trail is summer only.) The final ¼ mile to the peak climbs only 160 feet but seems like more. You can see the lookout tower with 1/8 mile to go.

At the top, you are rewarded with a 360-degree view of forest, mountains and sea. To the southwest is Kings Crest with its peaks from right to left: Blue Slide, Shubrick, Kings, Saddle and Horse. South-southwest is a notch where you can see the ocean on a clear day. From southeast to east sit the snowy summits of the Yolla Bollys: Hull, Sanhedrin, flat-topped Black Butte, Anthony, South and North Yolla Bolly, Black Rock and Four Corners Rock, the latter almost due east. South Fork Mountain runs miles north from near there. In the foreground are the vast forests of Humboldt Redwoods State Park, the Eel River and Highway 101. To the north-northwest is Eureka. And to the west are several ridges and peaks which extend all the way to Cape Mendocino (beyond view).

If you are on a day hike, be sure to leave enough time to hike the 8 miles back to Big Tree or 6¾ miles down Grasshopper Road before dark. Luckily, it is a downhill run.

## 52.
## SQUAW CREEK RIDGE
### BACKPACKING BULL CREEK BASIN

*Squaw Creek Ridge and the rest of Bull Creek Basin provide varied opportunities for day hikers, backpackers, equestrians and mountain bikers. The shortest route to Whiskey Flat Camp and points beyond is described below, the first 2¼ miles on Baxter Trail open only to hikers and equestrians. Baxter Trail was recently reworked into a well graded single track trail, so it no longer follows the steep old road. If you want to ride mountain bikes along the ridge, you must start at Grasshopper Trailhead. That route climbs 5/8 mile, then goes to the right on Squaw Creek Ridge Road climbing 5/8 mile, then contouring for one mile to meet the trail described below.*

*To stay at Baxter or Hamilton Barn Environmental Camps or at any of the trail camps, you must first register at Park Headquarters or Burlington Campground.*

Baxter Trail starts from Mattole Road opposite the gravel road to Hamilton Barn Environmental Camp, marked only by a sign, "HAMILTON BARN E CAMP." The trail heads east, soon encountering a small signpost confirming that this is Baxter Trail. Baxter Trail soon turns southeast, then south by 1/8 mile, crossing a flat gravelly area. On my autumn 2013 visit I saw no evidence of a trail forking left to head for Baxter Camp that is shown on some maps. Your trail soon veers left to a seasonal bridge/ford across Bull Creek. It was a dry-foot ford that early October.

Baxter Trail climbs the bank on the creek's east side, coming to a sign confirming no bikes are allowed on Baxter Trail, then climbs into second-growth forest. Stay right to climb northeast as a vague side trail heads north to Baxter Camp. As you climb you can spot the southernmost of Baxter Camp's two sites right below your trail. Ascend past redwoods to two feet in diameter, mixed with firs, tanoaks and maples.

Just beyond ¼ mile you ford a seasonal stream and pass another spur on the left that descends to Baxter Camp. Baxter Trail climbs north. Switchback left to ascend south at 3/8 mile, then veer left to climb along a small canyon.

At ½ mile your trail crosses the seasonal stream and continues to ascend. Baxter Trail winds across more gullies, as redwoods grow to three feet diameter with madrones, Douglas firs and abundant huckleberry shrubs joining the mix.

Switchback left at 5/8 mile and continue your winding climb. Switchback to the right at ¾ mile, then switch left and right again. Cross a bridge over a seasonal stream where poison oak vines up a bay tree. Your ascent eases as you switchback left. Douglas fir dominates the forest, with a mix of madrone and tanoak. You gain filtered views west to the high ridge that is a dominant feature of Humboldt Redwoods State Park.

Beyond one mile wood rose, hazel, starflower and salal join the ubiquitous huckleberry bushes. Cross a gully to contour through forest, then resume a gentle ascent passing ocean spray and ceanothus, mixed with hazel and thimbleberry, then raspberry. You pass Douglas firs to six-foot-diameter (though most are smaller), but no redwoods, although a few are nearby.

After switchbacking to the right, you soon gain vistas on your right of rolling grasslands and high wooded ridges. Make a long, steady ascent through forest, passing gooseberry. Baxter Trail switchbacks left around 1¾ miles. A volunteer spur trail from the switchback leads 150 feet to a ridge with a grand view of upper Bull Creek Basin. Below you, Mattole Road winds through a patchwork of shades of green mixed with golds in autumn. Due west and far below you can see Cuneo Creek Horse Camp.

Enjoy a short respite from climbing around 1 7/8 miles, then ascend moderately. Many large fir stumps attest to past logging here. By 2 miles you are nearing Squaw Creek

## SQUAW CREEK RIDGE:

DISTANCE: 8 miles round trip to Whiskey Flat Camp (add ¼ mile each direction from Grasshopper Trailhead.
One way to Hanson Ridge Camp: $6\frac{3}{8}$ miles.
To Grasshopper Camp: $7\frac{5}{8}$ miles.
TIME: To Whiskey Flat: 2 hours. Park backcountry ideal for 1- to 3-night backpack trips.
TERRAIN: Climbs to and traverses ridges. Possible peak climb and more.
ELEVATION GAIN/LOSS: From Baxter Camp or Grasshopper Road to Whiskey Flat; 1630 feet+ 120 feet-.
From Whiskey Flat to Hanson Ridge Road junction: 520 feet+/160 feet-.
To Hanson Ridge Camp: add 240 feet+/100 feet-.
From Hanson Ridge junction to South Prairie Trail: 860 feet+/760 feet-.
To Bull Creek Road and Camp: add 1200 feet-.
Preacher Gulch Road to Grasshopper Camp: 1320 feet+/340 feet-.
From Grasshopper Camp to peak: add 300 feet+.
BEST TIME: Spring and fall. Summer is hot, but Whiskey Flat Camp is always cool.
WARNINGS: No fires in backcountry. Watch for extensive poison oak. Permit required to camp at Whiskey Flat and other backcountry camps.
HOW TO GET THERE: Exit Highway 101 at South Fork/Honeydew (M.36.1 from north, M.35.5 from south). Go west on Mattole Road for 5.4 miles to Grasshopper Road (starting point for mountain bikes), 6.4 miles to Baxter Camp and Baxter Trailhead. (Environmental Camp and trailhead for hikers and equestrians only.) Park on the east side of the road where Baxter Camp trail heads east.
FEES: Environmental Camps: $20/night. Trail camps: $5/person/night.
FURTHER INFO: Humboldt Redwoods State Park (707) 946-2263, 445-6547.
OTHER SUGGESTIONS: LOOK PRAIRIE TRAIL (on north, 4.3 miles from highway) climbs to a grand view (up to $6\frac{5}{8}$ miles round trip). Mountain bikers can make an 11-mile loop by continuing steeply up Look Prairie Road to go left on Peavine Road along the ridge, then descending Thornton Multi-use Trail to Albee Creek. JOHNSON PRAIRIE TRAIL (on north, 4.6 miles from highway) climbs through prairie to a pioneer grave ($2\frac{3}{8}$ miles round trip).

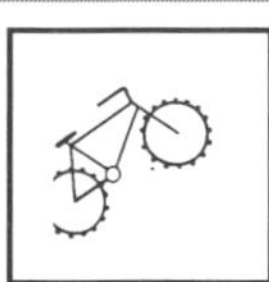

Ridge. Baxter Trail climbs east, encountering a pocket of virgin trees, with a six-foot-diameter redwood giant on the right side of the trail and others ahead and below.

Switchback right at 2¼ miles and climb 150 feet to Baxter Trail's end at Squaw Creek Ridge Road. Turn right on the wide road, climbing south past large redwoods, then contouring to 2½ miles. Squaw Creek Road then climb gradually to a saddle on the ridge at 2⅝ miles, where big redwoods grow with Douglas firs, tanoaks, madrones, huckleberries and irises.

Make an easy ascent along the ridge to 2⅞ miles, then descend to another saddle. Follow the ridge southwest as ceanothus, wild rose and salal join the understory. Beyond 3¼ miles you continue along the ridge with short ups and downs.

After a straightaway you start the last big climb to Whiskey Flat Camp. The climb eases at 3½ miles, then steepens as your trail bends left into virgin forest. Climb and wind to 3¾ miles, then descend into a grove of large redwoods, where rare western yew also grows.

Your road climbs to 4 miles where it enters Whiskey Flat Camp. In this beautiful spot redwoods of ten-foot diameter tower over woodwardia and sword ferns, salal, redwood sorrel and a babbling brook. A faucet at the camp entrance provides sweet water. The camp was named for a Prohibition-era still located here.

You can use Whiskey Flat Camp as a base for exploring the surrounding wilderness. It is 5¾ miles to Grasshopper Peak, an 11½-mile round trip with far less elevation change than from the Big Trees Day Use Area.

Another option is to use a different trail camp each night. From Whiskey Flat Camp, it is a steady climb to Hanson Ridge Road in 1¾ miles, 2⅜ miles to Hanson Ridge Camp with its wonderful views. From Hanson Ridge Road junction, it is 3⅝ miles via Preacher Gulch Road and Grieg Multi-use Trail to Grasshopper Camp, 6¼ miles to Johnson Camp. You can also descend to Bull Creek Trail Camp, but the lower part of Bull Creek Road no longer connects to the main road, and the lower part of Preacher Gulch Road has been closed by a big slide, so you must now descend via South Prairie Trail or Grieg Multi-use Trail. The options are many but you must plan ahead to get the required camping permits. All camps mentioned are accessible to hikers, equestrians and mountain bikers.

# THE LOST COAST

THE HEART OF KING RANGE WILDERNESS AREA

*Imagine 25 miles of wilderness beach backed by steep bluffs and cliffs rising to ten peaks over 2000 feet and cut by fifteen year-round streams. If you like such wild rugged country, plan a trip to the Lost Coast.*

*The King Range is the largest area of wilderness on the Pacific Coast between Olympic National Park and Point Reyes National Seashore. Popularly known as the Lost Coast, the 68,000 acres of King Range National Conservation Area include the wilderness coast and the steep mountains and canyons of the King Range. Happily, the King Range was formally designated as wilderness in 2006 and now includes 42,625 designated wilderness acres. You can get a free map of the areas roads and trails from the Bureau of Land Management office in Arcata, Whitethorn or Ukiah.*

**NOTE: BLM plans to implement a new permit system for overnight trips in King Range Wilderness Area, probably in place by summer 2015. The new system will likely require a fee for each overnight trip in the wilderness. BLM will likely also implement a quota system limiting entry of overnight visitors to about 60 people per day.**

We will post the new requirements ASAP at boredfeet.com under trail updates.

## 53. MATTOLE RIVER SOUTH

ALONG THE LOST COAST

*Most people enter this wild coast from the north or south end. Though these approaches avoid significant elevation change, the trek is not easy. Walking in strong winds over loose sand and uneven rocks demands hiking boots for backpackers. Currently six other trails reach the middle portion of the Lost Coast, all involving substantial elevation change: Cooskie Creek, Spanish Ridge, Kinsey Ridge (west end of Smith-Etter Road), Rattlesnake Ridge, Buck Creek, and Horse Mountain Creek. Consider them for shorter trips or as part of a loop only if you are in good shape.*

*Of the north and south trailheads, the mouth of the Mattole River on the north provides the most pristine approach. You may be exposed to strong winds for the 3-mile hike to Punta Gorda Lighthouse. Unless you time your hike with the tide as you pass Sea Lion Gulch, you must scramble over crumbling cliffs to stay out of the surf. The 1992 earthquake made the tidal passage there even tighter than it was before. Walking becomes easier as you pass the deep canyons of Cooskie, Randall and Spanish Creeks.*

*Prevailing winds blow from northwest to southeast. So the common lore is that you hike the Lost Coast from north to south, with the wind at your back. But unless you intend to go the whole 25 miles, you will likely have the wind against you in one direction or the other.*

*If you enter from the south via Shelter Cove (see Trail #58), note that the beach is no longer open to vehicles for the first 3 miles. North of 3 miles lies the most spectacular part of the Lost Coast, a narrow beach backed by high cliffs and steep canyons with lush vegetation and wildflowers.*

*Wherever you approach the Lost Coast, you will find solitude and physical grandeur to challenge your spirit, and a wondrous diversity of plant and animal life growing right to the ocean's edge. Be careful, watch for rogue waves, and treat the wilderness with respect.*

From the end of Lighthouse Road, walk west to the tide line, then head south along the broad, dark sand beach. The firm sand just above the water provides the best walking, except where a firmly packed old jeep trail follows the base of the bluffs. Sheep graze the steep grasslands on your left.

Before one mile the first of many year-round creeks cascades down the steep, grassy bluff. The beach gets rockier to the south. Stay on the beach to avoid a large slide on the bluff caused by the 1992 earthquake. Tidepools and sea stacks lie offshore. Beyond 1½ miles the broad beach narrows. Beyond a small point, several seasonal streams drop to the beach.

At 2½ miles an old ranch road winds steeply up the bluff. You immediately round Punta Gorda as the lighthouse comes into view. From here you can walk on a firm roadbed. You pass two cabins near Fourmile Creek at 2⅝ miles. After the ford, continue on a firm track across the grassy bluff, passing more dilapidated ranch buildings. The Cooskie Creek Trail forks left. That rugged track climbs to cross the headwaters of Sea Lion Gulch, then descends to ford Cooskie Creek about ⅝ mile from the coast before climbing to meet the end of the Telegraph Ridge Jeep Trail around 12 miles. Our description continues along the beach.

At 3 miles a path forks left to Punta Gorda Lighthouse ruin. The light station helped ships navigate this fogbound, rugged coast from 1911 to 1951. It was built after the wreck of the SS *Columbia* claimed 87 lives here in 1907. Today only the squat light tower remains, the keeper's quarters and fog signal house having been razed by BLM in 1970. The wind usually roars and whistles through the concrete tower.

You cross several small creeks in the next ½ mile as you

follow the old jeep road along the coast. After the creek at 3½ miles, you can climb a hill to stay on the road, or you can return to the beach. On the road you have another chance to return to the beach at 3¾ miles. Either way, you come to steep Sea Lion Gulch at 4 miles. Sea Lion Rocks lie just offshore, home to three dozen Steller sea lions and many cormorants and pelicans. The steep mouth of the creek provides shelter from the wind, views of the sea lions and wildflowers.

The beach narrows after the gulch. At 4½ miles beach

## MATTOLE RIVER SOUTH:

DISTANCE: 25 miles one way, or round trip of your choice.
TIME: Three to 4 days for entire hike. 4-hour day hike to ruins of Punta Gorda Lighthouse.
TERRAIN: Mostly level beach and headland, backed by precipitous cliffs and deep canyons. Some rough rock hopping.
BEST TIME: Spring. September and October next best. Summer also good but often foggy.
WARNINGS: Get a wilderness permit (required) at any Lost Coast Trailhead or local BLM office. Organized groups must apply to BLM for a permit in advance. Backpackers must now carry a bear canister, which may be available for rent from BLM's King Range office, Arcata office, Petrolia Store, or Shelter Cove stores. Purify all water, especially Cooskie Creek north and in Shelter Cove area. Watch for timber rattlers, especially near wood piles. Isolated country with no services. Difficult beach walking in soft sand and over rocks. Two or three points difficult or impassable at high tide.
HOW TO GET THERE: Exit Highway 101 at South Fork/Honeydew (M.36.1 from north, M.35.5 from south). Go west on Mattole Road for 23 miles to Honeydew, then right on Mattole Road for 14 miles to Lighthouse Road, just before Petrolia. Go left on Lighthouse Road to its end at the beach near the mouth of the Mattole River.
FURTHER INFO: Bureau of Land Management, Arcata (707) 825-2300, Southern Humboldt office 986-5400.
SHUTTLE SERVICE: Two companies currently offer to shuttle hikers and their gear to Lost Coast trailheads: call Lost Coast Shuttle (707) 986-7437 or (707) 223-1547, or Lost Coast Adventure Tours (707) 986-9895 or (707) 502-7514. If these change, they will be posted on the BLM website.

passage may be blocked at medium to high tide. If necessary, you might scramble over crumbling rock and mud slides on a steep, rough detour above the surf. You would do better to wait for the tide to drop below +1.0 foot, when the beach is passable. (Keep in mind that the tides here occur about 30 minutes earlier than the times for the mouth of the Mattole.) When the tide is out, uneven-sized rocks on the beach slow your progress.

You pass a barn and cabin above the beach at 4¾ miles. Then walking becomes easier at the base of steep cliffs. Around 5¼ miles Cooskie Creek Spur Trail forks left to climb to the Cooskie Creek Trail. At 6 miles the beach track meets the broad, deep canyon of Cooskie Creek. A sweat lodge of driftwood sometimes sits beside its mouth. Sheltered camps lie within ¼ mile upstream. Fishing is fair for trout to nine inches. You should purify drinking water. Private property lies about one mile upstream.

Continuing southeast, you must boulder-hop for a few hundred feet. Then footing improves as the beach widens. You pass small waterfalls and two narrow spots to 7 miles. From 7¼ to 7¾ miles, the cliffs above the beach have massive landslides. At 7½ miles large, uneven rocks on a steeply slanting beach make rough walking. The bluffs, however, are worse, cut by many little canyons. Beyond 7¾ miles loose sand and gravel slow progress.

About 8 miles from the trailhead, Reynolds Rock lies offshore. You pass a point showing greatly twisted rock strata. The geological folding continues to the mouth of Randall Creek at 8⅝ miles.

Narrower and more wooded than Cooskie Creek, Randall Creek also provides fair fishing. A pleasant camp lies a short walk upstream on the north side of the creek.

A road along the bluffs south of the creek provides firm footing. Just 250 feet from Randall Creek, the old Spanish Ridge Trail that once climbed from the beach has been abandoned. Your path climbs the rolling grassland at the base of the steep bluffs. At 8⅞ miles you cross a small stream where watercress grows. Offshore rocks line this stretch of coast. Near 9¾ miles a mostly level footpath crosses the lower bluff. Or you can walk the old road, which leads up and down along the upper bluff. You pass two more streams jammed with wildflowers, the second with watercress and mint.

At 10¼ miles the grassy headlands get broader and flatter as you come to the north end of Spanish Flat. If it is not too windy these lush grasslands provide good camping. At 10½ miles Spanish Ridge Trail forks left, climbing 2⅞ miles to meet Cooskie Creek Trail, 4.7 miles to Spanish Ridge Trailhead at the end of Telegraph Ridge Jeep Road. You walk the broad grassy flat, where wildflowers lie scattered through the grasslands. Woodwardia ferns grow at the base of the steep bluffs.

At 11⅜ miles you come to the broad flood plain of deep Spanish Creek Canyon. Several campsites lie in or near the canyon. Continue over mostly level grasslands. You pass an old corral, then come to pioneer Paul Smith's cabin, 12 miles from the trailhead. It overlooks a broad sandy beach.

At 12⅜ miles you cross Oat Creek. The creek cascades down its twisting, rocky gorge. Swallows dip and soar overhead. Mimulus, iris, sticky monkeyflower, columbine, yarrow, paintbrush, cow parsnip, penstemon and lupine grow in the sheltered canyon. You meet the Smith-Etter Road, here called Kinsey Ridge Trail, at 13 miles (see Trail #54).

The road continues southeast along the coast, crossing the broad, gravelly wash of Kinsey Creek in ¼ mile. It leads along grasslands below steep bluffs, passing the Etter cabin at 14 miles. The headlands narrow as a sandy track heads for Hadley Creek (also known as Big Creek), which you cross at 14⅝ miles. Dense forest in the deep, shady canyon shelter pleasant campsites.

Your trail continues in loose sand along a narrow beach. At 14⅞ miles the beach is backed by high sand dunes stacked against a steep grassy hill. A trail climbs the steep headlands to the south. It provides better walking than continued slogging in the sand. At 15 miles the faint double track is obliterated by a slide, but a narrow trail continues. Back on the grasslands the trail becomes vague; stay high on the headlands below steep bluffs. You cross a stream choked with watercress at 15⅛ miles. Then your trail descends to meet a gently rolling grassland, soon returning to an obvious dirt road.

You cross a small creek at 15¾ miles and come to Big Flat, which stretches along the coast for over a mile. The first of many Indian shell middens lies beside the road. It is unlawful to disturb these archaeological sites. The road provides easy walking for your sand- and rock-weary soles.

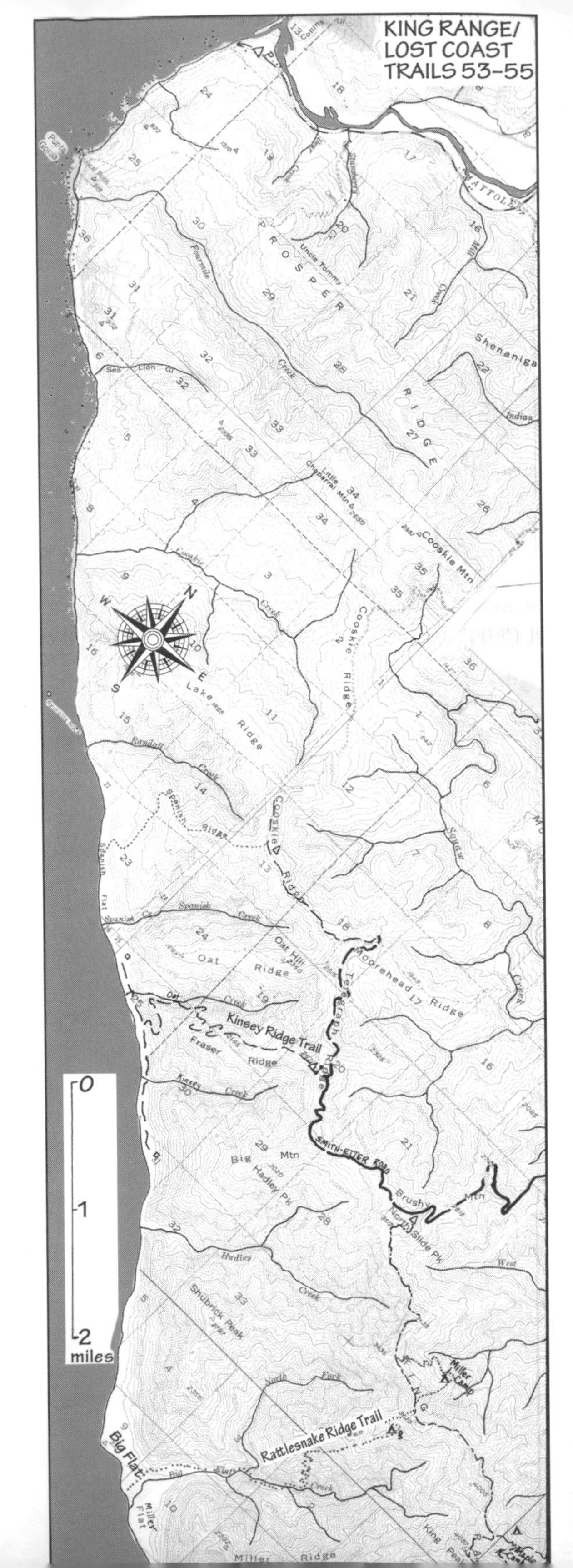
KING RANGE/
LOST COAST
TRAILS 53-55
Kinsey Ridge Trail
SMITH-ETTER ROAD
Rattlesnake Ridge Trail
Big Flat
0
1
2
miles
PROSPER RIDGE
Cooskie Mtn
Cooskie Ridge
Lake Ridge
Spanish Ridge
Oat Ridge
Fraser Ridge
Moorehead Ridge
Telegraph Ridge
Big Hadley Pk
Brushy Mtn
North Slide Pk
Shubrick Peak
Miller Camp
Miller Flat
Miller Ridge
King Peak

As Big Flat broadens to its widest point, the road draws away from the shore. At 16¼ miles your path crosses a landing strip used by the residents of the house ahead.

As you approach the canyon of Big Flat Creek, you meet the Rattlesnake Ridge Trail on the left. It climbs 5¾ miles to Kings Crest Trail east of the Miller Camp Trail. Watch for the small timber rattlesnakes that live on the flat and in the rocky wash of the creek. Other animals frequenting Big Flat include bear, deer, fox, badger, rubber boa snake (harmless) and various lizards. Douglas firs and cypresses grow along the edge of the flat.

After paralleling the runway, your trail forks. The roadbed continues along the runway, then heads into the canyon, where the most protected campsites lie among trees alongside the broad, gravelly wash. If you are continuing south or want to camp at Miller Flat, take the trail that forks right, crosses the runway, and follows the edge of the alder and willow forest near the beach. It passes two camps around 16I miles. The second one has a driftwood shelter tall enough to stand up in, with a nifty flag. From here you can look up Big Flat Creek Canyon to 4088-foot Kings Peak. Then you cross Big Flat Creek. Stay right of the trees on the far side. Watch for rattlers!

You come to Miller Flat, broader and more wooded than Big Flat. Wild rose, chemise, gooseberry, red alder and poison oak grow near the creek. Several campsites lie near the trail. More sheltered camps are in the forest to the northeast. Your trail turns east, climbing gradually up the broad flat, a favorite browse for deer. Easy walking across Miller Flat brings you to 17⅝ miles, where a short descent drops you back on the beach at 17¾ miles.

You again walk the beach at the base of steep bluffs. On your right lie many offshore rocks and tidepools. After a small, unmapped creek, the beach becomes very rocky. You round a small point at 18⅜ miles as the beach gets narrower.

Ahead lies another stretch where progress may be blocked at a tide of +4.0 feet or more. The rugged cliffs above have many small creeks, seeps and springs, supporting hanging gardens of wildflowers in spring and early summer. The narrowest point lies just before Shipman Creek at 18¾ miles.

Beautiful Shipman Creek has camps in the driftwood on either side of its mouth. The deep wooded canyon is a treat to explore. At low tide you can visit the rewarding tidepools west of its mouth. You are 6¼ miles from Shelter Cove.

You walk a broad beach until 19½ miles, where you cross a small creek. Round a point where the beach turns rocky and narrow. Pass Buck Creek at 20 miles and meet the Buck Creek Trail, which climbs 3300 feet in the 3⅝ miles to Kings Crest Trail (see Trail #57-OTHER SUGGESTION).

Many more creeks tumble down the cliffs on your way to Gitchell Creek at 21½ miles. A campsite sits beside its mouth. The vehicle users once allowed this far north on the beach from Shelter Cove had degraded the place with trash, but it is more pristine now.

After another mile of sandy beach, you can follow a dirt track along the bluffs. Around 23¼ miles, the Horse Mountain Creek Trail on the left climbs 4¼ miles to Horse Mountain Road about a mile north of Tolkan Campground. While Horse Mountain Trail gains 1700 feet, it is still one of the less challenging coast to crest routes.

At 23½ miles is the mouth of wooded Horse Mountain Creek, where the track returns to the beach. Big rocks lie along the beach at 23⅞ miles, before another steep creek. The beach broadens as you turn south, heading straight for Point Delgada. As you walk the beach or bluff road along the base of the rugged Kaluna Cliff, your thoughts may turn to the cold beer or ice cream available in Shelter Cove. You cross Telegraph Creek at 25 miles and come to the parking area.

## 54. SMITH-ETTER ROAD/KINSEY RIDGE TRAIL TO BEACH

STEEP SHORTCUT TO HEART OF LOST COAST

*This is the shortest hiking route into the heart of the Lost Coast. Although it entails a longer drive on dirt roads to get to this trailhead, the extra effort by vehicle allows you to hike just 4 miles to reach the middle section of the Lost Coast, 12 miles from the north and south trailheads. Remember that you must climb 2400 feet in elevation to return to your car from the beach.*

*The Smith-Etter Road was reopened to vehicle traffic in spring, 1987. When the road is open, generally April 1 to October 31, you can drive 9 steep, winding miles on the Smith-Etter Road, park at the locked gate, and hike to the beach.*

The locked gate blocks Smith-Etter Road at its junction with the Telegraph Ridge Jeep Trail. Park near the gate, being sure not to block traffic on Telegraph Ridge Jeep Trail (which four-wheelers can drive northwest for 2½ miles to the Spanish Ridge and Cooskie Creek Trails).

Behind the gate your route follows the Smith-Etter Road, now called Kinsey Ridge Trail, northwest, then west, below the summit of Telegraph Ridge. On your left the steep watershed of Kinsey Creek drops to the ocean far below. The trail climbs slightly for ½ mile. Beyond ¼ mile big Douglas firs grow where a little gully crosses the road. This pleasantly sheltered spot has room to camp on flat ground on either side of the road. When the wind dies down you can hear the roar of the surf.

At ½ mile your climb levels atop Kinsey Ridge, which you follow on the steady descent to the beach. A wide spot

## SMITH-ETTER ROAD/KINSEY RIDGE TRAIL TO BEACH:

DISTANCE: 3¾ miles one way.
TIME: Two to 3 hours each way.
TERRAIN: Descends road along Kinsey Ridge to beach. Steep climb back.
ELEVATION GAIN/LOSS: 140 feet+/2460 feet-, one way.
BEST TIME: Spring or fall.
WARNINGS: Road closed in wet weather, usually November to March; inquire. Unmaintained road requires high clearance vehicle, may require four-wheel drive. Bear canisters and permits required for overnight trips. See also warnings for Trail #53.
HOW TO GET THERE: Follow directions in Trail #53 to Honeydew. Then go left for 1.5 miles, then right on Smith-Etter Road. Drive 9 steep, rough and winding miles to trailhead.
FURTHER INFO: Bureau of Land Management, Arcata (707) 825-2300, Southern Humboldt office 986-5400.
OTHER SUGGESTION: SPANISH RIDGE TRAIL starts from Telegraph Ridge Jeep Trail, off Smith-Etter Road, descending 2000 feet in 3 miles to Spanish Flat.

on the ridge marks ¾ mile. The trail descends steadily from there. The low, brushy vegetation allows views northwest into deep Oat Creek Canyon and grassy Oat Ridge and Spanish Ridge beyond.

At one mile you have another view of the beach at the mouth of Kinsey Creek. Then your trail leaves the ridgetop, bending right to descend along its north face. Beyond 1½ miles you regain the top of the ridge as it descends steeply toward the shore. Wildflowers along the road include bush lupine, wild rose, sticky monkeyflower, Douglas iris, morning glory, thistle, and pennyroyal.

The road starts a series of long switchbacks at 1¾ miles. These descend into a dark forest of Douglas fir and live oak. Return to the ridge briefly at 2¼ miles, then switchback right to its north side. Many birds frequent this area. Poppy, coastal manroot and poison oak grow on the road shoulders.

At 3 miles you come to the westernmost bend in the road, high above the mouth of Oat Creek. Switchback sharply left here and descend steeply southeast. The wilderness coast stretches magnificently before you. The broad shoal of Big Flat lies 4 miles away. Far beyond it Point Delgada extends into the Pacific. You can see the Etter cabin to the south and Paul Smith's cabin not far to the north. The point where the road comes to the beach is also visible, still 800 feet below.

At 3¼ miles you switchback right and descend by five more steep switchbacks to the beach, 3¾ miles from the locked gate. Sticky monkeyflower, rattlesnake grass and beach morning glory grow at the junction.

From the junction a road runs south to Kinsey Creek in just ¼ mile. Big Flat is 4½ miles, while the southern trailhead at Shelter Cove lies 12 miles to the southeast.

Along the coast to the north, Paul Smith's cabin lies at the foot of Oat Ridge in one mile. Spanish Flat is 1¾ miles away. It is 10 miles to the Punta Gorda Lighthouse, 13 miles to the northern trailhead at the mouth of the Mattole River. See Trails #53 and 58 for more details on the Lost Coast.

## 55.
## KINGS CREST NORTH
### FROM SMITH-ETTER ROAD TO KINGS PEAK

*The Kings Crest Trail traverses the high ridge of King Range Wilderness Area. One of the more rugged hikes in the area, Kings Crest Trail provides spectacular views of the wilderness coast to the west. While this area burned in a summer 2004 wildfire, the trails were reworked in 2005. The route connects with spurs to designated campsites at Rattlesnake Ridge, Miller and Maple Camps, or you can dry-camp along the trail. After 5⅝ miles the trail reaches the 4088-foot summit of Kings Peak, where the views are unsurpassed. The trip to the peak is ideal for a backpack trip of one or two nights. It can also be done as a long, rigorous day hike of 11¼ miles. Experienced backpackers may make a 28¼-mile loop, continuing south beyond Kings Peak to descend the steep Buck Creek Trail, walk the beach, then ascend Kinsey Ridge Trail/Smith-Etter Road to the trailhead.*

*You will often have the Kings Crest to yourself. Carry water since there is none along the main trail and the sources at Miller and Maple Camps may dry up by summer. The Smith-Etter Road may be closed in wet weather, limiting access to the trailhead.*

The trail starts by climbing 200 feet on an old jeep road to a flat clearing with views east. Your trail then descends along the east face of North Slide Peak with fine views of the rugged ridge you follow southeast to Kings Peak. The path descends an open, brushy slope to ½ mile, then descends gradually along a shaded section.

At 7/8 mile make a big bend left and cross another barren stretch to the end of the old jeep track at one mile. A broad spot on the trail sits in a saddle of the ridgetop, a level spot for a dry camp. The trail turns east, climbing steadily for 1/8 mile to a summit where one-leaved wild onion grows.

Make a short, steep descent to 1¼ miles. Then your path contours for nearly ¼ mile before climbing steeply again along the razor ridgetop. More than a dozen steep, short switchbacks wind up a north face of the ridge. Meet the Miller Camp Trail at 1¾ miles, which forks left and descends 800 feet in 1 5/8 miles to the camp and a spring.

After the junction,your trail turns south and descends through burned forest, the result of a fire that you will see much evidence of along the rest of the route. You soon return to the ridgetop. Two miles from the trailhead, you come to a saddle with great views along the razor ridge and west to Shubrick Peak and into Hadley Creek Canyon. In spring wildflowers sprinkle the steep slide below you.

The next 3/8 mile offers some of the easiest walking in the King Range. Contour along the leeward side of the ridge, then climb gradually to meet the south end of the Miller Camp Trail beyond 2 3/8 miles (7/8 mile to Miller Camp on vague tread).

Kings Crest Trail climbs by six switchbacks through forest

## KINGS CREST NORTH:

DISTANCE: 11¼ miles round trip to Kings Peak, 12½ miles with Maple Camp loop; 10 miles one way to Buck Creek Trail.
TIME: Best as an overnight, though possible as long day hike.
TERRAIN: Up and down along a rugged ridge to top of Kings Peak.
ELEVATION GAIN/LOSS: One way to peak: 2210 feet+ /1380 feet-. Round trip: 3590 feet+/3590 feet-. Round trip with Maple Camp loop: 3800 feet+/4250 feet-.
BEST TIME: Spring is best. Summer or fall also good.
WARNINGS: Isolated country, no services. Watch for timber rattlers. May be snow on trail in winter or early spring. Road to trailhead may be closed in rainy season: November to March. Bear canisters and permits required for overnight trips.
HOW TO GET THERE: Follow directions for Trail #48, except that you come to the trailhead at 7.5 miles on Smith-Etter Road.
FURTHER INFO: Bureau of Land Management, Arcata (707) 825-2300, Southern Humboldt office 986-5400.

where Oregon grape, waterleaf, gooseberry and bear grass thrive, coming to a knob on the ridgetop at 2⁵/₈ miles. Make a shady descent, followed by a short uphill to 2⁷/₈ miles, where a shady dry camp sits astride the trail. Descend, then climb to the 3-mile point, where you meet the Rattlesnake Ridge Trail, marked by a plastic sign. The spur drops steeply south to a camp and reliable water source in ¾ mile, then continues 5 more miles to the coast at Big Flat.

The Crest Trail climbs steeply by seven switchbacks to a summit of 3620 feet at 3¼ miles. Then you descend steeply through a brushy area for ¼ mile. The trail follows the ridgetop up, down, up and down again in the next stretch with frequent views of Big Flat Creek and the blue Pacific 3000 feet below.

From 3⁷/₈ miles you leave the ridgetop to climb steeply again. At 4¹/₈ miles the trail becomes easier, contouring through a pleasantly shaded forest of Douglas fir, crossing steep slopes prone to slides. Around 4½ miles you have views of the Mattole Valley and the Yolla Bolly and Trinity Mountains.

Your trail climbs a bit, then crosses a talus slope before 4¾ miles. Return to the ridgetop briefly at a saddle with breathtaking views of the steep and rugged surrounding country. The headwaters of Big Flat Creek lie just ¼ mile to the south and 1000 feet below.

The trail climbs, then descends through fir and hardwood forests along a steep slope, then ascends steeply to a junction at 5¹/₈ miles. On the left the Lightning Trail (see Trail #56) descends 2 miles to its trailhead, with a spur branching right to reach Maple Camp in ⁵/₈ mile. On the right the Kings Crest Trail continues (see Trail #57) for 5¾ miles to end at Saddle Mountain Road. Turn right for the top of Kings Peak as well, ascending 600 feet in ½ mile to the summit. Trail #56 has a detailed description of the fantastic view from the peak.

# 56.
# LIGHTNING TO KINGS PEAK
## STEEP BUT SHADY ROUTE

*The Lightning Trail offers the shortest hike of the three routes to Kings Peak, with the easiest road access as well. It is the most accessible in winter, although the King Range Road may also be closed by slides in the rainy season. This route has two other advantages: it is the shadiest route, ideal in hot weather; it is the shortest route to Maple Camp, which has water in winter, spring and early summer. Although the route ascends 2000 feet to Kings Peak, it is well graded and pleasant.*

The Lightning Trail ascends from a new trailhead just before the old trailhead on the left side of King Range Road, just beyond a big curve left and a wide spot where you can park. Head southeast past a garbage can and a trail register. Sign in, please. The trail climbs through a hardwood forest of madrone and tanoak, with huckleberry in the understory.

Your path soon switchbacks left and heads east on faint tread. The trail steepens, climbing moderately through a series of lazy switchbacks. Just beyond ⅛ mile you pass through a sunny clearing surrounded by manzanita.

Climb steadily along a hardwood-covered ridge. At ¼ mile you pass an old Douglas fir and veer to the left. The trail runs southeast, then south, climbing the ridge with occasional switchbacks.

By ½ mile a steep drop lies on the right. Continue your climb, meandering in and out of virgin Douglas fir forest with much bear grass and salal as you approach the sound of a stream. Beyond ⅝ mile, a right fork leads to pretty Big Rock Camp, beside a stream with big, moss-covered rocks and Douglas firs eight feet in diameter.

Climb steeply by many switchbacks for the next ¼ mile. At ⅞ mile you switchback left and head southeast onto the relatively cool and wooded north side of the ridge. Regain the top of the ridge briefly at one mile, then climb west through the forest. After a straight, uphill stretch, your trail switchbacks left at 1⅛ miles. Salal and Oregon grape cover the forest floor.

You soon return to the dry ridge, where manzanita and canyon live oak mix with the fir forest. Climb the ridge, passing through a thicket of spiny whitethorn ceanothus, which has fragrant white flowers in May. At 1⅜ miles you climb through a dense forest of young Douglas fir.

Just 1⅝ miles from the trailhead, you come to a junction where gooseberry grows. The left fork leads to Maple Camp in ¼ mile (shady camp by a seasonal stream) and to Kings Crest Trailhead in 6 miles. Take the right fork northwest. It is one mile to the top of Kings Peak, 5½ miles to Smith-Etter Road.

The trail continues to climb through forest and brush

LIGHTNING TO KINGS PEAK:

DISTANCE: 2½ miles to peak, 1 7/8 miles to Maple Camp.
TIME: At least 3 hours to top and back.
TERRAIN: Ascends brush-and-forest covered ridge to summit of Kings Peak.
ELEVATION GAIN/LOSS: Round trip: 2000 feet+/2000 feet-.
BEST TIME: The best year-round trail to the peak, still nicest in spring.
WARNINGS: Watch for timber rattlesnakes and ticks. Isolated country with no services. Best to carry extra water in dry season when water sources are not reliable. Bear canisters and permits required for overnight trips.
HOW TO GET THERE: FROM NORTH: Leave Highway 101 at South Fork/Honeydew exit (M.36.1 from north, M.35.5 from south). Follow Mattole Road west for 23 miles to Honeydew and junction with Wilder Ridge Road. turn left and go 5 miles to junction with Horse Mountain Road. Turn right and go 3 miles on steep, winding Horse Mountain Road to junction with King Range Road. Take sharp right and go 6.6 miles to Lightning Trailhead.
FROM SOUTH: Leave Highway 101 at Garberville (M.10.8). Take Briceland Road from Redway (2.8 miles north of Garberville on Redwood Drive). Go 18 miles, then turn right onto unpaved Horse Mountain Road (aka Kings Peak Road). Follow this for 9.5 miles to junction with King Range Road, where you turn left and go 6.6 miles more to trailhead.
FURTHER INFO: Bureau of Land Management, Arcata (707) 825-2300, Southern Humboldt office 986-5400.
OTHER SUGGESTIONS: Two pleasant campgrounds are located on Kings Crest Road, TOLKAN CAMP and HORSE MOUNTAIN CAMP (respectively 3.8 and 7.0 miles from Shelter Cove Road). PARADISE ROYALE MOUNTAIN BIKE TRAIL offers a 14-mile loop through rugged country east of Horse Mountain Road. Find it's designated trailhead on east side of road 2.8 miles from Shelter Cove Road (one mile south of Tolkan Camp).

fields where white-veined shinleaf and tall prince's pine grow in the understory. As you meet the Kings Crest Trail at 2 miles, make a sharp left for the top of Kings Peak. The trail climbs by switchbacks, then follows a brushy ridge to 2¼ miles, where you turn right on the trail to the summit.

Climb a jagged ridge, with views down the west face of the peak to Big Flat and the ocean far below. Indian warriors brighten the way in spring with their bold, dark red flowers. Reach the summit less than ¼ mile from the turnoff. Suddenly you come out on top of the world.

The top, 4088 feet above sea level, consists of a 30-feet-by-40-feet semi-flat area, dropping off steeply on all sides. To the west the ocean glimmers in sunlight. Infinite waves roll toward the shore, reflecting light and heat over chilly ocean depths. Purplish streaks far offshore mark the deepest water, beyond which a snow-white fog bank often obscures the horizon.

The rugged King Range stretches northwest, ending just beyond view at Cape Mendocino, westernmost point in California. To the northeast lie the Trinity Mountains. The jagged Trinity Alps rise to 8000 feet beyond the lower Trinitys. On the clearest of days you can see the round bulk of Lassen Peak (10,487 feet) to the east-northeast, 141 miles away. Directly to the east, at half the distance, the 7000-foot peaks of the Yolla Bollys show in sharp relief.

As you look south down the coast, Saddle Mountain looms in the foreground. Shelter Cove juts seaward to its right. South of Shelter Cove fall (in order) Chemise Mountain, Mistake Point, Cape Vizcaino, Bruhel Point, then the white sands of Ten Mile Dunes. From here, Fort Bragg lies to the right of the dunes, with Point Arena stretching seaward beyond.

Take a moment to reflect on the geology of this place. Directly west of Kings Peak is Big Flat, 4000 feet below (just 3 miles as the crow flies). The San Andreas Fault lies just offshore. Over eons, as the onshore tectonic plate moves south, it collides with the Pacific plate moving north. This immense and powerful collision has uplifted these rugged mountains.

From the peak you can return to Lightning Trailhead in about one hour.

## 57.
## KINGS CREST SOUTH
### SADDLE MOUNTAIN TO THE TOP OF THE WORLD

*The southern end of the Kings Crest Trail follows the old Saddle Mountain Road for 3.1 miles, then the trail along the high ridge of the King Range to the top of Kings Peak. At 4088 feet, the peak is the highest point along the Northern California coast. Brush fields alternate with fir forests in this steep, rugged country. This route to the peak is a pleasant overnight hike (or a strenuous, 10¾-mile day hike) climaxing in spectacular views. Be sure to read HOW TO GET THERE to*

*prepare you for the drive to the starting point.*

*The Legend of Kings Peak claims that a Manila galleon was wrecked on the Lost Coast. Survivors or Indians carried away its gold, jewels and spices to a cave and hid them. Years later an earthquake sealed the cave and obliterated all traces of it. My own favorite treasure is the view from the peak.*

From the trailhead, your trail descends west to a trail register. Sign in, please. Then descend south on the old road through mixed forest of Douglas fir, tanoak and madrone. After a view south along the coast, the track climbs west as sugar pine joins the forest. The road switchbacks left at 1/8 mile, then right on a steady ascent.

Around 7/8 mile Buck Creek Trail forks left, climbing south before descending steeply to the beach (see OTHER SUGGESTION). The Kings Crest Trail descends gradually west. Beyond 1¼ miles you descend moderately, winding along the crest with views down to the mouth of Buck Creek and ahead to Kings Peak.

At 1⁵/8 miles your track bends right and resumes climbing. Live oak joins the forest, with whitethorn and coffeeberry in the understory. The route offers more vistas south along the coast until you switchback to the right around 2¹/8 miles and pass a dry camp.

Ascend moderately north with views east to the Yolla Bollys. Beyond 2¾ miles the road switchbacks right, then left to climb gradually. Descend west from 3 miles, coming to the old trailhead at 3¹/8 miles.

Descend gradually north as the trail narrows. For the next ¼ mile you descend through mixed forest of Douglas fir, sugar pine and hardwoods. Bear grass and spiky Oregon grape grow in the understory. The trail contours to 3½ miles, then descends past madrone, tanoak, canyon live oak and scattered fir.

You soon see the glimmer of the ocean through the trees on your left. To the north lie the steep slopes of Kings Peak,

KINGS CREST SOUTH:

DISTANCE: 10¾ miles round trip to Kings Peak, 11⅝ miles with Maple Camp loop; 5¾ miles one way to Lightning Trail junction, 10⅞ miles to Smith-Etter Road.

TIME: Best as an overnight, but can reach Kings Peak as a long day hike.

TERRAIN: Climbs a high, rugged coastal ridge to the top of Kings Peak; continues up and down along the ridge to Smith-Etter Road.

ELEVATION GAIN/LOSS: One way to peak: 2480 feet+/1420 feet-. Round trip 3900 feet+/3900 feet-.

BEST TIME: Clear weather. Spring is best; September and October next best.

WARNINGS: Isolated country without services. Last 3.6 miles of road are steep and rough, prone to washouts in winter. No water available on trail. Watch for ticks and timber rattlesnakes. May be snow on trail in winter, early spring. Bear canisters and permits required for overnight trips.

HOW TO GET THERE: Leave Highway 101 at Garberville (M.10.8) from the south (or Redway at M.14.6 from the north). Take Redwood Drive to Redway, then Briceland Road west for 18 miles (steep and winding, but paved). Go right on unpaved Horse Mountain Road (aka Kings Peak Road) for 6.5 miles. Then turn left on Saddle Mountain Road, marked "KINGS CREST TRAIL." The driving gets rough here. While most cars can make it to the trailhead, consider Lightning Trailhead as the "better road" alternative if your car has low clearance, a weak transmission or bad tires, or if you visit in winter. If you take the high road, drive slowly and alertly as it is steep, winding and poorly maintained. In one mile you top Horse Mountain Ridge. Go right, coming to Kings Crest Trailhead at 3.6 miles. The broad parking area on the right has room for a rudimentary camp but no water.

FURTHER INFO: Bureau of Land Management, Arcata (707) 825-2300, Southern Humboldt office 986-5400.

OTHER SUGGESTIONS: BUCK CREEK TRAIL forks left at ⅞ mile up the Kings Crest Trail. It descends 3300 feet to the beach at the mouth of Buck Creek in just 3⅝ miles. It is the shortest and steepest route to the beach from Kings Crest. Not recommended for a stroll to and from the beach. Experienced backpackers may choose to make a 29.5-mile CREST TO COAST LOOP: descend to beach at Buck Creek, head north for 9 miles, where you climb east on the Kinsey Ridge Trail/Smith-Etter Road for 6 miles. Then take Kings Crest Trail for 10⅞ miles to return to Kings Crest Trailhead. Trails #53, 54 and 55 provide further detail. You might do it in the opposite direction, but the climb from the beach to Saddle Mountain may conjure thoughts of an eternity in hell, even though the trail was recently reworked to provide fewer steep pitches (and making it a mile longer).

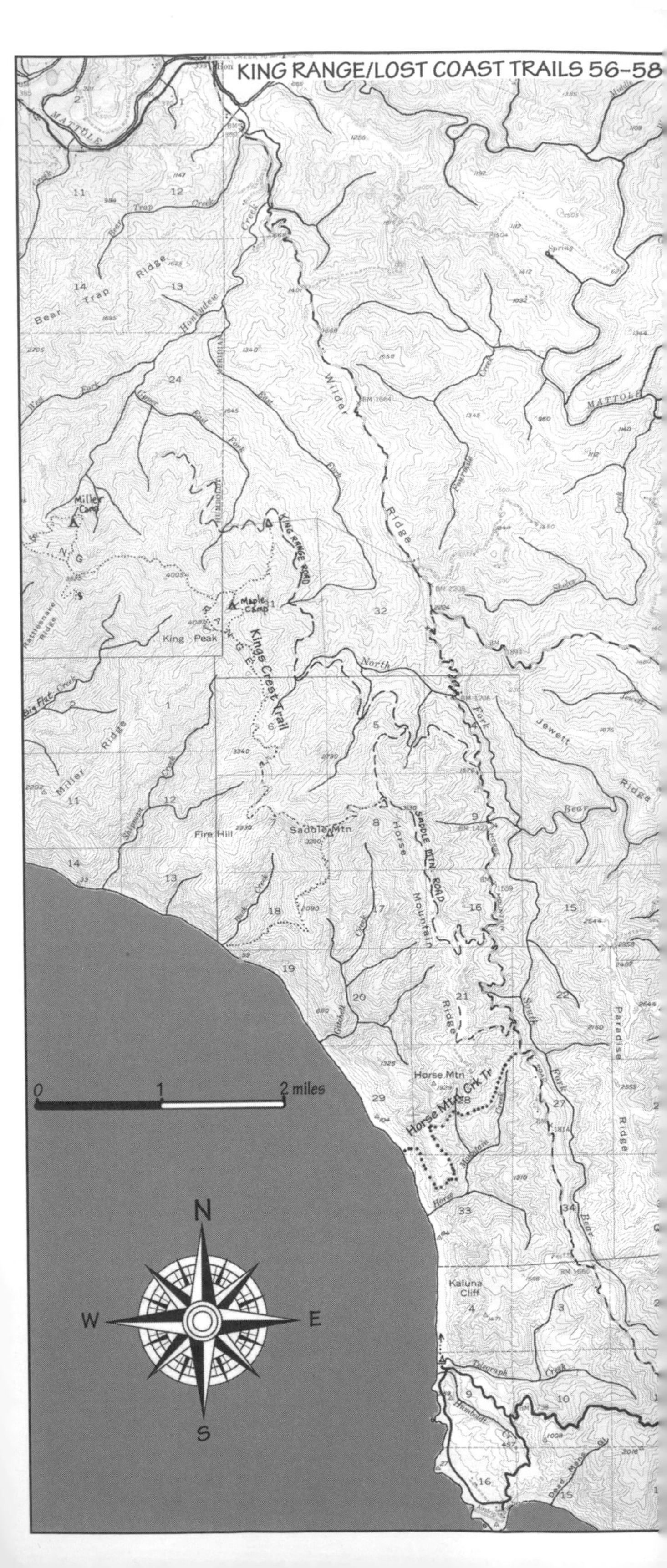

KING RANGE/LOST COAST TRAILS 56-58
MATTOLE
Bear Trap Ridge
Bear Trap Creek
Honeydew Creek
West Fork
East Fork
Wilder Ridge
Miller Camp
Maple Camp
King Peak
KING RANGE ROAD
Kings Crest Trail
Rattlesnake Ridge
Big Flat Creek
Miller Ridge
North Fork
Jewett Ridge
Fire Hill
Saddle Mtn
SADDLE MTN ROAD
Horse Mountain Ridge
Paradise Ridge
Horse Mtn
Horse Mtn Crk Tr
Kaluna Cliff
Telegraph Creek
Spring
0
1
2 miles
N
S
E
W

scarred by a massive landslide. Before 3¾ miles the trail starts to climb. Soon gnarled, gravity-defying canyon live oaks on the left afford views of the sheer drop to the headwaters of Shipman Creek. You might notice the massive roots of a tenacious Douglas fir down slope.

Now the climb starts in earnest, making ten switchbacks through madrone and oak forest. At 4⅛ miles a clearing provides the best views yet to the east and south.

For another ⅛ mile, you climb through manzanita brush fields with broadleaf ceanothus (can be unpleasant on a warm day). Then your climb eases as the trail plunges into cool mixed forest. At 4½ miles the trail levels on a brushy ridge. Views open up to the ocean far below and Kings Peak to the northwest.

Your trail returns to the east side of the ridge and climbs north. At 4⅝ miles you can see Wilder Ridge below you, dotted with houses and barns. Mattole River Canyon lies beyond the ridge. Beyond that, the parallel ridges of the Coast Range, bisected by the Eel River Canyon, stretch to the horizon.

Your climb steepens around 4¾ miles. You switchback twice to regain the brushy ridgetop. At 4⅞ miles you pass cabin-sized boulders surrounded by Fremont silktassel as the tread turns rough briefly. The Trinity Alps may be visible to the northeast beyond the very long and straight South Fork Mountain. Just up the trail you have views down the ocean side of the ridge. Make a steep, winding climb to a broad flat covered with low manzanita.

At 5 miles a steel sign marks the junction. The right fork descends ½ mile to Maple Camp, in a shady canyon beside a seasonal creek that rushes in winter and spring, and to Lightning Trailhead (2½ miles, 1000 feet below). Take the left fork. This leads to another junction at 5⅛ miles. From the junction you can see the simple shelter on the east face of Kings Peak. If you go left, the summit lies a brisk ¼ mile up the trail, 200 feet more in elevation. The thrilling view from the top is described in Trail #56.

Take the right fork to continue along the Kings Crest Trail. It climbs gradually west, then north across the east face of the peak. It soon descends, returning to the ridge and rejoining the peak trail by 5⅜ miles. Look northwest for a view along the rugged north end of the Kings Crest.

The trail descends north along the brushy ridgetop, then climbs east to 5½ miles. Descend through chaparral, then drop by seven switchbacks to another junction at 5¾ miles. The Lightning Trail on the right (see Trail #56) offers the last chance for Maple Camp.

Go left for the Kings Crest Trail. It descends to 6 miles, then contours along the ridgetop briefly, then across the shady east and north slopes of Peak 4005. You return to the ridgetop again around 7 miles. Climb, then contour along the ridge to 7⅜ miles. Climb steeply for ¼ mile,

then descend steeply by six switchbacks. You return to the ridgetop and meet the Rattlesnake Ridge Trail at 7⅞ miles.

The spur down Rattlesnake Ridge has been reworked since the 2004 fire. It descends moderately along the ridgetop for ½ mile, then turns steep and brushy for ¼ mile to reach a camp and a year-round water source in a swale at the headwaters of Big Flat Creek. Rattlesnake Ridge Trail descends all the way to Big Flat on the coast, about 5 miles from the camp.

Kings Crest Trail continues northwest along the main ridge. It passes the Miller Camp spur on the right at 8½ miles on its way to the northern North Slide Peak Trailhead at 10⅞ miles. See Trail #55 for details of the north half of the trail.

## 58. SHELTER COVE NORTH

LOST COAST, SOUTH END

*The subdivision of Shelter Cove sprawls over the steep, grassy bluffs of Point Delgada. It sits like a mirage, surrounded by the rugged wilderness peaks and canyons of the King Range. In the northwest corner of the subdivision, Beach Road ends at at the big parking lot just above Black Sands Beach, the southern trailhead for the 25 miles of wilderness beach called the Lost Coast. If you have forgotten anything, Shelter Cove has two small general merchandise stores.*

*The first 3½ miles of beach are no longer open to motorized vehicles, a happy commentary on the Bureau of Land Management's improved policies for this pristine wilderness and California generally.*

*This trailhead allows you to reach some of the most spectacular areas of the Lost Coast in an overnight hike. The virgin*

| SHELTER COVE NORTH: |
| --- |
| DISTANCE: Up to 25 miles; $5^1/_8$ miles to Buck Creek, 6¼ miles to Shipman Creek, 8 miles to Big Flat.<br>TIME: One or more days.<br>TERRAIN: Level beach walking, often in loose sand.<br>BEST TIME: Spring or fall.<br>WARNINGS: Watch for timber rattlers and rogue waves on beach. Wilderness permits and bear canisters are required for overnight trips.<br>HOW TO GET THERE: Follow directions in Trail #57, but stay on Shelter Cove Road about 21 miles. As you descend to Shelter Cove, take first right, Beach Road, which ends at trailhead parking lot.<br>FURTHER INFO: Bureau of Land Management, Arcata (707) 825-2300, Southern Humboldt office 986-5400. |

*canyon of Shipman Creek lies just 6¼ miles from the trailhead. Miller Flat and Big Flat are about 2 miles farther.*

You walk north on the broad beach, quickly crossing Telegraph Creek. At $^1/_8$ mile a hard-packed road on the bluffs parallels the beach. It climbs a short, steep hill sprinkled with wildflowers and soon descends to a campsite at the top of the beach at $^3/_8$ mile. Although the road climbs the bluff again, it soon ends at a rough crossing of the creek that comes off the steep face of Kaluna Cliff. Hike the broad beach north, crossing another creek at $1^1/_8$ miles, beyond which big rocks stand on the beach.

At 1½ miles you come to Horse Mountain Creek, a deep wooded canyon with a mouth bracketed by steep, grassy slopes. Soon the Horse Mountain Creek Trail forks right to climb 4¼ miles to Horse Mountain. The beach tapers to its narrowest point at 1¾ miles, then broadens. Before 2 miles a primitive road runs along the bluffs again. You can follow the bluff road for ½ mile, as the coast bends northwest. A washout near 2½ miles forces you to return to the beach.

Pass Gitchell Creek at 3½ miles. The broad beach narrows at $4^1/_8$ miles. You continue along the base of steep cliffs with many cascading streams. At $4^5/_8$ miles the beach tapers to a point that may be impassable at very high tide. Walk the narrow, rocky beach to Buck Creek at $5^1/_8$ miles. The Buck Creek Trail climbs east from the south side of the creek (see Trail #57—OTHER SUGGESTION).

Continuing along the beach, you quickly come to another rocky, narrow section of beach. It should be passable at all but the highest tide. The narrow beach continues past many offshore rocks. The high cliffs on your right have many springs and hanging gardens of wildflowers.

At 5½ miles a creek cascades to the beach, just short of a rocky promontory. It plunges 1600 feet in its short, ¾-mile course. Offshore lies the deep submarine trench of Delgada Canyon, which is 450 feet deep just ½ mile from shore. Beyond the rocky point, the beach becomes very broad.

You come to Shipman Creek 6¼ miles from the trailhead. Huge piles of driftwood lie in the protected mouth of the wooded canyon, which has camps on both sides. Clear pools and waterfalls lie upstream, while wildflowers thrive on the grassy bluff east of its mouth.

To continue along the beach, you need a tide lower than +4.0 feet. The narrow beach is backed by 10-foot cliffs topped by steep, grassy bluffs. Beyond 6⅝ miles the beach gets wider, though steep cliffs still tower overhead. At 7¼ miles a painted rock covered with iceplant marks a path that climbs onto rolling and grassy Miller Flat. You come to Big Flat Creek at 8 miles. The base of the Smith-Etter Road lies 4 miles beyond. For details of this area and the north end of the Lost Coast, see Trail #53.

## 59.
## HIDDEN VALLEY TO CHEMISE MOUNTAIN TO WHALE GULCH

### CONTINUING ALONG THE LOST COAST

*BLM reconstructed much of this old pack trail in the early 1990s. It connects the northern and southern sections of the Lost Coast Trail. You can now start backpacking at the mouth of the Mattole River, walk 25 miles along the beach to Shelter Cove, then hike or hitchhike 3 miles of paved road to Hidden Valley Trailhead. From there it is a 28-mile hike to the Usal Trailhead 6 miles north of Highway 1. The 4½ miles south from Hidden Valley Trailhead provide excellent walking. But the next 2½ miles descend the ridge steeply to the mouth of Whale Gulch.*

*You can also start this hike from pleasant Wailaki or Nadelos Campgrounds. This shortens the trip to Chemise Mountain or Whale Gulch by 2¼ miles. There is now a designated camp and reliable water source near the trail between Chemise Mountain and Whale Gulch. The Chinquapin Trail forks to the right south of Chemise Mountain, descending to a water source and Nick's Camp, then returning to the main trail.*

Walk past the gate heading southwest on an old road. Young Douglas fir mix with alder, bay laurel, hazel, and thimbleberry. Wild mint grows in the middle of the road. You will notice the harsh devastation of a forest fire on the left. This hike winds in and out of the area burned by the Chemise Mountain fire of 1973.

At 1/8 mile the road swings left and crosses a tiny, slow-flowing creek. In spring the purple shades of bush lupine, Douglas iris, and ceanothus brighten the path.

You quickly come to a lush green meadow stretching for ½ mile up a valley surrounded by chaparral and fire-scarred forest. Poppy and lupine sprinkle the heavenly meadow of

HIDDEN VALLEY TO CHEMISE MOUNTAIN TO WHALE GULCH:

DISTANCE: 8 5/8 miles one way to Needle Rock Visitor Center; 7 miles one way to Whale Gulch, 5 miles round trip to Chemise Mountain.
TIME: Three to 5 hours.
TERRAIN: Contours through chaparral to a lush meadow, climbs along edge of forest to ridge, which you follow to its summit. Descends ridge to mouth of deep canyon on the coast, climbs, then contours to Needle Rock.
ELEVATION GAIN/LOSS: One way to Whale Gulch: 1170 feet+/2880 feet-. Round trip to Chemise Mountain: 1040 feet+/1040 feet-.
BEST TIME: Spring. Summer and fall are also good.
WARNINGS: In winter and spring the ford of Whale Gulch Creek may be dangerous or impassable. No water on trail until Whale Gulch. Watch for timber rattlers and poison oak. Wilderness permits and bear canisters are now required for overnight trips. Nearest year-round facilities at Shelter Cove. South end of trail is very brushy; wear or carry long pants. Stay on trail and off private property.
HOW TO GET THERE: Leave Highway 101 at Garberville (M.10.8) from south or at Redway (M.14.6) on the north. Take Briceland Road from Redway (2.8 miles north of Garberville on Redwood Drive) for 17 miles. Go left on Chemise Mountain Road for ¼ mile to trailhead on right.
FURTHER INFO: Bureau of Land Management, Arcata (707) 825-2300, Southern Humboldt office 986-5400.
OTHER SUGGESTION: A shorter, easier route to CHEMISE MOUNTAIN leaves from Wailaki Campground, 1.5 miles south of Hidden Valley Trailhead on Chemise Mountain Road. WHALE GULCH can be reached from Briceland Road in Sinkyone Wilderness State Park.

Hidden Valley in spring. Views of the blue Pacific lie to the west and south. In the upper end of the valley an apple orchard marks the site of an old ranch.

At ¼ mile your road forks. Take the left fork; the right fork continues into Hidden Valley. Climb moderately with views of the valley and the ocean beyond. Before ½ mile you are above the upper end of the apple orchard. Your trail switches left and heads north, climbing steeply away from the road. As you climb by several steep, short switchbacks, you are rewarded with views of Hidden Valley.

Climb into unburned forest, then descend briefly back into the burn. The ascent resumes, entering hardwood forest at ¾ mile. It changes to fir forest by 7/8 mile. Then your steep climb winds to gain the ridge at one mile.

The ridge soon becomes brushy. Descend the ridge to 1¼ miles, where you return to forest. Climb briefly, only to descend again, with ceanothus along the trail. Your trail levels at 1 3/8 miles, then makes a steep, short climb to 1½ miles. Another level stretch leads to another short climb.

Climb steeply to 1¾ miles, then level at the junction with the trail from Wailaki and Nadelos Campgrounds. Turn right for Chemise Mountain and Whale Gulch. You climb gradually, heading south to gain the ridgetop.

In 5/8 mile your climb brings you to a sign marking the 2596-foot summit of Chemise Mountain on your left. A nar-

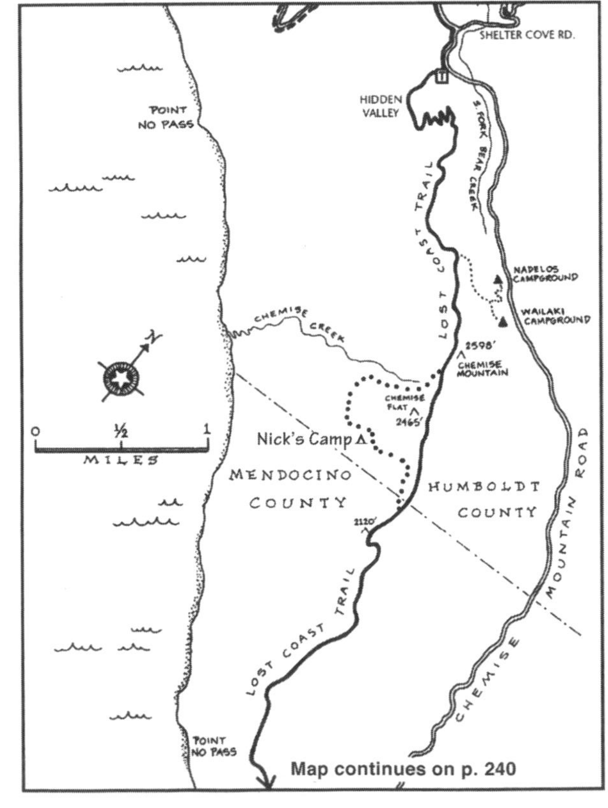

Map continues on p. 240

row, brushy trail winds to the very top in about 150 feet. The side trip is worthwhile because the brush opens to present fine vistas in all directions. Immediately to the south, Chemise Mountain drops off into the deep canyon of Whale Gulch, the route of the rest of this trail. The Sinkyone Wilderness and precipitous Anderson Cliffs lie just beyond. On a clear day you can spot at least 13 different coastal ridges to the south. The high peaks of the Yolla Bolly Mountains are to the east.

The main trail heads south along the ridge. Soon the Chinquapin Trail (2 1/8 miles) forks right, descending to Nick's Camp and the only water source near Chemise Mountain Ridge. It returns to the main trail one mile south of where it left it. The ridgetop trail continues south to the secondary peak of Chemise Flat at 2¾ miles.

The trail south descends briefly, then climbs to a brushy knob on the ridgetop at 2 7/8 miles. Then you descend gently on a rocky, well-cleared path until 3 1/8 miles. Your trail descends steeply, then moderately along the west side of the ridge before it climbs to a top at 3¼ miles where bay laurel grows. You descend again with more views south.

You may hear the distant roar of surf as you climb to another top at 3¾ miles. Then a shady portion of trail descends along the ridge before climbing briefly to the top called Manzanita, 4 miles from your trailhead. A USGS bench marker beside the trail indicates an elevation of 2120 feet. This is a good place to turn back if you are day hiking. From here the trail descends steeply to sea level in less than 3 miles.

What the heck, you say? Let's go! You can reach the

beach in an hour. Your trail descends southeast. By 4¼ miles you enter cool, mature Douglas fir forest. You leave the ridge to descend steeply into a gully by switchbacks, then contour to return to the ridge at 4³/₈ miles.

The trail descends steeply along the ridge, then levels briefly at a grassy clearing, a sign of what lies ahead. Your trail bends left and descends through mixed forest before climbing to another knob on the ridgetop at 4¾ miles. Your trail levels along the shady ridgetop, then descends gradually beyond 5 miles before leveling again. Wild rose, Douglas iris, sugar stick and huckleberry grow beneath the dense forest canopy.

Before 5½ miles you make a brief steep descent, then climb along the crest of the razor ridge, with grasslands to the west. This quickly brings you into a grassy clearing, with excellent views south into the Sinkyone Wilderness. Descend, then climb through the grasslands, then descend steeply through the forest for 1/8 mile. At 5 7/8 miles you again descend through grasslands sprinkled with poppy, yarrow, redwood sorrel, tall brodiaea, buttercup, purple bush lupine, sticky monkeyflower and paintbrush. You soon meet a road from the left that the trail follows, climbing to a flattop on the ridge at 6 miles. An unfinished hip-roofed building sits beside the trail. Horses or dogs are not allowed beyond this point. From here you should stay on top of the ridge or on its west face; private property lies to the east.

Enjoy the easy descent through the grasslands. The trail will soon turn steep and brushy. At 6¼ miles you return to the forest as you descend steeply along the narrow ridge. As you pass the bench marker called Red Hill (elevation 1418 feet), you can see a private house below on the left. Stay on the razor ridge to avoid the private property.

Beyond the house the trail steepens. Watch for poison oak from here to the bottom. At 6 3/8 miles the trail veers left and follows the east side of the ridge through hardwood forest. Return briefly to the ridge. Then, at 6½ miles, the trail descends east by switchbacks. Slink pod and hazel grow on the forest floor. The broad cleared path descends steeply, zigzagging toward Whale Gulch Creek.

At 6¾ miles your trail comes to a shady, slippery ford of the creek. Rock-hop across the creek, then follow the well beaten trail climbing east by switchbacks, then winding south through small gullies. You ascend to a summit and an overlook of Whale Gulch Creek.

Descend toward two small lakes, 7 miles from the Hidden Valley Trailhead. The trail soon climbs southeast, coming to Jones Beach Environmental Camp at 7 5/8 miles. Three campsites cluster around a eucalyptus grove beside a small creek. It is one mile farther south to Needle Rock Visitor Center, where you must register if you wish to camp.

If you plan to continue on the Lost Coast Trail to Usal, you must walk the dirt road south for 2¾ miles to its end at Orchard Creek. From there it is 16¾ miles to Usal. See Trail #60.

# SINKYONE WILDERNESS STATE PARK

*Located in the extreme northwestern corner of Mendocino County, the Sinkyone (sing-key-own) preserves a sample of the rugged wilderness that once existed all along California's North Coast. Though the Sinkyone was settled in the 1860s and was logged and ranched for much of the next century, it now stands as a largely pristine wilderness. The state park was established in 1976.*

*The Sinkyone Wilderness State Park (7937 acres) is unlike any other park in the state. It can be reached only by isolated unpaved mountain roads that are often impassable in winter. You must hike at least 200 feet to camp in the northern half of the park. The Visitor Center is located in a rustic old ranch house with no electricity or telephone.*

*The Sinkyone was named for the tribe that originally inhabited this corrugated country. They were the southernmost of the Athabaskan language tribes on the coast. Known for their backwoods skills, the Sinkyone tribe was small and loosely organized. They were quickly overrun by white settlers.*

*On the brighter side, a four-legged group of Sinkyone natives have recently been relocated in the park. At last count at least three dozen Roosevelt elk live within park boundaries. If you meet elk on the trail, give them plenty of room, especially in rut season in September. The half ton bulls may resent sharing their territory. When agitated, they can run as fast as 35 mph.*

*For more trails in Sinkyone Wilderness State Park, see* **The Hiker's hip pocket Guide to the Mendocino Coast.**

# 60. NEW LOST COAST

## HEART OF THE SINKYONE

*The New Lost Coast Trail traverses the most spectacular portion of the Sinkyone, a rugged untamed country. You pass remnants of century-old homesteads and logging camps, even walk through a ghost town abandoned in 1960. But most signs of habitation have been erased by the harsh climate and lush vegetation.*

*This trail, completed in 1986, only shows on the most recent USGS topo maps. One used to be able to drive 2.5 miles beyond the Visitor Center to the Orchard Creek Trailhead near Orchard Creek Camp. But in 2012, a slip-out on that dirt road caused State Parks to close the road permanently. So now one has to walk the 2½ miles of dirt road to reach the rest of the Sinkyone's Lost Coast Trail. Wilderness Press publishes* **California's Lost Coast Recreation Map**, *the best mapping of the trail to date. On the ground the trail is adequately marked. Map and compass are still recommended as is hiking with a friend. You must register to camp along the trail. The cost is $5 per person per night.*

Start at the Visitor Center or at the locked gate just beyond that bars vehicles from the closed road. Follow the narrow and unimproved dirt road south across coastal grasslands with superb ocean views. The road climbs and descends as it winds through several wooded canyons in the first mile. Descend to ford tiny Flat Rock Creek, then ascend to pass over the flank of High Tip around 1½ miles. Descend steeply with grand views down the coast to cross another creek,then descend gently along a lush valley to road's end and Orchard Creek Camp at 2½ miles.

From the road-end the trail crosses Orchard Creek on a small footbridge. The nearly level trail parallels the creek through lush, riparian vegetation. At 2⅝ miles a spur forks left to Railroad Creek Environmental Camp. Before 3 miles you come to the site of Bear Harbor Ranch, where Bear Harbor Environmental Camp lies near the beach.

The Lost Coast Trail heads east along a creek, passing a corral and trail register. Grasslands give way to forest as you begin to climb. At 3⅜ miles you cross the creek. Then you switchback to the right and climb steadily out of the canyon. Before 3¾ miles your trail joins the first of many old logging roads it follows. It climbs to grand views of the rugged coast.

At 4 miles the trail switches away from one logging road and promptly joins another. Redwood, huckleberry, wild rose, iris and slink pod grow along the path. You top a ridge, then descend into Duffy's Gulch. The trail leaves the logging road and joins a portion of the original Humboldt Trail, built in 1862 when the coast to the south was opened to homesteading. Settlers from Mendocino had to ride or walk the trail to Eureka to register their land claims.

As you descend east into Duffy's Gulch, you spot virgin redwoods. The trail switchbacks down to the creek crossing, passing ancient redwoods ten feet in diameter, grand fir, Douglas fir, bay laurel and bigleaf maple.

Take a minute to quench your thirst, fill your canteen, and marvel at the virgin beauty of this place. Along the creek grow five-finger, woodwardia, leather, sword and lady ferns. Pacific waterleaf and saxifrage thrive in this moist habitat, as does poison oak, which you should watch for. You have come 2¼ miles from Orchard Creek, 4¾ miles from Needle Rock gate.

At 5¼ miles you leave the forest for steep coastal grasslands. Your trail traverses the grassy bluffs through a series

NEW LOST COAST:

DISTANCE: One way: 19¼ miles to Usal; 6¾ miles to Wheeler, 11⅞ miles to Little Jackass, 14¼ miles to Anderson Gulch.
TIME: Up to 3 days.
TERRAIN: Many ups and downs over rugged coastal ridges and through canyons.
ELEVATION GAIN/LOSS: To Wheeler 1830 ft.+/1960 ft-. Visitor Center to Usal: 5690 feet+/5820 feet-.
BEST TIME: Spring. Summer and fall are next best.
WARNINGS: Road beyond visitor center was closed permanently in 2012 after a slip-out, so hikers now must start from the visitor center for all points south. Isolated country far from towns and services. Timber rattlesnakes, ticks, poison oak, stinging nettles all occur along trail; watch for them. You must have a permit to camp overnight on the trail. Camping allowed only in designated areas. Bear canisters are recommended but not required.
HOW TO GET THERE: Exit Highway 101 at Garberville (M.10.0) on the south or Redway (M.14.6) on the north. Take Briceland Road from Redway (2.0 miles north of Garberville on Redwood Drive). In 12 miles go left through Whitethorn. In 4.5 more miles you come to the junction known as Four Corners. Go straight,descending a steep and narrow,winding dirt road (impassable to RVs or trailers, may be closed after heavy rains). Park near the Visitor Center in 3.6 miles.
FEES: $5/person/day.
FURTHER INFO: Sinkyone Wilderness State Park (707) 946-2311, 247-3318.

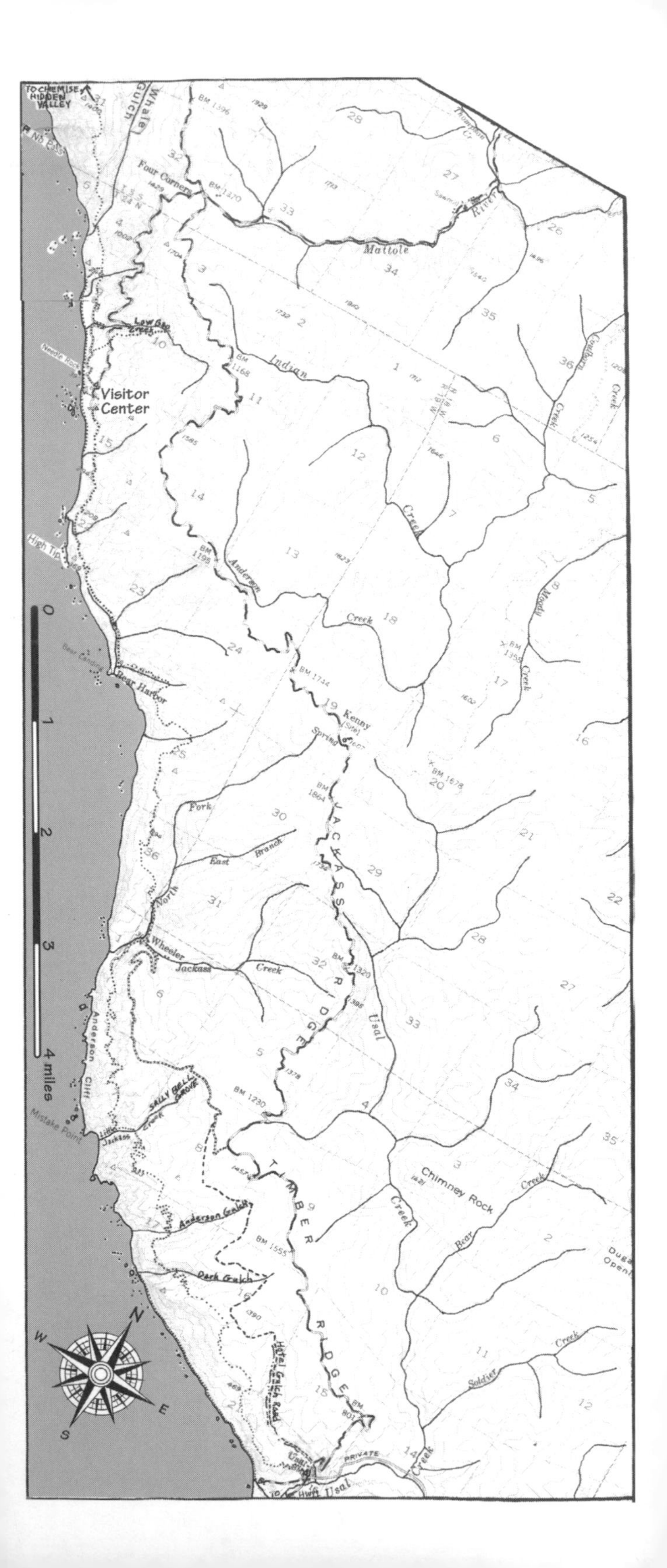
TO CHEMISE, HIDDEN VALLEY
Whale Gulch
Four Corners
Thompson Cr.
Sawmill
River
Mattole
Low Gap Creek
Needle Rock
Visitor Center
Indian
Creek
Anderson
Creek
High Tip
Moody
Creek
Bear Harbor
Kenny (Site)
Spring
JACKASS
RIDGE
Fork
East Branch
North
Wheeler
Jackass
Creek
Usal
Anderson Cliff
Mistake Point
SALLY BELL GROVE
Little Jackass Creek
Anderson Gulch
Dark Gulch
Hotel Gulch Road
TIMBER
RIDGE
Chimney Rock
Creek
Bear
Creek
Soldier
Creek
PRIVATE
Usal
Creek
0
1
2
3
4 miles
N
E
S
W

of small gullies and rises. Paintbrush, buttercup, blue-eyed grass, lupine and golden poppy add color as the roar of surf rises from below.

You soon plunge into the first of several dark forests along the ridge. After more grasslands, you enter another fir forest as you wrap around a sinkhole on your left. Notice the dense vegetation growing in its shelter. Pass a gnarled,wind-topped redwood, then come to more grasslands.

You come to a nice stand of redwoods at 5¾ miles. Your trail switchbacks left and climbs to the ridge. Climb steeply along the narrow ridge to its top (elevation 1000 feet), passing trillium, iris, redwood sorrel, one-leaved wild onion, slink pod, miners lettuce, toyon and columbine. You parallel an old fence before descending steeply east, then south. Climb steeply again to another top, then descend more switchbacks before climbing to a third top at 6¼ miles. From here you can look east into the heavily wooded canyons of Jackass Creek, site of the logging ghost town of Wheeler.

Descend gradually along the east side of the ridge through forest. Then you switch sharply right and descend bluffs of low brush and grass with foxglove, tall brodiaea, blue-eyed grass, sticky monkeyflower, beach strawberry and poison oak.

Parallel the edge of a forest around 6⅜ miles. At 6⅝ miles your trail leaves coast and ridge to descend southeast by a series of long switchbacks.

You soon pass two large redwoods surrounded by smaller redwoods, then descend into a fern-filled gulch. Come to big trees at the bottom of the canyon. This is known as Schoolmarm Grove, named for the teacher of the Wheeler schoolhouse once located nearby. A campsite sits beneath two large redwoods in a clearing beside North Fork Jackass Creek. A second campsite lies 200 feet downstream, near the creek crossing. A spring is in the gulch to the west.

Wheeler was established in 1950, one of the last company logging towns and probably the newest ghost town in the west. The town lasted 10 years, abandoned as improved roads allowed the logs to be hauled to larger mills. Wheeler housed 32 families who harvested the timber, worked in the sawmill, and hauled the cut lumber to Willits by truck. The modern town had electricity, telephones and a water system.

The trail into "town" crosses the creek on a large log, remnant of an old bridge. Then the trail heads south on the old road, passing crumbling foundations, rusting logging relics and side streets. Domesticated plants grow wild here: foxglove, spearmint, red hot poker and alyssum. About ¼ mile from the creek crossing, you come to the heart of town. The sawmill was located here at the confluence of the two forks of the creek.

The trail crosses the creek and heads south, paralleling the beach at 7⅜ miles. A large grassy flat and a lagoon lie between the trail and the beach. High cliffs guard the dark sand beach at both ends.

The trail turns southeast and climbs a grassy gulch where the bosses lived. At 7⅝ miles you come to a wildflower garden at the top of the cleared portion of the gulch. The trail climbs steeply through dense brush, then into tall forest. At 9¾ miles you climb by several switchbacks to top a ridge at 800 feet elevation.

Descend along the border between forest and grasslands. At 9¾ miles a vernal pool lies west of the trail. Continue your descent into a hanging valley of grasslands sprinkled with wildflowers. At 10 miles you approach the creek at an elevation of 450 feet. Be careful as you cross it because stinging nettles cover deep holes in the creek; one false step and they will sting you.

Then your trail climbs east, following the south fork of the creek. At 10⅛ miles you switchback right and climb a ridge at the top of Anderson Cliff by a dozen switchbacks. Several of the westernmost switchbacks have side trails that lead to the top of Anderson Cliff for magnificent views.

The long climb ends as you gain a grassy ridge at 10⅞ miles (1100 feet elevation). An old jeep track on your left climbs to meet the Wheeler Road. After a brief level stretch, your trail descends gradually east, then steeply south toward Little Jackass Creek. At 11⅜ miles you veer left and descend by several switchbacks through grasslands with great views. You might hear a herd of sea lions barking on the beach below. Wildflowers brighten the way: foxglove, paintbrush, yarrow, monkeyflower, poppy and brodiaea.

Come to the floor of the canyon at 11¾ miles, near an old corral, all that remains of a pre-1900 logging camp. An outhouse at the junction serves two adjacent campsites. The magnificent beach lies about ⅛ mile west, bordered by sea caves and the towering Anderson Cliff. A herd of sea lions sometimes lives on the south end of the beach. Please stay at least 200 feet from the wild animals.

The main trail heads up the canyon, crossing the creek at 11⅞ miles. In another 500 feet, you come to the upper camp with two more sites near the creek beneath large redwoods and maples.

The trail south starts climbing immediately, crossing the creek and ascending along it before switching right. Ascend steadily by six switchbacks into the upper canyon, a checkerboard of clearcuts and virgin stands. At 12¾ miles the trail meets an old road. Follow it east, then south above Northport Gulch. The road contours, crossing a small creek at 13 miles, then passing whole hillsides of sticky monkeyflowers.

Beyond 13⅜ miles you come to a broad flat where the road turns northeast. Your trail leaves the road here, descending south, with views down to the mouth of Northport Gulch. Switchback left, then descend steeply by eight switchbacks into Anderson Gulch. At 14¼ miles you reach the camp, with a view down to the mouth of Anderson Gulch.

Descend two more switchbacks to a ford of the creek. Climb steeply to precipitous, grassy headlands above the rugged shore. Then descend to fern-filled Dark Gulch, which you follow upstream, crossing the creek at 15 3/8 miles.

Now you make one last long ascent, climbing 900 feet in 1¼ miles to just below the 1320-foot summit of Timber Point. Your trail meanders south through the forest, crosses a seasonal creek, then descends to grasslands at 17¾ miles. An unusual red and green brodiaea called Chinese firecracker grows beside the trail in spring.

You follow the ridge southeast, with great views of the coast to the south and the wooded canyons of Hotel Gulch and Usal Creek to the east. In the last 7/8 mile, you descend east by 20 switchbacks to Usal Road, 19¼ miles from the northern trailhead.

# 61. SOUTHERN HUMBOLDT COMMUNITY PARK

## GENTLE NEW PARK CELEBRATES NATURE JUST OUTSIDE TOWN

*This welcoming 430-acre community park nestles in a gentle valley in the often rugged South Fork Eel River canyon. Located just outside Garberville, the unique natural beauty of the park features grasslands, upland forests, prime farmland, a one mile stretch of the "Wild and Scenic" river complete with playground and swimming beach, native redwoods, and a 20-acre hilltop across the river. Local businessman Stephen Dazey led a drive to raise $650,000 to buy the parklands, part of a nineteenth century ranch. The park opened in 2000 with the Meadow Loop Trail opening in 2003. The forest trails have been added since then.*

*Native peoples of local Sinkyone and neighboring tribes, especially the Wailaki and Wiyot used the park's lands for centuries, harvesting the abundant acorns and other native plants and catching fish from the river. After the California Gold Rush, Euro-American settlers disrupted the native ways of life, developing farms and ranches and harvesting the timber. The 1960s and '70s brought a new wave of settlers with their often countercultural ways. Today the park's restored habitats inspire deep appreciation and reverence for nature, and a chance to recreate in this lovely place.*

Park near the kiosk across from the farm residence. Follow the main trail, an old ranch road, as it heads west-southwest past the historic ranch house, two small barns and abundant willows. Continue along the broad dirt track, passing through a ranch gate and past two more weathered barns. Near the latter barn, the ranch road turns right, leading to a nearby chemical toilet and the Garberville Community Farm beyond the trees. Take the narrower double track that continues west-southwest past pennyroyal and a variety of farm vehicles, including a couple of electric ones. You pass invasive Himalayan blackberries and a skate ramp on your right. Beyond those stand a natural windbreak of black oaks and bay laurels.

You soon come to a junction where you can go either way. Our described hike turns right to follow the narrower path. You head northwest briefly, then merge with a narrow path from the main entrance. Veer left on the path that heads west through the grasslands. (Another trail veers right to explore the nearby woods, with madrones and

SOUTHERN HUMBOLDT COMMUNITY PARK:

DISTANCE: $2^{1}/_{8}$- to $3^{3}/_{8}$-miles on three connecting loops.
TIME: One to 2 hours.
TERRAIN: Mostly level grasslands and oak woodlands, with two optional wooded, steeper loops through mixed forest.
ELEVATION GAIN/LOSS: 120 feet+/120 feet- for main loop. Add 70 feet+/70 feet- for first forest loop, 100 feet+/100 feet- for New Forestry Loop.
BEST TIME: Spring and fall. Also pleasant in winter between storms.
WARNINGS: Watch for poison oak.
HOW TO GET THERE: Exit Highway 101 at Garberville/Sprowel Creek Road exit (MP.11.3 from north, MP. 10.9 from south). Go west on Sprowel Creek Road for 1.0 mile from Main Street (.9 mile from Freeway north) to park entrance on left. A second park entrance is .7 mile beyond the main entrance on the left side of Camp Kimtu Road.
FURTHER INFO: Southern Humboldt Community Park (707) 923-2287.
OTHER SUGGESTIONS: The park has other short trails in redwood forest across Sprowel Creek Road at Tooby Playground. You will also find a swimming beach there, ideal for a cool dip in the South Fork Eel River on a hot day. BENBOW LAKE STATE RECREATION AREA, about 2.5 miles south on Highway 101, offers about 2 miles of trails west of the highway and river. Pioneer Trail climbs to an old meadow now overrun with oak trees.

bigleaf maples joining the oaks and bays.) After passing the Southern Humboldt Labyrinth on your left, continue west along the edge of grasslands and woods. Douglas firs join the mixed forest, but it is the large black oaks that are a defining characteristic of the park.

Cross a metal footbridge over a seasonal stream. Toyon grows beside the bridge. Two short cross-park trails head south-southeast on either side of the deep stream channel. You can take either of these to the south side of the park if you prefer a shorter walk. Three other side trails fork right to explore the nearby woodlands. Continue west-southwest on the trail beyond the bridge. At ½ mile you pass a side trail on the right, the end of the last two side trails back at the bridge. Look for California poppies in spring.

At 5/8 mile you reach the secondary parking area on Kimtu Road, with another kiosk and chemical toilet. On your left, a picnic table is in a pleasant, shady spot beneath black oaks and madrones. A second picnic table is in a sunnier spot near the kiosk. South Fork Eel River flows by just across Kimtu Road.

Your trail continues, soon climbing south-southeast along the park boundary. The adjacent land owner allows park visitors to use this corner of his land. You pass a rose bush on your left that looks like an old-fashioned garden variety, then more Himalayan blackberry.

Cross a metal bridge over a small seasonal stream at ¾ mile, coming onto the land of the obliging neighbor. In 75 feet, turn right onto the narrow side path into the nearby woods. Beneath Douglas firs, bays and madrones grows an immense antique grape vine. With a base eight inches in diameter and its long vines, the grape has most of its foliage high above near the top of the tall madrone nearby. This vine and another about 40 feet away, seem to love madrone and avoid nearby bays and firs.

Your side trail promptly rejoins the main path, passing narrow-leaved mule ears on your left. Your trail meanders in and out of the woodland. You come to a very large Cali-

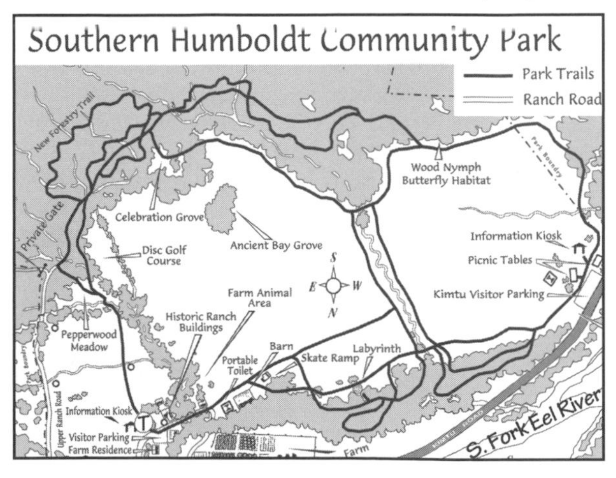

fornia buckeye, slouching like a teenager along the edge of the meadow. Honeysuckle and hedge nettle grow in shady corners of the grassland then native wood rose. Continue past irises and more buckeyes beneath black oaks and bays, with madrones nearby. Your track bends left and climbs to a pleasant vista across the park to surrounding ridges.

At 7/8 mile the trail bends left to head east past a rustic rest bench, promptly returning to park property. On your right you pass an old water trough and plum trees, growing along an old fence at this high point for the Meadow Loop. Honeysuckle, poison oak and blackberry, both Himalayan and California native, also abound. This area is prime wood nymph butterfly habitat.

Beyond one mile you come to a junction, with a rest bench just beyond. You can continue on Meadow Trail for a 2¼-mile-loop. Our described hike turns right to explore the woodland trails on this wilder side of the park. You climb gradually southeast, following the fence line into woods of black oaks, bay laurels, buckeyes and young Douglas firs. In 500 feet, ignore the fork on the left. Continue climbing, passing through the fence line. At 1/8 mile hop over a gully as you roughly parallel the fence. Coyote brush and sword ferns join the understory.

At a fork before ¼ mile, turn right to ascend into forest. (A left returns you to the place you left the Meadow Trail.) You quickly cross a small gully and enter a different ecological niche. California hazel, starflower, wild strawberry, twisted stalk, honeysuckle, polypody and sword ferns thrive beneath Douglas fir, madrone and bay. Then, having climbed to 315 feet in elevation, you descend past young bigleaf maples, wood rose, and lady ferns. Descend to the lower forest trail, then turn left to return to the Meadow Trail beyond ¾ mile.

Head east, then north on the Meadow Trail, coming to the first of the cross-park trails beyond 1 1/8 miles. A sign on your right marks "EDUCATIONAL CAMP" under large black oaks. Continue east on Meadow Trail, crossing a gully on a metal bridge (or a ford for equestrians). After meeting the second cross-park trail, find another rustic bench beside a sprawling bigleaf maple. Continue southeast along the ecotone, the boundary between meadow and forest. Across the meadow on your left, notice the immense ancient bay laurels, among the tallest in the park.

Around 1 3/8 miles, on your right you pass a signed old man's beard lichen (*Usnea longissima*) growing on a black oak above the gully you've been following. *Longissima* is the longest, and among the rarest, of this family of lichens. It's relative *Usnea barbata* also grows in the park. Have you noticed how deep the gullies in the park are? Apparently they became so during the monstrous 1964 flood. When you reach another fence line, look left for Celebration Grove, a venue for events. Your trail returns to the forest.

You come to a T junction around 1½ miles, with a rest

bench nearby. You can turn left here to finish the Meadow Loop. Our described route turns right. In just 150 feet go left on the New Forestry Trail. (If you go straight you meet the end of the earlier forest loop.) Climb east for 125 feet, then turn right as New Forestry Trail climbs southeast along the edge of a gully, easily the steepest ascent of any trail in the park. A sign indicates that New Forestry Trail is a project of the Institute for Sustainable Forestry, a local group. The trail tops out just beyond at about 400 feet, where Douglas firs grow to two feet in diameter, along with oaks and bays.

At ¼ mile you cross a gully that is more natural than the flood-scoured lower gullies. Descend to cross a rustic bridge over an even larger gully before 3/8 mile. This watercourse is narrow and fairly well vegetated here. Descend to a junction with the main trail. (The New Forestry Loop is ½ mile if you return to the point at which you started it.)

Our described route turns right to follow Meadow Trail north-northeast beneath forest. Ignore a maze of side trails unless you know where you're going. Stay on the broad trail as it descends gently north. You come to a park gate, usually closed unless maintenance is being done, at 1¾ miles, with another gate on adjacent private property just beyond. Go 200 feet, crossing a gully and nearing the private gate, then go left to head northwest.

Follow Meadow Trail as it passes coast live oak and rounds Pepperwood Meadow, where the birds often sing and human music sometimes happens. Go north across a bridge over a gully around 1 7/8 miles. Your trail winds left and right, passing through a fence line, then beelines north across the base of a seasonal wet meadow. A big steel water tank sits on the hill at the top of the meadow. You cross one more gully, then angle left to return to the main parking area and kiosk at 2 1/8 miles.

# 62. TANOAK SPRINGS DURPHY CREEK LOOP

EXPLORING RICHARDSON GROVE STATE PARK

*The Sinkyone people had a winter village on the South Fork of the Eel River near the present southern park boundary. The village of Kahs'chosoningibe had several houses constructed of slabs of redwood bark. The people of the village spent about six months of each year there, catching salmon and other fish. They lived near the coast for the rest of the year.*

*The Tanoak Springs/Durphy Creek Loop is the longest hike in 1772-acre Richardson Grove State Park. It explores a high ridge and a stream canyon in the southwest quadrant of the park. Other trails are listed in* OTHER SUGGESTIONS.

The trail heads southwest beside campsite 58. (In summer, unless you are camping here, you must park in Day-Use area and walk 3/8 mile up to the trailhead.) You climb gradually through mixed forest of redwood, Douglas fir, tanoak and madrone to a fork in 150 feet. Go left on the Lookout Point Trail, heading southeast. This trail climbs gradually, following the top edge of the river canyon. Soon you switchback to the right and climb up and around a steep side canyon. Cross it at ¼ mile and climb east.

In 300 feet you come to Lookout Point, where you have a fine view of the river and highway snaking below. Then climb gradually southwest. As you pass under a power line, the trail steepens, becoming gradual again beyond 3/8 mile.

TANOAK SPRINGS/DURPHY CREEK LOOP:

DISTANCE: 4 1/8-mile loop (add 3/8 mile from Day-Use area).
TIME: Two to 3 hours.
'l'ERRAIN: Climbs up to and along a wooded ridge, then descends a creek canyon.
ELEVATION GAIN/LOSS: 950 feet+/950 feet-.
BEST TIME: Spring for wildflowers. Nice anytime.
WARNINGS: Watch for poison oak and ticks along the trail. Carry water because the spring may be dry or fouled by animals.
HOW TO GET THERE: Turn west off Highway 101 at M.1.73 into Richardson Grove State Park. Go .1 mile to fork. Then go right to Madrone Campground, coming to trailhead in .4 mile, just past campsite 58. In summer, unless you are camping here, you must park in Day-Use area: go left at fork, then .3 mile to parking near river.
FEES: Day use/parking: $8/vehicle. Car camping: $35/night. Hike/Bike Camp: $5/person/night.
FURTHER INFO: Richardson Grove State Park (707) 247~3318.
OTHER SUGGESTIONS: HARTSOOK TRAIL climbs ½ mile from old Hartsook Inn (M.0.89) to meet main trail at Lookout Point. WOODLAND TRAIL offers an easy 1.6-mile loop through the northern portion of the park. In summer you can cross seasonal bridges over Eel River to reach the TOUMEY-BIG SPRINGS LOOP (2 miles).

You soon pass back under the wires and come to a fork. (You can turn right for a short 1¼-mile loop.) Our described trail goes left, meeting the Tanoak Springs Trail in 300 feet. Go right and head northwest. (The left fork descends almost ¼ mile to reach the Hartsook Giant, a venerable old redwood.) Tanoak Springs Trail climbs gradually at first, then winds and climbs steeply to gain the top of the ridge at ¾ mile. Douglas irises and tiny calypso orchids grow along the trail in spring.

You climb steeply between level stretches along the ridge to 1¼ miles, where the trail runs sidehill on the steep north slope. Descend to a saddle, climb again to 1 3/8 miles, then contour along the ridgetop to 1½ miles. Large madrones, tanoaks and Douglas firs grow along this part of the ridge.

Your trail stays on the ridgetop, climbing, descending to another saddle, then climbing into a young forest of firs at 1 5/8 miles. Then contour along the ridgetop.

Beyond 1¾ miles your trail switches right and makes a winding descent to meet the spur trail to Tanoak Springs at 1 7/8 miles. Walk the 350 feet to the springs, where a lush patch of woodwardia ferns thrives in the cool and wet.

Returning to the main trail, turn left and descend through thickets of huckleberries. The trail makes a steep and winding descent into the canyon of Durphy Creek. At 2 3/8 miles you hear the creek gurgling below as big Douglas firs line your path. Descend by about ten more switchbacks to 2¾ miles, where you head east, fifty feet above Durphy Creek.

The trail follows the shady, north-facing south bank of the creek. The cool, moist bank shelters iris, redwood sorrel, saxifrage, bay laurel and many ferns: sword, horsetail, woodwardia, maidenhair and five-finger. Just before 2¾ miles, you have easy access to the creek.

Your trail descends steps to a bridge at 3 1/8 miles, then quickly crosses two more bridges over side streams. Gooseberries grow here. The trail follows Durphy Creek, alternating between drier and wetter microclimates. Interior live oaks with prickly leaves grow in the drier spots, while ferns, redwood sorrel and even a few western yew trees grow in the moist spots.

At 3¼ miles you draw near the creek again, but it quickly

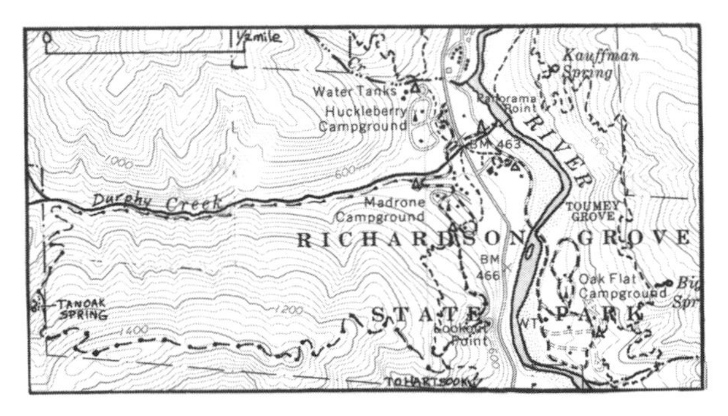

drops deeper into its canyon. Cross two more bridges around 3 3/8 miles, then return to redwood forest. At 3½ miles a 12-foot-diameter redwood stands to the left of the trail.

You then descend by short switchbacks to Durphy Creek Rest at 3 5/8 miles. A short spur leads to a small redwood grove in a level spot between creek and trail, where a bench provides a picnic spot. Trilliums, redwood sorrel and calypso orchids grow beneath the big trees.

The main trail crosses two more side streams, climbs briefly, then descends through a rocky area to reach the creek bed again. From there a broad trail climbs away from the creek, coming to the paved park road in 250 feet, just before your 4-mile point.

To return to the Madrone Campground trailhead, turn right on the paved road and climb the hill into the campground. Follow the road to campsite 58 for a total loop of 4 1/8 miles. (If you parked in the Day-Use area, turn left on the paved road and descend to your car.)

# CALIFORNIA COASTAL TRAIL

## BECOMING REALITY IN DEL NORTE, HUMBOLDT & NORTHERN MENDOCINO COUNTIES

*The California Coastal Trail is a proposed 1600-mile system of interconnected beach and coastal range trails running the length of the spectacular California coast from Oregon to Mexico.*

*-California Coastal Trails Foundation*

The California Coastal Trail is a work-in-progress, with an estimated 850 miles of trail already in place, providing public access. Although only the most avid coast hikers will hike the California Coastal Trail (CCT) in its entirety, its establishment will greatly expand coastal access for millions of hikers and coast lovers.

The northernmost segment of CCT is one of the most complete. Roughly 120 nearly continuous miles of the trail exist from Northern Del Norte County through Redwood National Park and beyond to Humboldt Bay. Partial segments of CCT exist from the bay south into Mendocino County. This report catalogs the current status of CCT development, from north to south.

From the Oregon border you can walk south along open beach through Pelican State Beach and Kamph Memorial Park to the mouth of the Smith River. Through hikers, having no way to cross the river at its mouth, must detour inland on Highway 101 and Fred Haight Drive. After crossing Smith River on the Highway 101 bridge, one may turn west on Lake Earl Drive, then Moseley Road to enter either Tolowa Dunes State Park via Pala Road or Lake Earl public lands via Kellogg Road. South of the river CCT continues along the beach or through the dunes of Tolowa Dunes

State Park and Lake Earl Wildlife Area (see Trails #1 and 2).

South of Lake Earl you can walk the beach and headlands around Point St. George, then follow Pebble Beach Drive into Crescent City. From Crescent City, you can follow the bike path to the Small Boat Basin, then walk south on Crescent Beach for two (or more) miles. The best route turns inland at Crescent Beach Picnic Area on two miles of trail to Enderts Beach Trailhead.

The Coastal Trail runs south continuously from there for 18 spectacular miles to Klamath Overlook near Requa (see Trails #6, 8, 9 and 10). Campsites along the way provide off-road camping: Nickel Creek at one mile and DeMartin Camp at ten miles. Redwood Hostel is now closed.

To continue on CCT from Requa, the Klamath River is an obstacle, as it was to early travelers. It is 7 miles by car to the start of the Flint Ridge Section of CCT. The distance can be halved if someone ferries you across the Klamath.

The Flint Ridge Section of CCT (see Trail #11) heads west 4½ miles to the coast, passing Flint Ridge Camp ¼ mile from the west end. Then CCT follows the Coastal Drive ( now partially closed to vehicles) for 4¼ miles to Carruthers Cove Trailhead (see Trails #12 and 13). A steep descent brings you to the beach at Carruthers Cove, where 8 miles of beach walking lie to the south. You must have a tide lower than +3.0 feet to walk the first mile. After you have synchronized with the tide, it is 5⅞ miles to the Gold Bluffs Hike/Bike Camp, where you register on the spot.

From Gold Bluffs Campground, it is 1¾ miles to Espa Lagoon, northern trailhead for the Skunk Cabbage Creek Trail (see Trail #23). That trail and its southern access road meet Highway 101 after 6⅛ miles at the current end of this length of CCT. After ⅝ mile along the shoulder of Highway 101, CCT veers left on a gated gravel road that follows the Redwood Creek levee through Orick. Shortly before the mouth of Redwood Creek, CCT turns south to Redwood National Park's Kuchel Information Center

From there you can walk the beach past Freshwater Lagoon. A segment of CCT from Stone Lagoon to Dry Lagoon adds 5 miles to CCT. It passes a walk-in camp beside Stone Lagoon. You may not be able to ford the seasonal outlets of Stone or Big Lagoons in winter or early spring. When the barrier beach is passable you can walk 6¼ miles from Dry Lagoon to Patrick's Point (see Trail #30).

After walking through beautiful Patrick's Point State Park (see Trails #30 and 31), you must walk Patrick's Point Drive to Trinidad, then Scenic Drive to Moonstone County Park at the mouth of Little River (see Trail #36).

From Little River to the mouth of Humboldt Bay lie 19 miles of beach and dunes (see Trail #38). You can walk onto the beach at Moonstone County Park, ford Little River, and walk the beach to Clam Beach County Park and the north end of the Hammond Trail, the designated CCT route. Then follow back roads to the city of Arcata. Eventually the Humboldt Bay Trail will be the CCT route south to Eureka. For now, you must follow the bike lane along busy 101. In Eureka the Waterfront Trail will eventually follow virtually all of the city's shoreline. For now, you can walk city streets to connect the completed portion of Waterfront Trail (see Trail #42).

Then you can walk the inactive railroad tracks south. To get around the Eel River delta, through hikers must detour inland on county roads to Fernbridge, then follow State Route 211 to Ferndale.

South of the Eel River, Centerville Beach provides 9 miles of beach and dune trekking (see Trails #45 and 46). The steep cliffs between False Cape and Cape Mendocino block passage south, but one might follow Mattole Road (see Trail #48) to reach the Lost Coast south of Petrolia.

The Lost Coast of the King Range may be the most famous stretch of CCT. It follows 25 miles of wilderness beach from the mouth of the Mattole River on the north to Shelter Cove on the south (see Trail #53).

From Shelter Cove, it is 3 steep miles on paved roads to the Hidden Valley Trailhead, starting point for a steep segment of CCT that climbs over Chemise Mountain, then descends into Mendocino County and Sinkyone Wilderness State Park (see Trail #59).

From Whale Gulch it is 1½ miles to the Needle Rock Visitor Center of Sinkyone Wilderness State Park. Then you walk 2½ miles on unpaved Briceland Road (this segment now closed to vehicles) to the New Lost Coast trailhead, start of another 16¾-mile section of CCT (see Trail #60).

The above trails include about 200 miles of coastal hiking, among the greatest and most complete portions of the California Coastal Trail. If you would like more information about CCT and what you can do to help, contact the California State Coastal Conservancy, 1330 Broadway, 13th Floor, Oakland, CA 94612 or COASTWALK, 555 S. Main St. Suite 1, Sebastopol, CA 95472

## WHAT KIND OF TRAIL ARE YOU LOOKING FOR?

continued from page 10

### TRAILS FOR EQUESTRIANS

32. Elk Head—see OTHER SUGGESTIONS
37. Hammond Section, Coastal Trail
38. Mad River Beach
39. Arcata's Community Forest—see map
40. Arcata Ridge
43. Elk River to Headwaters Forest—only to South Fork bridge
44. Table Bluff County Park
45. Centerville Beach North
46. Centerville Beach South
49. Avenue of the Giants
51. Grasshopper Peak—see map
52. Squaw Creek Ridge—see map
53. Mattole River South
54. Smith-Etter Road to Beach
55. Kings Crest North
56. Lightning to Kings Peak
57. Kings Crest South
58. Shelter Cove North
59. Hidden Valley to Chemise to Whale Gulch
60. New Lost Coast
61. Southern Humboldt Community Park

### BEACH WALKS (OR RUNS)

1. North to Yontocket & the Mouth of Smith River
2. Dead Lake Loop
3. North from Point St. George
6. Enderts Beach—see also OTHER SUGGESTION: Crescent Beach
10. Hidden Beach
12. Coastal Drive—see Dad's Camp
20.. Coastal Trail (and all of Gold Bluffs Beach)
23. Skunk Cabbage Creek (west portion)
29. Dry Lagoon to Big Lagoon—
see also OTHER SUGGESTION: Stone Lagoon
30. Agate Beach
32. College Cove
33. Trinidad State Beach
35. Indian Beach
36. Other Trinidad Trails
38. Mad River Beach and Dunes
44. Table Bluff County Park
45. Centerville Beach North
46. Centerville Beach South
48. Cape Mendocino
53. Mattole River South—the ultimate!
58. Shelter Cove North

# COMMON & SCIENTIFIC NAMES OF PLANTS ALONG THE TRAILS

*alyssum, *Lobularia maritima*

anemone (wind flower), *Anemone deltoidea, A. lyallii*

angelica, *Angelica hendersonii*

azalea (western azalea), *Rhododendron occidentale*

baby blue eyes, *Nemophila menziesii*

bay laurel, (California bay, pepperwood), *Umbellularia californica*

beach morning glory, *Calystegia soldanella*

beach pea, *Lathyrus japonicus* var. *glaber*

beach primrose, *Camissoniopsis cheiranthifolia*

beach strawberry, *Fragaria chiloensis*

bear grass, *Xerophyllum tenax*

bedstraw, *Galium* spp.

bigleaf maple, *Acer macrophyllum*

Bishop pine, *Pinus muricata*

black crowberry, *Empetrum nigrum*

black oak (California), *Quercus kelloggi*

bleeding heart (western), *Dicentra formosa*

blue dick, *Dichelostemma capitatum*

blue flag iris, *Iris purdyi*

blue gilia, *Gilia capitata*

*blue gum eucalyptus, *Eucalyptus globulus*

blue-eyed grass, *Sisyrinchium bellum*

blueblossom (California lilac), *Ceanothus thyrsiflorus*

Bolander's lily, *Lilium bolanderi*

bowl-tubed iris, *Iris macrosiphon*

bracken fern, *Pteridium aquilinum*

broadleaf ceanothus, *Ceanothus griseus*

brodiaea (tall brodiaea), *Brodiaea laxa*

brook foam, *Boykinia occidentalis*

brooklime, *Veronica americana*

buttercup, *Ranunculus repens*

California bee plant, *Scrophularia californica*

California blackberry, *Rubus ursinus*

California lace fern, *Aspidotis densa*

California ladyslipper orchid, *Cypridium californicum*

California polypody, *Polypodium californicum*

California poppy (golden poppy), *Eschscholtzia californica*

California rose, *Rosa californica*

California water hemlock, *Cicuta douglasii*

*calla lily, *Zantedeschia aethiopica*

calypso orchid, *Calypso bulbosa*

canyon gooseberry, *Ribes menziesii*

canyon live oak, *Quercus chrysolepis*

cascara sagrada, *Rhamnus purshiana*

cattail, *Typha* spp.

chamise, *Adenostoma fasciculatum*

checker lily, *Fritillaria lanceolata*

Chinese firecrackers, *Dichelostemma ida-maia*

chinquapin, *Castanopsis chrysophylla*

clintonia, *Clintonia andrewsiania*

coast buckwheat, *Eriogonum latifolium*

coast lily, *Lilium maritimum*

coast silktassel, *Garrya elliptica*

coastal broom-rape, *Orobanche californica* ssp. *californica*

coastal manroot (wild cucumber), *Marah fabaceus, M. oreganus*

coastal nemophila, *Nemophila menziesii* var. *atomaria*

coffeeberry, *Rhamnus californica*

Columbia lily, *Lilium columbianum*

columbine, *Aquilegia formosa*

common juniper, *Juniperus communis*

coral root orchid, *Corallorhiza* spp.

cordgrass, *Spartina foliosa*

*cotoneaster, *Cotoneaster* spp.

cow parsnip, *Heracleum maximum*

coyote brush, *Baccharis pilularis*
cream cups, *Platystemon californicus*
creek trillium, *Trillium rivale*
*creeping myrtle, *Vinca minor*
cypress, *Cupressus* spp.
dandelion, *Taraxacum officinale*
death camas, *Zigadenus venenosus*
deer fern, *Blechnum spicant*
deer oak, *Quercus sadleriana*
Del Norte pea, *Lathyrus delnorticus*
Del Norte wallflower, *Erysimum menziesii* ssp. *eurekense*
dogwood (Pacific), *Cornus nuttalli*
Douglas fir, *Pseudotsuga menziesii*
Douglas iris, *Iris douglasiana*
duckweed, *Lemna minima*
dune tansy, *Tanacetum douglasii*
elderberry (blue), *Sambucus cerulea*
elderberry (red), *Sambucus racemosa*
elk clover, *Aralia californica*
* English daisy, *Bellis perennis*
Eureka lily, *Lilium occidentale*
evergreen huckleberry (California huckleberry), *Vaccinum ovatum*
evergreen violet (redwood violet) *Viola sempervirens*
fairy bells, *Prosartes smithii*, *P. hookeri*
false lily of the valley, *Maianthemum dilatum*
false Solomon's seal (fat Solomon's seal), *Maianthemum racemosum*
fawn lily, *Erythronium oregonum*
fiddleneck, *Amsinckia intermedia*
* filaree (redstem storksbill), *Erodium cicutarium*
fireweed, *Epilobium* spp.
five-finger fern, *Adiantum aleuticum*
* foxglove, *Digitalis purpurea*
Fremont silktassel, *Garrya fremontii*
fringe cups, *Tellima grandiflora*
giant horsetail, *Equisetum temateia*
giant trillium, *Trillium chloropetalum*
godetia (farewell to spring), *Clarkia* spp.
goldback fern, *Pentagramma triangularis*
grand fir, *Abies grandis*
gum plant, *Grindelia stricta*
hairgrass, *Deschampsia cespitosa* ssp. *holciformis*
hairy cat's ear, *Hypochoeris radicata*
hairy honeysuckle, *Lonicera hispidula*
hairy manzanita, *Arctostaphylos columbiana*
hairy star tulip, *Calochortus tolmiei*
hazel (California), *Corylus cornuta* var. *californica*
hedge nettle (wood mint), *Stachys bullata*
hen and chicks, *Dudleya farinosa*
*Himalayan blackberry, *Rubus procerus*
*holly, *Aquifoliaceae aquifolium*
horsetail, *Equisetum* spp.
hound's tongue, *Cynoglossum grande*
huckleberry, *Vaccinum* spp.
huckleberry oak, *Quercus vaccinifolia*
*iceplant, *Mesembryanthemum* spp.
Indian pink, *Silene californica*
Indian plum (osoberry), *Oemleria cerasiformis*
Indian warrior, *Pedicularis densiflora*
inside-out flower, *Vancouveria planipetala*
Jeffrey pine, *Pinus jeffreyii*
johnny tuck, *Triphysaria eriantha*
kinnikinnick (bearberry), *Arctostaphylos uva-ursi*
knobcone pine, *Pinus attenuata*
knotweed, *Polygonum paronychia*
lady fern, *Athyrium felix-femina*
leather fern, *Polypodium scouleri*
leopard lily, *Lilium pardalinum*
licorice fern, *Polypodium glycyrrhiza*
lupine, *Lupinus latifolius*, *L. littoralis*, *L. nanus*, *L. polyphyllus*, *L. variicolor*, *L. rivularis*

madrone, *Arbutus menziesii*

manzanita, *Arctostaphylos* spp.

miner's lettuce, *Claytonia perfoliata*

mint, *Mentha* sp.

miterwort, *Mitella ovals*

monkeyflower, *Mimulus guttatus* ssp. *litoralis*

*Monterey cypress, *Cupresssus macrocarpa*

*Monterey pine, *Pinus radiata*

morning glory, *Calystegia* sp.

mouse-ear chickweed, *Cerastium arvense*

mugwort, *Artemesia douglasiana*

ninebark, *Physocarpus capitatus*

northem dune tansy, *Tanacetum douglasii*

ocean spray (cream bush), *Holodiscus discolor*

oenanthe, *Oenanthe sarmentosa*

one-leaved wild onion, *Allium unifolium*

Oregon crab apple, *Malus fusca*

Oregon grape, *Berberis nervosa*, *B. aquifolium*

* ox-eye daisy, *Leucanthemum vulgare*

Pacific silverweed, *Potentilla egedei* var. *grandis*

Pacific waterleaf, *Hydrophyllum teniupes*

paintbrush, *Castilleja latifolia*, *C. affinis*, *C. foliolosa*, *C. hololeuca*, *C. wightii*

*pampas grass, *Cortaderia selloana*

pearly everlasting, *Anaphalis margaritacea*

*pennyroyal (western), *Mentha pulegium*

penstemon, *Penstemon* spp.

pickleweed, *Salicornia virginica*

piggyback plant, *Tolmiea menziesii*

pinemat manzanita, *Arctostaphyllos nevadensis*

plantain, *Plantago* spp.

*poison hemlock, *Conium maculatum*

poison oak, *Toxicodendron diversilobum*

poppy, *Eschscholzia californica*

Port Orford cedar, *Chamaecyparis lawsoniana*

prince's pine (pippsissewa), *Chimaphila umbellatum*

raspberry, *Rubus leucodermis*

*rattlesnake grass, *Briza maxima*

rattlesnake plantain, *Goodyera oblongifola*

red alder, *Alnus rubra*

*red hot poker, *Kniphofia uvaria*

red huckleberry, *Vaccinium parvifolium*

red trillium, *Trillium chloropetalum*

red-flowering currant, *Ribes glutinosum*

redwood lily, *Lilium rubescens*

redwood sorrel, *Oxalis oregana*

redwood, *Sequoia sempervirens*

rein orchid, *Habenaria elegans* var. *maritima*

rhododendron, *Rhododendron macrophyllum*

rush, *Juncus sphaerocarpus*

salal, *Gaultheria shallon*

salmonberry, *Rubus spectabilis*

sand verbena, pink, *Abronia maritima*

sand verbena, yellow, *Abronia latifolia*

saxifrage, *Saxifraga* spp.

*Scotch broom, *Cytisus scoparius*

scouring rush, *Equisetum hyemale*

scythe-leaved onion, *Allium falcifolium*

*sea fig (ice plant), *Mesembryanthemum chilense*

sea lavender, *Limonium* spp.

*sea rocket, *Cakile maritima*

sea thrift, *Armeria maritima* var. *californica*

seaside daisy, *Erigeron glaucus*

sedge, *Carex* spp.

*self heal, *Prunella vulgaris*

serviceberry, *Amelanchier alnifolia*

shooting star, *Dodecathon hendersonii*

shore pine, *Pinus contorta* ssp. *contorta*

Siberian miner's lettuce (candyflower), *Claytonia sibirica*

silky beach pea, *Lathyrus littoralis*

silver beachweed, *Franseria chamissonis* ssp. *bipinnatisecta*

silverleaf phacelia, *Phacelia argentea*

silverweed, *Argentina anserina*

Sitka spruce, *Picea sitchensis*

skunk cabbage, *Lysichitum americanum*

slink pod, *Scoliopus bigelovii*

snow queen, *Synthyris reniformis*

snowberry, *Symphoricarpus alba*

soap root, *Chlorogalum pomeridianum*

*spearmint, *Mentha spicata*

star Solomon's seal (slim false Solomon's seal), *Maianthemum stellatum*

starflower, *Trientalis latifolia*

sticky monkeyflower, *Mimulus aurantiacus*

stinging nettle, *Urtica dioica*

sugar pine, *Pinus lambertiana*

sugarstick, *Allotropa virgata*

sundew, *Drosera rotundifolia*

sword fern, *Polystichum munitum*

tanoak, *Notholithocarpus densiflorus*

tarweed, *Madia madiodes*

thimbleberry, *Rubus parviflorus*

thistle, *Cirsium brevistylum*

tooth-leaved monkeyflower, *Mimulus dentalus*

trail plant, *Adenocaulon bicolor*

trillium, *Trillium ovatum*

twin flower, *Linnaea borealis*

twinberry, *Lonicera involucrata*

twisted stalk, *Streptopus amplexifolius*

vanilla grass (California sweet grass), *Anthoxanthum occidentale*

vanilla leaf (deer foot), *Achlys triphylla*

vetch, *Vicia* sp.

vine maple, *Acer circinatum*

watercress, *Nasturtium officinale*

wax myrtle (bayberry), *Myrica californica*

western coltsfoot, *Petasites palmatus*

western dog violet, *Viola adunca*

western hemlock, *Tsuga heterophylla*

western redcedar, *Thuja plicata*

western wood anemone, *Anemone lyallii*

western yew, *Taxus brevifolia*

white-veined shinleaf, *Pyrola picta*

whitethorn, *Ceanothus incanus*

wild ginger, *Asarum caudatum*

*wild mustard, *Brassica campestris*

wild rose, *Rosa* spp.

wild tobacco, *Nicotiana attenuata*

willow, *Salix* spp.

wintergreen, *Pyrola* spp.

wood fern, *Dryopteris arguta*

wood rose, *Rosa gymnocarpa*

wood strawberry, *Fragaria vesca*

woodwardia ( giant chain) fern, *Woodwardia fimbriata*

yarrow, *Achillea millefolium*

yellow globe lily (fairy lantern), *Calochortus amabilis*

yellow mat, *Sanicula arctopoides*

yellow pond lily, *Nuphar polysepala*

yerba de selva, *Whipplea modesta*

* Introduced species

# BIBLIOGRAPHY


Adams, Kramer, *The Redwoods*, Popular Library, New York, 1968.

Alt, David D. and Donald W. Hyndman, *Roadside Geology of Northern and Central California*, Mountain Press Publishing Co., Missoula. Montana, 2000.

Becking, Rudolph, *Pocket Flora of the Redwood Forest*, Island Press, Covelo, California, 1982.

Brown, Joseph B., *Monarchs of the Mist*, Coastal Parks Assoc., Pt. Reyes, California. 1982.

*California Coastal Access Guide*, Sixth Edition, University of California Press, Berkeley, 2003.

*California Coastal Resource Guide*,University of California Press, Berkeley, 1987.

Chase, J. Smeaton, *California Coastal Trails*, Tioga Publishing, Palo Alto, California, 1987, reprint, originally published: Houghton Mifflin, Boston, 1913.

Chronic, Halka *Pages of Stone: Geology of Western National Parks and Monuments: Sierra Nevada, Cascades and Pacific Coast, Volume 2*, Mountaineers, Seattle, Washington, 1986.

Coy, Owen C., *The Humboldt Bay Region 1850-1875*, California State Historical Association, Los Angeles, 1929.

Dawson, Ann, *Nature Bound Pocket Field Guide*, Omnigraphics Ltd., Boise, Idaho, 1985.

Dewitt, John B., *California Redwood Parks and Preserves*, Save-the-Redwoods League, San Francisco, 1982.

*Experience the California Coast: A Guide to Beaches and Parks in Northern California: Del Norte, Humboldt, Mendocino, Sonoma, Marin*, University of California Press, Berkeley, 2005

Grillos, Steve J., *Ferns and Fern Allies of California*, University of California Press, Berkeley, 1987.

*Handbook of North American Indians*, edited by William C. Sturtevant, Smithsonian Institution, Washington, D.C., 1978.

Hayden, Mike, *Exploring the North Coast*, Chronicle Books, San Francisco, 1982.

Hoopes, Chad L. , *Lure of the Humboldt Bay Region*, Wm. C. Brown Co., Dubuque, Iowa, 1966.

*Humboldt Redwoods Trail Guide, Revised*, Humboldt Redwoods Interpretive Association, Weott, California, 2012.

Jensen, Edward C., Warren R. Randall, ,Robert F. Keniston, A *Manual of Oregon Trees and Shrubs, Ninth Edition*, Oregon State University Bookstores, Corvallis, Oregon, 2008.

*Jepson Manual: Vascular Plants of California, Thoroughly Revised and Expanded*, edited by Bruce G. Baldwin, Douglas Goldman, David J. Keil, Robert Patterson, Thomas J. Rosatti, Dieter Wilken, University of California Press, Berkeley, 2012.

Keator, Glenn and Ruth Heady, *Pacific Coast Berry Finder*, Nature Study Guild, Berkeley, 2000.

Keator, Glenn and Ruth Heady, *Pacific Coast Fern Finder*, Nature Study Guild, Berkeley, 1981.

Kroeber, A.L., *Handbook of the Indians of California*, Dover

Publications, New York, 1976.

Lewis, Oscar, *The Quest for Qual-a-wa-loo* (Humboldt Bay), San Francisco, 1943, (no publisher cited).

Leydet, Francois. *The Last Redwoods and the Parklands of Redwood Creek*, Sierra Club, Ballantine Books. New York, 1969.

Little, Elbert, *The Audubon Society Field Guide to North American Trees, Western Region*, Alfred A. Knopf, New York, 1980.

Lyons, Kathleen and Mary Beth Cuneo-Lazaneo, *Plants of the Coast Redwood Region*, Shoreline Press, Soquel, California, 2003.

McConnaughey, Bayard H. and Evelyn McConnaughey, *Pacific Coast, Audubon Society Nature Guides*, Alfred A. Knopf, New York, 1985.

Munz, Philip A., *Introduction to California Spring Wildfiowers of the Foothills, Valleys, and Coast*, University of California Press, Berkeley, 2004.

Munz, Philip A., *Introduction to Shore Wildflowers of California, Oregon and Washington*, University of California Press, Berkeley, 2003.

Niehaus, Theodore F. and Charles L. Ripper, *Field Guide to Pacific States Wildflowers*, Peterson Field Guide Series, Houghton Mifflin, Boston, 1976.

Peterson, Roger Tory, *A Field Guide to Western Birds, Peterson Field Guide Series*, Houghton Mifflin, Boston, 1990.

Petrides, George A. and Olivia: *A Field Guide to Western Trees, Peterson Field Guide Series*, Houghton Mifflin, Boston, 1992.

Preston, Richard, *The Wild Trees: A Story of Passion and Daring*, Random House, New York, 2007.

Ransom, Jay Ellis, *Complete Field Guide to North American Wildlife*, Harper & Row, New York, 1981.

Russo, Ron and Pam Olhausen, *Pacific Intertidal Life*, Nature Study Guild, Berkeley, 1981.

Schrepfer, Susan R., *The Fight to Save the Redwoods*, University of Wisconsin Press, Madison, 1983.

Spellenberg, Richard, *The Audubon Society Field Guide to North American Wildlfowers, Western Region*, Alfred A. Knopf, New York, 1979.

Watts, Phoebe, *Redwood Region Flower Finder*, Nature Study Guild, Berkeley, 1979.

Watts, Tom, *Pacific Coast Tree Finder*, Nature Study Guild, Berkeley, 1973.

Whitney, Stephen, *Western Forests, Audubon Society Nature Guides*, Alfred A. Knopf, New York, 1985.

Yocum, Charles and Raymond Dasmann, *The Pacific Coastal Wildlife Region, American Wildlife Region Series*, Naturegraph, Happy Camp, California, 1965.

Young, Dorothy King, *Redwood Empire Wildflowers, Third Edition*, Naturegraph Publishers, Happy Camp, California, 1976.

# INDEX

A.W. Way County Park Campground, 192
Agate Beach, 131-134, 135, 137
Alder Basin Trail, 51
Arcata, 13, 18, 19, , 138, 152, 155-168, 213, 251
Arcata Community Forest, 155-160, 161
Arcata Marsh, 163-168
Arcata Ridge Trail, 155, 158, 159-162
Avenue of the Giants, 193-196, 201
Azalea State Reserve, 156

Baker Beach, 146
Bald Hills Road, 104-106, 110-111, 113, 115-122, 125
Bear Harbor, 238
Beith Creek Loop, 160
Benbow, 245
Big Flat, 215-217, 220, 222, 225, 230, 231, 232
Big Lagoon, 128-132, 133, 135, 251
Black Sands Beach, 230
Boat Creek Trail. 84, 99
Boat Ridge Trail, 84, 99
Boyes Prairie, 86-88
Boy Scout Tree Trail, 41-45
Brown Creek, 79-82
Buck Creek Trail, 211, 217, 220, 221, 225, 227, 231
Bull Creek, 193, 197-202, 203, 208, 209
Bull Creek State Wilderness, 195, 198
Butler Creek, 79, 84, 100

Cadre Point/McLaughlin Pond Loop, 28
Cal Barrel Road, 80, 82
California Coastal Trail, 14, 21-34, 45-49, 52-76, 79, 84-85, 97, 98, 100-101, 129-137, 146-152, 177-184, 189-192, 211-218, 234-243, 250-252
Canoe Creek Trail, 196
Cape Mendocino, 19, 63, 68, 132, 144, 184, 189-191, 207, 225
Carruthers Cove, 71, 72, 73-76, 79, 100, 251
Castle Rock, 30, 33, 34
Cathedral Trees Trail, 82, 86
Centerville Beach, 180-185, 252
Ceremonial Rock, 131, 132, 133, 137
Chemise Mountain, 211, 225, 232, 233-235, 252
Children's Forest Loop, 196
Chilula, 18, 35, 115, 116, 124
Clam Beach County Park, 148, 153, 251
Clintonia Trail 89, 90, 92, 93-94
Coastal Drive, 65, 66-72, 251
College Cove, 138, 139, 140
Cooskie Creek Trail, 211, 213, 215, 218
Crab County Park, 178
CREA Trail, 80
Crescent Beach, 45, 46, 250
Crescent City, 13, 21, 35, 45, 250
Crest to Coast Loop, 227

Damnation Creek, 46, 48, 49-52, 60
Davison Trail, 77, 78, 88, 101, 103-104, 114-115
Del Norte Coast Redwoods State Park, 35, 48-56
Del Norte County, 13, 14, 21-74, 152, 250-251
DeMartin Campground, 52, 54-55, 251
Devil's Gate, 190, 191
Dolason Prairie, 123, 124-125

Drury and Chaney Trail, 193-194
Dry Lagoon, 128-132, 251

Eel River 18, 19, 177-183, 187, 188, 190, 194, 229, 252
Eel River Wildlife Area, 177-180
elk, 17, 73, 75-76, 85-88, 98, 100, 101, 103, 107, 114, 237
Elk Prairie Trail, 82, 85-88
Elk River, 168-172, 173-176
Emerald Creek, 123, 126, 108
Emerald Ridge Trail, 120, 121, 123, 126, 127
Enderts Beach, 45, 46, 47
Eureka, 13, 19, 138, 168-172, 207, 239, 251
Eureka Waterfront Trail, 168-172, 251

Falk, 173, 174, 175
False Cape, 180, 185, 252
Fern Canyon,85, 90, 91, 93, 95-98
Ferndale, 13, 180, 181, 183, 185-191, 252
Five Allens' Trail, 194
Fleener Creek Trail, 181, 185
Flint Ridge Campground, 66, 68, 69, 251
Foothill Trail, 80, 82, 86
Fort Humboldt State Park, 169
Founder's Grove Loop Trail, 194-195
Friendship Ridge Trail, 84, 85, 93, 98-101

Garberville, 243-247
geology, 31, 63, 95, 132, 134, 142, 170, 214, 225
Gold Bluffs Beach, 64, 71, 73, 76, 89, 92, 95, 106, 107, 109, 251
gold discoveries, 18, 64, 89-91, 95, 128, 132
Grasshopper Peak. 193, 203
Grasshopper Trail, 96, 203, 207
Gregg, Josiah, 18-19, 138, 172
Guthrie Creek Trail, 181, 185

Hammond Interpretive Trail, 149-151
Hammond Trail, 147-152, 153, 251
Headwaters Forest, 173-174, 176-177
Hidden Beach, 56, 58-59
High Bluff Trail, 68, 69
Hiouchi Trail, 31
Hiller Park, 151
Hobbs Wall Trail, 51
Horse Mountain Creek Trail, 211, 218, 231
Houda Point, 144, 146
Humboldt Bay, 13, 18, 19, 89, 152, 153, 155, 166, 167, 168-172, 177, 178, 184, 190, 250
South Spit, 178
Humboldt County, 13, 14, 18, 76-235, 243-250
Humboldt Lagoons State Park, 128-131
Humboldt Redwoods State Park, 192, 193-210
Hupa, 60, 115, 116

James Irvine Trail, 84, 85, 89-93, 95, 98, 101
Jedediah Smith Redwoods State Park, 35, 36-45
Johnson (Cabin) Camp, 193, 203, 204, 206, 210
Johnson Prairie Trail, 209
Jones Beach Environmental Camp, 236

Karok, 60
King Range Conservation Area, 211-236
King Range Wilderness Area, 190, 192, 211-236,

Kings Crest Trail, 217, 220-222, 223, 224, 225-230
Kings Peak, 207,220, 221, 222, 223, 224
Kinsey Ridge Trail, 211, 215, 218, 220
Klamath Overlook Trail 64
Klamath River; 18, 58, 60, 63, 64, 66, 67, 68, 73, 89, 95, 132, 251

Lake Earl, 21, 28,32, 48
Lake Earl Wildlife Area, 21, 28, 250
Lanphere-Christensen Dune Preserve, 155
lighthouses, 23, 30, 144, 145, 177, 189, 211, 212, 213, 220
Lightning Trail, 222, 223-225, 227, 229
Little Bald Hills Camp, 38, 40
Little Bald Hills Trail, 36-41, 42
Little River, 60, 147, 152, 153, 251
Look Prairie Trail, 209
Lost Coast, 13, 190, 191, 211-243, 252
Lost Man Creek, 104-106
Luffenholtz Beach, 146
Lyons Ranch Trail, 126

Mad River, 18, 149, 151, 152-155
Mad River County Park, 152-155
Maple Camp, 220, 221, 222, 223, 224, 227, 229
Mattole, 18
Mattole River, 191, 192, 211, 213, 214, 220, 222, 229, 232, 252
McKinleyville, 147-152, 156
Mendocino County, 235-243, 250, 252
mileposts, how to use, 13-14
Mill Creek, 36, 40
Mill Creek Trail, 42, 51
Miller Camp, 217, 220, 221, 230
Miner's Ridge Trail, 90, 91, 93, 94-95
Moonstone Beach, 147, 153
Murrelet State Wilderness, 73, 77

Nadelos Campground, 232
Nature Trail (Prairie Creek), 82, 88, 91
New Lost Coast Trail, 238-241
Nickel Creek Camp, 45, 46, 251
Nickerson Ranch Trail, 42
Orick, 35, 121, 251
Ossagon Creek. 73, 75, 78, 100

Pacific Flyway, 130
Paradise Royal Mountain Bike Trail, 224
Patrick's Point State Park, 56, 63, 71, 130, 131-137, 251
Pelican Bay 30
Pelican State Beach, 250
Petrolia, 180, 190, 191, 213, 252
Pewetole Island, 139, 140, 141, 142
Pioneer Trail, 245
Point St. George, 27, 28, 29, 30-34, 45, 250
Prairie Creek Redwoods State Park, 2, 35, 66, 73-101
Prairie Creek Trail, 80, 82, 83, 85
Punta Gorda, 191, 211, 212, 213, 220

Randall Creek, 212, 214-215
Rattlesnake Ridge Camp, 220, 222, 230
Rattlesnake Ridge Trail, 211, 217, 222, 230
Redwood Creek. 35, 115-124, 125, 126, 127, 251
Redwood Creek Buckarettes, 117
Redwood National Park, 35-127, 250, 251

Revelation Trail, 86, 88
Rhododendron Trail, 80-82
Richardson Grove State Park, 247-250
Rock Creek Camp, 37, 41
Rockefeller Forest, 193, 194, 197, 198, 201
Rocky Gap, 120-121, 123
Russians, 18, 138

St. George Reef, 23, 30
San Andreas Fault, 225
San Francisco, 19, 138, 193
Save-the-Redwoods League, 35, 81, 197
School Road Multi-use Trail, 152
Shelter Cove, 212, 213, 217, 218, 220, 225, 230, 232, 233, 252
Shipman Creek, 217, 229, 231, 232
Sinkyone, 18, 237, 243
Sinkyone Wilderness State Park, 233, 235, 236, 237-243, 252
Siskiyou Wilderness, 36
Skunk Cabbage Creek,106-109, 251
Smith-Etter Road, 211, 215, 218, 219, 220, 221, 223, 227, 232
Smith, Jedediah, 18, 36, 60
Smith River, 21, 23, 25, 28, 29, 30, 32, 36, 39, 250
Smith River National Recreation Area, 36, 37, 38, 40-41
South Fork Trail, 80, 81-82
Spanish exploration, 18, 60, 138, 144, 189, 219
Spanish Ridge Trail, 211, 215, 218, 219
Stone Lagoon, 128, 129, 251
Stout Grove Trail, 37, 42
Streelow Creek Trail, 78

Table Bluff, 177-180, 182
Tall Trees Grove, 115, 117, 119, 121, 122-123, 124
Te-wo-lew Trail, 67, 69-72
Tolkan Campground, 218, 224
Tolowa,18, 21-23, 27, 30, 33, 35, 51, 60
Tolowa Dunes State Park, 21-29, 250
Toumey-Big Springs Loop, 248
Trees of Mystery, 56, 57-58, 62
Trillium Falls Loop, 35, 101-104, 114
Trinidad, 13, 18, 19, 60, 89, 138-147, 152, 251
Trinidad Head, 18, 139, 140, 142-144, 149, 151, 155, 190
Trinidad State Beach, 138-141
Trinity River, 18

Usal, 232, 236, 239, 243
Van Duzen River, 18
Wailaki, 243
Wailaki Campground, 232, 233, 234
West Ridge Trail, 82-85, 91, 98, 100
Whale Gulch, 232, 233, 234, 235, 236, 252
Whiskey Flat Camp, 207, 209, 210
Wilson Creek, 52, 53-54, 55, 56, 57, 60, 61
Winship, Jonathan, 18
Wiyot, 18, 168, 169-170, 177, 243
Woodland Trail, 248

Yolla Bolly Mountains, 207, 222, 225, 226, 235
Yontakit, 21-25
Yurok, 18, 22, 35, 51, 60-64, 67, 69, 76, 78, 96, 124, 128, 131-133, 134, 135, 136, 137, 138, 145, 177
Zig Zag Trail #1, 82, 83
Zig Zag Trail #2, 82, 83, 85

# ABOUT BORED FEET

We began Bored Feet Press in 1986 to publish *The Hiker's hip pocket Guides*. Today we publish more than a dozen other titles about California. We also distribute more than 200 other great books and 120 recreation maps covering outdoor recreation, nature, travel, history art, food/wine and more. The easiest way to see what's new at Bored Feet is to visit our user-friendly and accessible website: www.boredfeet.com. There you can read about and order any of our great products, view or print updates on our key publications, or give us your welcome feedback.

If you're not into computers, you can call us toll free weekdays at 888-336-6199 to place an order (Visa and MasterCard welcome), or to get a catalog or updates for our publications. Thanks for your support!

| | |
|---|---|
| *Hiker's hip pocket Guide to Sonoma County, 3rd ed.*, Lorentzen | $16.00 |
| *Hiker's hip pocket Guide to Humboldt-Del Norte Coast, 3rd ed.*, Lorentzen | 17.50 |
| *Hiker's hip pocket Guide to Mendocino Coast, 3rd ed.*, Lorentzen | 16.00 |
| *In the Company of Redwoods: 50 Redwood Community Plants*, Casterson | 16.96 |
| *Healing with Medicinal Plants of the West, 3rd ed.*, Garcia & Adams | 17.95 |
| *Mendocino Coast Glove Box Guide, 3rd ed.*, Lorentzen | 17.50 |
| *Hiking the California Coastal Trail, Vol. 2: Monterey-Mexico* | 19.00 |
| *Great Day Hikes . . . Napa Valley, 3rd ed.*/ Stanton | 16.00 |
| *Geologic Trips: San Francisco & Bay Area*/ Konigsmark | 13.95 |
| *Geologic Trips: Sierra Nevada*/ Konigsmark | 17.50 |
| *Trails & Tales of Yosemite & the Central Sierra, Revised*/ Giacomazzi | 19.00 |
| *Exploring Eastern Sierra Canyons: Bishop to Lone Pine*, " | 16.00 |
| *Exploring Eastern Sierra Canyons: Sonora Pass to Pine Creek*, " | 16.00 |
| *Wood, Water, Air & Fire: Anthology of Mendocino Women Poets* | 13.00 |

Please add $4 shipping for orders under $30,
$6.50 over $30 ($7.50/12 for rush orders).
For shipping to a California address, please add 7.625% sales tax.

PRICES SUBJECT TO CHANGE WITHOUT NOTICE

**Bored Feet Press**
P.O. Box 1832
Mendocino, CA 95460
www.boredfeet.com/ 888-336-6199